United Kingdom Association for European Law

University Association for Contemporary European Studies

THE EUROPEAN UNION AND WORLD TRADE LAW

After the GATT Uruguay Round

Edited by
Nicholas Emiliou
Senior Lecturer in Law, Jean Monnet Chair of European
Integration, University of Durham

David O'Keeffe
Professor of European Law, University College London

John Wiley & Sons
Chichester · New York · Brisbane · Toronto · Singapore

Published in the United Kingdom by
John Wiley & Sons Ltd
Baffins Lane, Chichester,
West Sussex PO19 1UD, England
National: Chichester 01243 779777
International: (+44) 1243 779777

Published in North America by
John Wiley & Sons, Inc.
7222 Commerce Center Drive
Colorado Springs CO 80919
USA

Other Wiley Editorial Offices

John Wiley & Sons, Inc., 605 Third Avenue,
New York, NY 10158-0012, USA

Jacaranda Wiley Ltd, 33 Park Road, Milton,
Queensland 4064, Australia

John Wiley & Sons (Canada) Ltd, 22 Worcester Road,
Rexdale, Ontario M9W 1L1, Canada

John Wiley & Sons (SEA) Plc Ltd, 37 Jalan Pemimpin #05-04
Block B, Union Industrial Building, Singapore 2057

British Library Cataloguing-in-Publication Data

A catalogue record for this book is available from the British Library

ISBN 0–471–95552–3

Typeset in 10½/12pt Baskerville by Dorwyn Ltd, Rowlands Castle, Hants
Printed and bound in Great Britain by Bookcraft (Bath) Ltd

This book is printed on acid-free paper responsibly manufactured from
sustainable forestation. At least two trees were planted for each one
used for paper production.

Contents

CONTENTS

Part 4: THE URUGUAY ROUND: EFFECT ON THE EC LEGAL ORDER

Customs Law

Services

Social Law

Agricultural Law

Environmental Law

Trade Law

Public Procurement

Part 5: THE EC'S EXTERNAL TRADE POLICY BEFORE THE COURT OF JUSTICE

Part 6: EC AND CHINA: A CONTINUING SAGA

Foreword

The "trade law" of the Community has occupied the Court of Justice in a number of important areas – some developed in much more detail than others. Thus the Competition rules which probably have the greatest relevance to those from non-European countries who set up companies, manufacture or sell in the Community have led to many important decisions. Even those concerned with companies operating only in the Member States give guidance as to how Articles 85 and 86 may be applied to cross Community-border transactions. The anti-dumping decisions of the Commission, as challenged before the Court, have produced important changes as to procedure and important rules as to the scale of the relevant provisions adopted under Article 113 of the Treaty.

Article 113, however, goes much wider and has raised in particular difficult questions as to the competence of the Community, in particular the Commission, and as to the inter-relationship of the competences of the Community and the individual Member States. The Court's statement on Opinion 1/78 on the draft International Agreement in Natural Rubber (1979 E.C.R. 2871) gave the direction: "A restrictive interpretation of the concept of common commercial policy would risk causing disturbances in intra-Community trade by reason of the disparities which would then exist in certain sectors of economic relations with non-Member countries".

Subsequent opinions developed the notion that the Community might have competence in regard to commercial policy not only where it had already adopted policies or taken action inside the Market but also in some cases where it had not. The recent opinion of the Court in Opinion 1/94 on the World Trade Organisation Agreement is of considerable significance in this area. How far it modifies earlier Opinions remains to be seen. Its detailed analysis of the movement of goods, of different kinds of services (e.g. those which can be compared with the movement of goods and those where the recipient goes to receive the services) and the increasingly important Trade Related Intellectual Property Rights is important.

The Court did not accept that certain specific provisions of the GATT before the Uruguay Round could be relied on directly in national courts, though GATT provisions and rulings might be relevant for the Court in deciding on the validity of Community measures. Those decisions as to direct effect were in part based on the specific terms of the provision in question and in part on the element of flexibility and discretion for Member States with a power of derogation and a dispute settlement procedure of its own. These latter factors may have indicated that GATT was not likely to be held to create rights for the citizen to enforce in national courts, but I do not believe that the Court ever said that it could never apply and it always seemed to me possible that one day some provision specific enough might get through.

Now we have the new Agreement and different considerations may apply and will have to be explored.

It is very timely that this collection of papers should be published since they trace the development of trade law before the Uruguay Round, explain many of the decisions reached insofar as they affect the Community and, in examining the questions which arise, indicate the way in which the law may be developed.

The list of authors speaks for itself. They are highly experienced and distinguished experts in Community Law. The papers in some respects consider the same questions from different angles but they all contain a wealth of material in this complex area – not only as to general principles but they give a detailed examination of the case law of the Court and they describe aspects of trade with China and Japan.

These papers are not "an easy read": a child's guide to the subject would not be much use. The papers contain a thoughtful and valuable treatment of many aspects of the subject. Dr. Nicholas Emiliou and Professor David O'Keeffe are to be congratulated on having put them together in this book.

SLYNN OF HADLEY

Introduction

This book has its origin in a conference on European Community Trade Law in the light of the GATT Uruguay Round, organised for the United Kingdom Association for European Law in conjunction with the University Association for Contemporary European Studies by the Centre for the Law of the European Union, University College London, where the conference took place on 6 May 1994. The Conference was chaired by the Right Hon The Lord Slynn of Hadley, President of the United Kingdom Association for European Law.

Subsequently, on 15 November 1994, the Court of Justice gave its Opinion 1/94 on the World Trade Organization Agreement, the implications of which are also considered in this book.

In view of the very topical nature of the subject, we decided to publish the revised conference papers at a later date, allowing for further reflection (unfortunately one speaker was unable to submit a paper for publication), together with contributions from other experts in the field.

The book has six parts. In Part 1, *Eileen Denza* discusses the International Personality of the EC, focusing on the Community's membership of international organizations. She states that the problems which the Community faces as a member of international organizations are slowly diminishing but notes that consistency may not easily be achieved, and that disputes among the Member States and the Commission over the determination of the Community's external competence show no sign of diminishing.

Part 2 deals with the legal framework of the Community's external trade policy. *Baroness Elles* writes on the role of the Institutions, and notes the efforts of the institutions to enhance their respective roles in trade policy. *Nicholas Emiliou* discusses the scope of the Community's external powers in relation to trade policy. *Damian Chalmers* analyses the issue of Legal Base and External Relations. He believes that although Article 113 of the EC Treaty may be a sufficient legal base for a considerable part of the Uruguay Round, in the future increasing use may have to be made of the Community's "internal powers". *Marise Cremona* raises the question of Human Rights and Democracy Clauses in the EC's trade agreements. She argues that the external trading relations of the Community can no longer be seen in purely economic terms but will increasingly be integrated into the overall policy making of the Union.

Part 3 contains evaluations of the Uruguay Round by *Jacques Bourgeois* and *Stephen Hyett*, considering its impact on the EC and the United Kingdom respectively.

In Part 4, ten articles discuss the effect of the Uruguay Round on different aspects of the Community legal system. *John Usher* and *Laurence Gormley* discuss the impact on Community Customs law. Gormley stresses the importance of legislative consolidation or codification in relation to both the internal and external effectiveness of the single market. *Wendy Kennett* discusses the General Agreement on Trade in Services. *Catherine Barnard* reviews the External Dimension of Community Social Policy. She concludes that the debate currently taking place in the Community about the desirability of setting standards at supra-national level is replicated and magnified at international level and that the creation of international labour standards is now firmly part of the Commission's agenda.

Joanne Scott discusses agricultural trade and the Common Agricultural Policy in the light of the Uruguay Round. *Martin Hession* and *Richard Macrory* discuss the principle of sustainable development and its interrelation with trade freedom. In a section dealing with trade law, *Mark Clough* and *Fergus Randolph* review recent developments in EC anti-dumping practice and the GATT, *Ernst-Ulrich Petersmann* analyses the GATT Dispute Settlement System as an Instrument of the Foreign Trade Policy of the EC, and *Hiroko Yamane* discusses the EC/Japan consensus on cars. Finally, *Mary Footer* examines public procurement and concludes that the new multilateral Government Procurement Agreement will strongly influence the external dimensions of the Community's procurement activity, although she notes that access remains largely dominated by a reciprocal approach.

Part 5 deals with the judicial review of the Community's external trade policy by the European Court of Justice. *Nanette Neuwahl* reviews the caselaw of the Court on the effect of the GATT for individuals. *Advocate General Francis Jacobs* considers the approach of the Court hitherto in reviewing commercial policy measures and raises the question what changes might be expected as a result of the Uruguay Round and the entry into force of the WTO Agreement. He concludes that the approach of the Court seems consistent with the liberal principles of trade policy laid down in the Treaty. *Anthony Arnull* analyses Opinion 1/94 and finds that it is one of "a growing catalogue of spectacular errors of judgment by the Commission". He notes that had the Court accepted the Commission's view that Article 113 extended to any international agreement which was liable to produce a direct or indirect effect on the volume or structure of commercial trade, the result would have been to transform the common commercial policy into a common policy on external economic relations, and that a Commission proposal along those lines had been rejected during the Maastricht Treaty negotiations.

Finally, in Part 6, *Francis Snyder* discusses the legal aspects of trade between the European Union and China. He concludes that the EU, as distinct from its Member States, is assuming an increasingly significant role. He notes that there remain a number of significant outstanding issues in trade relations between the EU and China, some of them structural, reflecting fundamental differences.

We are grateful to The Right Hon the Lord Slynn of Hadley for his encouragement for this project and for writing the Foreword to this book.

We would also like to thank The Right Hon The Baroness Elles, Vice-President of the United Kingdom Association for European Law, who was most helpful in suggesting themes for the conference, at which she was one of the commentators, and for this book.

One of the commentators on the papers presented at the conference was Professor Kenneth R Simmonds, one of the leading experts in this area, who has since died. We would like to recall his brilliant, stimulating and provocative commentary, which was a *tour de force*.

We would also like to thank Sue Jones, Executive Secretary of the United Kingdom Association for European Law, for her help in organising the conference, and her predecessor, Eva Evans MBE.

We would like to thank our publisher David Wilson for his co-operation and enthusiasm for the project.

Finally, we would like to thank the contributors to this book.

NICHOLAS EMILIOU
DAVID O'KEEFFE

List of Contributors

Anthony Arnull	Wragge Professor of European Law, University of Birmingham.
Catherine Barnard	City Solicitors' Educational Trust Lecturer in Law, Jean Monnet Chair of European Integration, University of Southampton.
Jacques H J Bourgeois	Partner, Baker & McKenzie (Brussels); Professor at the College of Europe, Bruges.
Damian Chalmers	Lecturer in Law of the European Union, London School of Economics and Political Science.
Mark Clough	Ashurt, Morris, Crisp, Brussels.
Marise Cremona	Senior Fellow, Centre for Commercial Law Studies, Queen Mary and Westfield College, University of London.
Eileen Denza	House of Lords.
Right Hon Baroness Elles	Member of the Select Committee and Sub-Committee E (Law and Institutions) House of Lords. "Of-Counsel" to Van Bael & Bellis, Brussels.
Nicholas Emiliou	Senior Lecturer in Law, Jean Monnet Chair of European Integration, University of Durham; Special Adviser on European Union Law, Ministry of Foreign Affairs, Nicosia, Cyprus; Member on the Panel of the Permanent Court of Arbitration, The Hague.
Mary E Footer	Program Legal Counsel, International Law Institute, Rome; Visiting Senior Research Fellow, Centre for Commercial Law Studies, Queen Mary and Westfield College, University of London.
Laurence W Gormley	Professor of European Law, Rijksuniversiteit Groningen; Visiting Professor of EC Law, University College, London; Barrister, Houthoff, Amsterdam & Rotterdam.
Martin Hession	Senior Research Scientist, Environmental Change Unit, University of Oxford.
Steven Hyett	Solicitor with the Department of Trade and Industry, London.
Francis G Jacobs	Advocate General, Court of Justice of the European Communities.
Wendy Kennett	Keele University.

Richard Macrory	Professor, Director, Environmental Change Unit, University of Oxford.
Nanette A E M Neuwahl	Professor of European Law, University of Liverpool.
David O'Keeffe	Professor of European Law and Director of the Centre for the Law of the European Union, University College London; Consulatant on EC Law to Coudert Brothers.
Ernst-Ulrich Petersmann	Professor of International, European and Swiss Public Law at the University of St Gallen; Visiting Professor at the Graduate Institute of International Studies at Geneva, Switzerland.
Fergus Randolph	Barrister, Brick Court Chambers, London and Brussels.
Joanne Scott	Lecturer in European Community Law, Queen Mary and Westfield College, University of London.
Lord Slynn of Hadley	Lord of Appeal in Ordinary; President United Kingdom Association for European Law.
Francis Snyder	Professor of European Community Law, European University Institute, Florence; Professor of Law, College of Europe, Bruges; Honorary Visiting Professor of Law, University College London.
John Usher	Salvesen Professor of European Institutions in the University of Edinburgh.
Hiroko Yamane	Professor of Law, Faculty of Law, Ritsumeikan University, Kyoto, Japan.

Tables

TABLE OF TREATIES

TABLE OF CASES

European Court of First Instance

European Court of Justice

TABLE OF EC REGULATIONS

TABLE OF EC DIRECTIVES

TABLE OF CONVENTIONS AND AGREEMENTS

TABLE OF NATIONAL LEGISLATION

Part 1

The International Personality of the EC

Chapter 1
The Community as a Member of International Organizations

Article XI of the Agreement establishing the World Trade Organization, signed at Marrakesh on 15 April 1994[1], provides as follows:

"Original Membership"

"1.   The contracting parties to GATT 1947 as of the date of entry into force of this Agreement, and the European Communities, which accept this Agreement and the Multilateral Trade Agreements and for which schedules of Concessions and Commitments are annexed to GATT 1994 and for which Schedules of Specific Commitments are annexed to GATS shall become original members of the WTO."

The entry into force of this provision will bring to an end the anomalies whereby GATT, one of the most influential and effective rule-making systems in the world, was not an international organization, and the European Communities never became Contracting Parties to the GATT. For the European Communities this is an important step forward in its struggle to win full acceptance as an international legal personality and so to achieve what the European Court of Justice has described as "the requirement of unity in the international representation of the Community".

Acceptance of the Communities as full members of an international organization has been a slower process than acceptance of their capacity to become party to multilateral agreements. Most of the significant international organizations were established in the 1940s, when the international legal personality of international organizations was hardly established, and their constitutions entitled only States to full membership. Even when the capacity of international organizations, and of the Communities in particular to assume international commitments came to be understood and accepted, there was little disposition to initiate the difficult and slow process of seeking to amend these constitutions. Representatives to the organizations usually tended to regard questions of membership and representation as political matters which distracted them from pursuing their proper functions. The Soviet Union and its allies were resolutely opposed to granting any enhanced status or rights to the Communities, and attempts to widen entitlement to membership would have led to argument over the entitlement of North Korea, for example, or East Germany. The Commission for many years accepted the status of "observer" in international organizations dealing with relevant subjects and concentrated on securing arrangements for representation and presentation of the Community's position which

---

[1] Cmnd 2571.

would reflect the internal division of competence between the Community and its Member States.[2]

The United Nations

Under Article 229 of the European Economic Community Treaty the Commission is given responsibility for maintenance of all appropriate relations with the organs of the United Nations, of its specialised agencies and of the General Agreement on Tariffs and Trade, as well as relations with other international organizations. In 1974 the General Assembly by Resolution[3] invited the Secretary-General to participate in the sessions and work of the General Assembly in the capacity of observer. This Resolution gave the Community as such the right to speak in debates, but not to vote. The particular interest of the Community at that time lay in the work of the Assembly in the elaboration of the instruments of the proposed New International Economic Order, such as the Charter of Economic Rights and Duties of States – work of obvious relevance to Community policies on development and on foreign investment. Co-ordination of the positions of Member States on matters within Community competence or of Community interest was established soon afterwards and took place both in Brussels, on a general basis, and in New York. The Economic and Social Committee of the United Nations had already extended a standing invitation to the European Economic Community, along with three other international organizations active in the economic and social field, to be represented by observers at meetings of the Council and to participate in debates, but without the right to vote.[4] Broadly similar arrangements were established in other United Nations bodies and in those specialised agencies dealing with matters of Community interest. The Commission tried consistently to obtain the right to speak on matters within Community competence, while the Presidency would speak on other matters, in both cases following consultation as appropriate among representatives of Member States. The practice however was not consistent across the different bodies.

---

[2] A summary of the nature of Community participation, with relevant texts, is contained in the Commission's publication *The European Community, International Organizations and Multilateral Agreements.* See also Schermers, *"International Organisations: Membership"*, in *Encyclopedia of Public International Law* (Kluwer).

[3] GA Resolution 3208(XXIX) of 11 October 1974.

[4] ECOSOC Resolution 1267(XLIII) of 3 August 1967, supplemented by a decision of 20 May 1971. The procedures of co-ordination in international negotiations generally are described in a Memorandum by the Foreign and Commonwealth Office to the House of Lords EC Committee, printed in the Select Committee's Report on *External Competence of the European Communities*, 16th Report 1984–85, HL 236.

The commodity organizations

The European Community first established a claim to full membership of an international organization with the negotiation of the International Wheat Agreement in 1971.[5] The Community as such negotiated its own accession to the Agreement, for matters within its competence, after that of the Member States and became a full member of the International Wheat Council and of the Food Aid Committee. There were a number of reasons why the commodity organizations were the first to accept the European Community as a full member. Most obviously, the agreements were concluded normally for a five-year period and all the legal arrangements could be revised on each occasion. The need for swift entry into force after agreement was reached, because of the link to commodity markets, led to the development of techniques of provisional entry into force, and generally to a somewhat more flexible approach to constitutional matters than prevailed in the case of older organizations. The developing countries were sympathetic to the Community's claims, and the Soviet Union and its allies found that they were unable to block the innovation. They did, however, make their displeasure known. The Soviet Union accompanied its instrument of accession to the International Wheat Agreement with a letter which stated that "its accession did not imply recognition of the EEC and created no obligations for the USSR with regard to the Community". The Presidency and the other Member States duly placed it on record that they did not accept this Declaration.[6]

The negotiation, between 1977 and 1979, of an International Natural Rubber Agreement brought out dispute among the Member States and the Commission over whether the Community was competent under Article 113 of the EEC Treaty to negotiate the proposed agreement alone. The Agreement had the usual objectives of stabilising trade in natural rubber by setting ranges of buying and selling prices and establishing a buffer stock in order to avoid extreme price fluctuations. It also provided for technological assistance, research, fair labour conditions and consultations on tax policies. The Council argued that some at least of these aspects took the draft Agreement outside the Community competence conferred by Article 113 in respect of the common commercial policy. This implied that the Commission delegation should be accompanied by separate national delegations who would under Article 116 of the EEC Treaty concert their positions, and that the Member States should become contracting parties to the Agreement along with the Community. The Commission, under Article 228 of the EEC Treaty, asked the European Court for an opinion on the compatibility of the draft Agreement with the

---

[5] OJ 1974 L219/25.
[6] Texts published in *The European Community – international organisations and multilateral agreements* (1983), 183–187.

Treaty and on the competence of the Community to conclude it. The Court in *Opinion 1/78, International Agreement on Natural Rubber*[7] held that:

"Article 113 empowers the Community to formulate a commercial 'policy' based on 'uniform principles' thus showing that the question of external trade must be governed from a wide point of view and not only having regard to the administration of precise systems such as customs and quantitative restrictions."

The links with development policy and with general economic policy, or the political importance of the product could not be a reason for excluding it from the domain of the common commercial policy. The provisions on technological assistance, research, labour conditions and tax consultations were of a "subsidiary or ancillary nature". Financing of the buffer stock on the other hand was an essential feature of the proposed agreement, and if financing was to come from national budgets, "that will imply the participation of those States in the decision-making machinery or, at least, their agreement with regard to the arrangements for financing envisaged and consequently their participation in the agreement together with the Community". In the event it was agreed that financial contributions should be made by Member States and so the Community became a contracting party to the Agreement and a member of the International Natural Rubber Organization along with the Member States. The Soviet Union once again declared that its participation in the Agreement along with the European Economic Community "would not give rise to any obligations on its part in relation to the Community". Financial contributions by Member States have continued to be standard for other commodity agreements, and so the Community and the Member States have continued together as members of the organizations.

The *Natural Rubber* case gave the Community and its Member States clear guidance on the cases where it was appropriate for the Community to seek to participate in a multilateral international agreement or apply for membership of an international organization. During the succeeding years the political obstacles to the Community being accepted as a member of an international organization diminished considerably. The two main difficulties to be overcome, once it was agreed in principle that the door would be open to Community membership, were those of voting and of the extent of Community competence. These two problems were linked. Where the Community remained an observer, or a non-voting member of an organization of which its Member States were also members, the possibility of double voting did not arise. Third states, while not objecting to the Community being given voting rights as a member were anxious that its vote should be a substitute for and not an addition to the votes of the Member States. It was also extremely difficult for them to understand and accept the concept that the boundaries of the Community's external competence would shift – usually outwards – following

---

[7] 1979 ECR 2871, at p 2913.

adoption of new Community rules or a subsequent judgment of the European Court. The solution usually adopted in commodity agreements is exemplified in Article 4 of the International Coffee Agreement 1994, which includes the following provision:

"3. Any reference in this Agreement to a Government shall be construed as including a reference to the European Community, or any intergovernmental organization having comparable responsibilities in respect of the negotiation, conclusion and application of international agreements, in particular commodity agreements.

4. Such intergovernmental organization shall not itself have any votes but in the case of a vote on matters within its competence it shall be entitled to cast collectively the votes of its Member States. In such cases, the Member States of such intergovernmental organization shall not be entitled to exercise their individual voting rights.

5. Such intergovernmental organization shall not be eligible for election to the Executive Board . . . but may participate in the discussions of the Executive Board on matters within its competence. In the case of a vote on matters within its competence . . . the votes which its Member States are entitled to cast in the Executive Board may be cast collectively by any one of those Member States."[8]

United Nations specialised agencies

In the Food and Agriculture Organization (FAO), as with other specialised agencies of the United Nations, the Community for many years was entitled to observer status only. The Commission was, however, permitted to speak and reply on matters of Community competence, which in the case of FAO activities were numerous. On other matters the Community position, following co-ordination under Article 116 of the EEC Treaty, was presented by the Presidency. The Commission, however, sought full membership for the Community first in regional fisheries organizations and later, in the context of the 1991 revision of the constituent agreement, membership of the FAO itself. The new provision contained in Article II of the FAO Constitution[9] is as follows:

"To be eligible to apply for membership of the Organization under paragraph 3 of this Article, a regional economic integration organization must be one constituted by sovereign states, a majority of which are Member Nations of the Organization, and to which its Member States have transferred competence over a range of matters within the purview of the Organization, including the authority to make decisions binding on its Member States in respect of those matters."

---

[8] OJ 1994 L222/1.
[9] Printed in *Basic Texts of the Food and Agricultural Organization of the United Nations* (FAO, 1992).

It will be seen that this provision, although not specific to the European Community, is tightly drawn in terms of majority FAO membership and in terms of legislative competence to make binding decisions.

In November 1991, the Community application was accepted by the FAO Conference and the Community acceded as a separate member. Under Article II 5 of the new Constitution of the FAO, the Community was required to lodge a general declaration specifying the matters within the FAO's fields of activity where competence had been transferred by the Member States to the Community, and Article II 7 required any change in the distribution of competence to be notified to the Director-General of the FAO. An appropriate declaration was annexed to the Council Decision authorising accession of the Community to the FAO.[10] Entry into force of the Treaty on European Union made it necessary to update the Community's Declaration of Competence – for example by setting out the Community's new policy on development co-operation as well as new powers on vocational training, public health and consumer protection.[11] The rules regarding voting by a member organization in the FAO are set out in paragraphs 8 to 10 of Article II of the new constitution. As with the International Coffee Organization, they make clear the alternative character of the Organization's voting rights – "A Member Organization shall exercise membership rights on an alternative basis with its Member States that are Member States of the Organization in the areas of their respective competences and in accordance with rules set down by the Conference". For the avoidance of any doubt, Article II 10 also says that "Whenever a Member Organization exercises the right to vote, the Member States shall not exercise theirs, and conversely". Member Organizations are expressly excluded from certain bodies of restricted membership, and under the General Rules of the FAO they are not entitled to hold office in the Council or in any subsidiary body of the Council. There are elaborate arrangements in the General Rules requiring the provision of information to other member nations of the FAO on the distribution of competence in respect of any question, both generally and before meetings on specific agenda items. Information has also to be provided for each agenda item on which, as between the member organization and its Member States, has the right to vote.

It is not surprising that these provisions have already led to dispute between the Commission and the Member States of the European Community over the right to vote. In November 1993 the Council of Ministers decided that a vote at the FAO Conference approving a draft Agreement to Promote Compliance with International Conservation and Management Measures by Fishing Vessels on the High Seas should be cast by the Member States rather than by the Commission. The Member States

---

[10] Annex II to the Council Decision of 25.11.1991 on the accession of the EC to the FAO.
[11] The proposed text is in SEC(94)437 final, Communication from the Commission to the Council.

maintained that the Commission, although entitled to accede to the Agreement, did not have exclusive competence over the subject matter. The European Commission has however challenged this decision before the European Court in Case C 25/94 *Commission* v *Council* OJ 1994 C90/6.

No other UN specialised agency has yet accepted the European Community as a full member of the organization. In the International Telecommunications Union (ITU), the Commission has been unable even to act as spokesman in discussions affecting matters which have been the subject of Community legislation.[12] Although a few years ago the Commission expressed the hope that in the International Civil Aviation Organization it should "gradually become the spokesman for the Community", a more recent Communication entitled *The Way Forward for Civil Aviation in Europe* makes clear that improved arrangements for representation in ICAO are not an immediate priority.[13]

The International Labour Organization is another specialised agency operating in a field where the Community has acquired extensive competence. The constitution of the ILO dates from 1919 and the European Community has observer status only, entitling it to speak on matters within Community competence, but not to vote. Full membership in the case of the ILO would raise special problems because of the nature of representation on the General Conference of the Representatives of the Members which is the principal organ of the organization. Representation is tripartite in character – each Member State has two Government representatives, one representative of its employers and one representative of its workers. The four representatives do not vote together as a national delegation – each is entitled to vote individually. The main task of the General Conference of the ILO is the adoption of international conventions and recommendations which are then opened for ratification under national procedures. Member States are required to communicate the convention or recommendation to the "competent national authority" for the purposes of implementation and to inform the Director-General of the International Labour Office of the authority regarded as competent and of the action taken by it. The Constitution of the ILO restricts ratification of ILO Conventions to states which are members of the organization. The Commission has in the light of these difficulties concentrated its efforts on devising a procedure which, so far as is possible, reconciles the conflicts between the rules of Community external competence and the constraints of the ILO Constitution.

The working procedures originally negotiated between the Community and the Governing Body of the International Labour Office envisaged that

---

[12] See Dehousse and Ghemar, "Le traité de Maastricht et les relations extérieures de la Communauté européenne", *European Journal of International Law* (Vol. 5, 1994, No. 2 p 151, esp. pp 164–168.

[13] COM(94)218 final. On the earlier Communication, see Report of the House of Lords Select Committee on the European Communities: *Conduct of the Community's External Aviation Relations*, 9th Report, 1990–91, HL Paper 39, at paras 70–72 and 105.

Member States would authorise the Commission to make proposals on their behalf, that they would inform the Director-General that the "competent authority" for the purposes of implementation was the Council and that ratification could take the form of 12 national notifications followed by a statement from the Council. During the preparation of ILO Convention No. 162 on Safety in the Use of Asbestos, dispute between the Commission and the Member States over the extent of Community competence led the Commission to bring an action before the European Court. This was withdrawn following adoption of a Council Decision of 22 December 1986 which set out procedures whereby full account would be taken during negotiations of the results of consultation with employers and trade union representatives, the Council would adopt a negotiating mandate and the Commission would speak to this in the Conference, supplemented where appropriate by national delegates. The Decision – which was not expressly approved by the ILO authorities – did not however apply to Conventions for which competence was shared between the Community and the Member States. In the case of ILO Convention No.170 concerning Safety in the use of Chemicals at Work, a number of Member States challenged the Commission's claim that the Community had exclusive competence over the subject matter. In 1991 the Commission sought the opinion of the European Court on the compatibility of the Convention with the EEC Treaty and on the competence of the Community to conclude it. In Opinion No. 2/91[14] the Court held that the subject matter of this Convention fell in part within the competence of the Community and in part within that of Member States. The main reason why exclusive Community competence could not be accepted was that the relevant internal Community rules constituted minimum standards and, pursuant to paragraph 3 of Article 118A of the EC Treaty, Member States were entitled to maintain or introduce more stringent measures for the protection of working conditions. The Court stressed the need for "close association between the institutions of the Community and the Member States both in the process of negotiation and conclusion and in the fulfilment of the obligations entered into". This co-operation was particularly necessary since the Community could not at present itself conclude ILO Conventions and must do so through the medium of the Member States.[15] The Court did not instruct the Member States and the Commission on how they should carry out their duty of co-operation.

It is likely, in view of the Court's reasoning and the insistence of many Member States that Community rules on health and safety of workers should take the form of minimum rules, that most of the future conventions drawn up by the ILO will be ones where competence is shared between the Community and its Member States. The Court's ruling, as in

---

[14] 19 March 1993, not yet reported. The earlier history is set out in the Opinion.
[15] Paragraphs 36 & 37.

the case of participation in commodity agreements, has clarified the Community law aspects, while leaving intact the difficulties of reflecting the law in suitable internal procedures and of reaching accommodation with third States within an international framework not designed for entities having the direct law-making powers of the Community. The Commission has proposed a Council Decision on the exercise of the Community's external competence at international labour conferences in cases falling within the joint competence of the Community and its Member States. In its Explanatory Memorandum the Commission states that "the intention is not to have the ILO Constitution or other internal rules governing the organization's bodies amended" and also stresses its wish to respect the independence of the two sides of industry and the principle of consulting the two sides of industry. Consultation at European level would have to be the subject of consultations to find a suitable formula, and would not be a substitute for consultations at national level.[16] The proposed procedures met with a hostile reaction from the United Kingdom Government, who commented that they were contrary to the principle of subsidiarity, and that "The Community's interests can be adequately represented in the ILO by close co-operation between the Member States".[17]

The Organization for Economic Co-operation and Development

Article 231 of the EC Treaty requires the Community to establish close co-operation with the Organization for Economic Co-operation and Development, "the details to be determined by common accord". The common accord was drawn up in 1960 as Protocol No. 1 to the OECD Convention, and provides that representation in the OECD of the three European Communities "shall be determined in accordance with the institutional provisions of those Treaties". The Commission is specifically given the right to take part in the work of the OECD. An Exchange of Letters between the International Energy Agency and the European Commission regarding research and development in the field of energy provided for Community participation in International Energy Agency programmes and projects, and for the negotiation by the Commission of implementing agreements "in accordance with the provisions of the Treaties establishing the European Communities".[18] The question of separate membership for the Community does not appear to have arisen – given the relatively

---

16 Council Doc. 4255/94; COM(94)2 final.

17 Explanatory Memorandum from the Minister of State, Dept of Employment, submitted to Parliament on 25.2.1994.

18 *Texts published in the EC, international organisations and multilateral agreements* (1983) pp 137–138.

informal procedures of the OECD it has perhaps not been a significant objective.

The Council of Europe

The EC Treaty envisages looser links between the Community and the Council of Europe than those with the United Nations and the OECD, requiring under Article 230 only the establishment of "all appropriate forms of co-operation". The Community has always been entitled to observer status in the Council of Europe on the basis of a 1951 Resolution of the Committee of Ministers applying generally to intergovernmental organizations. Under the terms of an Exchange of Letters of 1959 the European Commission is entitled to take part in relevant meetings of the Committee of Ministers and in meetings of government experts on problems of interest to the Community.[19] Most of the Conventions concluded within the Council of Europe framework were in areas such as criminal law and extradition where the Communities do not have competence. Council of Europe Conventions were not open to participation by the Community until the conclusion in 1976 of the Convention on the Protection of Animals kept for Farming Purposes. The Council of Ministers of the European Community, however, decided that the Community should not become a party to that Convention until all Member States had ratified. Rules of Procedure drawn up by the standing committee established by the Convention entitled the Community, once it was a party, to exercise on matters within its competence the votes of those Member States which were also parties. In 1989 the Commission in a Communication to the Council on development of relations between the EC and the Council of Europe, put forward practical suggestions for improved co-operation including possible wider participation by the Community in Council of Europe Conventions. The Foreign Affairs Council in March 1989 agreed to intensify political contacts between the two organizations.[20] In recent years the Commission, strongly supported by the European Parliament, has concentrated its efforts on securing accession by the Community to the European Convention for the Protection of Human Rights and Fundamental Freedoms. This raises institutional problems much wider than those of membership of the Council of Europe and of the institutions which supervise the Convention – problems which have been widely canvassed among lawyers and within the Community institutions and are now being argued before the European Court.[21]

---

[19] *Ibid.*, at pp 139–142.
[20] See Hansard HL Debates 22.3.1989 WA 623.
[21] The Commission Communication of 1990, SEC(90)2087 final, was the starting point for an enquiry by the House of Lords Select Committee on the European Communities, *Human Rights Re-examined*, 3rd Report, 1992–93, HL Paper 10.

The GATT

The GATT was originally intended to be an interim arrangement, pending establishment of an international trade organization by the Havana Charter. After the failure of the United States to ratify the Havana Charter, the GATT continued as a multilateral agreement. In 1955 there was a further attempt to establish an Organization for Trade Co-operation, with an assembly, an executive committee and a secretariat as well as powers to supervise the Agreement, but this was also rejected by the United States Senate. Kenneth Dam, in his book on the GATT[22], said that: "In legal and institutional patrimony, the GATT is one of the most humble, if not deprived, of the multitude of international bodies on the world scene. But in positive accomplishments, the GATT must surely rank near the top." Since the GATT had neither international legal personality nor members, the question of membership for the Community never arose. The original contracting parties were governments and accession was only open to governments. The contracting parties administered the GATT, and the Community never became a contracting party.

With the establishment of the EEC as a Customs Union, the Community as such became responsible for the rights and obligations conferred by the GATT and was *de facto* given the right to participate fully in sessions of the contracting parties, working groups and committees for matters within EEC competence. In practice, the Commission acted for the Community in most areas of GATT business, although the Member States retained competence over budgetary matters. International agreements concluded under GATT auspices were always open to conclusion by the Community, leaving the Community's internal procedures to settle any dispute as to whether the Community should sign and conclude them alone, or together with the Member States. The situation was described by the European Commission in its 1988 pamphlet "The European Community in the world" in the following, somewhat provocative terms: "In the GATT and in the North Atlantic Fisheries Organization, the Community, through the European Commission, takes the place of Member States and speaks on their behalf ".[23]

The Final Act Embodying the Results of the Uruguay Round of Multilateral Trade Negotiations, signed at Marrakesh on 15 April 1994[24] begins the process which should convert the European Community into a full member of the new World Trade Organization. The European Communities are listed among the members of the Trade Negotiations Committee which drew up the Agreement establishing the World Trade Organization

---

[22] *The GATT: Law and International Economic Organization*, (1970, University of Chicago Press). See also Simmonds, "Closing the Uruguay Round", in *Essays in Honour of Henry Schermers, Vol. II, Institutional Dynamics of European Integration* (Kluwer, 1994).

[23] 16/88.

[24] Cmnd 2570.

with its accompanying Declarations, Decisions and Understanding.[25] The representatives agree to submit the WTO Agreement "for the consideration of their respective competent authorities with a view to seeking approval of the Agreement in accordance with their procedures". This wording will of course leave it to the Community institutions to determine the extent to which Community conclusion of the Agreement should be accompanied by national ratifications and the legal base or bases for Community participation. The Agreement was signed on behalf of Member States as well as on behalf of the Community. The Final Act, and Article XI of the Agreement establishing the World Trade Organization, make clear that as a non-contracting party to the GATT 1947 the Community will require as a condition of original membership of the WTO to negotiate terms of accession to GATT, including Schedules of Concessions and Commitments.

Under Article 228 of the European Community Treaty, the Commission sought the opinion of the European Court on the question of competence to conclude the Agreement. Of particular relevance was the Commission's argument that if competence were shared between the Commission and the Member States, interminable arguments would threaten the unity of the Community's external action and impair its negotiating strength. The Court said that the division of competence could not be determined by practical difficulties – there was an imperitive requirement on the Member States and the institutions to co-operate within the WTO. Concurrent negotiations took place in the Council for an agreement on an acceptable code of conduct to determine representation within the WTO of the Community and Member States.[26]

Article IX of the Agreement establishing the World Trade Organization, on decision-making, begins as follows:

"The WTO shall continue the practice of decision-making by consensus followed under GATT 1947. Except as otherwise provided, where a decision cannot be arrived at by consensus, the matter at issue shall be decided by voting. At meetings of the Ministerial Conference and the General Council, each Member of the WTO shall have one vote. Where the European Communities exercise their right to vote, they shall have a number of votes equal to the number of their member States which are Members of the WTO. Decisions of the Ministerial Conference and the General Council shall be taken by a majority of the votes case, unless otherwise provided in this Agreement or in the relevant Multilateral Trade Agreement."

This provision follows the precedent of the more recent commodity agreements and eliminates the possibility of third states being prejudiced by the exercise of rights by the Community rather than by the Member States. (A footnote to Article XI spells out that the number of votes of the European Communities and the Member States shall in no case exceed the number of the Member States.)

---

[25] Cmnd 2571.
[26] Press Release of Foreign Affairs Council, 4 October 1994.

Conclusion

This summary of the extent to which the Community has achieved membership status in a few of the more important international organizations shows that the problems which it faces are slowly diminishing. General political opposition to the Community by third states, or to the exercise by the Community of international legal rights has now largely disappeared. Where constitutional revision, followed by national ratifications is required for the Community to be admitted to membership of an organization, the process may be postponed indefinitely. It will always be easier for the Community to become a member of a new international organization or one which, like the commodity organizations, is radically renewed at intervals of a few years. The problem of voting is capable of being resolved by the formula used for the recent International Coffee Agreement and the Agreement establishing the World Trade Organization. Third states can shrug off the fear that they cannot accept the Community as a potential voting member without understanding the arcane doctrines of Community external competence. The most difficult problem, and one which is not susceptible to easy resolution, is that of liability for non-performance of treaty obligations. This arises with Community participation in any international agreement, regardless of whether it is drawn up in the framework of an international organization. It is becoming standard practice, where this may cause difficulties for third states, for a statement of Community competence to be demanded as the price of Community participation. These statements, if they are not to be worse than useless, require constant updating, and given the tension between the Commission and the Member States where demarcation of competence is involved, the process of revision is likely to be time consuming and perhaps divisive.

Article C of the Treaty on European Union requires the Union to "ensure the consistency of its external activities as a whole in the context of its external relations, security, economic and development policies". Community membership in international organizations whose activities are to a significant extent within Community competence will to some extent contribute to this objective and will certainly help to increase the understanding among third states of the nature and limits of the powers of the Community as an international actor. But there is no indication that the task of consistency will easily be achieved or that the disputes among the Member States and the Commission over the determination of the Community's external competence will diminish either in number or in importance.

EILEEN DENZA

Part 2

The General Legal Framework of the EC's External Trade Policy

Chapter 2
The Role of EU Institutions in External Trade Policy

Introduction

Increasingly over the last four years, many parts of the world hitherto trading under state-controlled systems have opened up to European trade – for example, Russia, Commonwealth Independent States, Central and Eastern European states – with the result that recently there have been a number of trade and association agreements concluded between the EC and third countries.

Contemporaneously, the completion of the internal Single European Market following the coming into force of the Single European Act (SEA) on 1 July 1987, has led to a greater centralising of powers over, *inter alia*, EC external trade relations. The removal of intra-state trade barriers is having an influence on existing bilateral voluntary restraint agreements between Member States, such as those relating to the import of cars from Japan.

The significance of this evolution in the pattern of world trade has been reflected to some extent in the provisions of the Maastricht Treaty (Treaty on European Union or TEU) affecting the roles of the institutions in relation to their powers over the conduct of trade relations. One result which has emerged from the application of the principle of subsidiarity has been the review by the Commission of pending proposals for new directives, following the Edinburgh Summit of December 1992. These modifications have included for instance the temporary importation of motor vehicles and amendments to the Sixth VAT Directive.

The Commission also reacted to this non-exhaustive list of changes by reorganising its portfolios for the Commissioners appointed in January 1993, with a division of the portfolio for external relations – Mr van den Broek to be responsible for external political relations and Sir Leon Brittan, formerly responsible for Competition policy to become responsible for external economic relations. Mr Marin continued to cover Co-operation and Development, together with Southern Mediterranean, Middle East, Near East, Latin America and Asian matters, as well as the Lome Convention and Humanitarian Aid Office. The Directorate General 1 remained responsible for the two external relations portfolios, with Directorate General VIII retaining responsibility for Development issues.

A further recent change has been the setting up of the European Economic Area which will have affected trade procedures for EFTA Member States. As from 1 January 1995, there have been further changes with the accession of Austria, Finland and Sweden to the European Community, thereby increasing the number of Member States to 15 and Commissioners to 20.

Development of EC external trade

The EC, following the removal of internal tariffs between the Member States, has taken full part in multilateral international trade negotiations, including successive GATT rounds, resulting in a common external tariff with a weighted average of about 5%. With over 140 countries with diplomatic representation accredited to the EC about 120 trade and other agreements have been concluded between the EC and third countries as well as about 30 multilateral agreements.

As the world's leading trading area, with exports of goods and services amounting in 1992 to 20% of world exports (United States 18% and Japan 12%) and 21.5% of world imports (United States 19% and Japan 8%), the EC also remains the world's largest food importer and second largest food exporter. Not only has there been a rapid expansion in world trade over 20 years but there has also been a dramatic increase in the number of countries which are now engaged in world trade.[1]

It is inevitable that with this development in which the EC is one of the leading players, there should be shifts in balance between the Community's institutions, with demands for greater scrutiny and openness by both national parliaments and the European Parliament (EP) and with tensions arising between the Commission and the Council of Ministers regarding the final decision-making process and the powers and functions to be exercised at the conclusion of negotiations.

For the purposes of this chapter, consideration will be given to the provisions of the European Economic Community and amending Treaties, excluding the relevant articles in the Euratom Treaty. In this latter Treaty, there is different provision, under Article 101, for the negotiating and concluding of external agreements, whereby they are both carried out by the Commission, in some cases being approved by a qualified majority vote of the Council and in other cases subject only to the Commission keeping the Council informed.

The Common Commercial Policy

When considering the powers of the Community's institutions, it should be recalled that although EC law has supremacy over the national laws of

---

[1] GATT estimates.

Member States, the EC itself is not a sovereign state and consequently does not have all the powers of sovereign states to conclude international agreements. At the same time, Member States, in accordance with the provisions of the EEC and amending Treaties have conceded some of their treaty-making powers to the Community. The caselaw of the European Court of Justice has also affected their powers. The Community therefore claims the right to negotiate and conclude international treaties, covering an ever-widening number of sectors of Community activity and to participate, either together with, or on behalf of, Member States, in international organizations set up under such treaties. The participating role of the Community will vary according to the terms of the treaty concerned, and can be limited to participation without vote, with vote, on behalf of or with Member States.

The provisions of these treaties, once concluded in conformity with the required formalities, have binding effect on Member States, can – in certain circumstances – have direct effect on individuals, and can have a limiting effect on the individual actions of Member States once the Community has exercised its external competence.[2]

It is the function of the Commission to negotiate trade agreements, as set out in Article 113 of the EEC Treaty and amended by the TEU:

"1. The common commercial policy shall be based on uniform principles, particularly in regard to changes in tariff rates, the conclusion of tariff and trade agreements, the achievement of uniformity in measures of liberalization, export policy and measures to protect trade such as those to be taken in the event of dumping or subsidies.

2. The Commission shall submit proposals to the Council for implementing the common commercial policy.

3. Where agreements with one or more states or international organizations need to be negotiated, the Commission shall make recommendations to the Council, which shall authorize the Commission to open the necessary negotiations.

The Commission shall conduct these negotiations in consultation with a special committee appointed by the Council to assist the Commission in this task and within the framework of such directives as the Council may issue to it.

The relevant provisions of Article 228 shall apply.

4. In exercising the powers conferred upon it by this Article, the Council shall act by qualified majority."

Following the entry into force of the TEU, the Article 113 procedure now applies also to multilateral agreements and to agreements with international organizations.

The new drafting of Article 238 contains the provision that:

---

[2] Art 228 (7) TEU.

"[T]he Community may conclude with one or more States or international organizations agreements establishing an association involving reciprocal rights and obligations, common action and special procedures."

The former Article 238 required that such agreements should be concluded by the Council by unanimous vote. This requirement is now contained in a revised Article 228 TEU.

This article confers treaty-making powers on the institutions, and refers to the Community's common commercial policy, with the following distinction. In Article 228(2), second sentence:

"the Council shall act unanimously [not by qualified majority] when the agreement covers a field for which unanimity is required for the adoption of internal rules, and for the agreements referred to in Article 238."

Article 228 (7) also confirms that "Agreements which are concluded under the conditions set out in this Article are binding on the institutions of the Community and on Member States".

These three articles set out the conditions under which the Community can undertake to negotiate and conclude external agreements on behalf of the Member States.

Interpretation of express powers

It is not always clear under which Article an international agreement is to be negotiated and concluded. Under Article 228 (6), the Council, the Commission or a Member State may obtain the opinion of the Court of Justice as to whether an agreement envisaged is compatible with the provisions of the Treaty. The European Court of Justice (ECJ) has had to consider the scope of Article 113, whether the proposed agreement was within the terms of the common commercial policy of the Community and whether the Member States had or did not have concurrent powers with those of the Community institutions. The first case of its kind to come before the ECJ, the *Local Cost Standard Case*[3], concerned the negotiation in the OECD of an agreement to limit the amount of aid or support national authorities could give to the production or supply of goods for export. The Court concluded that this agreement came within the common commercial policy and consequently within the external competence of the Community. The *National Rubber Agreement Case*[4] concerned the negotiation of a commodity agreement to regulate international trade in natural rubber. The Court recognised that although the Community's competence in external matters dealt with tariffs and customs duties, it was possible for it to include the stabilisation of trade in particular commodities. It

---

[3] Opinion 1/75, [1975] ECR 1355.
[4] Opinion 1/78, [1979] ECR 2871.

had to be considered within the context of the overall aims of the common commercial policy. However, the Court also decided that Article 113 did not apply to matters such as the establishment, storage and financing of buffer stocks which were matters for Member States. This case is an example of frequent "mixed agreements" which contain provisions within Community competence but also those which remain within the competence of Member States and for which they retain sole responsibility.

Implied powers

The express powers granted to the Community under Articles 113 and 238 have been influenced and extended through the caselaw of the ECJ.

i) It has been held that every internal power implies a power on the international plane, the Treaty thereby establishing the principle of parallelism. The international commitment must, however, be necessary for the attainment of a specific object.[5] Whether an international commitment is necessary is for the Council to decide and where there is an unresolved conflict between the Council and the Commission, resort may be had for the opinion of the ECJ under Article 228 (6).

Where the Community has not exercised its internal powers a residual power is retained by Member States to assume international commitments essential to achieve a Community objective. Such action does not prevent the Community from taking any action in the same sphere in the future, a principle which is very relevant to the development of the Community's external aviation relations.

ii) Where the Treaties contain powers to regulate specific matters internally, even where internal rules have not been adopted, the Community may have competence to conclude international agreements.[6] In this case, concerned with international road transport, the Commission claimed exclusive Community competence on the ground that Article 75 EEC gave the Community power to regulate internally corresponding matters.

Negotiating procedure

Where it is perceived that there is a Community interest in opening negotiations with one or more third countries or with an international organization, the Commission proposes that it should initiate such negotiation and submits a mandate covering the Community's objectives. The Council, following consideration by its working groups, will authorise the

---

[5] See *Laying-Up Fund for the Rhine*, Opinion 1/76, [1977] ECR 741.
[6] Case 22/70, *Commission* v *Council* (AETR), [1971] ECR 263.

opening of negotiations and decides on the mandate to be given to the Commission. Where the legal base is Article 113 (3), a special committee is established, known as the 113 Committee, on which Member States are represented, generally by officials from the government department concerned with the substance of the agreement to be considered. It has happened that the Council refused to grant a mandate, though this is rare. In the process of negotiation the Commission may propose changes to the mandate or require a wider mandate, for which the Council must give its agreement. Before doing so the Council may consult with COREPER (the Committee of Permanent Representatives) or working groups. At the conclusion of the negotiations, the agreement may be signed or may be followed by a formal "conclusion", equivalent to ratification of the agreement by a state.

While this outline reflects the textbook procedure, recently there have been lapses from these formalities, which have been subject to justified criticism by Sub-Committee E of the House of Lords Select Committee on the European Communities. The Council has failed to issue a formal Decision authorising the opening of negotiations and identifying the legal base under which the agreement should be considered, but has confined its action of authorising negotiations by means of an entry in the Council Minutes. This practice leads to the result that such agreements are not subject to Parliamentary scrutiny and do not clarify the legal base of the proposed agreement.[7]

The negotiating process differs in the case of those agreements which do not fall solely within Community competence, that is mainly under Article 113(3).[8]

The legal base

The failure to define the base at the outset of negotiations raises the question of which institutions (in particular the EP and national parliaments) will be enabled to scrutinise the negotiations and vote on the terms achieved during the negotiations and also as to whether the vote in the Council will be by unanimity or by qualified majority.

There will inevitably be a tendency for the Commission to claim that the appropriate legal base is Article 113 and to argue effectively that the subject matter of the agreement falls within the definition of EC trade. Under this article, the EP is not consulted, and the vote in Council is by qualified majority. Where for, example, the appropriate legal base is

---

[7] See Correspondence with Minsters, House of Lords Reports: House of Lords, Session 1989–90, 26th Report. House of Lords, Session 1991–92, 5th Report.

[8] See Denza, "The Community as a Member of International Organizations", in this volume at pp 3–15.

Article 235, requiring unanimity, and the Council is not able, unanimously, to adopt a negotiating mandate, it is obvious that the Commission may decide not to proceed, at any rate for the time being, or will alter or modify its original proposal.

The role of the EP

As in the case of the Commission, playing a greater role in the negotiating and conclusion of agreements, and in the case of the Council, also seeking to hold on to its powers, so the EP, in its striving to play a more important role in the affairs of the Community, has increased its powers in relation to external trade policy.

The role of the EP prior to the adoption of the SEA in 1987 was limited to informal procedures. The Luns procedure applied to agreements under Article 113, and the Westerterp procedure in the case of association agreements under Article 238. There are four stages to these procedures.

i) Before negotiations are opened, the EP may hold a debate in its plenary session on the subject matter of a proposed agreement. These debates are often "blind" to the extent that the EP is not generally informed on an official basis either on an impending agreement or on the terms on which the Community is to negotiate. The EP therefore may or, more likely, may not influence the negotiating stance of the Commission.

ii) The relevant EP committees (*i.e.* the External Relations Committee or REX as it is known, generally the Foreign Affairs Committee, the Budgets Committee where there are financial implications, and the Development and Co-operation Committee) are kept informed of the progress of the negotiations.

iii) Once the negotiations are over, but before the agreement is signed, the President of the Council or a representative, will inform the appropriate committee(s) in confidence and unofficially of the substance of the agreement. This information is generally circulated in the form of a brief note.

iv) In the case of trade agreements, the Presidency of the Council informs the EP in plenary sitting of the content of the agreement, after it has been signed but before conclusion. This procedure is now applied to all major international agreements adopted by the Community following the Stuttgart Declaration in 1983.

The consultative role of the EP in relation to all international agreements, with the exception of those falling within the provision of Article 113(3), is now set out in Article 228(3) TEU. Procedural rules concerning the timetables to be observed are also set out.

The assent of the EP, a power first granted by Article 238 as modified by the SEA, is now required, under Article 228(3) as modified by the TEU in the case of all agreements which are:

"referred to in Article 238, other agreements establishing a specific institutional framework by organizing co-operation procedures, agreements having important budgetary implications for the Community and agreements entailing amendment of an Act adopted under the procedure referred to in Article 189b [Co-Decision Procedure], shall be concluded after the assent of the European Parliament has been obtained."

The assent procedure, which requires the agreement of the absolute majority of the component members of the EP has already been effectively exploited in the last Parliament. The EP by failing to provide the absolute majority required, rejected proposed protocols to the EC agreement with Turkey.[9] A few months later, the EP failed to produce the required majority to give its assent to a protocol to the association agreement between the EC and Israel. In both cases the grounds for refusal were based on considerations of non-observance of human rights. In both cases, the EP later gave its assent.

The EP's right to use the assent procedure in the case of accession treaties, formerly granted under Article 237 as modified by the SEA, is now contained in Article O, TEU. The absolute majority of positive votes has been raised from 260 out of 517 in the Parliament before the 1994 Elections, to 284 out of 567 as from June 1994 and now stands at 314 out of 627 since the accession of Austria, Finland and Sweden on 1 January 1995.

New forms of agreements have recently been concluded with Central and Eastern European states, known as "Europe Agreements". These agreements include new provisions to encourage the economies of these states to grow and enable them in the future to accede to the EC. Also included are provisions relating to political dialogue based on democratic processes, observance of human rights and progress towards a market economy.[10]

A significant agreement which came before the EP towards the end of its last five-year period concerned the extension of the general tariff preferences in respect of certain products originating in developing countries with additions to the list of beneficiaries. It had been necessary to extend the present Generalised Preference Scheme until the GATT negotiations were concluded. While the substance remained unchanged, seven new countries had been added to the list: Liberia, Zaire and Zambia as well as countries of the former Soviet Union. On this latter issue the EP Committee on Development and Co-operation expressed some reluctance to admit Russia and the Ukraine to the system, as they already enjoy infrastructures and trading and industrial capacities far in advance of those in many developing countries. It was argued that their entry to the system could erode some of the benefits which accrue to developing

---

[9] EP plenary session, December 1987.
[10] Agreements concluded with Poland, Hungary, Czech and Slovak Federal Republic.

countries by reason of their membership. Despite the tabling of the requisite amendment, this was turned down by the Commission in the January plenary session of the EP. Ten other republics of the former Soviet Union were admitted to the list without objection.

The role of the ECJ

The role of the ECJ has already been discussed in relation to implied powers. There are other aspects of the Court's role which should be recognised in relation to the development of the external trade law of the EC.

(i) The principle of direct effect was considered early on in the history of the EEC. The question was asked as to whether the EEC Treaty conferred rights on the citizens of Member States which they could invoke before the Courts. The ECJ, in the *Van Gend en Loos* case[11], stated that the direct application of international treaty provisions depended on the spirit, the general scheme and the wording of the provisions. The case was brought by a company before a Netherlands court challenging an increased rate of import duty charged by the national revenue authorities on certain products which they had imported from Germany. The company claimed that this increase contravened the prohibition on increases in customs duties on imports or exports between Member States, in Article 12 of the EEC Treaty, applicable from 1 January 1958. The Court held that the Community constitutes a new legal order of international law. Independently of the law of Member States the Community imposes not only obligations on individuals but is also intended to confer on them rights which become part of their legal heritage. The wording of Article 12 was clear and unambiguous and no further legislation was necessary for its implementation.

In contradistinction to the above case, in the *International Fruit Company* joined cases[12], concerning a request to obtain certificates to import eating apples, authorisation had been refused under a Commission Regulation. The company challenged the Court on the basis that the Regulation contravened Article XI of the GATT. It was necessary, held the ECJ, to establish first that the Community was bound by the relevant international treaty obligations and second that they were capable of conferring rights on individuals which they could invoke before the courts. The Court held that the flexible arrangements written into the GATT established general principles subject to negotiation between the parties, and that consequently Article XI of the GATT was not capable of conferring on citizens of the Community rights which could be invoked before the courts.

---

[11] Case 26/62, [1963] ECR 1.
[12] Joined Cases 21 to 24/72, [1972] ECR 1219.

ii) Trading procedures. The agreement between the EEC and the Republic of Cyprus of 19 December 1972 had laid down certain protective measures against the importing into the EEC of organisms harmful to plants or plant products. The exporting authority was the Republic of Cyprus, responsible for empowering experts to check and guarantee the issue of the appropriate phytosanitary certificate. The Court held, in the case of *The Queen* v *Minister of Agriculture, Fisheries and Food, ex parte S.P. Anastasiou (Pissouri) Ltd and Others*[13], that the national authorities of the importing company should preclude the imports covered by certificates issued by authorities other than the competent authorities of the Republic of Cyprus.

iii) The Court once again has held that there must be observance of the proper roles of the institutions in their conduct of affairs concerning the external trade relations of the Community. The Court decided that an antitrust agreement signed between the European Commission and the United States Government was void. According to the Court, the agreement should have been concluded by the Council of Ministers. The Commission claimed that such agreements only required administrative approval and that the Council would soon give its approval to the deal.[14]

This case highlights the continued jostling between the institutions for an increase in their powers in, *inter alia*, the conduct of external affairs. The ratification of the Uruguay Round under the GATT has shown the involvement of all four institutions. The Council claimed that the provisions of the GATT cover not only trade but also other matters for which the Commission does not have responsibility under Article 113, such as services, transport and intellectual property rights which remain within the competence of the Member States. The EP has insisted, and this has not been denied to it, the right under Article 228(2) to give its assent to the proposed terms of the agreement. The Commission, under Article 228(6), has applied to the ECJ to deliver an opinion on the competence of the European Community to conclude the Agreement establishing the World Trade Organization and in particular: (a) whether the draft General Agreement on Trade in Services (GATS) and the draft Agreement on Trade-Related Aspects of Intellectual Property Rights including Trade in Counterfeit Goods (TRIPS) should be concluded on the basis of Article 113 of the EC Treaty alone or on the basis of that provision in conjunction with Articles 100a and/or 235 of the EC Treaty; (b) on the extent of that competence as regards products and/or services falling within the scope of the ECSC and EAEC(Euratom) Treaties; and (c) on the consequences which that would have on the capacity of the Member States to conclude the WTO Agreement.[15]

It was questionable whether the Court would give its reply without delaying the ratification process. The Presidency therefore drew up a proposal

---

[13] Case 432/92 [1994] ECR I-3087.
[14] Case 327/91 *France* v *Commission* [1994] ECR I-3641.
[15] Opinion 1/94 [1994] ECR I-5267.

28

for a "Code of Conduct" which would clarify the roles of the Council and the Commission in relation to the ratification process, but also and more importantly, the way in which future negotiations on behalf of the Community are to be carried out and the role of Member States in relation to the many important issues, for instance labour, which do not come within the parameters of trade.

The practical and political solutions sought to this problem should enable the Commission to negotiate and the Member States and the EP to retain their respective roles, maintaining a sensitive balance between them.

In the event, the ECJ gave its response to the request of the Commission for an opinion on 15 November 1994, so enabling the respective institutions to fulfil their appropriate roles in the ratification process.

Although the Commission had been mandated the power to negotiate on behalf of the Community this did not prejudge the question as to the competence of the Community or the Member States in relation to particular issues.

In an extensive analysis of the respective powers of the institutions in regard to ratification of the GATT Uruguay Round agreements, the main conclusions of the Court were as follows.

The EU has exclusive competence to conclude international agreements relating to goods. The EU also has competence to conclude such agreements on products which are covered by the Euratom Treaty. Member States have exclusive competence for products covered by the ECSC Treaty since this Treaty was concluded in 1951, before the setting up of the European Economic Community in 1957. Since an examination of the Multilateral Agreements on Trade in Goods showed that they did not relate specifically to ECSC products, the EU retained sole competence under Article 113 EC to conclude those agreements.

Arguments submitted by the Council that both the Agreements on Agriculture and on the Application of Sanitary and Phytosanitary Measures should fall within the competence of the Member States were rejected by the Court. Even if commitments entered into under the terms of the Agreements required, in one instance, internal measures under Article 43 EC, and in the other, the establishment of a multilateral framework of rules and disciplines, these Agreements could be concluded on the basis of Article 113.

Similarly, the Court ruled that the Agreement on Technical Barriers to Trade could be concluded by the EU.

The ruling of the Court departed from the stand of the Commission in relation to the General Agreement on Trade in Services (GATS) and on Trade-Related Aspects of Intellectual Property Rights (TRIPS). If the Commission relied on the generally non-restrictive interpretation of the Court to the provisions of the Treaty, they were to be disappointed.

The nature of the GATS was not homogeneous. It could be accepted by the Court that trade in cross-frontier supplies is not unlike trade in goods and could therefore fall within the concept of the Common Commercial Policy (CCP). This analogy could not be applied to the three other modes of supply of services covered by GATS (consumption abroad, commercial presence and the presence of natural persons).

A matter of considerable interest is that aspect of the ruling dealing with the services comprised in transport. The Court had, in the *ERTA* judgment[16], ruled that the Community had competence to conclude international agreements not only under Articles 113, 114 and 238, but also where measures had been adopted by the Community institutions. In the present case, the Court made it clear that transport services did not fall within the CCP.

The TRIPs Agreement also came under close examination by the Court. It could be accepted that since measures concerning the free circulation of counterfeit goods can be autonomously adopted by the Community institutions, the Community alone could conclude international agreements on those matters.

In summary, in reply to arguments put forward by the Commission, the Court ruled that both the Community and the Member States were jointly competent to conclude the GATS and the TRIPs.

In conclusion, the Court stressed the need for close cooperation between the Community and the Member States in the implementation of the WTO Agreement and its annexes.

The Community and the Member States subsequently, in accordance with their own procedures, ratified the Agreements which came into force on 1 January 1995.

The EP, for the first time exerting its newly acquired power under Article 228, paragraph 3 TEU to ratify the results of a multilateral agreement, granted its assent by an overall majority of members.

The practical, legal and political solutions sought to clarify the problem of ratification will no doubt throw up new divergences in the future as the institutions strive to enhance their respective roles in an ever-expanding area of Community activity.

DIANA ELLES

---

[16] See n 6 *supra.*

Chapter 3

The Allocation of Competence Between the EC and its Member States in the Sphere of External Relations

Introduction

The EC's extensive involvement in external relations under the EC Treaty raises several difficult legal issues. First, there is the question of authority. On what basis does the EC exercise its external relations activities? To what extent do Treaty provisions explicitly grant such power to the EC and to what extent may the existence of such powers be implied from more general Treaty provisions? In the cases where external relations powers are explicit, how broadly is the grant of power to be interpreted. Second, there is the question of exclusivity. To what extent can the Member States act independently of, or participate jointly with, the EC in an area where the EC has competence under the Treaty? Third, it is necessary to consider how the EC's external relations powers are divided among the Community institutions. May the Commission act independently of the Council? What is the Parliament's role?

The Court of Justice bases the *capacity*[1] to enter into binding agreements with other subjects of international law, over the whole area of objectives set out in Part A of the EC Treaty, on Article 210 EC which confers legal personality on the EC. Whether the EC has the *authority* (competence) to enter into an agreement in a particular case depends on the question whether a Treaty provision expressly[2] or impliedly provides the authority to do so.

Express powers

Two of the most significant express treaty-making powers relate to: (i) commercial agreements under Article 113 EC; and (ii) association agreements under Article 238.

---

[1] Capacity appears to relate to the EC's legal power to enter into an agreement.
[2] See *e.g.*, Articles 113, 114, 229–231 and 238 EC.

31

The concept of commercial policy

Article 113 does not contain a definition of commercial policy but provides a non-exhaustive[3] list of uniform principles on which it is to be based:

"particularly in regard to changes in tariff rates, the conclusion of tariff and trade agreements, the achievement of uniformity in measures of liberalization, export policy and measures to protect trade such as those to be taken in case of dumping and subsidies".[4]

The Council has taken the view that only measures relating to the volume or flow of trade fall within the scope of the common commercial policy. The Commission, on the other hand, has argued on many occasions that the assessment must primarily be made by reference to the specific character of the measure as an instrument regulating international trade.[5] The Court has not yet taken a clear position on this dispute. However, its case-law has contributed to further detailing the scope of the common commercial policy.

The starting point is that the concept of commercial policy has:

"the same content whether it is applied in the context of the international action of a State or to that of the Community".[6]

Thus, there is no apparent reason to interpret the concept of commercial policy more narrowly in the case of the Community. On the contrary, the proper functioning of the customs union justifies a wide interpretation of Article 113 and of the powers conferred thereby on the Community institutions:

"to allow them thoroughly to control external trade by measures taken both independently and by agreement".[7]

Following this logic, the Court concluded that aid for exports to third countries, referred to in Article 112, and in particular measures concerning export credits necessarily fell within the scope of "export policy" under Article 113(1).[8] Also the definition of uniform principles described in Article 113(1) included:

"the elimination of national disparities, whether in the field of taxation or of commerce, affecting trade with third countries".[9]

---

[3] See Kapteyn and Verloren van Themaat (English edition by Gormley), *Introduction to the Law of the European Communities* (Kluwer, 1989, 2nd ed), p 788. *Cf.* Opinion 1/78, [1979] ECR 2871, at 2913.

[4] See Art 113(1).

[5] These views are fully set out in Opinion 1/78, *supra*, n 3 at 2880–2894. See also Att-Gen Lenz's Opinion in Case 45/86, *Commission v Council*, [1987] ECR 1493. There the Commission presented a more elaborate argument based on the transparent and specific regulation of trade with third countries. See also Bourgeois, "The Common Commercial Policy – Scope and Nature of Powers", in Völker (ed), *Protectionism and the European Community* (Kluwer, 1987, 2nd ed), pp 4–6.

[6] Opinion 1/75, [1975] ECR 1355, at 1362.

[7] Case 8/73, *Massey Ferguson*, [1973] ECR 897, at 908.

[8] Opinion 1/75, *supra*, n 6 at 1362.

The Court has also held that it is:

"not possible to lay down, for Article 113 of the Treaty, an interpretation the effect of which would be to restrict the common commercial policy to the use of instruments intended to have an effect only on the traditional aspects of external trade to the exclusion of more highly developed mechanisms"[10]

such as the more recent international commodity agreements which are associated with UN resolutions concerning the development of a new international economic order. If it were otherwise, observed the Court, the common commercial policy:

"would be destined to become nugatory in the course of time. Although it may be thought that at the time when the Treaty was drafted liberalization of trade was the dominant idea, the Treaty nevertheless does not form a barrier to the possibility of the Community's developing a commercial policy aiming at a regulation of the world market for certain products rather than at a mere liberalization of trade".[11]

Moreover, according to the Court, the EC system of generalised tariff preferences for developing countries:

"reflects a new concept of international trade relations in which development aims to play a major role".[12]

Thus, the EC Regulations applying the system of generalised tariff preferences need no legal base in the Treaty other than Article 113 itself, since that system falls within the scope of the common commercial policy. However, a general reference to the EC Treaty is insufficient while recourse to the general clause of Article 235 is not acceptable.

In Opinion 1/78[13], concerning the Community's authority to enter into an international rubber agreement which was to be concluded under the auspices of UNCTAD, the Court saw no reason to exclude the agreement from the sphere of the common commercial policy because of its possible repercussions on certain sectors of economic policy such as the supply of certain raw materials to the Community, or price policy or because the building up of stocks of a product could be of political importance. It also appears from the same Opinion that the description of an agreement:

"must be assessed having regard to its essential objective rather than in terms of individual clauses of an altogether subsidiary or ancillary nature"

such as technological assistance, research programmes, labour conditions

---

[9] Cases 37 & 38/73, *Social Fonds voor de Diamantarbeiders*, [1973] ECR 1609, at 1623.
[10] Opinion 1/78, *supra*, n 3 at 2913.
[11] *Ibid.*
[12] Case 45/86 *supra*, n 5 at 1521, *per curiam.*
[13] *Supra*, n 3 at 2915.

in the industry concerned or consultations relating to national tax policies which could have an effect on the price of the product concerned.[14]

The Court shed more light on the interpretation of the concept of commercial policy (which falls within the exclusive competence of the Community) in Opinion 1/94[15] concerning the competence of the Community to conclude the agreement resulting from the Uruguay Round of GATT. This agreement, which establishes the World Trade Organization (WTO) includes annexes incorporating the Multilateral Agreements on Trade in Goods, the General Agreement on Trade in Services (GATS) and the Agreement on Trade-Related Aspects of Intellectual Property Rights (TRIPS), including trade in counterfeit goods. The Commission submitted to the Court a request for an Opinion under Article 228(6), which centred mainly on the question whether the Community had exclusive power to conclude these Agreements.

The Court held that, under Article 113, the Community had exclusive jurisdiction to conclude the Multilateral Agreements on Trade in Goods. These powers covered the Agreement on Technical Barriers to Trade and also extended to agricultural products and tariff regulation of products covered by the Euratom and ECSC Treaties. With regard to GATS, the Court ruled that the power to conclude the Agreement was shared between the Community and the Member States. The Court confirmed that the concept of common commercial policy must be given a broad and non-restrictive interpretation and explicitly concluded that services may fall within the scope of Article 113. However, it pointed out that, of the four modes of supplying services envisaged in the GATS[16], only the cross-border supplies were not "unlike trade in goods, which is unquestionably covered by the common commercial policy within the meaning of the Treaty".[17] There was therefore no particular reason why a cross-frontier supply of services should not fall within the concept of the common commercial policy. The other three modes of service were excluded from the scope of Article 113 as they involved the movement of natural and legal persons and were covered by a Treaty objective distinct from that of establishing a common commercial policy.

As far as the TRIPS was concerned, the Court ruled that intellectual property rights did not fall within the scope of Article 113, except as regards Community measures prohibiting the release for free circulation

---

[14] *Ibid.*, at 2917.

[15] [1994] ECR I-5267.

[16] The Court explained that the definition of "trade in services" given in Art I(2) of GATS comprised four ways in which services could be supplied: "(1) cross-frontier supplies not involving any movement of persons; (2) consumption abroad, which entails the movement of the consumer into the territory of the WTO member country in which the supplier is established; (3) commercial presence, *i.e.* the presence of a subsidiary or branch in the territory of the WTO member country in which the service is to be rendered; (4) the presence of natural persons from a WTO member country, enabling a supplier from one member country to supply services within the territory of any other member country." *Ibid.*, at 5401.

[17] *Ibid.*

of counterfeit goods. The Court observed that even though there was a connection between intellectual property rights and trade in goods, those rights enabled those holding them to prevent third parties from carrying out certain acts. This was not enough to bring them within the scope of Article 113 since intellectual property rights did not relate specifically to international trade; they affected internal trade just as much, if not more, than international trade. Thus, the power to conclude the TRIPS Agreement was shared between the Community and the Member States.

The common commercial policy, it is respectfully submitted, embraces all measures (autonomous[18] or conventional[19]) which serve to regulate economic relations with third countries and concern free movement of goods and related traffic in services and payments.[20] Classification of agreements as commercial policy agreements should depend therefore on their essential objective and not on what is also covered by them as subsidiary or ancillary matters.[21] The Court's caselaw makes it clear that the concept of commercial policy is a dynamic one. It is not a static concept written in stone in 1957. Development objectives may play a significant part in a modern commercial policy. The scope of the common commercial policy embraces new instruments for the development of international trade, even if they are designed more to regulate than merely to liberalise the flow of trade.

The exclusivity of Community competence in the field of commercial policy

The Court's caselaw demonstrates that the Community has exclusive competence in relation to conventional as well as autonomous measures; indeed after the end of the transitional period national commercial policy measures are only permissible by virtue of specific authorisation from the Community.[22] In Opinion 1/75[23] the Court based this concept of exclusivity on the ground that the common commercial policy was conceived:

"in the context of the operation of the Common Market, for the defence of the common interests of the Community, within which the particular interests of the Member States must endeavour to adapt to each other".

"Quite clearly", continued the Court,

---

[18] *i.e.*, unilateral measures concerning imports and exports.

[19] *i.e.*, agreements with third countries in the sphere of commercial policy.

[20] The Commission has always taken the view that Article 113 also covers the exchange of services (and connected payments). See Bourgeois, *supra*, n 5 at 4.

[21] In Opinion 1/75, *supra*, n 6 at 1363, the Court said that: "a common commercial policy is in fact made up by the combination and interaction of internal and external measures, without priority being taken by one over the others. Sometimes agreements are concluded in execution of policy fixed in advance, sometimes that policy is defined by the agreements themselves".

[22] See Case 41/76, *Donckerwolcke*, [1976] ECR 1921, at 1937.

[23] *Supra*, n 6 at 1363–1364.

"this conception is incompatible with the freedom to which the Member States could lay claim by invoking a concurrent power, so as to ensure that their own interests were separately satisfied in external relations, at the risk of compromising the effective defence of the common interests of the Community".[24]

If such a parallel competence were to be accepted, that:

"would amount to recognizing that, in relations with third countries, Member States may adopt positions which differ from those which the Community intends to adopt, and which would thereby distort the institutional framework, call into question the mutual trust within the Community and prevent the latter from fulfilling its task in the defence of the common interest".[25]

No obstacle to the Community's common commercial policy authority arises from the fact that the obligations and financial burdens inherent in the execution of an envisaged agreement are borne directly by the Member States; such obligations and burdens do not necessarily have to be transferred to the Community institutions.[26]

The Community has the power to undertake financial obligations arising from an instrument of commercial policy which falls on the EC budget. This is the case even if these obligations are not incidental or subsidiary, but are an essential part of the system set up, such as, for example, in the case of buffer stock mechanism which was to be financed as part of the regulatory system of an international commodity agreement.[27]

It appears that if the financial obligations arising from an agreement fall on the Member States then the exclusive competence of the Community cannot be envisaged.[28] In Opinion 1/78, concerning the natural rubber agreement, it was accepted that although the issues covered by the agreement fell within the scope of the common commercial policy, it was the Member States which would bear financial responsibility for the implementation of the agreement, and so they had to be allowed to conclude the agreement alongside the Community. Two considerations led the Court to this conclusion. First, the extent and the detail of arrangements for the financial undertakings which the Member States would be required to satisfy affected to a great extent the possibilities and efficiency of intervention by the buffer mechanism. Second, the Court pointed out that price decisions to be taken by the International Rubber Council which was to be set up would have immediate repercussions on the use of the financial resources put at that body's disposal.

The Court stated that if the financing was to be assumed by the participating Member States that would imply their participation in the decision-making machinery or at least their agreement with regard to the envisaged

---

[24] *Ibid.*, at 1364.
[25] *Ibid.*
[26] *Ibid.*
[27] Opinion 1/78 *supra*, n 3 at 2918.
[28] *Cf.* Opinion 1/75, *supra*, n 6 at 1364.

financial arrangements; this consequently meant their participation along with the Community in the agreement.

Other expressly conferred powers

The Treaty confers an express power on the Community to enter into association agreements with third countries and international organizations.[29] These are concluded with third countries either in preparation for full membership[30] or as an alternative to membership.[31] Article 238 provides that the Community may conclude agreements "establishing an association involving reciprocal rights and obligations, common action and special procedures" with other countries or international organizations.

Article 238 was apparently initially intended to permit the Community to enter into agreements establishing a Europe-wide free trade area, but it has been used by the Community to enter into a wide variety of agreements with many countries. Article 238 could serve as a basis for attributing a general foreign policy power to the Community, but the Court has tended to base its expansive decisions in the field of external relations on other grounds and Treaty provisions. Since the adoption of the Single European Act, association agreements must be approved by an absolute majority of the members of the Parliament.

The power of the EC in external relations was addressed in the Single European Act. Article 130m[32] authorises the Community to enter into international agreements providing for co-operation with third countries in EC research and development programmes, such agreements to be negotiated and concluded pursuant to Article 228. A similar provision with respect to environmental matters is contained in Article 130r(4). The Treaty on European Union has added provisions on international agreements in the context of monetary union[33] and of development co-operation.[34] Two other Treaty provisions relate to external relations. First, as to the responsibility for representing the EC in international organizations, the EC Treaty provides that the Commission shall maintain relations with the UN and other international organizations, and, in particular with the GATT.[35] Although the Treaty contains no specific provisions on

---

[29] See Art 238.

[30] This was the case with Greece, Spain and Portugal. See also the "New Europe Agreements" with the Central and Eastern European countries which are considered as prospective EC Members.

[31] See *e.g.*, Turkey whose membership application has been effectively set aside.

[32] Art 130n has been renumbered 130m by the Treaty on European Union.

[33] See Art 109.

[34] See Art 130y. In some cases, these provisions state that they are without prejudice to Member State rights to negotiate and conclude international agreements; see Arts 109, 130r(4), 130y. A declaration attached to the Final Act adopted at Maastricht notes that these provisions do not affect the principles resulting from the Court's *ERTA* judgment.

[35] Art 229. Arts 230 and 231 provide for co-operation between the EC and the Council of Europe and the OECD.

diplomatic relations, in 1994 the Commission maintained over 100 delega-tions in foreign countries and at various international organizations (for example, it has observer status at the UN), and there were diplomatic missions from approximately 130 countries accredited to the EC. Second, Article 131 provides for the association with the EC of the non-European territories of the Member States. When the Treaty initially came into force in 1958, there were many such territories. Over time, almost all of them have become independent and their relations with the EC are no longer dealt with in Part IV of the Treaty[36], but rather through such arrange-ments as the Lomé convention.

Implied powers (the doctrine of "parallelism")

A first glance at Article 228 would justify the view that the power of the Community to enter into international agreements is limited. According to this provision, the Commission is to negotiate agreements "where this Treaty provides for the conclusion" of such agreements.[37] Thus, on its face, the EC Treaty adopts the model of enumerated powers; (*compétence d'attribution*) by allocating specific powers to the Community with the non-allocated powers remaining with the Member States.[38]

The Court, however, in its first major judgment given on the matter in the *ERTA* case[39] rejected the principle of enumerated powers in favour of the doctrine that Community treaty power is co-extensive with its internal powers (*in foro interno, in foro externo*)[40], and thus it cuts across all areas of its internal competence listed in Article 3.[41] In its cardinal judgment in *ERTA*, the Court established four important principles which were further elaborated and expanded in subsequent judgments. These principles delineate the scope of the EC treaty-making power and may be summarised as follows:[42]

(i) The principle of general powers. Article 210 provides that the Com-munity has legal personality which "means that in its external relations the Community enjoys the capacity to establish contractual links with third countries over the whole field of objectives defined in Part One of the Treaty".[43]

---

[36] Arts 131–136a.

[37] See Arts 109, 113, 130m, 130r(4), 130y and 238.

[38] This view was supported by A.G. Dutheillet de Lamothe in his opinion in Case 22/70, *Commission* v *Council* (*Re E.R.T.A.*), [1971] ECR 263, at 274–276.

[39] *Ibid.*

[40] This expression has been used extensively by Pescatore to illustrate the extent of Community powers in the field of external relations. See *e.g.,* (1979) 16 CMLRev. 615, 618.

[41] See Stein, "External Relations of the European Community: Structure and Process", in Clapham (ed.), *Collected Courses of the Academy of European Law 1990* (Martinus Nijhoff, 1993), vol. I, book I, p 146. The list of Community activities included in Art 3 is formidable and seems ever expanding since other areas have been added in practice and confirmed by the Single European Act and more recently by the Treaty on European Union.

[42] See *The Oxford Encyclopedia of European Community Law* (1990), Vol I, *Institutional Law*, by A G Toth, pp 521–531.

[43] Case 22/70, *supra*, n 38 at 274, *per curiam*.

(ii) The principle of implied powers. In order to determine in an individual case the Community's authority to enter into international agreements:

"regard must be had to the whole scheme of the Treaty no less than to its substantive provisions. Such authority arises not only from an express conferment by the Treaty . . . but may equally flow from other provisions of the Treaty and from measures adopted, within the framework of those provisions, by the Community institutions".[44]

(iii) The principle of exclusivity. Each time the Community, with a view to implementing a common policy envisaged by the Treaty, has adopted common rules, whatever form these may take:

"the Member States no longer have the right, acting individually or even collectively, to undertake obligations with third countries which affect those rules. As and when such common rules come into being, the Community alone is in a position to assume and carry out contractual obligations affecting the whole sphere of application of the Community legal system".[45]

In Opinion 1/76[46], the Court ruled, apparently reversing its view in *ERTA*, that the external competence is not dependent on the actual adoption of internal measures. Consequently, the Community enjoys external competence even though internal measures in a specific area have not been enacted, provided that and in so far as:

". . . the participation of the Community in the international agreement is . . . necessary for the attainment of one of the objectives of the Community".

However, in Opinion 1/94[47], the Court confirmed its *ERTA* judgment[48] with respect to GATS[49], to the effect that Member States lose their powers to the benefit of the Community as and when common rules come into effect which could be affected by international obligations. The Court acknowledged that the Community may use powers conferred on it under the Treaty provisions on the right of establishment and the freedom to provide services in order to lay down internal rules on nationals of non-member countries. It therefore concluded that the Community would acquire exclusive external powers whenever it included in internal legislative Acts provisions relating to the treatment of nationals of non-member countries, or expressly conferred on its institutions powers to negotiate

---

[44] Case 22/70, *ibid.*, at 274, paras 15–16 *per curiam* cited verbatim in Cases 3, 4, & 6/76, *Kramer*, [1976] ECR 1279, at 1308, paras 19–20 *per curiam*. See also Opinion 1/76, [1977] ECR 741, at 755, para 3 *per curiam*.

[45] Case 22/70, *supra*, n 38 at 274.

[46] *Supra*, n 44 at 755.

[47] *Supra*, n 15.

[48] Case 22/70, *supra*, n 38.

[49] This part of the Opinion concerned the modes of supplying services as defined in GATS (see *supra*, n 16) other than cross-border supplies of services which fell squarely within the scope Article 113.

with non-member countries or again where the Community had achieved complete harmonisation of the rules governing access to a self-employed activity. As harmonisation was not yet complete in all these fields, the Court held that the power to conclude the GATS was shared between the Community and the Member States.

With regard to the TRIPS, the Court, following the same line of reasoning, ruled that the power to conclude the agreement was shared between the Community and its Member States as the harmonisation of the regime of different intellectual property rights was only partial or, in some fields, completely non-existent. Thus, in areas of intellectual property law other than the prohibition of release for free circulation of counterfeit goods which fell within the scope of Article 113, the Community's external powers depended upon the extent of internal harmonisation. However, the Court pointed out that the Community did have external powers to harmonise national rules which could have a direct effect on the establishment and functioning of the common market; in that respect, there was no reserved domain for Member States.

Thus, while treaty-making powers expressly conferred on the Community by the Treaty are exclusive irrespective of whether they have been exercised or not[50], this is not the case where Community treaty-making power exists by implication. As long as an implied treaty-making power has not been used, Member States retain residual authority to enter into international agreements necessary to achieve a Community aim subject to certain conditions.[51]

(iv) The principle of parallelism. According to the Court "the system of internal Community measures may not be . . . separated from that of external relations".[52] However, after *ERTA*, some Member States have opposed certain internal measures in the Council on the ground that their adoption may give rise to Community treaty-making power in the same subject-matter.[53] Moreover, except for agreements falling squarely within the area of commercial policy, the Council has preferred not to rely on Community powers as declared in *ERTA* and Opinion 1/76. It has opted instead to invoke the less controversial general clauses of Articles 100 and 235 either exclusively[54] or in conjunction with other Treaty provisions conferring specific powers on the institutions.[55] As to the form in which Community agreements are concluded, the Council has clearly favoured

---

[50] See Opinion 1/75, *supra*, n 6 at 1364.

[51] See Cases 3, 4 & 6/76, *supra*, n 44 at 1310–1311.

[52] Case 22/70, *supra*, n 38 at 274.

[53] This is particularly true in certain sensitive areas such as sea and air transport measures under Article 84 EC. See House of Lords Select Committee on the European Communities, *External Competence of the European Communities* (1985), 16th Report, 104–106.

[54] See *e.g.*, in the field of environmental protection the Bonn Convention (1976), OJ 1977 L240/35.

[55] Mainly Arts 43 and 113. For examples see Stein, "European and US Foreign Affairs Systems Compared", in Cappelletti, Secombe, Weiler (eds), *Integration Through Law: European and the American Federal Experience* (Walter de Gruyter, 1986), Vol I, book 3, pp 50–51.

"mixed agreements" in which the Community is joined by the Member States as parties. This practice:

". . . confirms the acute sensitivity of the Member Governments when it comes to recognizing the foreign affairs powers of the Community".[56]

Thus, in cases in which there is an apparent overlap between Community and national powers, the primary problem is to establish whether a given matter comes under the jurisdiction of the Community, and if so whether the competence is exclusive.

The role of the political institutions

Article 228 deals generally with the roles of the various EC institutions in the conclusion of international agreements. According to the Court:

". . . Article 228 constitutes, as regards the conclusion of treaties, an autonomous general provision, in that it confers specific powers on the Community institutions".[57]

With a view to establishing a balance between those institutions, it specifies that where the EC Treaty provides for conclusion of international agreements by the Community, the agreements shall be negotiated by the Commission and concluded by the Council, after consulting the European Parliament where required by the Treaty. Since the coming into force of the Treaty on European Union, the Council is authorised to act by qualified majority with two exceptions. Unanimity is required for Article 238 association agreements and agreements covering a field for which unanimity is required for the adoption of internal rules.

However, the power to conclude agreements is conferred on the Council under Article 228 "subject to the powers vested in the Commission in this field". The Court had the opportunity to clarify the meaning of this expression in *France* v *Commission*.[58] In its decision, the Court declared void the agreement entered into by the Commission and the Government of the United States on the enforcement of their respective competition rules. In its judgment the Court recognised that the exercise of the powers vested to the Commission was an exception to the general rule stated in Article 228 that the Council was responsible for the conclusion of international agreements. Furthermore, the Court pointed to Article 4 which provides that the institutions must only act within the powers conferred on them. No practice, even if such practices existed under the terms of the Euratom Treaty, could override the express wording of the EC Treaty. In this case the Commission also argued for a kind of parallelism of powers for itself. It argued that having had specific powers in the sphere of

---

[56] See Stein, *ibid.*
[57] Case C-327/91, *France* v *Commission*, [1994] ECR I-3641, at 3675.
[58] *Ibid.* For a comment see Burrows, (1995) 20 ELRev 210.

competition law, it had the power to enter into international agreements in relation to this specific subject matter. This argument failed to impress the Court which held that the fact the Commission was responsible for the enforcement of the competition rules within the Community did not give it the authority to negotiate agreements with third countries on the question of the enforcement of competition rules. Clearly, the principle of parallelism does not extend this far. The outcome of this case makes clear that the Council, not the Commission, has the authority to enter into international agreements, and that there are no general powers in the field of external relations vested in the Commission.

The extent to which the Parliament must assent to or be consulted in respect of international agreements has been a subject of controversy. Article 228 originally required consultation only in respect of association agreements under Article 238. In the case of agreements concluded under Article 113, no parliamentary consultation was required. However, under the *Luns-Westerterp* procedures, the Council voluntarily committed itself to inform the Parliament prior to commencing negotiations and prior to signing and formally concluding association agreements (1964) and commercial agreements (1973).[59] In addition, the Stuttgart European Council concluded in 1983 that, as a matter of policy, Parliament should be consulted prior to the conclusion of all significant international agreements.[60]

The Single European Act made the Parliament's assent necessary for the conclusion of association agreements under Article 238. The Treaty on European Union generally requires consultation of the Parliament prior to conclusion of all agreements, except those concluded under Article 113(3). The assent of the Parliament should be obtained for the conclusion of association agreements under Article 238; other agreements establishing a specific institutional framework by organising co-operation procedures; agreements having important budgetary implications for the Community; agreements entailing the amendment of an act adopted under the procedure provided for by Article 189b (co-decision).

Article 228 has two other important features. First, it provides that agreements concluded in accordance with its provisions shall be binding on the Community and the Member States. It also establishes a reference procedure. This procedure allows the Commission, the Council or a Member State to obtain an Opinion by the Court as to whether an envisaged agreement is compatible with the Treaty. The Court has used this provision to issue opinions on the scope and exclusiveness of the Community powers to enter into international agreements.

The view of the treaty-making competence of the EC initially favoured by the Member States in the Council was that the EC only possessed those treaty-making powers which had been expressly granted by the Treaty.

---

[59] Bull. EC 1973–10, p 90.
[60] Solemn Declaration on European Union, para 2.3.7., Bull. EC 1983–6, pp 26–27.

This approach led to a restrictive interpretation of Articles 228 and 238, that association agreements were limited to tariffs and trade.

Major agreements which clearly exceeded the limited commercial sphere, such as the Lomé Convention, were concluded as "mixed agreements" jointly by the Community and the Member States. Such agreements require ratification by the Member States according to their constitutional rules and approval by the Council on behalf of the EC. As a result there have been several disagreements between the Council and the Commission about who has the authority to negotiate international agreements.

Conclusions

Since the judgment of the Court in *ERTA* it is well established that the Community's treaty-making powers arise not only from the provisions giving express authority to enter into agreements but also, by implication, from other provisions granting the Community power to act internally and even from action undertaken in the application of such provisions by the Council and the Commission. As to the question of exclusivity it is now well established that so long as the Community has not exercised its power in a given area, the Member States may both take internal measures and enter into international agreements with third countries, subject to the obligations imposed on them by Article 5, and where applicable, Article 116 of the Treaty.[61] Once Community rules have been adopted internally, the Member States cannot, outside the framework of the Community institutions, assume any obligations likely to affect those rules or alter their scope.[62]

The Court, however, had failed to make clear whether the treaty-making powers of the Member States were always excluded whenever the Community had made use of its powers whether internally or internationally. The *ERTA* judgment was rather ambivalent on this issue. Although in paragraph 31 it was stated that the Community power excluded the possibility of a concurrent power of Member States, in paragraphs 17 and 22 the Member States were only barred from assuming obligations likely to affect or to alter the scope of the rules laid down by the Community. Does this mean that, even after Community rules have been adopted, the Member States may enter into agreements with third countries concerning the same matters, as long as in so doing they do not affect those rules or modify their scope?[63]

---

[61] See Cases 3, 4 & 6/76, *supra*, n 44; Case 61/77, *Commission* v *Ireland*, [1978] ECR 417.

[62] See Case 22/70, *supra*, n 38 at 274–276.

[63] This question has been raised and discussed by Waelbroeck, "The Emergent Doctrine of Community Pre-emption – Consent and Re-Delegation", in Sandalow and Stein (eds), *Courts and Free Markets* (OUP, 1982), Vol II, pp 569–571.

This question had not been addressed by the Court before Opinion 2/91.[64] Most legal writers, however, had answered this question in the negative.[65] Timmermans argued that, even in areas such as the common organisations of the market where, according to the caselaw of the Court, Member States retained a parallel power to adopt national measures provided that they did not jeopardise the objectives and the functioning of the common organisation, their power to enter into international agreements was precluded. Indeed, because of the doctrine of supremacy of Community law, national measures were less likely to pose a serious obstacle to the realisation of Community policy than international agreements entered into by the Member States which the Community could not unilaterally disregard.

This may hold true in the areas in which the Community has the power to make common policies. However as Kapteyn argued[66], in those areas in which the Community could only co-ordinate national policies there was no reason to adopt such a restrictive approach. Thus, if a harmonisation directive provided that Member States must enact legislation containing certain minimum provisions, but left them free to impose more stringent provisions, there seemed no reason why a Member State should not have the right to agree with third countries as to such provisions.

The Court in Opinion 2/91 confirmed Kapteyn's view. Since Article 118(3), provided for the adoption of minimum requirements to apply within the Community and did not forbid the adoption of more stringent measures by the Member States there was nothing to prevent the latter from adopting such measures either unilaterally or under international agreements. It would appear though, that joint competence in external matters seems to result from the setting of minimum requirements within the Community. On the other hand, in areas where powers are shared between the Communities and Member States, measures must be "common" and must involve close co-operation both in the process of negotiation and conclusion and the fulfilment of obligations entered into, and must also ensure "unity in the international representation of the Community".[67]

In Opinion 2/91 the Court also clarified the scope of the principle of exclusivity as enunciated in the *ERTA* ruling. It made clear that the *ERTA* ruling, in this respect, is not only confined to common policies but also covers all rules adopted within the framework of the objectives of the

---

[64] Opinion of 19 March 1993, nyr.

[65] See Kovar, "La Contribution de la Cour de justice au développement de la condition internationale de la Communauté Européenne", [1978] *Cah. dr. eur.* 527, 541; Timmermans, [1978] *S.E.W.* 582, 586.

[66] [1978] *S.E.W.* 276, 286–288. I would like to extend my thanks to Professor L. Gormley for the translation from the Dutch original.

[67] Opinion 2/91, para 36. See also Opinion 1/94, *supra* n 15 at 5419–5421; there the Court stressed that the obligation to co-operate was all the more important in the case of the WTO as the agreements were "inextricably intertwined" as demonstrated by the "cross-retaliation" mechanism.

Treaties. In other words, the scope of the principle of exclusivity as derived from the *ERTA* judgment cannot be restricted to instances where the Community has adopted rules within the framework of a common policy, but is applicable in all areas corresponding to the objectives of the Treaty.[68] The Court stressed, however, that exclusivity cannot be based (i) on any difficulties that may arise for the legislative function of the Community should the Member States retain concurrent competence in an area where the Community has adopted minimum requirements; and (ii) on Community measures adopted under Article 100. Moreover, in Opinion 1/94, the Court confirmed that Articles 100a and 235 cannot in themselves confer exclusive competence on the Community.[69] Different considerations might apply though for measures adopted on the basis of one of the general provisions of Articles 100, 100a and 235 in conjunction with a specific Treaty provision, such as Articles 43 or 113.

The question of division of power between the Community and the Member States in the field of external relations is a particularly thorny one. The EC Treaty is mostly silent on this issue. As a result the Court which has been dealing with this question has formulated essential structural principles which "were forcefully proclaimed and pertinaciously reiterated since its inception".[70] In this process the Court has been anxious to preserve not only the unity of Community law at its present stage but also to preserve the possibilities for future developments as they are designed by the Treaty. It is clear from Opinions 2/91 and 1/94, that further development of Community law and, particularly the cardinal concepts of effectiveness and unity of EC law require "close association between the institutions of the Community and the Member States both in the process of negotiation and conclusion and in the fulfilment of the obligations entered into".[71] This may constitute a means "whereby Community and Member States gain in international strength simultaneously and become among themselves even further inextricably linked [and may] be regarded as a contribution to a strengthening of the overall framework of European integration".[72]

NICHOLAS EMILIOU

---

[68] See para 10.

[69] *Supra* n 15 at 5414, 5418.

[70] See Barav, "The Division of External Relations Power Between the European Economic Community and the Member States in the Case Law of the Court of Justice", in Timmermans (ed), *Division of Powers Between the European Communities and their Member States in the Field of External Relations* (Kluwer, 1981), p 29.

[71] Opinion 2/91, para 36; Opinion 1/94, para 108.

[72] See Weiler, "The External Legal Relations of Non-Unitary Actors: Mixity and the Federal Principle", in O'Keeffe and Schermers (eds), *Mixed Agreements* (Kluwer, 1983), p 83.

Chapter 4
Legal Base and the External Relations of the European Community

Introduction

Trade liberalisation has led to the internationalisation of the dilemmas of the mixed economy. For as states see the national regimes they have established to protect against market externalities being undermined by free trade, so the need for transnational solutions has become more apparent. Within the European Community harmonisation of laws has therefore become inextricably linked with the development of policies to cope with market failure.[1] The conclusions of the Uruguay Round suggest, moreover, that such a high degree of economic integration is an unnecessary precondition for such interaction. The description of substantive intellectual property rights in the Agreement on Trade Related Aspects of Intellectual Property Rights (TRIPS),[2] the draft Decision on the establishment of a programme of work to identify the relationship between trade and the environment,[3] and the belated attempt by France and the United States to incorporate commitments towards the safeguarding of employee rights within the Round all indicate that increased global trade liberalisation will result in increased international commitments for states to intervene positively in their economies. The increasingly multifarious nature of international trade regulation has not been reflected, however, in the debate on EC competencies in this field, focusing, as it has, predominantly on the ambit of Article 113 EC.[4] The purpose of this piece is to suggest that a far more nuanced approach has to be taken towards Community competence in the field of trade liberalisation. Within such an arrangement, it will be argued, the practice of the Court and the mixed nature of the Community should result in Article 113 EC not being seen as the predominant base for the Community's trade relations, but merely as one piece in an evolving jigsaw.

---

[1] Most recently Case C-359/92 *Germany* v *Council*, 9 August 1994.
[2] GATT Secretariat, MTN/FA II-A1C.
[3] GATT Secretariat, MTN.TNC/W/123.
[4] On this debate see Emiliou in this Volume at pp 31–45.

 **FALLOUT**

ADMISSION £1 ALL NIGHT
[OPEN 10PM TILL 2AM]
PINTS/SHOTS £1*
BOTTLES £1.50*

**BRINGING YOU ALL THE BEST IN
CHART NU/METAL/ROCK/ALT
AND YOUR OLD FAVORITES**

THURSDAY NIGHTS
WEAR WHAT U WANT

L E

K E P I

B L A N C

L E

K E P I

B L A N C

PLYMOUTH
UNIVERSITY

LE KEPI
BLANC

ITS A
SCREAM

MONEY
CENTER

 K

LE KEPI BLANC, 27-31 COBURG STREET
PLY TEL. 01752 251 122
*OFFERS ON SELECTED LINES
MANAGEMENT RESEVRE THE RIGHT TO BE SELECTIVE

Sources of reasoning and sources of competence within the external relations law of the European Community

The importance of non-semiotic sources of law is particularly apparent in the instance of Article 113 EC. The wording of the Article is terse[5] and, therefore, broadly indeterminative.[6] Furthermore, there has been a recognition since the First General Report of the Commission that the policy is not an end in itself, but instrumental to realisation of some further objective.[7] Whilst the two principal sources of reasoning used to interpret Article 113 EC are prepositive,[8] therefore, in that they only give rise to rights and duties in so far as they are given concrete expression in Article 113 EC, their common leitmotif is that it is their development and interpretation that has shaped this Article.

Potentially the most activist strain of reasoning within Article 113 EC is that the commercial policy of the Community should have the *same content as that of a state*.[9] At the root of this reasoning is a federalist logic. The comparison with states suggests, first, that the Community is politically indivisible. Second, it detaches Community external competencies from internal competencies not merely through the recognition of a seperate legal base but through the suggestion that a more general external

---

[5] Article 113(1) EC reads: "The common commercial policy shall be based on uniform principles, particularly in regard to changes in tariff rates, the conclusion of tariff and trade agreements, the achievement of uniformity in measures of liberalisation, export policy and measures to protect trade such as those taken in case of dumping or subsidies."

[6] The wording of Article 113 EC has been used by both the advocates and opponents of its being interpreted to cover trade in services. Vigneron and Smith, "Le Fondement de la Compétence Communautaire en matière de Commerce International de Services" (1992) 28 *CDE* 515 at 537; Perreau de Pinninck, "Les compétences communautaires dans les negotiations sur le commerce des services' (1991) 27 *CDE* 390 at 401.

[7] "This common commercial policy, which embraces all aspects of the economic relations with the outside world, is not an end in itself. Like the common external tariff it is a prerequisite for the good functioning of the common market." *First General Report of the Commission (1958)* paragraph 145.

[8] Articles 2, 3 & 5 EC can not independently give rise to individual rights, Joined Cases C-78–83/90 *Compagnie Commerciale de l'Ouest* v *Réceveur Principal des Douanes de la Pallice Port* [1992] ECR I -1847; [1994] 2 CMLR 425; Case C-18193 *Corsica Ferries Italia* v *Corpo dei Piloti di Genova* [1994] ECR I. 1783; Case C-323/93 *Société Civil Agricole d'Insemination de la Crespelle* v *Cooperative d'Eleraje et d'Insemination Artificielle du Département de la Mayenne* [1994] ECR I. 5077. On prepositive norms within the EC legal order see Dauses, 'The Protection of Fundamental Rights in the Community Legal Order' (1985) 10 ELRev 398 at p 405.

[9] Opinion 1/75 *Opinion on an Understanding on a Local Costs Standard* [1975] ECR 1361; [1976] 1 CMLR 8; Opinion 1/78 *Opinion on the International Agreement on Natural Rubber* [1979] ECR 2909;[1979] 3 CMLR 639; Case 45/86 *Commission* v *Council* [1987] ECR 1493; [1988] 2 CMLR 131.

competence might exist which extends beyond a mere reflection of its internal competencies.[10]

It is difficult to gauge how widely Article 113 EC can be interpreted on the basis of this principle. The federalism incipient in the EC Treaty is integrative federalism.[11] In areas, such as external relations, the process is heavily dependent upon positive integrative measures such as the establishment and maintenance of common policies by the legislative bodies of the Community. Judicial activism is limited by the risk of dysfunction, if national instruments are prohibited without suitable replacement Community mechanisms being put in place.[12] In this respect at the Intergovernmental Conferences prior to the Treaty on European Union the Commission attempt to push Article 113 EC to its federal conclusions, by proposing it as a basis for Community competence in the more general field of external economic relations was rebuffed.[13] In the wake of such resistance and in the light of national sensitivity over areas such as direct investment, qualifications and immigration[14], the reasoning has lain rather undeveloped. In *General System of Preferences*[15], the Court examined only that state practice which had been conducted within the framework of the UNCTAD. More recently, in *Opinion 1/94*[16], the Court relied on state practice to find that trade in services prima facie fell within Article 113 EC. The practice it examined, however, was the Agreement establishing the World Trade Organization, and its assorted annexes. These Opinions suggest that *only* that part of commercial policy which states are willing to have circumscribed by international treaties, that is, that over

---

[10] This is specifically alluded to in *Opinion 1/78* [1979] ECR 2909; [1979] 3 CMLR 639: "the Treaty does not form a barrier to the Community's developing a commercial policy aiming at regulation of the world market for certain products rather than at a mere liberalisation of trade." On the propensity for federal bodies to have external powers that go beyond a reflection of their internal powers see Weiler, "The External Legal Relations of Non-Unitary Actors: Mixity and the Federal Principle" in O'Keefe and Schermers, *Mixed Agreements* (1983, Kluwer, Deventer).

[11] Lenaerts, "Constitutionalism and the Many Faces of Federalism" (1990) 38 AJCL 205 at p 220 describes this as "a constitutional order which strives at unity in diversity among previously independent or confederally related component entities".

[12] On "negative policy integration" see Pelkmans, "Economic Theories of Integration Revisited" (1980) 18 JCMS 333 at p 342; Pelkmans and Heller, "The Institutional Economics of European Integration" in Capelletti, Seccombe and Weiler, *Integration Through Law: Volume 1: Methods, Tools and Institutions* (1986, Berlin, New York, De Gruyter) p 324. For judicial recognition of this see Advocate-General Verloren Van Themaat in Case 59/84 *Tezi Textiel* v *Commission* [1986] ECR 887; [1987] 3 CMLR 64 and Lenaerts, "Some Thoughts about the Interaction between Judges and Politicians in the European Community" (1992) 12 YEL 1 at pp 10 *et seq.*

[13] In its commentary on its proposals the Commission stated "Article Y17 (the proposed new competence), like Article 113 EC, which preceded it, becomes the nucleus of the external economic policy, the basis for the Union's exclusive competence in the field of external economic relations." *EC Bulletin* Supplement 2/91 at p 108. On the negotiations see Maresceau, "The Concept 'Common Commercial Policy' and the Difficult Road to Maastricht" in Maresceau (ed), *The European Community's Competence after 1992: The Legal Dimension* (1993, Kluwer, Deventer).

[14] Mengozzi, "Trade in Services and Commercial Policy" at pp 241–242 in Maresceau (ed), *The European Community's Competence after 1992: The Legal Dimension* (1993, Kluwer, Deventer)

[15] Case 45/86 *Commission* v *Council* [1987] ECR 1493, [1988] 2 CMLR 131.

[16] Opinion 1/94, *Opinion on the World Trade Organization*, Opinion of 15 November 1994, [1995] 1 CMLR 205.

which they wish to limit their sovereignty, and which is therefore the least sensitive area of their external economic relations[17] will fall therefore within Article 113 EC, a meaning that is far more restricted in its scope.

The other source of law used in developing Article 113 EC is that of the logic of the *common market*. Initially referred to by the Commission in its First General Report[18] it received judicial recognition in *Opinion 1/75*:

"Such a policy is conceived in that article [Article 113 EC] in the context of the operation of the common market, for the defence of the common interests of the Community, within which the the particular interests of the Member States must endeavour to adapt to each other".[19]

The Court then stated that the unilateral granting of export credits by Member States would "distort competition between undertakings of the various Member States in external markets"[20], language clearly analogous to that used in judgments such as the *Titanium Dioxide*[21] that a precondition for the internal market is an area in which the conditions of competition are not distorted. The distortion of competition remit is wide indeed. In the field of EC competition law, competition within the single market will be considered to be distorted not merely by practices restricting imports into the Community[22] but also practices regulating exports, where there is a substantial chance that the goods will re-enter the Community[23] or wherever a deflection of trade occurs, which leads to Community undertakings gaining a competitive advantage.[24]

Despite its wide reach, the single market suffers, however, from a contradiction. It requires the development of other policies, regional, social, environmental, consumer, monetary, industrial, to be both attainable and socially acceptable.[25] The development of these policies results in the Community being a less technocratic and more recognisable political community. Yet the emergence of these policies results in the common market no longer being pre-eminent but merely *primus inter pares*. These policies now not only support the single market, they subsume it. They do so internally and the doctrine of parallelism has resulted in their also so

---

17 It is through this reasoning that the Commission has traditionally argued that Article 113 EC should be extended to trade in services. Commission Communication on "Community Relations with Third Countries in Aviation Matters" COM (90) 17 final, 23 February 1990 at paragraph 20.

18 *Supra* n 7.

19 Opinion 1/75 *Opinion on an Understanding on a Local Costs Standard* [1975] ECR 1361; [1976] 1 CMLR 85.

20 See also Advocate-General Darmon in Case C-62/88 *Greece* v *Council* [1990] ECR I-1542 who states that the purpose of the common commercial policy includes preventing distortions of competition in dealings with non-member countries.

21 Case C-300/89 *Commission* v *Council* [1991] ECR I-2867; [1992] 3 CMLR 281; Case C-202/88 *Commission* v *France* [1991] ECR I-1223; [1992] 5 CMLR 552.

22 Examples include *Re Franco-Japanese Ballbearings Agreement* OJ 1974 L 343/19; *Re French and Taiwanese Mushroom Packers* OJ 1975 L 29/26; *Re Aluminium Products* OJ 1985 L 92/1; *Siemens/ Fanuc* OJ 1985 L 376/29.

23 *BBC Brown Boveri – NGK* OJ 1988 L 301/68.

24 *French-West African Shipowners Committees* OJ 1992 L 134/1.

25 Pelkmans and Robson, "The Aspirations of the White Paper" [1987] 25 JCMS 185.

doing externally. This doctrine was most clearly enunciated in *Opinion 2/91*,[26] where the Court clarified the scope of the *Kramer*[27] judgment:

"The Court concluded, in particular, that whenever Community law created for the institutions of the Community powers within its internal system for the purpose of attaining a specific objective, the Community had power to enter into the international commitments necessary for the attainment of that objective even in the absence of an express provision in that connection."

The rationale for this is stated in *Germany* v *Commission*:[28]

". . . it must be accepted that if that provision [the express provision] is not to be rendered wholly *ineffective* [author's italics] it confers on the Commission necessarily and *per se* the powers which are indispensable in order to carry out that task."

This doctrine was interpreted widely there to include not only the existence of powers necessary to the exercise of express legislative powers, but also those powers that are necessary to the exercise of any task or objective that has been assigned to a Community institution.[29]

The constraint of "necessity" imposed on the ambit of these powers, is, moreover, a weak one. In the above instance Article 118(2) EEC required the Commission to arrange consultations in the social field. It followed from this, stated the Court, that the Commission must necessarily be able to require information from the Member States in order to identify the problems and to pinpoint possible guidelines for future action.[30] Hartley points out, however, that it is not necessary for the Commission to have such powers, as it is perfectly possible to arrange consultations without imposing obligations on Member States.[31]

In areas where the Council has legislated, the constraint is weaker still, the Court considering the matter to be one of Council discretion.[32] In areas where prior internal legislation exists, the constraint of necessity has been effectively dispensed with and replaced by a straightforward application of the principle of parallelism. In *Opinion 2/91* the coincidence of

---

[26] Opinion 2/91 *I.L.O. Convention 170 on Chemicals at Work*, [1993] ECR I-1061 [1993] 3 CMLR 800. See also Advocate-General Jacobs in Case C-316/91 *Parliament* v *Council* [1994] ECR I-626 at paragraph 38.

[27] Cases 3,4 & 6/76 *Kramer and Others* [1976] ECR 1921; [1977] 2 CMLR 535.

[28] Cases 281/283–5,287/85 *Germany, France, Netherlands, Denmark and United Kingdom* v *Commission* [1987] ECR 3203; [1988] 1 CMLR 11.

[29] Hartley, *The Foundations of European Community Law* (1994, 3rd ed., Clarendon, Oxford) p 111. In Opinion 1/94 the Court stated that it would only find implied external powers to be *exclusive* where these were "inextricably linked" to the exercise of internal powers. It has been argued that *this* marked a more restrictive interpretation of the concept of "necessary". The Court was only commenting, however, on the quality and not the remit of Community competencies. See *contra* Bourgeois "The EC in the WTO and Advisory Opinion 1/94: An Echternach Process" [1995] CMLRev 763 at 780–781.

[30] *Ibid.* paragraph 28.

[31] Hartley, "The Commission as Legislator" (1988) 13 ELRev 122 at p 124.

[32] *e.g.* Case C-359/92 *Germany* v *Council*, 9 August 1994. For discussion and possible reasons why this is so see Dehousse, "Community Competences: Are there Limits to Growth?" in Dehousse (ed), *Europe after Maastricht: An Ever Closer Union?* (1994, Munich, Law Books in Europe).

subject matter of ILO Convention 170, whose purpose was to protect employees from chemically induced illness, and certain Directives was sufficient to found Community competence.[33]

In turn, if the principle of effectiveness, which determines the extent of these powers, is not to be a rhetorical device, it must be assessed by reference to external sources, most importantly the prepositive norms set out in Articles 3 and 3A EC. In *Continental Can*[34] the Court referred explicitly to the link:

"As may further be seen from subparagraphs (c) and (d) of Article 86(2), the provision is not only aimed at practices which may cause damage to consumers directly, but also at those which are detrimental to them through their impact on an **effective** competition structure, such as mentioned in Article 3(f) of the Treaty."

The parallels between the external aspects of the policies and activities articulated in Articles 3 and 3A EC, and the relationship between Article 113 EC and the single market are thus fairly apparent. Just as the *telos* of the common market, with its derived requirements of avoidance of trade deflection and competitive distortion, has been used as a basis for development of the commercial policy, so similar methodology has been used to extend the remit of these other policies. As a consequence, in each instance the symbiotic link between internal and external competence is emphasised. Internal Community competencies in each instance constrain Community external competencies, not so much from not extending beyond what is necessary, as the limits placed here have been weak, but as the basis for the latter's enlargement and development.

The common commercial policy and the flanking and horizontal policies of the European Community

This proliferation of legal bases reflects more accurately the mixed nature of the Community economy but leads to problems of disharmony. Within the "internal context" this has manifested itself in the burgeoning caselaw on "legal base"[35] and in instances of "conflicts of

---

[33] *Ibid.* paragraph 17. See also more recently Opinion 1/94, *Opinion on the World Trade Organization*, Opinion of 15 November 1994 [1995] 1 CMLR 205 at para 77 where the Court suggests straightforward parallelism as the establishment of internal rules will lead straight away to exclusive Community external competence in that field.

[34] Case 6/72 *Europeemballage Corporation and Continental Can Co Inc. v Commission* [1975] ECR 495; [1976] 1 CMLR 587.

[35] Scott Crosby, "The Single Market and the Rule of Law" (1991) 16 ELRev 451; Weatherill, "Regulating the Internal Market: Result Orientation in the House of Lords" (1992) 17 ELRev 299; Barents, "The Internal Market Unlimited: Some Observations on the Legal Basis of Community Legislation" (1993) 30 CMLRev 85; Chalmers, "Environmental Protection and the Single Market: An Unsustainable Development. Does the EC Treaty need a Title on the Environment?" (1995/1) LIEI 65; Emiliou, "Opening Pandora's Box: The Legal Basis of Community Measures Before the Court of Justice" (1994) 19 ELRev 488.

norms".[36] There has, however, been remarkably little general discussion on this point within the external context. This is possibly because of the view expressed by Advocate-General Lenz in *Harmonised Commodity System* that, in the external relations of the Community:

"If a power is expressly conferred on the Community to conclude an agreement . . . then it is no longer permissible to fall back upon a residual competence which is not expressly referred, does not mention a power to conclude agreements."[37]

This reasoning is unconvincing, and has been flatly contradicted by *Opinion 1/94*[38], where the Court stated that international transport agreements, nothwithstanding that they affect trade, should be based upon the transport provisions rather than Article 113 EC.[39] Even prior to this Opinion, the reasoning of the Advocate-General assumed, first, a divisibility about these other legal bases, whereby they have a "noyau dur" which governs their internal remit, but their external remit is residual and subsidiary. This contradicted the tenor of the quote taken from *Germany* v *Commission*, which with its emphasis on parallel powers falling *per se* within the remit of any competence if the competence is not to be *wholly* ineffective. Such reasoning could also be turned against Article 113 EC. Like every legal base, it has relied upon non-semiotic criteria for its development. If these criteria are residual and subsidiary, one would be forced to accept the self-defeating proposition that Article 113 EC has a "noyau dur", only within which it enjoys the preeminence suggested by Advocate-General Lenz.

The reasoning that governs choice of internal legal base must therefore also be applied to external relations.[40] Formally, some legal bases – those on education, culture, health, consumer protection, industry, develop-

---

[36] Case C-2/90 *Commission* v *Belgium* [1992] ECR I-4431, [1993] 1 CMLR 357. In that instance the Court reinterpreted the non-discrimination principle not in terms of whether the objects were economically substitutable but whether they had comparable effects on the environment, thereby shifting the function of the principle away from protecting comparative advantage towards protecting the environment. For further analysis see Chalmers, *supra* n 35.

[37] Case 165/87 *Commission* v *Council* [1988] ECR 5545 at paragraph 26. See also Eeckhout, *The European Internal Market, A Legal Analysis* (1994, Clarendon, OUP) pp 41–46; A more qualified approach is taken by Völker, *Barriers to External and Internal Community Trade* (1993, Kluwer, Deventer) pp 196 *et seq.*; Mengozzi, "Trade in Services and Commercial Policy" and Eeckhout, "The External Dimension of the Internal Market and the Scope and Content of a Modern Commercial Policy" in Maresceau (ed) *The European Community's Commercial Policy after 1992: The Legal Dimension* (1993, Kluwer, Deventer).

[38] Opinion 1/94, *Opinion on the World Trade Organization*, Opinion of 15 November 1994, [1995] 1 CMLR 205.

[39] Paragraph 48.

[40] This is not to say that because internal measures implementing an international agreement are based, say upon Article 43 EC, the international agreement should be based upon that Article. The principles which underline the agreement and the principles underlying its internal implementation may occasionally differ, which may justify differing legal bases being used. See Opinion 1/94, *Opinion on the World Trade Organization*, Opinion of 15 November 1994, paragraph 29. The principles for determining legal base are identical, however, whether the measures are internal or external.

ment co-operation[41] – and Article 235 EC, are explicitly stated to be of a residual nature. Others, notably environment, have been so characterised by the Court.[42] Sectoral policies, such as agriculture and fisheries[43] and transport[44], are taken to be *leges speciales* and to take precedence over more general legal bases such as Articles 100 EC and 100a EC.[45] Yet this formal hierarchy has been overturned by the insistence of the Court that the question of legal base is dependent upon the aim and content of the measure.[46] This requirement stems from the "guarantee" function of legal base, namely that it ensures that choice of base is not decided purely upon institutional compromise but correlates to the measure in question and is subject to judicial review upon this point.[47] The requirement has been applied aggressively by the Court, so that the correct legal base will depend upon where, having regard to its aim and content, the centre of the measure falls. If it falls predominantly within the remit of the "subservient" legal base, it should be based upon that competence even if the ancillary aims and content of a measure could normally justify its being based upon a "predominant" legal base.[48] Only in the rare instance where the Court will adjudge that a measure is equally centred upon two legal bases, will the formal hierarchy apply.[49] In all other circumstances it has been effectively dismantled, and a new egalitarianism introduced.

Adoption of the Uruguay Round by the Community therefore revolves around what is the *appropriate* legal base. Choice of legal base being dependent upon not only the content of the measure but also its aim, delimitation can not be determined purely by reference to the effects of the measure upon trade. The mere fact that a measure concerns imports

---

[41] Articles 127(4) EC, 128(5) EC, 129(4) EC, 129A(1)(b) EC, 130(3) EC and 130W(1) EC respectively.

[42] Case C-300/89 *Commission* v *Council (Titanium Dioxide)* [1991] ECR I-2867; [1993] 3 CMLR 359; Case C-62/88 *Greece* v *Council* [1990] ECR I-1527; [1991] 2 CMLR 649; Case C-405/92 *Etablissements A. Mondiet* v *Société Armement Islais* [1993] ECR I- 6133. It is also likely that the Title on Economic and Social Cohesion, Articles 130A EC -103D EC, would be so characterised, as the language in Article 130B EC on integration of that policy into other policies is remarkably similar to the language in Article 130R(2) EC which was used as a basis for the residuary nature of the Environment Title.

[43] Case 68/86 *United Kingdom* v *Council* [1988] ECR 855; [1988] 2 CMLR 543; Case 131/86 *United Kingdom* v *Council* [1988] ECR 905; [1988] 2 CMLR 364; Case 11/88 *Commission* v *Council* [1989] ECR 3743.

[44] Case 167/73 *Commission* v *France* [1974] ECR 359; [1974] 2 CMLR 216.

[45] On the difference between horizontal and sectoral policies see Barents *supra* n 35 at pp 97–102.

[46] In the field of external relations this reasoning has been used in Case 45/86 *Commission* v *Council* [1987] ECR 1493; [1988] 2 CMLR 131. and Case 62/88 *Greece* v *Council* [1990] ECR I-1527; [1991] 2 CMLR 649. It was also arguably implicit in Case 131/87 *Commission* v *Council* [1989] ECR 3743. It was also raised in Case C-187/93 *Parliament* v *Council,* [1994] ECR I-2857 but the point on Article 113 EC was dismissed at the stage of admissibility.

[47] On this function of legal base see Barents *supra* n 35 at p 92.

[48] Case C-70/88 *Parliament* v *Council (Chernobyl)* [1991] ECR I-4529; [1992] 1 CMLR 91; Case C-155/91 *Commission* v *Council (Waste Directive)* [1993] ECR I-939; Case C-187/93 *Parliament* v *Council (Waste Shipment),* [1994] ECR I-2857.

[49] *e.g.* Case C-300/89 *Commission* v *Council (Titanium Dioxide)* [1991] ECR I-2867.

into the Community will not make Article 113 EC automatically applicable.[50] It is suggested rather that the *principles*, which characterise and differentiate these policies, serve as the point of delimitation.[51] The legal base of a measure should be determined by the principles it predominantly follows and articulates. In the instance of some policies, such as, for example, Environment and Development Co-operation, these principles are fairly well articulated within the Treaty.[52] In the case of others, notably consumer protection, they have not been articulated and may require development by the Court.

This approach is also taken by the Court. Most notably in the *Waste Directive* judgment[53] the Court considered that Directive 91/156 EEC on waste was correctly based upon Article 130S EC, rather than Article 100A EC because the Directive aimed, by permitting prohibitions on the movement of waste and encouraging self-sufficiency in waste disposal, at implementing the principle that environmental damage be rectified at source rather than the principle of free movement of goods. More recently in its *Waste Shipment*[54] judgment, the Court found that Regulation 259/93, on the regulation of the shipment of waste within the Community and foreign trade in waste between the Community and third countries, was correctly based on Article 130S(1) because it implemented the principles of proximity, priority for recovery of waste and self-sufficiency at both Community and national level.

The external relations of the single market

It is beyond the scope of this paper to examine the principles that govern the external ambit of each Community policy. With regard to sectoral, horizontal or flanking policies, whilst there will inevitably be difficulties with borderline cases, the kernel of most policies is relatively clear. The position is more opaque with regard to those provisions, notably Articles 54(2) EC, 57(2) EC, 59(2) EC, 100 EC and 100(A) EC, whose concern, like Article 113 EC, is the establishment of the single market. The risk of considerable, if not complete, overlap with Article 113 EC and consequent dysfunction is at its greatest here. If Advocate-General Lenz's proposition that express external competences trump parallel competences is to apply at all, this must be the arena in which it operates. There are arguments, however, which refute it even here.

---

[50] Case 131/87 *Commission* v *Council* [1989] ECR 3743.

[51] The author would therefore reject any approach which relies even partially on instrumentalism. Ehlermann, ''The Scope of Article 113 EEC Treaty'' in *Etudes de Droit des Communautés Européennes – Mélanges Offertes à Pierre-Henri Teitgen* (1984, Paris) 145.

[52] Articles 130(R)(1) & (2) EC and 130U(1) & (2) EC.

[53] Case C-155/91 Commission v Council [1993] ECR I-939.

[54] Case C-187/93 Parliament v Council [1994] ECR I-2817.

First, Article 59(2) EC states that the benefits of the Chapter on Services may be extended by the Council, acting by qualified majority on a proposal from the Commission, to third country nationals established within the Community. Article 113 EC can not therefore provide the sole basis for regulation of the external relations of the single market.

Second, whilst there have been some celebrated examples of the Community concluding agreements with third countries in the field of services on the basis of Article 113 EC[55], in the case of autonomous measures legislative practice has been to use Article 57(2) EC as a legal base not merely for subjecting third country nationals or enterprises to the same sytem of regulation as EC nationals or enterprises, but also as a base for the former's exclusion from the single market. Procedures have thus been put in place on the bases of Articles 57(2) and 66 EC to exclude third country operators from the Community market if it considers that Community operators are not granted equivalent treatment in those operators' country of origin. In the fields of banking[56], investment services in securities[57] and life[58] and non-life assurance.[59]

Third, if the Court were to consider Article 113 EC to be the sole legal basis for regulating the external relations of the single market, this would also be a reason for it to adopt Professor Timmermans' suggestion that the remit of Article 113 EC be co-extensive with that of Article 30 EC. Member States would therefore be precluded from taking any measures against third country imports, which, if applied to EC imports, would fall within Article 30 EC subject to the rule of reason, where, as in the instance of the *Cassis de Dijon* jurisprudence, they could take those measures that are necessary to secure an objective recognised by Community law.[60] Such parallels were not drawn by the Court in *EMI*[61], when it stated that the provisions on commercial policy did not *extend* to measures having equivalent effect. In the context of Article 95 EC, the reason for this has been given that Article 113 EC is insufficiently precise to allow assessment of such measures.[62] Yet there is an umbelical link between the economic

---

[55] Notably the bilateral agreements on services concluded with Argentina OJ 1971 L33/2, Uruguay OJ 1973 L249/18, Brazil OJ 1974 L102/23, Mexico OJ 1975 L247/2 and China OJ 1978 L125/1. Most recently see the Agreement on Government Procurement between the European Community and the United States which covers, *inter alia*, services, OJ 1993 L125/1.

[56] Directive 89/646 EEC, OJ 1989 L386/1, Article 7.

[57] Directive 93/22 EEC, OJ 1993 L141/27, Article 7.

[58] Directive 90/619 EEC, OJ 1990 L330/50, Article 9. (as amended by Directive 92/96 EEC, OJ 1992 L360/1).

[59] Directive 90/618 EEC, OJ 1990 L330/44, Article 4, as amended by Directive 92/49 EEC, OJ 1992 L228/1.

[60] Timmermans, ''Common Commercial Policy (Article 113 EEC) and International Trade in Services'' in *Du droit international au droit de l'intégration: Liber Amicorum Pierre Pescatore* (1987, Baden Baden, Nomos).

[61] Case 52/75 *EMI* v *CBS* [1976] ECR 811, [1976] 2 CMLR 235. On this question see Völker, *Barriers to External and Internal Community Trade* (1993, Kluwer, Deventer) pp 102–108.

[62] Case 266/81 *SIOT* v *Ministero delle Finanze* [1983] ECR 731; [1984] 2 CMLR 231; Case C-130/92 *OTO SpA* v *Ministero delle Finanze*, [1994] ECR I-3281.

freedoms within the Treaty and the provisions outlined above, as it is the function of the latter to secure the former, and the former can only be fully realised through legislation based upon the latter. These provisions (*i.e.* Article 57(2) EC, 100A etc) therefore must have a wider remit than Article 113 EC.

As the starting point for delimitation, this author, unlike Vigneron and Smith[63], does not consider that the division of external competences can be seperated from that of internal competences. The focus on the external dimension of internal legislative powers has obscured the fact that Article 113 EC has a parallel internal dimension, not merely through its circumscribing the ambit of Article 115 EC, but also from its being an emanation of the principle of unity of the single market.[64]

The principle of market unity, firstly, explains the exclusive nature of Article 113 EC. For, if Member States could unilaterally impose restrictions on imports from third countries, this unity will be equally compromised. Such restrictions, to be effective, would require parallel restrictions on intra-Community trade if trade deflection were not to occur. This would have an extremely disruptive effect not just on third country trade circulating within the single market, but on all trade, as *all* trade would be subject to verification as to its place of origin. Secondly, and more fundamentally, restrictions on the entry of goods or the provision of services on to part of the single market, which are available in other parts of the single market is fundamentally at odds with the concept of a single market as an area, where any factor of production lawfully present in one part can move around to any other part.

Thus, although the Court has stated four times that Article 113 EC is an exclusive power[65], that exclusivity stems from the obligation to establish a single market.[66] Only in *Opinion 1/75*, therefore, where the Court was considering export credits, whose object was to secure the competitive position of Community undertakings, was Article 113 EC interpreted to preclude national action. Yet central to such a finding was the view that unilateral action would undermine the common market. Where the other source, that of international State practice, has been used, the practice of the Court has been more circumspect. In *Opinion 1/78*, the Court found that the building of buffer stocks for commodity agreements, in this instance rubber, fell within the ambit of Article 113 EC, yet still found that

---

[63] Vigneron and Smith *supra* n 6 at pp 539–540.

[64] This was recognised in *Opinion 1/75* where the Court stated: "A commercial policy is in fact made up by the interaction of internal and external measures, without priority being taken by one over the others".

[65] Opinion 1/75 *Opinion on an Understanding on a Local Costs Standard* [1975] ECR 1361; [1976] 1 CMLR 8; Case 41/76 *Donckerwolcke* v *Procureur de la République* [1976] ECR 1921; [1977] 2 CMLR 535; Opinion 2/91 *I.L.O. Convention 170 on Chemicals at Work,* [1993] ECR I-1061 3 CMLR 800. Opinion 1/94, *Opinion on the World Trade Organization,* Opinion of 15 November 1994, [1995] 1 CMLR 205.

[66] Communication of the Commission to the Council and the European Parliament, *The Principle of Subsidiarity* SEC (92) 1990 final p 7.

Member States could participate in the agreement without Community authorisation, the division of competencies being drawn according to who was financing the buffer stock. In its judgment on *Aid to ACP States*[67], despite having previously concluded in its *General System of Preferences* judgment that there was a large overlap between trade and development and that, consequently, a large body of development policy fell within the remit of Article 113 EEC, the Court concluded that development aid was an area of mixed competence. Whilst the latter concerned preferential tariff arrangements rather than explicit aid, the rationale for those arrangements was that they were a form of development aid. The two situations are therefore indistinguishable, and the only conclusion can be that where the federalist argument of state practice is used, the principle of exclusivity is not necessarily applicable but rather that the exclusivity of Article 113 EC finds its roots in the single market and the language of distortion of competition.

Internally, the common commercial policy finds its parallel in the principle that there should be no discrimination on grounds of nationality. The latter's function as a socio-economic principle of the single market is synonymous with that of comparative advantage[68], whereby, unless the situation is purely an 'internal' one, which does not concern imports or exports, a state can not give a direct competitive advantage to one product over another.[69] It is unique in Community law in that it binds not just the host state and the Community institutions but also the home state. Member States can not therefore treat their export trade differently from their domestic trade.[70] Unlike the principle of mutual recognition, this principle does not serve to delimit national competence from areas of Community competence in any way but regulates all areas of state activity. If taken to its logical extremes it would go a long way towards outlawing state intervention in the economy.[71] As such, it is the internal manifestation of the principle of market unity for, taken to its limits, the principle requires states not to intervene in the market place in a manner which either restricts trade or compels, encourages or reinforces anticompetitive conduct.[72] Gyselen has suggested in a seminal article, therefore, that to

---

[67] Case C-316/91 *Parliament* v *Council* [1994] ECR I-625.

[68] Joined Cases 32–33/58 *SNUPAT* v *High Authority* [1959] ECR 123; Schwarze, *European Administrative Law* (1992, Sweet & Maxwell, London) pp 602–605; Chalmers, "Free Movement of Goods within the European Community: An Unhealthy Addiction to Scotch Whisky" (1993) 42 ICLQ 269 at 284; Chalmers, 'Repackaging the Internal Market – The Ramifications of the *Keck* Judgment' (1994) 19 ELRev 385 at 397.

[69] It is therefore distinct from "reverse discrimination", which stems from a Member State not granting to its product or citizens rights enjoyed by others under Community law, not from differential treatment between two comparable situations by the Member State concerned. Similarly a state that engages in regulatory competition, whilst placing economic agents from other jurisdictions at a competitive disadvantage, is not "discriminating" against them as it does not have jurisdiction to set the standards that form the basis of their disadvantage.

[70] Case 15/79 *Groenveld* v *Produktscap voor Vlees en Vlees* [1979] ECR 3409; [1981] 1 CMLR 207.

[71] Barents, "The Community and the Unity of the Common Market" (1991) 30 GYIL 9 at pp 12–13.

[72] Case 267/86 *Van Eycke* v *ASPA* [1988] ECR 4769.

prevent too restrictive a regime, the state action must, to be illegal, additionally, *specifically* aim at regulating competition.[73] In *Peralta*,[74] therefore, the Court held that an Italian law which prohibited only vessels flying the Italian flag from discharging hydrocarbon solutions in territorial waters was not illegal because the prohibition it lays down is "sufficient in itself". The wording is opaque but suggests that this line of reasoning is also being followed by the Court and that changes in competitive structures resulting from legislation do not render that legislation illegal unless that legislation aims to secure those advantages.[75]

Gyselen suggests that such anti-competitive conduct should be justifiable, either where it pursues genuine economic or monetary policy objectives, or where it pursues classic *Cassis de Dijon* legitimate objectives. He is no doubt here trying to tie in the caselaw on Articles 5 and 85 EC with that on Article 30 EC. The analogy drawn is not an accurate one. Where measures are found to fall within the remit of Article 30 EC and are found to be justified, either under the "mandatory requirements" doctrine or Article 36 EC, it is because they are found to pursue, in a proportionate manner, objectives recognised under Community law. A measure that has pursued the principle of securing comparative advantage for some at the expense of others has never been held to be legal, for the simple reason that it could not then be aiming to secure an objective justified under Community law.

Both the exclusive nature of the common commercial policy and the non-discrimination principle are therefore centred around the concept of direct competitive advantage. Member State conduct that falls foul of either is in principle outlawed. It is submitted that this parallelism is reflected in the remit of Article 113 EC. As an instrument of the single market, *Article 113 EC therefore only covers those measures which, from their aim and content, directly seek to secure the competitive position of Community goods or producers vis-à-vis third country goods or producers.*

No such parallel can be drawn between the common commercial policy and the principle of mutual recognition established in *Cassis de Dijon*. The latter principle requires that importing Member States recognise the capacity of the exporting Member State to protect the interests in question. As the host state must take account of the standards of the state of origin, the home state, there is a presumption that the home state, within this structure, is the state which has the central role, in so far as it can, in the setting of standards within the single market. Host states can only therefore regulate trade in so far as they can show that either the home state is unable to regulate the point in question or has not done so to a satisfactory level.

---

[73] Gyselen, "Anti-Competitive State Measures under the EC Treaty: Towards a Substantive Legality Test" (1994) 19 EL Rev CC55 at CC66.

[74] Case C-379/92 *Peralta*, [1994] ECR I-3453.

[75] See also Case C-2/91 *Meng* [1993] ECR I-5171. For further analysis see Reich, "The 'November Revolution' of the European Court of Justice: *Keck, Meng* and *Audi* Revisited" (1994) 31 CMLRev 459. See also Case C-2/91 *Meng* [1993] ECR I-5751; Case C-55/93 *Van Schaik* [1994] ECR I-4837; Case C-412/93 *Leclerc Siplec* v *TFI Publicité*, Judgment of 9 February 1995.

The principle serves to further integration but, in the absence of harmonisation, it also serves to allow diversity by protecting home state control. In so far as it delimits jurisdiction it can not therefore be said to be linked to the objective of market unity, for in the absence of harmonisation, and subject to the non-discrimination principle outlined above, Member States have autonomy to set regulatory standards. Regulatory competition, and therefore differences in competitive conditions, whilst not being actively encouraged, is permitted by the *Cassis de Dijon* line of reasoning.

Third country trade benefits from this principle of home state control, in that whilst the four freedoms do not extend to trade with third countries, third country goods will profit from it if they have been put into free circulation in one of the Member States.[76] The setting of "internal" standards has, thus, the inevitable external dimension that foreign actors will have to abide by those standards on entering the jurisdiction. This would seem to suggest that Member States clearly have jurisdiction *vis-à-vis* the setting of indistinctly applicable technical regulations. As such the establishment of such matters should fall outside the remit of Article 113 EC.

Opinion 1/94 is somewhat eliptical upon this. On the one hand the Court refused to accept Article 113 EC as the correct legal base for the conclusion of the Agreement on Trade-Related Aspects of Intellectual Property Rights (TRIPS). This Agreement describes substantive intellectual property rights that signatories must make available to traders on a non-discriminatory basis within their jurisdictions. The Court ruled that the Agreement fell outside Article 113 EC on the grounds that intellectual property rights did not bear down specifically upon international trade, but affected internal Community trade equally, if not primarily. The Agreement therefore also resulted in a partial harmonisation of intellectual property rights which directly contributed to the establishment of a common market. Article 100A EC was as such the correct legal base for the conclusion of such an Agreement. This suggestion therefore, that any measure that affects the harmonisation process should fall outside Article 113 EC, follows the line of reasoning outlined above.

Whilst the most developed part of the Opinion supports my contentions, there are two Agreements which the Court found the Community had competence to conclude on the basis Article 113 EC, neither of which are directly concerned with competitive advantage and which are problematic. These are the Agreement on Sanitary and Phytosanitary Measures

---

[76] Article 9 EC Case 41/76 *Donckerwolcke* [1976] ECR 1921; [1977] 2 CMLR 535; Case 59/84 *Tezi Textiel* v *Commission* [1986] ECR 887; [1987] 3 CMLR 64; Case 212/88 *Levy* [1989] ECR 3511. Albeit in the context of a Community secondary legislation, the Court has also suggested that the principle of Home State control equally applies to services. Case C-154/93 *Tawil-Albertini* v *Ministre des Affaires Sociales* [1994] ECR I- 451. See also Tedegar, "Applying the Cassis de Dijon doctrine to goods originating in third countries" (1994) 19 ELRev 86 who suggests that there might be further requirements before a third country good can benefit from the free movement provisions.

and the Agreement on Technical Barriers to Trade. In both instances the rationale given was that their purpose was to liberalise trade. Both Agreements cover indistinctly applicable measures. In the former Agreement members must ensure that any sanitary or phytosanitary measure is applied only to the extent necessary to protect human, animal or plant life or health.[77] Similarly, technical regulations must not be more trade-restrictive than is necessary to fulfil a legitimate objective.[78] These Agreements can be distinguished from the TRIPS Agreement on the grounds that these latter Agreements are primarily concerned with negative integration, the removal of impediments to trade, whereas the TRIPS Agreement focuses, in the development of substantive rights, on positive integration and the facilitation of trade that involves. If the implication of *Opinion 1/94* is that technical standards fall within Article 113 EC the exclusive nature of Article 113 EC means that national measures that fall within its ambit are only legal if authorised by the Commission.[79] The requirement of Commission authorisation not only goes against the principle of home state control but is thoroughly undesirable in policy terms. It would result in an overburdened Commission finding an ever increasing amount of its time spent dealing with difficult technical matters, a Community that could not react swiftly to risk regulation, as everything would have to be considered both by national authorities and the Commission, and to increasing tensions between the Member States and the Commission, as the former find their room for manoeuvre controlled. It is hoped, given the lack of argument on this in the Opinion that the matter is reviewed.

The confusion has been compounded by the recent Opinion, given on 7 March 1995, *Opinion 2/92* on Community participation in the Third Revised OECD Decision on national treatment. The OECD Decision provides for equal treatment of foreign-owned undertakings to that given to nationals in measures concerning government procurement, official aids and subsidies, access to finance, fiscal obligations and rules applicable to investment other than direct investment. The Court considered that the national treatment rule was predominantly concerned with the conditions for the participation of foreign-controlled undertakings in the internal economic life of the Member States where they operate. It should therefore be governed by the internal market rules rather than Article 113 EC. The Opinion, first, makes a dichotomy based on the material subject-matter of the agreement – that is, whether it is predominantly concerned with internal matters or with trade between States – which makes its reasoning in respect of the Agreements on Technical Barriers and Phytosanitary Measures even harder to understand. The Opinion is also odd in that, secondly, if predominantly internal measures fall outside Article 113 EC that would throw into doubt the Community's participation in the GATT

---

[77] GATT, MTN/FA II-A1A-4, Article 6.
[78] GATT, MTN/FA II-A1A-6, Article 2.2.
[79] Case 41/76 *Donckerwolcke* v *Procureur de la République* [1976] ECR 1921; [1977] 2 CMLR 535.

which deals, *inter alia*, with internal taxation. Thirdly, the internal/external distinction suggested is replete with difficulties. Trade in services, for example, is often only evidence through investment flows. Yet the Opinion suggests such matters as they concern integration in the internal life of a Member State fall outside Article 113 EC. Finally, a commercial policy should concern not merely access to a market for foreign goods but also the terms under which they compete on that market. If it does not concern the latter, as this Opinion suggests, not only is the access rendered illusory but the unity of the market is affected as foreign goods may be subjected to different terms of competition within different parts of the single market.

Conclusion

The borderline between Article 113 EC and the "internal" single market competences may be difficult to draw in the field of external relations, in particular as many technical and regulatory standards have the *effect* of securing a competitive advantage for particular undertakings. In this respect, it should be remembered that it is the principles upon which a measure is based and which it seeks to achieve which should be determinative. The author would also observe that, in parallel with the requirement that an internal measure must specifically aim at altering the competitive structure to be illegal, a measure should only fall within the ambit of Article 113 if it acts *directly* to secure the competitive position of Community undertakings. Countervailing and anti-dumping measures, safeguards and measures against illicit trade practices therefore all clearly fall within Article 113 EC as they all attempt either to secure the competitive position of Community undertakings or to protect against anti-competitive practices. Measures protecting intellectual property rights are less clearcut as although they aim to protect markets, this stems from the rationale of the need to protect property rights.

Despite Article 113 EC being a sufficient legal base for a considerable part of the Uruguay Round, the Round may well represent its apogee. With, in particular, the servicisation of the world economy, the principal obstacles to trade are increasingly being seen as differences in national regulatory regimes, most of which have been set up to secure some objective of general interest.[80] For liberalisation of these regimes, which will involve the establishment of minimum standards or the acceptance of the principle of mutual recognition, Article 113 EC is unlikely to be a sufficient legal base and the Community will have to rely increasingly on its other so-called "internal" powers.

DAMIAN CHALMERS

---

[80] As an example of the wide variety of interests that this can cover see Case C-275/92 *Her Majesty's Customs and Excise* v *Schindler Brothers* [1994] ECR I-1039.

Chapter 5
Human Rights and Democracy Clauses in the EC's Trade Agreements

Introduction

The Fourth Lomé Convention which came into force in 1991[1] contains a striking innovation. This was the first appearance within a Community agreement of what may be termed a "human rights clause". The Preamble contains phrases familiar from many other Community agreements of the 1970s and 1980s, affirming respect for human rights and containing references to specific instruments such as the Universal Declaration of Human Rights and the European Convention. However these statements also find expression in Article 5 of the agreement itself:

"1. Co-operation shall be directed towards development centred on man, the main protagonist and beneficiary of development, which thus entails respect for and promotion of all human rights. Co-operation operations shall thus be conceived in accordance with the positive approach, where respect for human rights is recognised as a basic factor of real development and where co-operation is conceived as a contribution to the promotion of these rights.

In this context development policy and co-operation are closely linked with the respect for and enjoyment of fundamental human rights. . . .
2. . . . The rights in question are all human rights, the various categories thereof being indivisible and inter-related each having its own legitimacy: non-discriminatory treatment, fundamental human rights, civil and political rights, economic social and cultural rights."

The Community had been seeking the inclusion of a human rights clause since the negotiations for the second Lomé Convention in 1979, proposals which had foundered on the ACP states' fears of political interference and on differing approaches to human rights. This last factor explains both the unusually full "shopping list" of conventions in the Preamble and the reference to the "indivisible" nature of the different aspects of human rights in Article 5 itself. Since 1991, when the fourth Lomé Convention came into force, a human rights clause has become a regular feature of Community agreements: trade agreements as well as association agreements. As we shall see, even in this short period, the standard form of

---

[1] Fourth Lomé Convention signed Lomé Togo 15 December 1989; concluded by Decision of EC Council and Commission OJ 1991 L229/1. In force 1 September 1991.

clause has evolved into a potentially powerful weapon raising questions as to the relationship between political objectives and trade policy.

The direct impetus for generalising the inclusion of the human rights clause – especially in agreements which have a development component – was the European Council Resolution of 28 November 1991 on human rights, democracy and development[2] which was itself a response to a Commission initiative.[3] This document in addition explicitly links human rights with democracy. Development is "based on the central place of the individual" and is thus linked to civil and political liberty and specifically to "representative democratic rule" based on respect for human rights. Priority is expressly given to a positive approach[4], involving active support for projects designed to advance good governance, but significantly the Resolution envisages the possibility of action in cases of "grave and persistent violations" of human rights or serious interruption of democratic processes. A graduated response may range from "confidential or public *démarches*" to "when necessary, the suspension of co-operation with the states concerned". This approach is to be supported by the introduction of human rights clauses in future co-operation agreements.[5]

The Treaty on European Union, negotiated during the same months, formalises the Community's own position in Article F which not only reaffirms previous declarations of respect for fundamental human rights "as general principles of Community law"[6] but also expressly refers to the principles of democracy on which the systems of government of the Member States are founded. This is then carried through into the Union's relations with third states, as Article J.1(2) includes among the objectives of the Common Foreign and Security Policy "to develop and consolidate democracy and the rule of law, and respect for human rights and fundamental freedoms". The link between human rights, democracy and development has also been introduced into the EC Treaty itself in the provisions on development co-operation using words that are virtually identical to those used in Article J.1(2).[7] In 1992 the EC Commission said:

---

[2] Resolution of the Council and of the Member States meeting in Council on human rights, democracy and development, 28 November 1991, Bulletin of the EC 11–1991 p 122.

[3] Commission Communication to Council "Human Rights, Democracy and Development Co-operation Policy" 25 March 1991 SEC(91)61/6.

[4] *cf.* Article 5(1) of Lomé IV *supra*.

[5] Resolution of the Council and of the Member States meeting in Council on human rights, democracy and development, 28 November 1991, see n 2 *supra*, at para 10.

[6] For example the Joint Declaration by the European Parliament, the Council and the Commission of 5 April 1975; and the Declaration by the Foreign Ministers on Human Rights of 21 July 1986. Fundamental rights are expressed in terms of the European Convention for the Protection of Human Rights and Fundamental Freedoms 1950, and the constitutional traditions of the Member States.

[7] Article 130u(2) EC: "Community policy in this area shall contribute to the general objective of developing and consolidating democracy and the rule of law, and to that of respecting human rights and fundamental freedoms".

"Community development aid has become conditional on effective observance of human rights and real progress towards democracy, although any decision to suspend aid does not affect humanitarian operations."[8]

In its report on the implementation during 1993 of the November 1991 Resolution, the Commission covers both the positive action envisaged in the Resolution and the range of sanctions which may be employed in cases of serious violation. It goes beyond the scope of this paper to analyse the measures of positive action in detail; however they have included support for electoral processes (logistical and technical assistance as well as the presence of teams of observers) in several countries (Malawi, the Central African Republic and others); action to strengthen the rule of law, such as support for Ministries of Justice, Constitutional Courts and legal aid; assistance to identified vulnerable groups (detainees, political prisoners and minorities, for example) through legal assistance, aid centres and ombudsmen's offices.[9] Negative measures or sanctions available are listed on a rising scale:

- confidential or public *démarches*;

- change in the content of co-operation programmes or channels used;

- deferment of decisions needed to implement co-operation;

- reduction of cultural, scientific or technical co-operation programmes;

- deferment of joint committee meetings;

- suspension of high-level bilateral contact;

- postponement of new projects;

- refusal to act on partner's initiatives;

- trade embargoes;

- suspension of co-operation with the states concerned.[10]

Where there is no trade or co-operation agreement with the state concerned, the legal basis for such action can be found in Article 130u(2) EC and, more generally, Article F and J.1(2) TEU. The imposition of sanctions in the context of a trade agreement raises further questions which will be considered below.

These developments have of course taken place against a background of immense political change in Europe. One result of the collapse of the Communist regimes has been an increased confidence in democracy as a

---

[8] 26th General Report 1992 (point 901).

[9] Report from the Commission to the Council and European Parliament on the implementation in 1993 of the Resolution of the Council and of the Member States meeting in the Council on human rights, democracy and development adopted on 28 November 1991, COM(94)42 final, 23 February 1994. During 1993 EC financing for 143 projects totalled ECU 39.2 million.

[10] *Ibid.* at p.11.

system of government able to provide stability and support economic development. Since 1989 the emerging democracies of Europe have been acutely conscious of the need for good governance based on the rule of law as a basis not only for the protection of fundamental human rights but also for the transformation of their economies. These priorities have been recognised also by the European Community. Article J.1(2) TEU includes references to the principles of the Helsinki Final Act (to which both the Community and the Member States are party) and the objectives of the Charter of Paris. On 16 December 1991, the EC Foreign Ministers adopted a highly significant Declaration on the recognition of new states in Eastern Europe and the former Soviet Union.[11] The Declaration adopts a series of conditions for recognition, among them respect for the provisions of the UN Charter, Helsinki Final Act and the Charter of Paris, "especially with regard to the rule of law, democracy and human rights" and guarantees for the rights of ethnic groups and minorities. As well as forming prior conditions for recognition (in a departure from previous practice) these commitments "could be laid down in agreements". The way was thus paved for the inclusion of specific human rights and democracy clauses in EC agreements with the emerging states of Eastern Europe and the former Soviet Union.

Against this background, human rights and democracy clauses – in various forms – have appeared increasingly frequently in Community agreements since 1991. In order to illustrate the way in which these underlying trends have translated themselves into specific agreements a brief survey follows of three groups of EC agreements: (1) Latin America, (2) Asia and (3) Central and Eastern Europe and the former Soviet Union. The different forms taken by these clauses are a reflection of differences in the political and economic bargaining power of the contracting parties, as well as of the development of Community policy itself over the last five years.

Latin America

Prior to 1990, Community agreements with Latin American states merely contained generalised references in their preambles to fundamental human rights and "international co-operation based on equality, justice and progress".[12] However the new generation of co-operation agreements

---

[11] Declaration on Guidelines on the Recognition of New States in Eastern Europe and in the Soviet Union, 16 December 1991. For a discussion see Rich, "Recognition of States: The Collapse of Yugoslavia and the Soviet Union" (1993) 4 EJIL 36.

[12] *e.g.*, the 1984 Co-operation agreement with the Cartagena states (Bolivia, Colombia, Equador, Peru, Venezuela). OJ 1984 L153. See also the 1986 Co-operation agreement with the parties to the General Treaty on Central American Economic Integration (Costa Rica, El Salvador, Guatemala, Honduras, Nicaragua) and Panama. OJ 1986 L172. The bilateral agreements with Uruguay (OJ 1973 L333), Mexico (OJ 1975 L247), and Brazil (OJ 1982 L281) are similarly limited.

signed since 1990 have almost all included a human rights and democracy clause. The first was the Framework Agreement for Co-operation with Argentina[13], which in 1990 was anxious both to prove its democratic credentials and to normalise its trading relations with the Community. Article 1 states:

"Co-operation ties between the Community and Argentina and this agreement in its entirety are based on the respect for democratic principles and human rights which inspire the domestic and external policies of both the Community and Argentina. The strengthening of democracy and regional integration are the basic principles of this agreement and are a concern shared by both parties."

Framework agreements for co-operation have also been signed with Chile in 1991[14], Paraguay in 1992[15] and Uruguay also in 1992[16] containing virtually identical clauses. The theme is continued by the Council Regulation on financial assistance to Asia and Latin America.[17] Co-operation is to involve financial and technical development assistance and economic co-operation:

"In this connection, the Community shall attach the utmost importance to the promotion of human rights, support for the process of democratization, good governance, environmental protection, trade liberalization and strengthening the cultural dimension, by means of an increasing dialogue on political, economic and social issues . . ."

Two departures from this pattern are worth noting. The Trade and Co-operation Agreement signed with Brazil in 1992[18] contains an interesting addition. Article 1 provides that respect for democratic principles and human rights "constitute an essential element of the agreement". The reasons for and implications of this "strong version" of the clause will be considered below.

In contrast, the Framework Agreement with Mexico of 1991[19] does not contain any human rights or democracy clause at all even in its weaker form. The Preamble itself merely considers that "the main beneficiary of co-operation is man, and that respect for his rights should therefore be promoted". One can only speculate as to the reasons for this omission.

---

[13] The Framework Agreement for Co-operation with Argentina OJ 1990 L 295/66. These Latin American agreements are essentially non-preferential as far as trade is concerned, being based on MFN and GATT principles; they do however form a basis for financial and technical assistance.

[14] OJ 1991 L79.

[15] OJ 1992 L313/71.

[16] OJ 1992 L94/2.

[17] Council Regulation 443/92 OJ 1992 L52/1; Article 1.

[18] COM(92)209 final.

[19] OJ 1991 L340/1.

Asia

In the Asia agreements, a similar pattern emerges. Pre-1990 co-operation agreements with India[20], Pakistan[21] and Bangladesh[22] as well as ASEAN[23] do not contain human rights and democracy clauses although the preambles all refer, as did the Latin American agreements, to co-operation based on "freedom, equality and justice". However the Trade and Co-operation Agreement with Macao of 1992[24] contains in Article 1 the weaker version of the human rights and democracy clause:

"Co-operation between the Community and Macao and the implementation of this agreement are based on respect for the democratic principles and human rights which inspire the policies of both the Community and Macao."

The Trade and Co-operation Agreement with Mongolia of the following year has an almost identical clause.[25] However, also in 1993, the strong version of the clause emerges in other Asian agreements: respect for human rights and democracy is an "essential element" of the agreements with both Sri Lanka in 1993[26] and India in 1994[27]:

"Co-operation ties between the Community and Sri Lanka and this agreement in its entirety are based on respect for the democratic principles and human rights which inspire the domestic and external policies of the Community and Sri Lanka and which constitute an essential element of the agreement."[28]

The European Parliament has also requested that a similar clause be included in the projected trade and co-operation agreement with Vietnam and a new agreement envisaged with ASEAN.

However, in spite of these signs, the Commission displays some ambivalence in its approach to human rights, democracy and trade issues in Asia. In its recent paper outlining its views on the Community's strategy towards Asia[29] the Commission states that the development and consolidation of democracy and the rule of law and respect for human rights and fundamental freedoms form a "major objective" of the Union's external policy (*cf.* Article J.1(2) TEU). In translating that objective into action,

---

[20] EEC – India Agreement for Commercial and Economic Co-operation OJ 1981 L328/5.

[21] OJ 1985 C81/3.

[22] OJ 1976 L319.

[23] Co-operation Agreement with ASEAN (Indonesia, Malaysia, Philippines, Singapore, Thailand) OJ 1980 L144.

[24] OJ 1992 L404/26.

[25] OJ 1993 L41/45.

[26] Co-operation Agreement between EC and Sri Lanka on Partnership and Development COM(94)15 not yet in force.

[27] Co-operation Agreement between EC and India on partnership and development OJ 1994 L223/23. In force 1 August 1994.

[28] Co-operation Agreement between EC and Sri Lanka on Partnership and Development, see n 26 *supra*, Article 1.

[29] Communication from the Commission to the Council, "Towards a New Asia Strategy" 13 July 1994, COM(94) 314 final.

however, although mention is made of positive measures including support for elections and a free media, no express link is made between trade and human rights or democracy and there is no reference to the human rights clauses to be found in the newer Asian trade agreements. In fact the Commission reflects a general perception by referring to the recent United States decision to extend MFN status to China as a "delinking" of trade and human rights. It is tempting to speculate whether the Commission envisages adopting an independent stance more consistent with its own general policy by attempting to include such a clause in any new agreement with China[30], but caution is evident. In developing its Asia strategy, the Union "will not be able to take for granted automatic acceptance of European values and ways of doing things. Universal human rights are recognised in Asia as in Europe, but the manner in which these are advocated and defended is crucial."[31] The Commission concludes by including human rights as an explicit part of the *political* dialogue with Asian countries, but remains silent on human rights as a basis for economic co-operation.[32]

Central and Eastern Europe and Former Soviet Union

A parallel development can be found in the second and third generation agreements concluded between the EC and central and eastern Europe, as well as the new states of the former Soviet Union. The first association agreements (known as "Europe" agreements) signed with Poland[33] and Hungary[34] and (the then) Czechoslovakia in December 1991, contain no human rights or democracy clause although the Preamble, in addition to explicit references to the Conference on Security and Co-operation in Europe (CSCE), the Helsinki Final Act and the Charter of Paris, refers to the process of "transition to a new political and economic order based on the rule of law and human rights, including the legal and economic framework for market economy and a multi-party system with free and democratic elections". The second wave of Europe Agreements, signed during 1992 and 1993 with the new Czech and Slovak Republics[35], Bulgaria[36] and Romania[37],

---

[30] The existing Trade and Co-operation Agreement with China contains no such clause; OJ 1984 1985 L250/2.

[31] Communication from the Commission to the Council, "Towards a New Asia Strategy" 13 July 1994, COM(94) 314 final, at p 18.

[32] *Ibid.* at p 24.

[33] Europe Agreement with Poland signed 16 December 1991, in force 1 February 1994, OJ 1993 L348.

[34] Europe Agreement with Hungary signed 16 December 1991, in force 1 February 1994 OJ 1993 L347.

[35] The new Agreements were signed 23 June 1993, in force 1 February 1995 OJ 1994 L359 and L360.

[36] Europe Agreement with Bulgaria signed 22 December 1993, in force 1 February 1995 OJ 1994 L358.

[37] Europe Agreement with Romania signed 1 February 1993, in force 1 February 1995 OJ 1994 L357.

all contain human rights and democracy clauses. This clause was therefore deliberately (and controversially as far as the Czechs and Slovaks were concerned) added to the otherwise little-altered agreement with Czechoslovakia following the break up of the federation. The clause takes the "strong" form, and is also linked in a regionally relevant manner to the CSCE process:

"Respect for the democratic principles and human rights established by the Helsinki Final Act and the Charter of Paris for a 'new Europe', as well as the principles of market economy and the support by the Community through this agreement, inspire the domestic and external policies of the Parties and constitute an essential element of this Agreement."[38]

The Co-operation Agreement with Slovenia[39], which is much less ambitious in its scope than the Europe Agreements (although it does envisage a Europe Agreement as a future possibility[40]) contains an almost identical clause, as do the Partnership and Co-operation Agreement with the Ukraine[41], the Partnership and Co-operation Agreement with Russia[42], and the agreements on trade and commercial and economic co-operation which the Community signed with the three Baltic states[43] and with Albania[44] during 1992. These Agreements also refer expressly in their Preambles to the protection of the rights of minorities, one of the Recognition conditions referred to above.[45]

The 1992 Baltic and Albanian agreements represent an interesting further development. Unlike the Asian and Latin American agreements, and unlike the Lomé Convention, they contain an express reference to the possibility of immediate unilateral action in case of breach of the human rights clause. The agreement with Albania, for example, provides (in addition to the possibility of denunciation with six months notice):

"The parties reserve the right to suspend this Agreement in whole or in part with immediate effect if a serious violation occurs of the essential provisions of the present Agreement."[46]

The Baltic agreements of 1992 contain identical provisions. The reference to "essential provisions" is clearly intended to refer to the human rights clause, and the appearance of this provision for unilateral suspension raises some more general questions concerning the enforceability of

---

[38] Article 6 Europe Agreement with Romania.

[39] Co-operation Agreement with Slovenia signed 5 April 1993 OJ 1993 L189/1, Article 1(2).

[40] Europe Agreement with Slovenia, initialled 15 June 1995, COM(95)341 final. This Agreement contains the "strong" form of clause, almost identical to that in the Europe Agreement with Romania.

[41] Partnership and Co-operation Agreement with the Ukraine, signed 14 June 1994, COM(94)226 final, Article 2.

[42] Partnership and Co-operation Agreement with Russia COM(94)257 final, Article 2.

[43] Trade and Commercial and Economic Co-operation Agreement with Estonia OJ 1992 L403/1; Latvia OJ 1992 L 403/10; Lithuania OJ 1992 L403/19.

[44] Trade and Commercial and Economic Co-operation Agreement with Albania OJ 1992 L343/1, Article 1.

[45] Declaration on Guidelines on the Recognition of New States in Eastern Europe and in the Soviet Union, 16 December 1991. See above at n 11.

[46] Article 21(3).

the human rights and democracy clauses, which are considered in the following section.

Nevertheless one cannot conclude that the suspension provision will now always accompany the human rights clause. It is striking that the free trade agreements with the Baltic states which were signed in June/July 1994 and which are designed to replace the trade provisions of the 1992 co-operation agreements, contain the "strong" human rights and democracy clause but do not repeat the provision on unilateral suspension. The legal implications of this omission will be considered below. It may be linked to the inclusion of a reference in Article 1 to the agreement as a "decisive step towards the early conclusion of a Europe Agreement"[47] and in the Preamble to the "ultimate objective" of membership of the EU for the Baltic states. In other words, the possibility of unilateral suspension of the agreement is not compatible with the degree of integration with the EU envisaged in the formation of an association with a view to membership.

This approach would be consistent with the lack of such a "suspension" clause in the Europe Agreements. Indeed, in those cases where a state has proved its democratic credentials by ratifying the European Convention for the Protection of Human Rights and Fundamental Freedoms and becoming a member of the Council of Europe, the Commission has proved reluctant even to be drawn into a discussion of an alleged breach of democratic principles or to criticise a law adopted by "the freely and democratically elected Parliament". As citizens have remedies available under the Convention, "no action on the Community's part is called for".[48]

Enforcement and sanctions

As we have already seen, the Council Resolution on Human Rights, Democracy and Development of November 1991 envisages the possibility of a range of "appropriate responses" to human rights violations.[49] Public statements by the Union and Member States were made on a number of occasions during 1993, for example, notably concerning Angola in January, Togo and Zaire in February, Nigeria in June and Haiti in September.

---

[47] Europe Agreements with the Baltic States were initialled in April 1995. COM(95)207. Like the free trade agreements they contain the "strong" human rights and democracy clause but no provision for unilateral suspension.

[48] See Commission answer to EP Question E-3159/93 OJ 1994 C240/52. The allegation concerned a Hungarian law banning the use of certain symbols in public (including the swastika, the hammer and sickle and five-pointed red star); it was pointed out by the MEPs asking the question that the latter two symbols are used by legal parties with democratic representation in EU Member States. In addition to the points referred to in the text, the Commission stated that the Hungarian law applied to domestic organizations only, and therefore did not affect political organizations within the EU. There is no human rights or democracy clause in the EC – Hungary Association Agreement, although this point was not alluded to by the Commission.

[49] Resolution of the Council and of the Member States meeting in Council on human rights, democracy and development, 28/11/91, Bulletin of the EC 11–1991 p 122 (see text above at n 10).

A decision to defer further decisions on co-operation with Guatemala was also taken in May following the dissolution of Parliament and the Supreme court by the President.[50] The Commission has stated that the Community and Member States, in response to the situation in Chad (a Lomé signatory), have "strongly petitioned the Chadian authorities" to restore order and put a stop to human rights violations; the authorities have also been informed that a favourable response would be forthcoming to any request for financial assistance under Lomé IV for human rights training for civil servants and members of the security forces.[51] This illustrates the limitations of this type of response: it is frequently dependant on a degree of co-operation from national authorities which is likely to be absent in exactly those circumstances where human rights abuses occur.

The efficacy of verbal protests and cancellation of meetings may be limited but action going beyond this and involving the suspension of trade links and/or financial assistance, is problematic where it takes place in the context of an agreement imposing treaty obligations on the Community. It is not at all clear whether the "weak" form of human rights clause, such as Article 5 of Lomé IV, would justify the unilateral suspension of the agreement in case of its breach by one party, in particular without any notice.[52] In spite of the fact that the Council Resolution of November 1991 refers to the possibility of suspension of co-operation, the Community has in fact been cautious in taking action under Lomé IV, as the case of Haiti demonstrates. After the September 1991 coup against President Aristide the Committee of Ambassadors of the ACP states in Brussels recommended that all Lomé parties suspend their trading relations with Haiti and an EC condemnation in October was followed up by an EPC decision in December 1991 to impose a trade embargo.[53] However, a formal embargo was not implemented until after a UN Security Council resolution in 1993 removed any problem caused by the possible incompatibility of economic sanctions with the Lomé Convention.[54] The 1993 EC Regulation imposing an oil embargo is explicitly based on the Security Council Resolution and the preamble states that "therefore the fourth ACP-EEC Convention to which the Community and Haiti are parties, does not pose an obstacle" to the implementation of the Resolution.[55] In 1994, a further Security

---

[50] Report from the Commission to the Council and European Parliament on the implementation in 1993 of the Resolution of the Council and of the Member States meeting in the Council on human rights, democracy and development adopted on 28 November 1991, COM(94)42 final, at pp 12–14.

[51] See Commission answer to EP Question E-2903/93 OJ 1994 C240/37.

[52] See Kuyper, "Trade Sanctions, Security and Human Rights and Commercial Policy" in Maresceau (ed), *The European Community's Commercial Policy after 1992: The Legal Dimension* (Nijhoff, 1993), for a discussion in particular in relation to measures taken by the EC against former Yugoslavia.

[53] See Kuyper, *op cit* at p 418.

[54] UN Security Council resolution 841(93). Art 103 of the UN Charter obliges members to set aside prior treaty obligations which conflict with obligations imposed by Security Council Resolutions.

[55] Regulation 1608/93 OJ 1993 L 155/2. The embargo was then suspended, again in accordance with Security Council Resolution 861(93) by Regulation 2520/93 OJ 1993 L 232/3; the suspension was repealed by Regulation 3028/93 OJ 1993 L 270/73, pursuant to Security Council Resolution 873(93).

71

Council Resolution formed the basis for additional trade sanctions: the discontinuation of economic and financial relations with Haiti, prohibition of the satisfaction of contractual claims by Haitian authorities, and freezing of assets and financial resources. These measures apply equally to rights and obligations under international agreements entered into prior to the Resolution.[56] Exceptions are made for commodities supplied for humanitarian purposes. The scope of these sanctions is similar to those imposed on Iraq, Libya, Serbia and Montenegro, also the result of UN Resolutions.[57]

The Community has more room to manoeuvre where an agreement contains an element of co-operation and (especially) financial assistance. It is possible to delay or defer decisions on programmes for financial assistance in response to, for example, a breakdown in the rule of law, without a formal breach of existing treaty obligations.[58] Before imposing a formal trade embargo, however, and in the absence of a "strong" human rights and democracy clause, the Community clearly prefers to have Security Council backing. However, the Commission takes the view that the strong version, stipulating that the clause constitutes an essential element of the agreement, provides a legal basis and a justification in international law for taking retaliatory measures, which might include a suspension of obligations under the agreement. In the explanatory memoranda attached to its proposal to conclude the agreements with Russia and the Ukraine (which it will be recalled contain such a "strong" human rights clause but not the explicit provision for unilateral suspension found in the Albanian agreement) the Commission nevertheless states that "the Agreement contains a clause which allows it to be suspended, even unilaterally, if it is considered that there has been a breach of the essential elements underlying the agreement *i.e.* respect for democracy, human rights and the principles of the market economy."[59]

It is significant, therefore, that in the opening of the mid-term review of the Lomé Convention in May 1994, the Community has as a key objective "to ensure that the Convention asserts the principles of democracy, the rule of law and good governance, alongside existing references to respect for and enjoyment of human rights."[60] It is clear that the Community

---

[56] UN Security Council Resolution 917(94); Regulations 1263 & 1264/94 OJ 1994 L139/1. It is worth noting that these Regulations are based on a Council Decision establishing a common position under Article J.2 TEU: Decision 94/315/CFSP OJ 1994 L139/10.

[57] See, *e.g.*, Regulation 2340/90 OJ 1990 L213 (Iraq); Regulation 990/93 OJ 1993 L102 (Serbia & Montenegro); Regulations 3274 & 3275/93 OJ 1993 L275 (Libya).

[58] See for example the suspension of aid to Malawi in May 1992, resumed in July 1993 together with substantial financial support for the referendum: see Commission Report cited above at n 9. See also JA McMahon, "Lomé IV – A Blueprint for the Future or a Relic of the Past?" paper given at EC Law Forum on "The legal regulation of the Community's external relations after the completion of the internal market" held in Bristol May 1994.

[59] Commission explanatory memorandum to its proposal to conclude the Partnership and Co-operation Agreement with Ukraine, COM(94)226 final.

[60] See Press Release IP/94/404, 19 May 1994.

would wish to see these principles established as "essential elements" of the Convention. It is less clear whether this should be accompanied by a provision for immediate unilateral suspension in case of breach. The most recent agreements, with the Baltic states, Ukraine and Russia, show that this provision has not become an invariable part of Community practice (such practice being in any case far from consistent). As we have seen, at least in the view of Commission, an explicit clause may not be essential. For the Community, the advantage is that by allowing for an immediate suspension, normal notice periods and consultation practices are avoided. However there are strong arguments based on due process in favour of providing, alongside such a clause, transparent criteria and decision-making procedures for the application of unilateral sanctions. The criteria contained in the Resolution of 1991 and the Commission's Reports on its implementation are not only imprecise but also represent unilateral policy decisions by the Community, not policy mutually agreed in advance with treaty partners.

An important limitation to the imposition of full economic sanctions must also be considered: the Community's international obligations under the GATT. In respect of those trading partners who are party to the GATT, even the strongest form of the human rights and democracy clause will only justify a suspension of preferential trading conditions granted by the specific trade agreement. It would not *per se* justify the suspension of underlying GATT-based free-trade obligations, thus ruling out full economic sanctions.[61] The same is also true of sanctions imposed against GATT parties who are not party to any bilateral trade agreement with the Community.

There is thus further support for Community reliance on a UN Security Council Resolution when imposing a full trade embargo. Following a UN Resolution, the Community would be able to rely on Article XXI GATT, which expressly allows contracting parties to take action in pursuance of obligations under the UN Charter for the maintenance of international peace and security.[62]

As far as the internal decision-making procedure is concerned, any interruption or reduction of economic relations with one or more third states is now governed by Article 228a EC (pre-TEU decisions on sanctions were based on Article 113 EC), which would appear to require – or at least assume – a prior decision in the context of the Union's Common Foreign and Security Policy (whether or not preceded by a UN Resolution). The

---

[61] It would be difficult to construe the general exceptions clause of the GATT to cover protection of human rights: Article XX GATT makes no mention of human rights or democracy as justifications for trade barriers.

[62] It should perhaps be said that although a breach of GATT obligations would render the Community liable to action under the GATT/WTO dispute resolution procedure, it cannot be assumed that the European Court of Justice would annul the Community legislation imposing the sanctions, even if contrary to GATT obligations: see case C-280/93 *Germany* v *Council*, judgment of 5 October 1994, not yet reported.

link between trade policy and the political objective underlying the human rights and democracy clause is thus made clear.

Human rights, democracy and trade policy

It is this link which raises the most difficult questions. As a matter of policy, it may be debated whether the insistence on "linkage" between development assistance and respect for human rights, fundamental freedoms and democracy is of real benefit to developing states. It may, as the Commission insists, support the development of individuals as well as democratic structures within the partner state and contribute to respect for the rule of law. However it is also perceived as the creation of yet another condition attached to aid, with the effect of penalising individuals for the violations of these principles by their governments, while also being powerless to prevent human rights violations by agencies outside government control.[63] Whatever position is taken on this issue, it is clearly *legally* defensible, particularly in the light of Articles F and J.1(2) TEU, for the Community to identify respect for human rights and fundamental freedoms and the consolidation of democracy and the rule of law as a major objective in its development policy. This provides a legal basis for the "positive action" programme of financial assistance to which priority has been given as well as for the withdrawal of support where serious violations occur.

It is also now well established that respect for these principles, and possession of a "system of government founded on the principles of democracy" are conditions of membership of the Union.[64] It is therefore reasonable to put such objectives at the heart of an agreement which is expressly designed to prepare a state for membership. The Europe association agreements would fall into this category. The Conclusions of the Presidency at the Copenhagen summit in June 1993 stated:

"the associated countries in Central and Eastern Europe that so desire shall become members of the European Union. Accession will take place as soon as the associated country is able to assume the obligations of membership by satisfying the economic and political conditions required.

Membership requires that the candidate country has achieved stability of institutions guaranteeing democracy, the rule of law, human rights and respect for and protection of minorities, the existence of a functioning market economy as well as the capacity to cope with competitive pressures and market forces within the Union . . ."[65]

---

[63] For a full discussion, see K Tomasevski, *Development Aid and Human Rights Revisited* (Pinter, 1993).

[64] Article F TEU. The Commission has stated that "a state which applies for membership must . . . satisfy the three basic conditions of European identity, democratic status and respect of human rights." "The Challenge of Enlargement" Supplement 3/92 Bulletin of the EC 1992.

[65] Conclusions of the Presidency, Copenhagen June 1993, point 7A(iii).

At this point a distinction can be made between respect for fundamental human rights and respect for "democratic principles". It will be recalled that Article 5 of Lomé IV, although containing an extensive description of various types of human rights, does not refer to democracy. Indeed Article 2 of the Convention expressly reserves such issues to the domestic policy of the parties:

"ACP–EEC co-operation . . . shall be exercised on the basis of the following fundamental principles:
. . . the right of each state to determine its own political, social, cultural and economic policy options; . . ."

The addition proposed by the Community as part of the mid-term review of Lomé would therefore not only strengthen the status of the human rights clause but also add the political dimension which is now explicitly present in the Community's development policy.[66] Association with (as well as membership of[67]) the Union appears now to require adherence to a specific form of government if not (yet) to market economy principles.

If the high level of integration – both political and economic – with the Community which these agreements envisage justifies the inclusion of a human rights and democracy clause, the case is not so clear in the context of trade and cooperation agreements of the type concluded with the states of Latin America and Asia.

By including as a matter of general practice the "strong" version of the human rights and democracy clause in its trade agreements[68], the Community is adopting a policy of linking these principles to its trade policy. There is a clear difference between choosing certain principles as a basis for positive action and financial assistance, and (expressly or impliedly) threatening the suspension of trading links in cases of serious (how serious?) violation. A new "uniform principle" is being added to the Community's developing common commercial policy – a principle which did not in general form a part of the commercial policy of the individual Member States. More significantly, as we seen it does not yet form part of the Community's international trade obligations under the GATT.

The Community is thus entering the arena of the debate which has surfaced in the context of the GATT Uruguay Round negotiations. Although outside the scope of this paper, the new "incentive clauses"

---

[66] Article 130u EC and the November 1991 Resolution on human rights, democracy and development. In this context it is relevant that the Community also proposes to create a mechanism for political dialogue within the EC-ACP Council of Ministers, as is the case with more recent Association Agreements, such as the Europe Agreements.

[67] Within the Union, although "respect for the national identities" of the Member States is guaranteed, this is on the basis that they are "founded on the principles of democracy" (Article F TEU).

[68] Agreements with Latin America, Asia, Central and Eastern Europe and the former Soviet Union have been mentioned. In negotiating new Association agreements with the Mediterranean states the Community is also seeking to include the human rights clause: see "Euro-Med" Agreement with Tunisia COM(95)235.

appearing in the Community's autonomous legislation, such as the new Generalised System of Preferences, furnish another example of this process.[69] Should trade concessions be linked to compliance with standards in areas such as consumer protection, social policy and environmental protection, and if so should these be nationally or internationally defined standards? Is the Community (or any other trading nation or bloc) entitled to use its economic weight in order to export its own standards to less powerful trading partners? Not only are there widely differing views between the developed and the developing world on this issue, but also an evident lack of consensus within the industrialised world.

Extending linkage from the current issues of debate, such as environmental and labour standards, to the protection of fundamental human rights is on the one hand easier to justify in that internationally accepted standards are more readily identified (and it is difficult *not* to be seen to support human rights). On the other hand, the link with trade is less immediately obvious, particularly in the case of civil and political (as opposed to social and economic) rights. If there are arguments against linking political objectives to development aid, they are even more acute in the case of general trade policy. As far as the Community is concerned, awkward but valid questions may also be raised. Although it has been a prime mover in the move towards international recognition of technical standards through its own policy-making and internal legislation, as a supporter of human rights and democracy its own record is more questionable. In spite of all the declarations in favour of the protection of fundamental human rights, the Community itself is still not a party to the European Convention and subjection to the discipline of the Convention's enforcement procedures may cause difficulties for the Community legal order.[70] In spite of its support for democracy in Member and non-Member States, the democratic deficit in the Community's own decision-making processes is notorious and has not been significantly altered by the Treaty on European Union. If the Community (and Union) gives a higher profile to political objectives in its external policy it must expect such comparisons to be made and the practical manifestations of its own commitment subject to scrutiny.

This is, however, a pragmatic reason for the Community to support such political objectives through its trade policy. At present, economic power is by far the most formidable weapon it has. The political dimension of the Union is increasing; political dialogue is now regularly included in partnership and association agreements (and is likely to be strengthened in the Lomé Convention as part of the mid-term review). Linkage between

---

[69] Under the new GSP Regulation incentives are available for complying with (still limited) labour and environmental standards: Regulation 3281/94 OJ 1994 L348/1, Articles 7 and 8.

[70] See the request by the Council to the European Court of Justice under Article 228(6) EC for an opinion as to whether accession by the Community to the European Convention would be compatible with the EC Treaty; Opinion 2/94 OJ 1994 C174/8.

the political and the economic is even implied by the requirement of consistency in Article C TEU:

". . . The Union shall in particular ensure the consistency of its external activities as a whole in the context of its external relations, security, economic and development policies . . ."

The external trading relations of the Community can no longer be seen in purely economic (GATT-based) terms, or even solely as an emergent foreign economic policy[71] but will increasingly be integrated into the overall policy-making of the Union in all its aspects. The Union may not yet be an effective international actor[72], but its external economic policy is likely to provide the firmest foundation on which to build.

MARISE CREMONA

---

[71] Kuyper, *op cit* at p 422.
[72] *cf.* Hill, "Conceptualizing Europe's International Role" [1993] 31 JCMS 305.

Part 3

The Uruguay Round: An Evaluation

Chapter 6

The Uruguay Round of GATT: Some General Comments from an EC Standpoint

I shall refrain from commenting on the results of the Uruguay Round from a trade policy perspective. Trade policy being the result of conflicting economic interests between the GATT Contracting Parties and, as is known, within the European Community (hereinafter: EC) and between the various sectors of the economy, this is a subject more suitable for robust political debate than for legal analysis.

Two main points are to be covered:

- the rule-making dimension of the agreements resulting from the Uruguay Round
- legal aspects of conclusion and implementation by the EC of the agreements that result from the Uruguay Round.

The rule-making dimension of the Uruguay Round

One could sum up the results by saying that there are three substantive agreements and two institutional procedural agreements.

1. Review of GATT Articles and of existing implementing agreements (codes) and negotiation of new codes. The review of the GATT articles, which had somewhat inappropriately been called FOG, concerns rules on BOP, state-trading enterprises, customs-unions and free-trade areas and withdrawal of tariff concessions; there are moreover clarifications of minor importance.

Most of the existing codes were reviewed. One of the major changes will occur in the so-called Subsidies Code. An American lawyer, who followed the negotiations closely, claimed that the EC had managed to include Article 92 EC in the Code. There finally is a definition of "subsidy" and other important clarifications.

Among the new codes, the Code on Safeguards and the Code on Origin Rules are to be mentioned in particular.

In the Code on Safeguards, there are two points of particular interest. First, negotiations on "selectivity", a major bone of contention between the EC and many other negotiating parties, have led to a sort of compromise: Members taking safeguard measures must apply them to products from all origins, however "quota modulation" will be permitted. Second, so-called "grey area" measures must be phased out. The European Community may keep the agreement with Japan on Japan's "voluntary" export restraints for cars until it runs out.

As to the Code on Origin Rules, two points can be stressed. First, the EC managed to keep out of the Code the so-called "preferential origin rules" by which it tailors the benefits of its preferential arrangements to the perceived needs of the beneficiary countries and to its own absorption capacity. Second, this Code contains clauses whereby the Members commit themselves to introduce a sort of prospective "ruling" to be given by customs authorities at the request of importers and an appeals procedure. This is an interesting development in that it shows an increasing concern at the international level for procedural guarantees to the benefit of economic agents.

2. The second substantive agreement is the Agreement on Trade in Services (the GATS). This is unquestionably a breakthrough, even though, as the EC experience shows, general principles, such as most-favoured nation treatment and transparency, will not bring about liberalisation of trade in services to the same extent as for goods under the GATT. The negotiators were well aware of this and drafted the GATS as a framework agreement with pledges to grant "national treatment" and/or "market access" and "schedules of initial commitments". Regretfully the USA could in the end not accept the MFN treatment for financial services.

The GATS as well contains obligations designed to offer procedural guarantees to private parties: Members are to maintain or institute judicial, arbitral or administrative tribunals or procedures for the purposes of providing review and remedies for administrative decisions affecting trade in services.

3. The third substantive agreement is the Agreement on Trade Related Intellectual Property Rights (TRIPS). It is interesting to note that this Agreement resembles an EC Directive of the "new approach" *i.e.* it sets substantive objectives for the protection of copyright, trademarks, geographical design, patents, topographies of integrated circuits and business secrets, while leaving it to individual members to work out how these objectives are to be reached.

The whole of Part III of the TRIPS Agreement deals in 20 articles with enforcement of intellectual property rights and covers such matters as civil and administrative procedures and remedies, special requirements related to border measures and criminal procedures.

One of the expected advantages of including TRIPS in the WTO framework is the possibility to use the WTO dispute settlement procedures.

4. The first institutional/procedural agreement is the Understanding on Rules and Procedures Governing the Settlement of Disputes, which significantly improves the existing system of dispute settlement. The main aspects are: first, the creation of a standing Appellate Body to which a Member which is dissatisfied with a Panel report can put its case, and

second, the ruling of the Standing Appellate body is final unless a committee of WTO Members, the Dispute Settlement Body, rejects this ruling by consensus.

This Understanding calls for three brief remarks.

First, while it is true that in the past the adoption of relatively few Panel reports was blocked, the very fact that a Panel report could be blocked led GATT Contracting Parties more often than not to find a compromise. From a legal perspective the improved system appears almost too good to be true: a Member cannot refuse a dispute settlement and it can no longer block the adoption of a Panel report which it does not like. Of course, the Appellate Body will be wise but there are bound to be circumstances in which it will be unable to avoid a ruling that the losing Member is likely to consider as politically unacceptable.

Second, Article 23 of the Understanding contains a commitment which excludes expressly unilateral measures. The EC considered this clause as an essential part of the package.

Third, the dynamics of international negotiations sometimes are unpredictable and full of surprises. Two statements made at the start of the Uruguay Round and positions taken at the end of the Round may illustrate this.

At the start of the Round, the United States stated:

"For many years in the GATT, panel reports were adopted but there was no mechanism to assure that countries complied with panel decisions. The United States would like to see countries agree to a political pledge to abide by GATT decisions."

The EC stated:

"The Community should reaffirm its readiness in the search for more effective procedural formulae in the area of dispute settlement *based on consensus.*"

At the end of the negotiations Sir Leon Brittan hailed the improved dispute settlement as a major achievement and he is supported by the EC Member States, including France. Mickey Kantor, the United States Trade Representative, is defending *inter alia* the view that the improved dispute settlement does not take away the sovereign rights of the United States to take unilateral measures.

5. The second institutional/procedural agreement is the Agreement establishing the Word-Trade Organization, which is designed to provide "the institutional framework for the conduct of trade relations among its Members in matters related to the agreements and associated legal instruments included in the Annexes to the Agreement" (Art II(i)).

The WTO Agreement calls for some general comments.

First, although the GATT as an organization has in its present form, and notwithstanding its present form, managed to adjust fairly well to the increasing demands on it, its transformation into a genuine international organization will put it on par with the IMF and the IBRD. Whether this in itself will result in a co-ordination, via these international organizations, of trade and financial/monetary policies remains to be seen. In addition, some commentators expect that the WTO, being an international organization created by an international treaty, formally approved according to each member's constitutional rules and properly ratified, will have a greater political weight. Again, whether this will result in more and better compliance remains to be seen. It is true that the WTO Agreement contains a clause providing that "(e)ach Member shall ensure the conformity of its laws, regulations and administrative procedures with its obligations as provided in the annexed Agreements" (Art XVI (4)). Arguably from an international law point of view this clause is superfluous. One may wonder what the effect of such clause will be in practice. At the international law level, it is unclear whether this clause could be enforced against a Member under the Understanding on Rules and Procedures Governing the Settlement of Disputes. At the national law level, it is doubtful that this clause would enable, more than in the past, courts to review national laws, regulations and administrative procedures on their consistency with the WTO agreements.

Second, there are two categories of legal instruments:

a) "Multilateral Trade Agreements"
   – the 1994 GATT
   – the 1994 GATT Tariff Protocol
   – the existing and the new "Codes"
   – the GATS
   – the Agreement on TRIPS
   – the Understanding on Dispute Settlement – the Trade Review Mechanism

   These "Multilateral Trade Agreements" are an integral part of the WTO Agreement and are designed to be binding on *all* WTO Members as a "single undertaking". Contrary to the case of the Tokyo Round agreements, Members cannot "pick and choose" the agreements which suit them. This may raise a problem for the EC, if the Council of the European Union were to reject the European Commission's view that the whole of the WTO Agreement comes within the scope of the EC's external powers. In the end this problem did not arise as the EC Member States managed to conclude the WTO Agreement alongside the EC in due time.

b) "Plurilateral Trade Agreements" which are not an integral part of WTO and are only binding on those WTO Members that have accepted them. (In fact four of the revised Tokyo Round Codes: Trade in Civil Aircraft, Government Procurement, Dairy Agreement and Bovine Meat Agreement).

Third, the article relating to decision-making (Art IX), refers to the continuation of the practice of decision-making by consensus, which a footnote defines as: "no Member, present at the meeting when the decision is taken, formally objects to the proposed decision". For certain matters, decision-making by a qualified majority is provided, albeit it that a "heavier" majority will now be required for a "waiver". The decision-making on certain amendments is a real puzzle (Art X, paras 2 to 6).

Fourth, there are some complicated provisions on the relationship between the 1947 GATT, the 1994 GATT and the WTO Agreement and the rights and obligations of the 1947 GATT contracting parties and the WTO members. There is an interesting clause: the 1947 GATT contracting parties as of the date of entry into force of the WTO Agreement and the European Community are the original members of the WTO, *provided inter alia* they have schedules of concessions and commitments annexed to the 1994 GATT *and* to the GATS (Art XI (1)). One may wonder whether the European Community could become a WTO member, should the Court of Justice of the European Communities – in the advisory opinion which the European Commission requested – be of the view that the European Community does not have the necessary powers, or should the Council of the European Union decide that it is up to the EC Member States rather than the EC to conclude the GATS.

Conclusion and implementation by the European Community

On the occasion of the review of the whole structure of the GATT and the creation of a WTO the question arose whether the time had not come to draw with respect to the EC's status in the GATT the consequences from the developments that had taken place both in the EC and in the GATT. In addition, as was to be expected – the same thing happened at the end of the Tokyo Round – there are disagreements within the EC on the question whether the matters covered by the various instruments come within the external powers of the European Community. Finally, there is the question of the effect of the WTO Agreement and the agreements annexed to it in the EC legal system.

1. As is well known the substitution of the European Community to the Member States in the GATT – whether this is something akin to state succession is left aside here – has been recognised by the Court of Justice of the European Communities in a series of cases. This 'substitution' has been accepted *de facto* and in many instances *de jure* by the other GATT contracting parties, all this notwithstanding the fact that formally the European Community Member States remained GATT contracting parties.

The creation of the WTO offered the opportunity to draw the formal international law consequences from these developments and to formally replace the EC Member States by the EC. The WTO text leaves this arguably open: the contracting parties of the GATT and the European Communities shall become original members of the WTO provided they fulfil the requirements mentioned earlier (Art XI).

However, two political considerations led the European Commission not to stand up for this: first the matter was discussed in a Council meeting in November 1993 *inter alia* after the Treaty on the European Union entered into effect with some difficulty, and it was thought wise not to push this issue at that stage. Second, around this time the last hurdles had to be cleared and Sir Leon Brittan, followed by the European Commission, thought it preferable not to put another contentious issue on the table and not to upset an apple cart that was already in danger of being out of balance.

It is not necessary for EC Member States to be members of the WTO. Of course, it is important for governments of EC Member States to be able to show the flag, for government ministers to be seen signing the Marrakesh Final Act and to have their pictures taken. However, from a practical point of view in the internal EC framework Member States are at any rate legally bound at least to act in common. Granted, in the WTO the advantage for the EC as a whole of Member States being members of WTO is that the EC has the 12 votes of its Member States. But that is the sort of reasoning one would expect from Russia and the other states of the CIS; this reasoning is unworthy of Member States forming the largest trading power in the world.

This is also deplorable. The European Community has thus missed the opportunity to formally show to the whole world that it is more than a club of states.

Finally, this is unwise. In the past there has been the pragmatic acceptance by the other contracting parties of the European Community as a single entity; this acceptance was obtained by using the argument that one should not review the GATT for the purposes of formally substituting the European Community for its Member States. There now is a risk that all the efforts of the past in this respect will come to nought. One wonders whether the other WTO members will continue to show the same forebearance. What was in the GATT a patient acceptance of a passing excentricity may turn in the WTO into a lingering handicap for EC policy making in the WTO.

2.   The second point deals with the question whether the matters that form the subject of the legal instruments that result from the Uruguay Round come within the scope of the EC's external powers.

The Commission has submitted to the Court of Justice a request for an advisory opinion under Art 228, para 6 of EC. Politically, it is not surprising that the issue has arisen: the proper scope of the EC's external powers have often led to discussions and tensions between the Commission and some Member States and resulted from time to time in disputes that the Court of Justice had to resolve. That goes from Opinion 1/75 on the OECD Arrangement on Local Cost[1] to the case brought by Greece against the Council on the so-called Chernobyl regulation.[2] It goes from the

---

[1] [1975] ECR 1364.
[2] [1990] ECR I-1527.

difficult acceptance of the ERTA doctrine[3] to the latest advisory opinion on the ILO agreements.[4] The vague and open-ended definition of the trade policy-powers of the EC in the EEC Treaty is well known and the Maastricht Treaty left Article 113 for what it was.

The conflicting theories defended in the past by the Council and the Commission which are set out in the Court's 1/78 Opinion on the International Rubber Agreement are not satisfactory, as C D Ehlermann demonstrated convincingly.[5] It is noteworthy that the Court has always avoided endorsing either one of the theories and has prudently decided each case on the merits. Quite rightly so: as Lenz A-G noted in one of the GSP cases[6] Council and Commission deploy the different theories according to where their interest lies.

Other theories are possible and have been put forward. One of these is simply to see trade policy as the external face of the common market and common policies.

As the main objections of certain EC Member States against the EC's powers under Article 113 EC concern the GATS, it is appropriate to test this theory by looking at the GATS. The legal argument of the EC Member States probably is that services are not goods. C Timmermans has developed the argument[7] that the function of a common trade policy in the EEC (now EC) Treaty is to make free circulation of goods originating in third countries possible within the common market; services do not circulate; *ergo*, Article 113 does not include powers to regulate trade in services with third countries. This argument is flawed. The common trade policy cannot only have the function of making free circulation of goods originating in third countries possible. When Member States transferred these powers to the EC they obviously and necessarily entrusted the EC with the task to do more than just ensuring that goods originating in third countries circulate freely within the EC. Moreover, later developments have shown – *e.g.* the Second Banking Directive[8] – that the proper functioning of the common market in banking also may require a common external policy.

This legal argument is also flawed for another reason. The Court has made the point, *inter alia* in its Opinion on the Rubber Agreement[9], that the notion of ''commercial policy'' has a dynamic and evolutionary character and thus that the EC must have the possibility, under its powers to

---

3 [1971] ECR 263; J Temple-Lang, ''The ERTA-judgment and the Courts Case-law on Competence and Conflict'', 6 YBK EUR L 183 (1987).

4 19 March 1993, nyr.

5 ''The Scope of Article 113 of the EEC Treaty'' in *Melanges Offerts a Pierre-Henri Teitgen* (Pedone, Paris, 1984), p 145.

6 CJEC, judgment of 26 March 1987 (*Commission* v *Council*, 1987, ECR 1493).

7 ''Common Commercial Policy and Trade in Services'' in *Du Droit International au Droit De L'integration – Liber Amicorum Pierre Pescatore* (Nomos, Baden-Baden, 1987), p 675.

8 OJ 1989 L 386/1.

9 Opinion 1/78, [1979] ECR 2871.

conduct a trade policy, to take account of new needs and new developments. According to figures mentioned by the Commission in its report to
the Council, at present 60% of the EC GDP is accounted for by services,
and foreign trade in services represents 30% of trade in general. In addition, there now is an increasing body of opinion among economists according to which the distinction between trade in goods and trade in
services makes less and less sense.

It is furthermore submitted that the aims of GATS fall squarely within
the objectives of the EC's "commercial policy" as defined in Article 110
EC. Moreover, one should bear in mind that trade in services has become
an integral part of the trade policies of states, a criterion on which the
Court of Justice has relied in the past to define the scope of the EC's trade
policy powers laid down in Article 113 EC. It is true that the GATS also
deals with other matters, such as the movement of persons to the territory
of another member for the purpose of supplying a service. However, these
matters are included as ancillary to the supply of services. If one were to
hold that on account of ancillary provisions an agreement does not come
within the scope of the EC's trade policy powers, quite a few of the agreements concluded by the EC under these powers would rest on a shaky
legal basis. The tail should not be allowed to wag the dog.

It is to be hoped that in its advisory opinion the Court of Justice will,
consistently with earlier pronouncements, hold that GATS can be properly concluded by the EC under its trade policy powers.[10]

If it were to consider that the ERTA doctrine applies and that the GATS
agreement can only be concluded on the basis of the EC's powers to
regulate services and, as the case may be establishment, within the EC, it
would quite probably create more problems than it would resolve. One
should bear in mind that the existence of external powers is then subject
to a finding that, were the EC Member States to conclude the GATS, the
obligations that they assume would affect the internal EC rules in these
fields or alter their scope. The Court of Justice would probably merely lay
down the principle and would leave it to the Council of the European
Union to make such finding. This would quite probably give rise to interesting debates. On the basis of past experience such decision would be
essentially political and would very likely be a compromise designed to
allow EC Member States to conclude the GATS alongside the EC. This is
not new. There have been other so-called "mixed agreements" but none
in an area such as GATS, where the "flou artistique" of this peculiar
phenomenon is likely to raise practical problems for other WTO members
and for businesses engaged in international trade in services.

---

[10] For a convincing demonstration see P Eeckhout, *The European Internal Market and International Trade: A Legal Analysis* (Clarendon Press, Oxford, 1994), pp 20–34. After this paper was
written, the Court rendered its opinion ([1994] ECR I-5267) in which it held that only cross-
frontier services are covered by Article 113 EC. For a comment see JHJ Bourgeois, "The EC in the
WTO and Advisory Opinion 1/94: an Echternach Procession", 32 CMLRev 763 (1995).

If the EC were not to conclude the GATS (and, for that matter, the TRIPS) which would then be concluded by the individual EC Member States a paradoxical situation would be obtained. At world level these matters are recognised to be dealt with in a fashion similar to the way in which trade in goods is regulated. At EC level they would be considered as not being covered by the EC's external powers and would be dealt with by EC Member States individually. The steps taken at world level towards more integrated economic relations would be followed by steps at EC level towards an atomisation of these economic relations.

3. The effect in the EC legal system. The caselaw of the Court of Justice of the European Communities on the direct effect of GATT, *i.e.* the possibility for private parties to rely on it in an EC Member State court, and the tests on which the Court of Justice relies to reject such direct effect in the case of the GATT, ought to be reconsidered in the light of the improvements resulting from the WTO Agreement and in particular from the Understanding on Dispute Settlement.

The path towards a change of attitude has been eased by *Nakajima*[11] which appears to distinguish between enforcing GATT in EC Member States courts and review by the Court of Justice itself of EC legislation on its consistency with GATT obligations. Moreover one of the reasons why the Court of Justice rejected direct effect of GATT and in so doing prevented national courts from setting aside EC legislation and EC measures on account of their inconsistency with GATT obligations has disappeared. In *Foto Frost*[12] the Court of Justice held that national courts faced with a claim of illegality of EC legislation and measures can either reject such claim or submit the question for preliminary ruling to the Court of Justice. *Tertium non datur.*

In view of these developments in the caselaw it is disappointing, though not surprising, that the Council Decision on the conclusion of the results of the Uruguay Round, states in its preamble:

". . . these are intergovernmental agreements and it is therefore necessary to ensure that the above agreements and arrangements cannot be directly invoked in Member State or Community courts by private individuals who are natural or legal persons".

Quite apart from the wording of this statement and the antediluvian underlying approach, it is noteworthy that such language does not appear in the operative part of the proposed Decision. The statement may very well, if the Council of the European Union adopts this Decision as proposed, reflect the intent but there is no corresponding rule in the operative part. It is true that in *KUPFERBERG I*[13] the Court of Justice held that:

---

[11] CJEC, judgment of 7 May 1991 (*Nakajima All Precision Co Ltd* v *Council of the European Communities*) [1991] ECR I-2069.

[12] CJEC, judgment of 22 October 1987 (*Foto Frost* v *HZA Lübeck-Ost*) [1987] ECR 4199.

[13] CJEC, judgment of 26 October 1982 (*HZA* Mainz v *C.A. Kupferberg & Cie*) [1982] ECR 3641.

". . . the effects within the Community of provisions of an agreement concluded by the Community with a non-member country may not be determined without taking account of the international origin of the provisions in question. In conformity with the principles of public international law Community institutions which have the power to negotiate and conclude an agreement with a non-member country are free to agree with that country what effect the provisions of the agreement are to have in the internal legal order of the contracting parties".

The Court of Justice added, however:

"Only if that question has not been settled by the agreement does it fall for decision . . . by the Court of Justice . . . in the same manner as any question of interpretation relating to the application of the agreement in the Community".

It would appear that the question of the effect of the WTO Agreement in the internal legal order of the Contracting Parties has not been settled by the WTO Agreement. This alone would suffice for the Court of Justice to disregard the statement in the preamble of the proposed Decision.

This is not a plea for an unconditional and unqualified internal effect of the WTO Agreement "lock, stock and barrel". It is a plea for keeping the possibility of judicial review open. Quite simply, what is in the end the use of making law, also international law, designed to protect private parties, if these private parties cannot rely on it?

Tentative conclusions

From an international law standpoint, the WTO Agreement marks on the whole a significant progress, in particular with respect to dispute settlement, the inclusion of TRIPS and the GATS. The increased concern for procedural guarantees resulting in international obligations in many areas covered by the Uruguay Round agreements should be welcomed by private practitioners and their clients.

From an EC standpoint these developments should on balance – negotiations always are a give and take – be considered as a favourable outcome. For purely internal reasons that were given undue weight, the EC missed a unique opportunity to succeed its Member States formally as a full member of the WTO. The usual internal dispute about the external powers remains to be settled. How it will be settled depends to a significant extent on the advisory opinion which the European Commission has requested, provided the Court of Justice manages to render its opinion on time.

The Court of Justice ought to disregard the apodictic statement on the "non-invocability" of the WTO Agreement.

JACQUES HJ BOURGEOIS

Chapter 7

The Uruguay Round of the GATT: The United Kingdom Standpoint[1]

This paper considers some of the European Community law issues which arise from the conclusion of the GATT Uruguay Round and which are important to the Member States and the institutions of the Community. It looks first at the content of agreements giving· effect to the Uruguay Round and then considers some of the principles of EC law which apply to the conclusion of those agreements by the Community and the Member States. The latter raises the question of the balance of powers between the Community and the Member States and between the institutions of the Community.

Outline of the Uruguay Round Agreements

The UK Government has been an enthusiastic advocate of a successful outcome to the GATT Uruguay Round. The successful conclusion of the Round will enlarge the scope for the expansion of world trade and investment. It should provide a substantial boost to world trade and international prosperity. It reduces the risk of protectionism and trade wars and introduces more effective means for the settlement of trade disputes. Tariffs have been cut on a wide range of products, and countries have undertaken not to raise them again on 95% of world visible trade. The changes in tariffs are very much a develoment of the existing GATT. Where the Uruguay Round has constituted a qualitative leap is in the new areas covered. First, multilateral rules will apply to services, which form an increasingly important component of output for the developed world. Second, the Round reached agreement on certain aspects of intellectual property. Third, a World Trade Organisation is established.

Services

The General Agreement on Trade in Services (the GATS) covers measures applied by members of the World Trade Organisation (the WTO)

---

[1] The views expressed are those of the author and do not necessarily represent the views of the United Kingdom Government.

WTO

affecting trade in services. The GATS rules include a requirement that regulations and agreements affecting trade in services should be transparent (members are required to publish all relevant measures promptly and make them generally available). A Council for Trade in Services is to be set up to facilitate the operation of the agreement and services will be covered by the general dispute settlement arrangements. Perhaps most importantly, the GATS introduces Most Favoured Nation (MFN) and National Treatment non-discrimination principles to trade in services for the first time. It is hoped that the GATS rules will provide valuable increased security and stability to United Kingdom exporters of services.

The GATS rules recognise that the process of liberalisation of trade in services will be a progressive one. The MFN and national treatment principles are therefore not applied unconditionally in all circumstances. Dealing first with Most Favoured Nation treatment. Countries are allowed to take derogations from the MFN principle for specific measures. The Agreement enables a member to maintain a measure inconsistent with the Most Favoured Nation principle provided that the measure is contained in a list submitted to other participants and meets the conditions for exemptions. Most countries have taken MFN derogations for some measures – the European Community, for example, has taken derogations which will enable it to continue to apply discriminatory measures relating to broadcasting services in the 1989 Broadcasting Directive.

So far as national treatment is concerned, the position is somewhat different. The Agreement provides for specific commitments. The obligation to provide national treatment to foreign service suppliers applies only in relation to the service sectors which countries have listed in the schedules of commitments negotiated with other parties during the Round and subject to the limitations described in those schedules. The Commission, being the negotiator for the Community and the Member States, submitted a Schedule of Commitments on their behalf.

The process of negotiating specific commitments in the various services sectors was a key part of the Round. The coverage achieved varies greatly between countries, with most developed countries covering all the major service sectors and some smaller developing countries' schedules covering no more than hotels and tourism. The GATS provides for further negotiations on these schedules to take place no later than five years after it enters into force with a view to achieving a progressively higher level of liberalisation. This will enable barriers to exports of services to be reduced progressively over a number of years in the same way that the GATT has reduced barriers to trade in goods in the decades since its inception.

Intellectual property

The second major new element is the Agreement on Trade-Related Aspects of Intellectual Property – the TRIPS Agreement. For the first time there will be a set of agreed rules requiring basic standards of protection for intellectual property. These rules are based on existing internationally accepted norms, but improve on them in several important respects, including a requirement to establish or maintain effective civil and criminal remedies. This should provide significant benefits for European businesses which have often been prejudiced by the failure of some countries to provide protection for intellectual property rights. Businesses have also often found that, even where intellectual property rights existed, they have frequently been impossible to enforce in some countries. More generally, the agreement should help to reduce growing tensions over trade in counterfeit goods.

The TRIPS Agreement contains two sets of obligations. First, it provides that each member is to accord nationals of other members treatment no less favourable than it accords to its own nationals with regard to the protection of intellectual property. This is subject to exceptions already provided in the relevant international Conventions governing intellectual property. In addition, it provides that, subject to certain exceptions, any advantage, favour, privilege or immunity granted by a member to nationals of any other country shall be accorded immediately and unconditionally to the nationals of all other members. Second, Part II of the TRIPS Agreement provides that members are to grant in their law basic standards for the protection of intellectual property rights. The Agreement sets out minimum standards in the fields of copyright, trade marks, geographical indications, industrial designs, patents etc. Consequently the Agreement goes beyond the effect of intellectual property rights on trade in goods. It goes beyond dealing with the movement of counterfeit goods. Rather, it deals with the intellectual property rights themselves. Although there is an increasing number of Community instruments in the field of intellectual property, they all acknowledge the continued existence of domestic rights. For example, so far as trade marks are concerned there is a Community trade mark but it exists in parallel with national trade marks.

Part III contains provisions on enforcement. It imposes on members obligations to provide civil and administrative procedures and remedies – these include a requirement that judicial authorities should be able to grant injunctions and award damages. These are all matters within the competence of the Member States, not the European Community.

World Trade Organization

The third major development is the establishment of the World Trade Organization, the WTO. Overseeing the agreements giving effect to the Round will be the World Trade Organization which will provide the common institutional framework for the conduct of trade relations among its members. It provides for a Ministerial conference to meet at least once every two years. A General Council is established. One of its most important functions will be to discharge the responsibilities of the Dispute

Settlement Body. There will also be Councils on Trade in Goods, Trade in Services and Trade Related Aspects of Intellectual Property.

This framework of agreements clearly covers a wider area than any other international agreement. Its wide coverage means that it raises different issues to those raised by the existing GATT. The starting point for a lawyer considering these issues is to look at the legal framework which will govern the agreements, and this paper now focuses on the caselaw of the Court of Justice on the external competence of the European Communities.

Judicial activity

This is an area of increasing concern to the institutions of the Community and the Member States. This is evidenced by the spate of cases there has been before the Court of Justice recently. After over a decade when there were only one or two cases, in the last year or so the Court has given its Opinions on Convention No 170 of the International Labour Organisation concerning safety in the use of chemicals at work (Opinion 2/91);[2] on the Community's conclusion of the decision of the OECD on national treatment (Opinion 2/92);[3] and on the competence of the European Community to enter into the agreements giving effect to the Uruguay Round (Opinion 1/94).[4] It has also given judgment in the case C-316/91 *Parliament* v *Council*[5] on the Lomé Convention.

In addition there were three cases pending before the Court which raise questions on the law relating to external relations, in particular the scope of Article 113. The first two, *Commission* v *Council*[6] were challenges by the Commission of certain Council Decisions. In the actions the Commission sought the annulment of Council Decisions relating to the conclusion of agreements between the EC and Hungary and Czechoslovakia on transit. The Council had adopted them under Article 75, which is in the transport chapter of the Treaty, but the Commission maintained that they should have been adopted under Article 113, as being concerned with the common commercial policy. The third case is *Parliament* v *Council*[7], in which the Parliament challenges the use of Article 113 as the Treaty base for an agreement between the EC and the United States on public procurement.

---

[2] Opinion 2/91, [1993] 3 CMLR 800 (ILO Convention No 170 concerning safety in the use of chemicals at work).

[3] Opinion 2/92 of the Court of Justice, 24 March 1995, nyr.

[4] Opinion 1/94 of the Court of Justice, [1995] 1 CMLR 205.

[5] [1994] ECR I-625.

[6] Cases C-74 & 75/93. Withdrawn by the Commission.

[7] Case C-360/93.

Importance of legal base

Why are these cases important to the institutions of the Community and the Member States? Dealing first with the concerns of the Parliament. If an agreement is concluded on the basis of Article 113 the Parliament has no right under the Treaty to be consulted. In most other areas of Community activity the Parliament has increased powers through the co-operation procedure or, since the Treaty on European Union, through the co-decision procedure. However, in the external field if an agreement is based on Article 113 the Parliament has no right to be consulted although in practice it is often consulted on a voluntary basis. There is a possible exception introduced by Article 228, as amended by the Treaty on European Union, where the Agreement establishes a specific institutional framework in organising co-operation procedures and for agreements having important budgetary implications for the Community or entailing amendment of an Act adopted under the co-decision procedure. In these cases the assent of the Parliament is required but it is not clear whether this applies to agreements adopted under Article 113.

Turning to the Member States, why are these legal issues important? The answer lies in pronouncements of the Court of Justice on the effect of holding that something is within the external competence of the Community. Before looking at those cases, I will take a step back and look at the principles governing the question of external competence.

Power of European Community to enter into international agreements

The Treaty itself confers an express power for the Community to enter into international agreements in a number of cases. For example, under Article 113 the Community may enter into agreements with one or more states or international organisations where they are needed as part of the common commercial policy. In addition, under Article 238 the Community may conclude association agreements.

The cases where the Treaty confers an express power is not the end of the matter because the Court has held that the Community has an implied power to enter into external agreements in certain cases. This was first established in the Opinion 1/76[8], and recently reasserted in Opinion 2/91.[9] In that Opinion the Court said:

". . . authority to enter into international commitments may not only arise from an express attribution by the Treaty, but may also flow implicitly from its provisions."

The Court went on to say:

---

[8] [1977] ECR 741.
[9] *Supra*, n 2.

"in particular, whenever Community law has created for the institutions of the Community powers within its internal system for the purposes of attaining a specific objective, the Community has authority to enter into the international commitments necessary for the attainment of that objective even in the absence of an express provision in that connection".

What is the consequence for Member States when the Community has the power to act externally? Can they also enter into international agreements? Where the Community's competence is based on Article 113, the answer the Court has given is no. In a line of cases the Court has held that where a matter is covered by the common commercial policy the Member States do not have the power to act in the Community sphere or in the international sphere. The Court has said, for example in Opinion 1/75[10], that the exercise of concurrent powers by the Member States and the Community is impossible where a matter falls within the common commercial policy.

The consequence is that the Member States lose the power to enter into international agreements. In many cases this will not be a problem. This is because the Member States no longer act on their own; instead they act through the Community. This can give the Member States greater power in dealing with, for example, the United States and Japan. Where it is a problem is where a Member State takes a different view to that of other Member States and this arose in the course of the Uruguay Round in a number of well-publicised areas. It would also be a problem if the common commercial policy were to cover matters which, in the internal field, are not matters where the Community has exclusive competence. This would mean that the Member States would have less power, or competence, externally than they have within the Community. Indeed they would have no power to act externally although they retained the power to act internally, unless, following the reasoning in Opinion 1/75, the consequence was that they also lost the power to act internally.

Turning to the case where competence is implied – what is the position? Can the Member States continue to act or can only the Community act? From the caselaw of the Court the answer seems to be as follows. If the Community has adopted internal rules and the international agreement in question might affect those rules or alter their scope, the Member States do not have the power to act; only the Community can assume obligations which might affect the Community's internal rules or alter their scope. This was decided by the Court in the *ERTA* case.[11] This clearly gives the Member States greater scope for continuing to act because the area where the Community has exclusive competence is more circumscribed. It has exclusive competence only if the agreement in question would affect the Community's internal rules or alter their scope.

What this means in practice is illustrated by Opinion 2/91. The Convention in issue in that case concerned, *inter alia*, matters relating to the

---

[10] [1975] ECR 1355, at 1364.
[11] Case 22/70, *Commission* v *Council* [1971] ECR 263.

health and safety of workers. In the internal sphere the Council has power under Article 118A to adopt measures relating to health and safety at work. That article expressly provides that it does not prevent any Member State from maintaining or introducing more stringent measures for the protection of working conditions. The directives that can be adopted are therefore minimum standards directives. In view of the power in Article 118A to adopt health and safety measures the Court recognised that the Community enjoys an internal legislative competence in the area covered by the relevant ILO Convention. It also recognised that there were several directives adopted under Article 118A which were relevant to the Convention.

However, the Court concluded that the provisions of the Convention were not of such a kind as to affect rules adopted pursuant to Article 118A. The way the Court put it was this. If, on the one hand, the Community decided to adopt rules which were less stringent than those set out in the Convention, the Member States could still adopt more stringent measures (because Article 118A is concerned with minimum standards) and this could include applying for that purpose the provisions of the relevant ILO Convention. If, on the other hand, the Community decided to adopt more stringent measures than those provided under the ILO Convention, there was nothing to prevent the full application of Community law by the Member States because the ILO Constitution itself allows its Members to adopt more stringent measures than those provided for in its Conventions. Therefore, in respect of this aspect of the Convention, the competence of the Community was not exclusive and the Member States were entitled to participate in the Convention in their own right.

By way of contrast there are a number of Community directives adopted in the areas covered by the Convention, which are more than minimum requirements. They are harmonisation measures dealing with such matters as classification, packaging and labelling of dangerous substances. The approach of the Court in respect of this area of the Convention was that the area was one which was already covered to a large extent by Community rules. Those rules had been progressively adopted since 1967 with a view to achieving an ever greater degree of harmonisation. They were designed, on the one hand, to remove barriers to trade resulting from differences in legislation from one Member State to another and, on the other hand, to provide protection for human health and the environment. The Court concluded that, in those circumstances, the commitments in that area of the Convention were of such a kind as to affect the Community rules laid down in the dangerous substances directives. Consequently, the Member States could not themselves undertake those commitments. They could do so only through the framework of Community institutions.

In looking at the competence of the Community where its power to act is implied, I have dealt so far with the case where the Community has the power to act externally because it has exercised a Community power internally. What of the case where it has the power to act internally but has not yet done so? In those circumstances can it act externally and what are the powers of Member States? These are important questions when dealing with agreements which have the scope of the agreements giving effect to the Uruguay Round. In a number of areas covered by those agreements, for example in connection with services and intellectual property, the Community has the power to act internally but has not yet done so. In that case does it have the power to act externally and, equally importantly, if it does, is this power exclusive so that Member States do not themselves have the power to act?

So far as the first question is concerned – the power of the Community to act – the Court of Justice has held in Opinion 1/76 that whenever Community law has created for the institutions of the Commnity powers within its internal system for the purposes of attaining a specific objective, the Community has authority to enter into international commitments necessary for the attainment of that objective. It will be noted that the Court referred to a specific objective. What this means is not clear where the power in question does not on its face or of necessity have an external aspect. Opinion 1/76 was concerned with transport and *Kramer*[12] with fisheries, both of which have a clear external aspect. On the other hand the chapters on establishment and services are concerned only with intra-Community matters.

So far as the second question is concerned – the question whether Member States can act – some guidance is provided by *Kramer*.[13] That case was a preliminary reference from the Dutch courts concerning a prosecution of fishermen for breach of Netherlands law which had been adopted to fulfil commitments entered into by the Netherlands as a party to the North East Atlantic Fisheries Convention. One of the questions referred by the national court asked the Court of Justice to rule whether the Netherlands had authority to be a party to the Convention or whether the Community alone had authority to be a party to it.

The Court of Justice held that the Community did have the power to enter into the Convention because it had the power to establish the necessary rules on the internal level. However, the Community had not at the relevant time made any rules. This being so, the Court held that the Member States had the power to enter into the Convention. But the Court went on to say that the power of the Member States was of a transitional nature. What this seems to mean is that the Member States can continue to act externally until the Community has adopted internal rules. This is, of course, subject to the obligation in Article 5 that the Member States must abstain from any measure which could jeopardise the attainment of the objectives of the Treaty.

In the writer's view the principle laid down in *Kramer* is important. It recognises that the external competence of the Community should move

---

[12] Cases 3, 4 and 6/76, [1976] ECR 1279.
[13] *Ibid.*

in step with what happens internally within the Community. As internal Community legislation increases and more areas become governed by Community law so the power of the Community to act externally increases. However, until the internal power is exercised, the Member States retain the power to act. This is sensible in constitutional terms; it is also sensible in practical terms. If something on the internal level is a matter for Member States, the expertise will tend to be with the Member States. It is therefore difficult for the Commission to be an effective negotiator if it has not yet developed an expertise in the subject matter. As competence is transferred on the internal level, the Commission will acquire expertise and be better able to be the negotiator.

It follows from what has been said above that an international agreement which covers a wide area could contain elements which are within the exclusive competence of the Community, as being part of the common commercial policy or as a result of implied competence applying the *ERTA* case or as a mixture of both. In addition, it could contain elements where the Member States have the power to be a party because exclusive competence has not passed to the Community or because the subject matter is of its nature outside Community competence. In those circumstances both the Community and the Member States should be parties. There is a large number of mixed agreements and in Opinion 2/91 the Court accepted the validity of such agreements. Indeed, on the facts of that case the opinion of the Court was that the conclusion of the Convention in question was a matter which falls within the joint competence of the Member States and the Community.

How do these principles apply to the Uruguay Round Agreements?

If the whole subject matter of the Uruguay Round agreements is within Article 113, the Community has exclusive competence. Therefore, although the Member States would be members of the WTO, that membership would be formal so far as matters at present within the scope of the WTO are concerned. So far as the substance of the matters was concerned, the Community alone would have the power to act. Therefore, the Community would act in matters such as services and intellectual property and not the Member States. This would be the case although there is comparatively little Community legislation concerning intellectual property and, in respect of both intellectual property and services, the Member States retain the competence to act internally, subject, of course, to Community law.

The implications go beyond the World Trade Organisation. If the Community has exclusive competence in respect of services and intellectual property for the purposes of the WTO, it would do so for other purposes as well. The implication of Opinion 1/75 seems to be that the Member States no longer have the power to conclude international agreements in these areas. This would be the case although Community law on intellectual property is undeveloped compared with the domestic laws of the individual Member States.

In the writer's view the respective powers of the Community and the Member States would be better recognised by applying the principles of implied external competence developed by the Court of Justice in such cases as *ERTA* and Opinion 2/91. Applying these principles the Member States would retain the power to act until the Community had adopted internal rules which would be affected by the international agreement in question. This would enable Community action to develop externally in parallel with its development internally. It is somewhat bizarre for the Community to develop externally more rapidly than internally. It would remain possible for the Council to decide in an appropriate case that the Community should enter into a particular agreement although the Community had not yet adopted internal rules. This would be an application of the principle in Opinion 1/76 and *Kramer*. But this would be a decision by the Council in a particular case, not an automatic application of Community rules.

In the last few years the Commission has argued that the common commercial policy should cover not only trade in goods but also trade in services. It now argues that it should include intellectual property rights. The consequence would be that the Community would have exclusive external competence in respect of those areas. However, goods are different to services and intellectual property rights both in fact and in their treatment in Community law. Goods exist physically. They can be moved physically from one Member State to another. So far as Community law is concerned, goods from a third country in free circulation within a Member State are treated in the same way as goods originating in a Member State for the purposes of the provisions of the Treaty of Rome on the free movement of goods.[14]

Services are different. They do not physically exist and services originating in a third country and provided in one Member State do not have the same right to move within the Community as do goods. This is reflected in the fact that the regulation of services concentrates on the provider of the service rather than the service itself. This in turn is reflected in the provisions of Articles 52 and 59 which refer to nationals of Member States. Nationals of a Member State established in a Member State may establish a secondary establishment in another Member State and nationals of a Member State may provide services in another Member State.

This means that problems of trade diversion do not arise as they do with goods. A third country national whose right to provide a service is recognised in one Member State does not thereby have the right to provide that service in all Member States. This was recognised by the Court of Justice in *Abdullah Tawil-Albertini*.[15]

---

[14] See Art 9.
[15] Case C-154/93, [1994] ECR I-451.

In that case Tawil-Albertini, a French national, obtained a diploma of doctor of dental surgery in Lebanon in 1968. In 1979 the relevant Belgian Ministry recognised his Lebanese qualification as equivalent to the Belgian diploma of graduate in dental science; this authorised him to practice in Belgium. Relying on the fact that this qualification had been recognised as equivalent in another Member State, Tawil-Albertini applied to the relevant French Ministry to practice his profession in France. That application was refused. The refusal was upheld by the Court of Justice which said that recognition by a Member State of qualifications awarded by non-Member States did not bind the other Member States.

Furthermore, the development of Community law in the field of services recognises the joint competence of the Community and the Member States. Some areas are unregulated by Community rules. But where there is regulation it is largely based on mutual recognition and minimum standards.

The position is more stark so far as intellectual property is concerned. Here Community rules do not oust national rules. There is now a Community trademark, established by the Trade Mark Regulation[16] but that mark exists in parallel with the national marks. In other areas of intellectual property there has been some harmonisation of national laws but harmonisation has been only partial leaving substantial matters to national law.[17] Finally, there are some intellectual property rights which are not subject to any harmonisation at Community level, *e.g.*, copyright and patents.

Duty of co-operation

Clearly in cases where both the Member States and the Community are parties to an agreement it is important that the Member States and the Community co-operate. As the Court of Justice put it in Opinion 2/91:

"When it appears that the subject matter of an agreement falls in part within the competence of the Community and in part within that of the Member States, it is important to ensure that there is a close association between the institutions of the Community and the Member States both in the process of negotiation and conclusion and in the fulfilment of the obligations entered into."

This flows in part from the obligations imposed by Article 5 of the Treaty. The obligation to co-operate has become more explicit in the Treaty on European Union. Article C provides for the Union to ensure the consis-

---

[16] Council Regulation 40/94 on the Community Trade Mark, OJ 1994 L11/1.

[17] See, for example, the Semi-Conductor Topography Directive (87/54); the Trade Mark Directive (89/104); the Directive on the Legal Protection of Computer Programmes (91/250); the Directive on Rental Rights and Lending Rights (92/100); and the Directive on the Co-ordination of Certain Rules Concerning Copyright and Rights Related to Copyright Applicable to Satellite Broadcasting and Cable Retransmission (93/83).

tency of its external activities as a whole in the context of its external relations, security, economic and development policies. In the case of agreements where competence is mixed, the practical working out of these principles of co-operation and consistency will be important. This is clearly an area that the Community and the Member States will need to address as a matter of urgency if they are to have an effective voice internationally. In many respects the practical issues that will need to be addressed are a development of those that arise at present in ensuring that the Community position on matters within exclusive competence is properly arrived at and in a way that most effectively achieves the Community's objectives.[18]

STEPHEN HYETT

---

[18] This contribution was sent to the editors on 6 October 1994. The oral hearing before the Court of Justice in Opinion 1/94 on the competence of the Community to conclude the Uruguay Round Agreements took place on 11 October. The oral hearing in Opinion 2/92 on the OECD National Treatment Instrument was on the same day. The Court's opinions have anwered many of the questions raised in this paper and will have a major impact on the balance of power between the Community and the Member States. Opinion 1/94 is reported at [1995] 1 CMLR 205; Opinion 2/92 is not yet reported.

Part 4

The Uruguay Round: Effect on the EU Legal Order

Chapter 8
Consequences of the Customs Union

Introduction

The completion of the Uruguay Round negotiations makes it particularly appropriate to consider the status of the EC as a customs union, to examine the legal consequences of that customs union, and to see what, if any, changes or developments may be expected.

The customs union and the internal market

Basic principles under the EC Treaty

The EC Treaty makes it clear at the outset, in Article 9, that the internal free movement of goods is linked to the adoption of a common customs tariff as part of a customs union. In turn, the common customs tariff was linked to the development of a common commercial policy towards third countries in the original Article 3, which set out the objectives of the Treaty. However, the Maastricht amendments to Article 3 have, rather oddly, deleted the reference to a customs union, although they maintain the reference to a common commercial policy.

Very simply, the concept of a customs union as exemplified in the EC Treaty means that third country goods should receive the same customs and commercial policy treatment wherever they enter the Community (and the directly applicable instrument of the Regulation provides a mechanism capable of achieving this aim), and that within the customs union both goods produced within the Community and goods legitimately imported from third countries should be able to move from Member State to Member State without being subject to customs duties and charges equivalent thereto[1], without being subject to quantitative restrictions or measures equivalent thereto[2], and without being subject to discriminatory or protective internal taxation.[3]

This aim may be contrasted with that of a free trade area, as under Article 4 of the Convention establishing the European Free Trade Association (EFTA). This does not establish a common customs tariff, and only

---

[1] Arts 9–16.
[2] Arts 30–36.
[3] Art 95.

treats goods as eligible for "area tariff treatment" (*i.e.*, free trade) if they are of "Area origin" as there defined. However, following the Accession of the United Kingdom, Ireland and Denmark to the European Communities in 1973, the EC as a single unit entered into free trade agreements with the remaining EFTA countries. This has developed to the point where the Customs Union of the EC is the centre of a wider free trade arrangement with the EFTA countries, using the same model transit documents[4], and in 1990 negotiations began on the creation of a European Economic Area involving the EC, and the EFTA states, involving the application of the internal market rules of the EC by the EFTA countries. The resultant Treaty finally entered into force on 1 January 1994, without the participation of Switzerland.

The logic of the Customs Union is not however at first sight always followed by the Treaty provisions on the free movement of goods. The provisions on internal taxation are set out in Article 95, which is contained in the Chapter on Tax Provisions in Part III of the Treaty, whereas the rules on customs duties and charges having equivalent effect and on quantitative restrictions and measures having equivalent effect are set out in Chapters 1 and 2 of Title I of Part II of the Treaty. The importance of this is that on a literal reading of Article 9(2), it is only provisions falling within those two Chapters which are expressly stated to apply not only to products originating in Member States but also to products coming from third countries which are in free circulation in Member States. Indeed, Article 95 itself only refers in terms to products "of" other Member States. There was therefore doubt as to whether products in free circulation could benefit from the provisions on internal taxation. However, faced with a case actually involving third country goods in free circulation in the Community, the Court took a different approach and used the opportunity to interpret Article 95 so as to parallel the other free movement of goods rules. This was in *Cooperativa Co-Frutta*[5], which involved Italian taxation of bananas imported through other Member States. The Court invoked the principles underlying the common customs tariff and the common commercial policy, which are intended to ensure both uniform treatment of goods imported from third countries and to enable such goods to circulate freely within the Community once they have been legitimately imported, to hold that the Treaty prohibitions on discriminatory and protective internal taxation under Article 95 must also apply to such goods.

Problems under the ECSC and Euratom Treaties

It must however be emphasised that the Customs Union is technically a concept of the EC Treaty. The common tariff under that Treaty may be

---

[4] See Council Regulation 2011/89 on the simplification of formalities in trade between the EEC and EFTA countries. OJ 1989 L 200/1.

[5] Case 193/85, [1987] ECR 2085.

contrasted with the common customs tariff originally established under Article 94 of the Euratom Treaty, which was introduced as scheduled, only a year after the entry into force of that Treaty, on 1 January 1959, but by virtue of an agreement between the Member States reached on 22 December 1958.[6] Nonetheless, the Euratom tariff had been reproduced in the appropriate headings of the table setting out the EC tariff from the beginning. That table also lists for convenience the nomenclature of products falling within the ECSC Treaty, and the current version makes a bracketed reference to the ECSC to indicate the products subject to that Treaty.

Article 72 of the ECSC Treaty allows for the Member States themselves to determine tariffs within certain limits; by virtue of the transitional provisions, however, the Member States reached agreement on 19 November 1957 as to a harmonised, but not common, ECSC tariff to be applied from 10 February 1958.[7] That the duties under this tariff were not common is evidenced by the recitals to the Commission Recommendation[8] which since 1964 has fixed the minimum duties on iron and steel products; these recitals justify the Recommendation on the ground that it was necessary to raise the duties imposed by the other Member States to the level already applied by Italy under the "harmonised" tariff so as to increase external protection. This Recommendation was enacted, *inter alia*, under Article 74 ECSC, which allows the Commission to take protective measures in certain circumstances, but since an ECSC recommendation is binding only as to the result to be achieved, the actual charge is still imposed by national legislation.

It may be wondered whether this is a distinction without a difference; Article 31 of the 1972 Act of Accession, like the corresponding provisions of the subsequent Acts of Accession, refers to the "ECSC unified tariff" for ECSC products other than coal as a target to which new Member States must move, and successive Decisions of the Representatives of the Governments of the Member States of the ECSC meeting within the Council provided that the nomenclature and conventional duties (*i.e.*, the duties applying to imports from parties to GATT and the states benefitting from most-favoured-nation treatment) for ECSC products set out for convenience in the EC common customs tariff should be applied by the Member States of the ECSC.[9] Eventually Decision 86/98/ECSC[10] declared that the Community provisions to ensure the uniform application of the common customs tariff should apply to the products falling within the province of the ECSC Treaty, and express reference is made to this fact in the new tariff introduced in 1987.[11]

In the analogous field of anti-dumping duties, where the ECSC legislation is also made under Article 74 ECSC and traditionally also took the

---

[6] JO 1959 p 408.

[7] *ECSC 6th General report*, p 82.

[8] Recommendation 1/64, JO 1964 p 99 as amended.

[9] See Decision 79/35/ECSC, OJ 1979 L 10/13 replacing Decision 72/1, JO 1972 L 1/383.

[10] OJ 1986 L 81/29.

[11] Council Regulation 2658/87, OJ 1987 L 256/1.

form of a Recommendation, the current ECSC legislation is contained in a Commission Decision[12] which is directly applicable as Community law and thus parallels the EC Council Regulation[13] on the same matter. Article 74 ECSC empowers the Commission to take measures which are in accordance with the Treaty and to make any necessary recommendations to the Member States. However, presumably taking a broad view of "any measures" in Article 74 ECSC, the explanation given in the recitals is that "it is appropriate to ensure that the legislation governing external trade should be as homogeneous as possible in the two Communities". By parity of reasoning, it may be wondered whether the ECSC customs tariff will eventually take the form of a directly applicable Decision.

Whatever the legal status of the ECSC tariff, however, there have been a couple of recent illustrations that the ECSC is something less than a customs union with regard to goods imported from third countries. In the coal sector, the Court of Justice has actually upheld a differential tariff applying to imports into a particular Member State in relation to imports occurring in the late 1970s. This happened in *Mabanaft* v *HZA Emmerich*.[14] The question there at issue related to the validity of a Recommendation dating back to 1959[15] under which Germany could impose customs duties on imports of coal originating in non-Member States and destined for Germany, subject to a maximum rate of 20 DM per tonne; in this particular case, the coal, although of non-Community origin[16], was in free circulation in the Netherlands, and imported from the Netherlands into Germany. Unlike Articles 9 and 10 of the EC Treaty, the ECSC Treaty contains no provision expressly stating that products of third countries in free circulation in a Member State benefit from the prohibition on customs duties and charges having equivalent effect in trade between Member States, although Article 4(a) ECSC does contain such a basic prohibition. Nevertheless, the Court repeated the principle it had laid down in *Vloeberghs*[17] that ECSC products originating in non-Member States and released into free circulation in a Member State do benefit from internal free movement, a principle recognised by the old High Authority in a letter it sent to the governments of the Member States as early as May 1955.[18] However, having stated that principle, and having described the ECSC as "more akin in its structure to the principle of a Customs Union" than a mere free trade area, the Court emphasised that Article 4(a) ECSC only prohibited import duties and other restrictions "as provided in this

---

[12] The change took place in 1984 with the enactment of Commission Decision 2177/84, OJ 1984 L 201/17. The current version is in Commission Decision 2424/88, OJ 1988 L 209/18.

[13] Currently Council Regulation 2423/88, OJ 1988, L 209/1.

[14] Case 36/83, [1984] ECR 2497.

[15] Amtsblatt, OJ German Edition 1959 p 197.

[16] It would appear that, as in so many of the leading cases in this area, the true origin of the coal was not declared at the time of importation; nothing turned on this, however.

[17] Cases 9 and 12/60, [1961] ECR 197.

[18] See [1961] ECR at 215.

treaty", and noted that subparagraph (3) of Article 74(1) ECSC authorises the Commission, if coal or steel products as defined in the Treaty are "imported into the territory of one or more Member States in relatively increased quantities and under such conditions that these imports cause or threaten to cause serious injury to production within the common market of like or directly competing products" to make Recommendations to Member States.

It was agreed between the parties that the relevant circumstances authorising the Recommendation did exist in Germany between 1959 and 1963, and the Court found that, with short-term exceptions, the situation had continued until 1978, when the last of the importations in question occurred, so that the Recommendation was still valid at that date, 16 years after its initial enactment. No consideration appears to have been given in the judgment to the compatibility of the Recommendation with the Decisions of the Representatives of the Member States mentioned above, concerning the use of the EC Common Customs Tariff nomenclature and conventional duties, nor was its continued operation considered in the light of GATT obligations despite the fact that by reference to the second paragraph of Article 71 ECSC, Article 74 ECSC requires that the Recommendation of the Commission may not exceed the powers accorded to Member States under the international agreements to which they are parties. On the other hand, it may be observed that following the Tokyo Round negotiations, Recommendation 1/64 on iron and steel duties was amended by Recommendation 81/772[19] to the effect that the Recommendation would not apply where it would entail disregard of the bound tariff concessions accorded to contracting parties to GATT, including obligations resulting from tariff agreements concluded within the framework of GATT by the Community or its Member States acting in agreement. Whilst it would be naive to pretend that there is complete free movement of imported goods under the EC Treaty, given the continued use of Article 115, at least the restrictions used do not include differential customs duties imposed on goods already in free circulation.[20]

A second illustration of the differences between the EC and ECSC Treaties may be more briefly explained. At a time when the Court was holding that goods imported into the Community under a quota allocated to a specific Member State under the EC commercial policy must nevertheless be regarded as in free circulation under the EC Treaty, the Commission adopted Decision 85/415 which, by way of derogation from Recommendation 1/64, authorised tariff quotas for the import of certain special steels into Germany, the Benelux countries and France, but expressly required those Member States to ensure that the products in

---

[19] OJ 1981 L 285/33.

[20] In Cases 80 and 81/77, *Ramel* v *Receveur des Douanes*, [1978] ECR 927, a provision of an EC Council Regulation was held invalid in so far as it authorised Member States to impose charges equivalent to customs duties.

question were not re-exported to other Member States. In any event, of course, Article 71 ECSC states that national powers with regard to commercial policy are not in principle affected by the Treaty, but here a more positive aspect (at least for those who wish to promote integration) of the judgment in *Mabanaft*[20a] may be reported. In that case, the German Government in fact argued that by virtue of Article 71 ECSC, a Member State could not only pursue an independent commercial policy but could itself avoid deflections of trade by means of customs duties levied on imports from another Member State which have originated in non-member countries. This argument was rejected by the Court in its limited acceptance of the principle of free circulation under the ECSC Treaty. Perhaps the Court's view could be summarised as being that the ECSC is sufficiently akin to a customs union for its Member States not to be able unilaterally to impose customs duties on goods in free circulation in other Member States, but it is not sufficient of a customs union for its institutions to be prohibited from authorising Member States to impose such customs duties.

The inconvenience caused to international negotiations by Article 71 ECSC are well known, and the external pressures which may lead to its circumvention are well illustrated in the arrangements made with the United States in the matter of the export of Community steel products.[21] The solution eventually adopted was a series of Commission Decisions[22] made under Article 95(1) ECSC, the "everything else" provision of that Treaty, roughly equivalent to Article 235, which requires unanimous Council approval. The recitals to these Decisions make interesting reading:

"whereas the decision to conclude such an arrangement is necessary in order to attain, in the context of the functioning of the common market for steel, the objectives of the Treaty are set out, in particular in the second paragraph of Article 2 of this Treaty;[23] whereas the Treaty did not make provision for all the cases covered by this Decision; whereas this Decision does not affect the powers of the Member States in matters of commercial policy referred to in Article 71 of this Treaty."

In other words, in order to reach an agreement with the United States, the Community used Article 95 ECSC to give itself a power which not only was not conferred upon the Community but was expressly conferred upon the Member States – a process repeated in later arrangements with the United States – whilst at the same time boldly asserting that the powers of the Member States were not affected.

However, in *Opinion 1/94*[24] on the EC's competence to enter the Uruguay Round Agreements, the European Court has strongly reasserted its view that Article 71 ECSC Treaty only reserves competence to the Member

---

[20a] Case 36/83 [1984] ECR 2497.

[21] See Benyon and Bourgeois, "The EC/US Steel Arrangement" (1984) 21 CMLRev 305.

[22] Decisions 2871–2873/82, OJ 1982 L 307/11.

[23] Which refers, *inter alia*, to bringing about "the most rational system of production" whilst taking care not to provoke fundamental and persistent disturbances in the economies of the Member States.

[24] [1994] ECR I-5267.

States as regards agreements relating *specifically* to ECSC products, and that agreements of a general nature which happen to include ECSC products fall within Article 113 of the EC Treaty.

Whatever its intrinsic deficiencies as a customs union, the ECSC Treaty nonetheless clearly illustrates in this area the way in which developments may be made in Community law without formal amendments to the treaties.

Agricultural trade

Agricultural trade is an area where, irrespective of the changes which will result from the Uruguay Round, internal and external markets are inextricably interlinked. With the notable exception of the market in oils and fats under Council Regulation 136/66[25], where such protection takes the form of relatively low customs duties, an integral part of the classic EC support scheme is a minimum price for the import of third country goods defended by an import levy designed to raise the price to that level.

The basic pattern of a fully developed common organization is to be found in that governing the market in cereals. At the heart of the system were a target price and an intervention price. The target price indicated the level of price it was hoped Community producers would receive, and as a matter of law was fixed for Duisburg in West Germany as being the centre of the area with the greatest deficit of cereals in the Community (even though the same nominal prices apply throughout the whole Community). The intervention price on the other hand has traditionally represented the price at which national authorities, such as the United Kingdom Intervention Board for Agricultural Produce, are legally required to purchase products subject to the price system which are offered to them, and was fixed for Ormes in France, as being the production area having the greatest surplus of cereals in the Community. Under the 1992 reforms, the target and intervention prices had no geographical links, and were fixed by Council Regulation 1766/92[26] so as to be reduced by fixed amounts over a three-year period, starting from a lower level than that previously applied. There has also, however, been a move away from product support towards producer support, culminating in Council Regulation 1765/92[27] on a support system for producers of certain arable crops. This sets up a system of compensatory payments for EC producers of arable crops with effect from the 1993–1994 marketing year. In general it is linked to an obligation to set aside 15% of the relevant area, but for "small" producers (those with an area less than that needed to produce 92 tonnes of cereals) there is no set-aside obligation.

The relevance of fixing a geographical location for the target and intervention prices was that the difference between those prices included an

---

[25] JO 1966 p 3025.
[26] OJ 1992 L 181/21.
[27] OJ 1992, L 181/12.

element to allow for the costs of transport between Ormes and Duisburg. Geography also played a role in the external aspects of the price structure. In order to ensure that the price structure was not upset by lower-priced imports, a threshold price was fixed, notionally for the port of Rotterdam, representing the minimum price at which the relevant goods may enter the Community. This threshold price was calculated not from the intervention price but from the higher target price (thus ensuring that the intervention price was not likely to be undercut), and the difference between the target price and the threshold price again included an element to allow for the cost of transport between Rotterdam and Duisburg. Like the target and intervention prices, under the 1992 version of the common organization the threshold price had no geographical link, and was fixed by Council Regulation 1766/92 so as to be reduced by fixed amounts over a three-year period. However, it may be observed that the new threshold prices were consistently higher than the target price, which would appear to mean that imports would be unable to compete at the price level anticipated for Community products. While the threshold price itself no longer had an express geographical link, it had still to be compared with a world price fixed for Rotterdam.

If (as was usually the case) the world price, calculated on a CIF basis for Rotterdam, was lower than the threshold price, the difference had to be covered by an import levy. In the converse situation, if a Community producer wishes to export into lower-priced world markets, there is power under the Community legislation to pay an export refund to cover the difference; provision was also made for the advance-fixing of both import levies and export refunds.

It would appear that the EC agreed to accept free or low-duty imports of all oilseeds, proteins and grain substitutes in exchange for United States acceptance of the concept of the variable levy[28], and the caselaw of the Court was insistent that this levy was not a customs duty. The Court pointed out in *Neumann* v *Hauptzollamt Hof*[29] that, whatever similarities import levies may have to customs duties, a levy is a charge regulating external trade connected with a common price policy and not a customs duty as such.

This, and much of the rest of the system has been changed as a result of the Uruguay Round Agreement on Agriculture. Under Article 6, domestic support (*e.g.*, intervention purchasing) is required to be reduced, in the EC's case by a global 20%, but taken from a 1986–1988 base (although under Article 6(5) and Annex II payments under production-limiting programmes (*e.g.*, set-aside) and decoupled income support do not need to be reduced). Under Articles 3(3) and 9, export refunds are to be reduced, in the EC's case by an average of 36% in amount and 21% in volume from a 1986–1988 base. Most importantly from the point of view of

---

[28] EC Commission, "Disharmonies in EC and US Agricultural Policies" (1988), Summary of Results, 9–12.

[29] Case 17/67 [1967] ECR 441.

external protection, under Article 4, import levies are required to be converted into tariffs, and in the EC's case reduced by an average of 36 per cent from a 1986–1988 base. It may be wondered how such a reduction could be reconciled with current prices which were higher even than the target price, but in the base years EC prices were relatively higher and world prices were relatively lower, giving a high tariff to start from, and the move within the EC away from a system of product support (intervention) to a system involving an element of producer support (*e.g.*, set-aside) will automatically reduce both the amount of internal support which is taken into account for GATT purposes, and the level of export refunds and external protection which will be required to maintain the internal price system.

The necessary legislative changes were made, or enabled to be made, by Council Regulation 3290/94[30], which for the cereals market abolished the concept of the threshold price, and provided for Common Customs Tariff duties to apply in principle. However, it is nevertheless provided that for most cereal products the import duty should be equal to the intervention price, increased by 55%, minus the c.i.f. price for the consignment in question, provided this does not exceed the Common Customs Tariff duty. Under this system, the target price no longer serves any useful purpose, and it also was eventually abolished by Council Regulation 1128/95[31].

External consequences

External competence

Under Article 23(3) EC, the common customs tariff was due to be established by the end of the original transitional period (1 January 1970), but by a Council Decision of 26 July 1966[32], the original Member States agreed to apply a common tariff as from 1 July 1968, 18 months before the deadline.

In one sense, therefore, it becomes possible to talk of the Community as a single unit in world trade from the introduction of the common customs tariff. In so far as judgments of the Court may be relevant in the matter, a detailed analysis of the relationship of the EC to the General Agreement on Tariffs and Trade (GATT) was made in the judgment in *Italian Finance Administration* v *SPI and SAMI*.[33] In that judgment it is stated that while the Community took part in the so-called Dillon round in 1960 to 1961, the General Agreement on Tariffs and Trade could only be regarded as having become an act of the Community institutions (rather than of the Member States) for the purposes of a reference for a preliminary ruling under Article 177 as to its interpretation, from 1968. From that year, following the

---

[30] OJ 1994 L 349/105.
[31] OJ 1995 L 148/3.
[32] JO 1966 p 2971.
[33] Cases 267–269/81, [1983] ECR 801, at 824.

introduction of the common customs tariff, the Community is taken by the Court to have succeeded to the rights and obligations of its Member States under GATT and under the International Customs Conventions.

Thus, under the 1950 Customs Co-operation Council Nomenclature Convention, the Community was held[34] to have replaced the Member States in their commitments arising under this Convention and was bound by those commitments, in particular the obligation to make no changes in the chapter or section notes in that Nomenclature in such a manner as to modify the scope of the chapters, sections and headings laid down in the Nomenclature. On the other hand, it has recently been made clear in *Germany* v *Council*[35], in relation to the EC banana regime, that

"it is only if the Community intended to implement a particular obligation entered into within the framework of GATT, or if the Community act expressly refers to specific provisions of GATT, that the Court can review the lawfulness of the Community act in question from the point of view of the GATT rules".

Charges equivalent to customs duties

Just as the EC Treaty made no express provision for the enactment of common rules on the valuation for goods for customs purposes or on the determination of the origin of goods for customs purposes, so also it contains no express prohibition on Member States imposing charges equivalent to customs duties[36] on imports from third countries after the common customs tariff entered into force. In practice, the agricultural legislation of the Community does usually expressly prohibit such charges, and such a prohibition is also contained in some of the specific trade arrangements negotiated by the Community, but there is still no general legislative prohibition on such charges. Hence, this is a matter in which the general principles have been laid down in the caselaw of the Court of Justice.

The matter came before the Court in 1973 in the context of Belgian legislation imposing a charge on imports of rough diamonds from non-Member States for the benefit of the Belgian social fund for diamond workers.[37] Having determined that this was a charge levied only by reason of importation, therefore equivalent in its nature to a customs duty, the Court held that it was clear from the objectives of the common customs tariff that Member States could not alter the level of protection defined by that tariff by means of charges supplementing the common customs tariff duties. Furthermore, the Court noted that even if the charge were not protective in nature, nevertheless its very existence could hardly be reconciled with the requirements of a common commercial policy. The Court therefore concluded that Member States could not, following the establishment of the common customs tariff, introduce in a unilateral

---

[34] Case 38/75, *Nederlandse Spoorwegen* v *Inspecteur der Invoerrechten*, [1975] ECR 1439.
[35] Case C-280/93, [1994] ECR I-4973.
[36] In effect, a charge other than a customs duty as such levied by reason of crossing a frontier.
[37] Cases 37 and 38/73 *Diamantarbeiders* v *Indiamex* [1973] ECR 1609.

manner new charges on goods imported directly from third countries or raise the level of those in existence at the time the tariff was introduced. The basic tenor of the Court's judgment appears to be that a common customs tariff and a common commercial policy require uniform external protection at the external frontiers of the Community's single market.

However, the problems of achieving this objective by caselaw in the absence of express legislation came clearly to a head in *Simmenthal* v *Italian Finance Administration*[38], which involved charges levied under Italian legislation in relation to the health inspection of meat imported into Italy from Uruguay. The Court here recognised that it was the Community policy of achieving a uniform external protection which prevented Member States from imposing their own charges having equivalent effect to customs duties on imports from non-Member States, but it accepted that the Council and Commission could create exceptions or derogations for the prohibition on charges having equivalent effect to customs duties provided that the charges involved had a uniform effect in all Member States in trade with third countries. However, in this case the Court was faced with the difficulty that health inspections would have been required in Community internal trade and that under the relevant Community legislation, national provisions relating to imports from third countries were not to be more favourable than those governing intra-Community trade. The Court therefore found itself having to accept that a Member State must hold inspections and charge for them where such inspections would be held and could be charged for in internal Community trade. In internal Community trade, such charges are in principle permissible if they do not exceed the actual cost of carrying out the inspection, but the Court in *Land Berlin* v *Wigei*[39] had to accept that in order to avoid reverse discrimination against Community products, the charges imposed for the inspection of products imported from non-Member States could exceed those levied on inspections of Community products provided they were not manifestly disproportionate. Subsequently, the Court has expressly accepted that the lawfulness of imposing a charge for a health inspection could not be subject to the existence of comparable charges in all the other Member States, at least where the charge corresponded to the cost of the inspection;[40] hence, this would appear to amount to an admission that there can be different treatment of imports from non-Member States depending on the Member State into which they are imported.

Whilst the Court may not, to judge from what it said in *Germany* v *Council*[41], regard GATT as a general criterion of the validity of Community action, it may nevertheless be observed that the view that the charges imposed for the inspection of products imported from non-Member States could exceed those levied on inspections of Community products

---

[38] Case 70/77, [1978] ECR 1453.
[39] Case 30/79, [1980] ECR 151.
[40] Case 1/83, *Intercontinentale Fleischhandelsgesellschaft* v *Bavaria* [1984] ECR 349.
[41] Case C-280/93, *supra*, n 32.

appears now to be incompatible with the Uruguay Round Agreement on the Application of Sanitary and Phytosanitary Measures, Annex C 1(f) of which requires that any fees imposed for the procedures on imported products should be equitable in relation to any fees charged on like domestic products and should be no higher than the actual cost of the service.

Furthermore, in the context of discriminatory internal taxation, the Court went so far as to say that the EC Treaty did not prohibit discrimination in the application of internal taxation to products imported from third countries, subject to any treaty which may be in force between the Community and the country of origin of the product.[42] This hardly seemed consonant with the concept of the common customs tariff[43], but despite holding in the *Co-Frutta*[44] case that the internal taxation rules apply to third country goods in free circulation within the Community, the Court has maintained its view that it is legitimate to discriminate against direct imports of third country goods[45], which appears to be an open invitation to distortions of trade. It also appears to conflict with Article III:I GATT requiring internal taxes and regulations not to be applied to imported or domestic products so as to afford protection to domestic production.

Measures equivalent to quantitative restrictions

A particular difficulty relates to the extent to which a Member State may still impose measures equivalent to quantitative restrictions on goods whose import is not subject to any quantitative restrictions as such. Here, there is a terminological difference between the free trade agreements with other European countries and the successive Lomé Conventions on the one hand, and the general rules governing imports on the other. In the free trade agreements, there is indeed an express prohibition on measures having an effect equivalent to quantitative restrictions, but there is no such express prohibition in the general rules on imports.

When it considered the matter in the light of the 1974 version of the common rules on imports[46], the Court held[47] that the Treaty provisions on commercial policy did not lay down any obligation on the part of the Member States to extend to trade with third countries the binding principles governing the free movement of goods between Member States, and in particular the prohibition of measures having an effect equivalent to quantitative restrictions. Having noticed the different drafting of the free trade agreements, the Court stated that the binding commitments undertaken by the Community with regard to certain countries could not auto-

---

[42] Case 148/77, *Hansen* v *HZA Flensburg* [1978] ECR 1787.
[43] See Usher, "The Single Market and Goods Imported from Third Countries" *Yearbook of European Law* (1986), 159, at 167.
[44] *Supra*, n 5.
[45] Cases C-228–234 etc/90, *Simba*, [1992] ECR I-3713.
[46] Council Regulation 1439/74, OJ 1974 L 159/1.
[47] Case 86/75, *EMI* v *CBS*, [1976] ECR 871, at 905–906.

matically be extended to others. The case in fact involved the use of trademark rights by a trading undertaking to keep out direct imports from the United States. In this context the Court had no difficulty in holding that the principles governing the common commercial policy did not prevent the owner of the trademark from exercising his rights in order to prevent the importation of similar products bearing the same mark coming from a third country. However, it should be observed that in discussing the differences between the general rules on imports and the specific rules governing the free trade agreements, the Court talked in terms of the commitments undertaken by the Community with regard to imported goods and did not talk in terms of the powers left to the Member States. In any event, even where a free trade agreement does expressly prohibit not only quantitative restrictions but also measures having effects equivalent to quantitative restrictions, it is clear that the same interpretation of that phrase need not be given in the context of trade with a third country as will be given in the context of trade between Member States, since there is no intention to create a single market under free trade agreements.[48]

The mechanisms of the common tariff

Nomenclature and tariff

As has been mentioned above, the single external tariff was introduced 18 months early, on 1 July 1968, and is built upon common rules on nomenclature, valuation and origin. No doubt for practical reasons, the geographical area to which it applies is defined in detail by secondary legislation.[49] The nomenclature was in fact originally based on the 1950 Customs Co-operation Council Nomenclature Convention, to which all the Member States were parties. In the eyes of the Court[50], the Community replaced the Member States in their commitments arising under this Convention and was bound by those commitments, in particular the obligation to make no changes in the chapter or section notes in that Nomenclature in such a manner as to modify the scope of the chapters, sections and headings laid down in the Nomenclature. Although Regulation 950/68[51] was made under the EC Treaty, it also listed the products

---

[48] Case 270/80, *Polydor* v *Harlequin*, [1982] ECR 379.

[49] Originally Council Regulation 1496/68, JO 1968 L238/1, replaced by Regulation 2151/84, OJ 1984 L197/1 as amended. It is this secondary legislation, rather than any Treaty provision, which excludes Gibraltar from the scope of the Common Customs Tariff.

[50] Case 38/75, *Nederlandse Spoorwegen* v *Inspecteur der Invoerrechten*, [1975] ECR 1439.

[51] JO 1968 L 172/1.

falling under the EURATOM Treaty[52], and, for convenience, products falling within the ECSC Treaty.[53]

The Community itself was a party to the negotiations leading to the International Convention on a Harmonised Commodity Description and Coding System, which has formed the basis of the nomenclature from 1 January 1988, following the adoption of a decision by the Council concluding the Convention on behalf of the Community in April 1987 and the enactment of Council Regulation 2658/87 on a common nomenclature and tariff.[54] The structure of the new nomenclature is in fact broadly similar to the old one, the analysis of products being largely based on a progression from raw materials to processed products, although there are changes in detail, and the codes for each classification are now entirely numerical, to aid computerised transactions.[55]

Valuation

The legislation on the valuation of goods for customs purposes shows a similar progression from the Community taking over an agreement previously binding on its Member States to the Community actively negotiating a new international agreement. In this case, the original Regulation in 1968[56] was based on the 1950 Customs Co-operation Council Valuation Convention, to which all the Member States were parties, and this was replaced in 1980 by Regulation 1224/80[57] based on the agreements reached on the implementation of Article VII GATT in the context of the Tokyo Round negotiations in 1979, negotiations to which the EC as such was party. It may be observed that the EC Treaty contains no express authority empowering the institutions to issue rules governing the valuation of goods for customs purposes. Hence, the 1968 Regulation was enacted under Article 235, which enables the Council to act where the Treaty has not provided the necessary powers. In one of the very first cases to be referred to the Court on the question of the valuation legislation[58], the

---

[52] Set by an agreement between the Member States of 22 December 1958, JO 1959 p 408.

[53] ECSC duties are technically imposed by the Member States pursuant to Commission Recommendation 1/64, JO 1964 p 99, but successive Decisions of the Representatives of the Governments of the Member States of the ECSC meeting within the Council have provided that the nomenclature and conventional duties (*i.e.*, the duties applying to imports from parties to GATT and from countries benefiting from most-favoured nation treatment) – see *e.g.*, Decision 79/35/ECSC, OJ 1979 L10/13. This pattern has been continued after the introduction of the new nomenclature and tariff by Decision 87/597/ECSC, OJ 1987 L363/67. The view that the ECSC Treaty creates something less than a full customs union for the products falling within its scope was expressed by the Court in Case 36/83, *supra*, n 14; see Usher, *supra*, n 40.

[54] OJ 1987 L256/1. Consolidated amended texts are issued by the Commission.

[55] For a more detailed discussion of classification problems, see Usher, "Uniform External Protection – EEC customs legislation before the European Court of Justice", (1982) 19 CMLRev 389.

[56] Council Regulation 803/68, JO 1968 L148/6.

[57] O.J. 1980 L134/1.

[58] Case 8/73, *HZA Bremerhaven* v *Massey Ferguson*, [1973] ECR 897.

argument was put that since all the Member States were already parties to the 1950 Valuation Convention, there was no necessity for action by the Community under Article 235. However, the Court found that, as was stated in the recitals to the Regulation, the definition of value and the interpretative notes set out in the 1950 Convention had been embodied into the legislation of the Member States in differing ways, and also certain optional provisions of the interpretative notes were being applied differently in different Member States. The Court, therefore, held that the fact that the Member States had all signed the Customs Co-operation Council's Valuation Convention would not lead to the necessary extent to the uniform determination of the valuation for customs purposes of imported goods required for the functioning of a customs union. It therefore held the use of legislation under Article 235 to be justified.[59]

The fundamental distinction between the system of valuation derived from the 1950 Convention and that derived from the 1979 Tokyo Round agreement is that whilst the former was based on the concept of a hypothetical normal price, in other words the price which the goods would fetch in a sale on the open market between a buyer and seller independent of each other, the Tokyo Round agreement is based on the concept of transaction value, which is defined as the price actually paid or payable for the goods when sold for export to the country of importation.[60] Important as this change may be, the concept of the normal price was not always taken to its logical conclusion; in particular, in *Chatain*[61] the Court refused to accept that the declaration of a price above the normal price on importation breached the Community rules. It was there alleged by the French authorities that the French subsidiary of Sandoz had declared goods supplied by its Swiss parent as having a value nearly twice the normal price when imported into France.[62] Although Advocate General Capotorti suggested that the concept of a normal price meant that an overvaluation should be reduced just as much as an undervaluation should be increased, the Court held that the essential aim of the legislation was to prevent goods being undervalued and that the adjustments permitted to the price paid or payable were all intended to avoid undervaluation. Similarly under the current system, it appears that, in circumstances where the invoice price cannot wholly be relied upon, Article 8 of Regulation 1224/80[63] only allows for additions to the price actually paid or payable.

---

[59] While this is still authority for the proposition that the Community needed its own rules on customs valuation, it may be wondered whether, following Case 165/87, *Commission v Council*, [1988] ECR 5545, the requisite powers were not already contained in Article 28 on the common customs tariff and Article 113 on the common commercial policy.

[60] A definition maintained in Article 1(1) of the Uruguay Round Agreement on Implementation of Article VII GATT.

[61] Case 65/79, [1980] ECR 1345.

[62] It was further alleged that this was done to ensure that profits were made in Switzerland rather than France (a practice commonly referred to as transfer pricing), so as to avoid the payment of French tax.

[63] OJ 1980 L134/1.

119

The essential aspect of the valuation of goods for customs purposes under Community law is that goods are valued at their point of entry into the Community. This means that costs incurred within Community Territory, such as warehousing costs[64], or transport costs (even if the bulk of the transport costs are within the Community)[65], are not included in the value provided they can be distinguished from the price paid or payable. On the other hand, factors such as the cost of obtaining an import licence or an unused share of a quota are also, perhaps more surprisingly, not taken into account in the assessment of value on importation.[66]

It may finally be observed that the EC rules on valuation, like those on origin which will be considered next, have been brought together in Council Regulation 2913/92 on the Community Customs Code.[67]

Determination of origin

The third basic element of the Community customs legislation concerns the determination of the origin of goods for customs purposes.[68] Here, the Community legislation is autonomous, because there was no international agreement on the matter in 1968 when the Community rules were enacted, although provisions on the matter are contained in the 1973 Kyoto Convention on the simplification and harmonisation of customs procedures.[69] Again, Article 235 was invoked as authority for the enactment of this legislation, but in conjunction with the Treaty provisions regulating the common commercial policy. Recent amendments have been based on the latter provisions alone[70], as was the codifying Regulation 2913/92.[71]

The linguistic problems to which such common rules can give rise were illustrated when a group of British trawlermen wished to obtain some cod, for which they were not allowed to fish in Community waters, but which did happen to be available in the area of the Baltic over which Poland claimed exclusive fishing rights, and where British trawlers had no right to fish.[72] At the same time Polish trawlermen needed herring and mackerel, which were not available in the Polish area of the Baltic, but which could be caught in Community waters – except that Polish boats had no right to fish there. A group of British trawlers therefore set off for the Baltic laden with herring and mackerel, and met the Polish trawlers off the Polish

---

[64] Case 38/77, *Enka* v *Inspecteur der Invoerrechten*, [1977] ECR 2203.

[65] See *e.g.*, Case C-17/89, *HZA Frankfurt am Main-Ost* v *Olivetti*, [1990] ECR I-2301.

[66] Case 7/83, *Ospig* v *HZA Bremen-Ost*, [1984] ECR 609.

[67] OJ 1992 L302/1.

[68] Council Regulation 802/68, JO 1968 L148/1.

[69] The relevant Annexes (D1 to D3) were accepted by the Community by Council Decision 77/415, OJ 1977 L166/1.

[70] See *e.g.*, Council Regulation 1769/89 on certificates of origin, OJ 1989 L174/11.

[71] OJ 1992 L302/1.

[72] Case 100/84, *Commission* v *United Kingdom*, [1985] ECR 1170.

coast. The British trawlers cast their empty nets into the sea, and these nets were then taken over by the Polish boats, which trawled them but did not take them on board. After the trawl was completed, the Polish trawlers passed the ends of the nets to the British trawlers, and the cod was landed onto the British trawlers; in return for this, the British boats transferred the herring and mackerel to the Polish boats.

When the British trawlers returned to the United Kingdom, the customs authorities treated the cod as being British, and therefore not liable to pay common customs tariff duties. The reason for this was that under the EC Regulation determining the origin of goods for customs purposes, fish are treated as wholly obtained in one country if they are "taken from the sea" by vessels registered in that country and flying its flag. The British view essentially was that since the nets were actually pulled from the sea by the British trawlers, the fish were "taken from the sea" by the British trawlers, whereas the Commission's argument was that fish were taken from the sea when the net closed round them, irrespective of when they were physically hauled out of the sea.

Faced with this dispute, the Court first looked at the texts of the Regulation, and noted that the French version used the phrase *extraits de la mer*, which appeared to support the British argument, whereas, for example, the German version used the word *gefangen*, meaning caught, which tended to support the Commission's argument. After referring also to the Greek, Italian and Dutch versions, but not, it would appear, the Danish (!), the Court concluded that a comparative examination of the various language versions did not enable a conclusion to be reached in favour of any of the arguments put forward, and so no legal consequences could be based on the terminology used. It therefore expressly turned to consider the purpose and general scheme of the Regulation determining the origin of goods for customs purposes, and came to the conclusion that in the context of a fishing operation carried out by a number of vessels registered in different countries, the origin should in principle depend on the flag flown by the vessel which performed the essential part of the operation of catching them. Faced with the fundamental question of legal philosophy as to when a free object becomes property, the Court took the view that the essential part of catching fish is locating the fish and separating them from the sea by netting them, and that simply hauling the nets out of the sea is not the essential part of the operation. Whatever may be thought of the Court's analysis, this judgment at least illustrates its general approach to such problems.

The central provision of this legislation is what was Article 5 of the original Regulation and is now Article 24 of the Customs Code. This states that:

"goods whose production involved more than one country shall be deemed to originate in the country where they underwent their last substantial, economically justified processing or working in an undertaking equipped for that purpose and resulting in the manufacture of a new product or representing an important stage of manufacture".[73]

It may be observed that this definition does not make any reference to percentages of added value, leaving scope for interpretation of what may be regarded as a "substantial process". It is clear that cleaning, grinding and packing a product does not confer origin.[74] On the other hand, it would appear from the *Yoshida* cases[75] that assembly operations which are economically justified, carried out in specially equipped premises and resulting in a new product or an important stage of manufacture, may well confer origin. Those cases involved the manufacture of slide fasteners, and it would appear that the assembly plants within the Community wove, bound and dyed tapes, pressed metal scoops or nylon interlocking spirals, fixed the scoops or spirals to the tapes, fixed the end lugs, inserted the slider, and cut the fasteners into separate slide fasteners. What they did not do was to manufacture the actual sliders, which were imported from Japan. The Court stated that what was done led to the manufacture of a new product which, unlike the products from which it was made, was a method of joining material together which could be repeatedly done up and undone; the slider itself was only one element in this, its price was hardly decisive, and although it was a characteristic of a slide fastener it was of no use until incorporated into the whole unit. Hence the sliders were of Community origin. In the light of this, the enthusiasm of Japanese manufacturers to set up car assembly plants within the Community may be understood.[76]

Despite the absence of any express reference to added value in the definition, it is an important element in determining whether a process is substantial, particularly where the finished product has not changed its intrinsic nature. It has thus been held that the gassing, mercerising, dyeing and spooling of cotton yarn, which on the evidence added 159% to its value, could confer origin, even though the ultimate product was still cotton yarn.[77] On the other hand, in *Brother International* v *HZA Giessen*[78] it was held that an added value of less than 10% was clearly not enough, and the Court referred to the Kyoto Convention as authority for the proposition that simple assembly operations, which do not require a skilled workforce or specially equipped premises, do not confer origin. In so far as it may be relevant in this context, the provisions of the EC anti-dumping legislation (whatever its compatibility or otherwise with GATT) which enable duties to be imposed on products assembled in the Community if

---

[73] It may be observed similarly that the Uruguay Round Agreement on Rules of Origin refers in its Article 3(b) to the "last substantial transformation" where more than one country is involved.

[74] Case 49/76, *Uberseehandel* v *Handelskammer Hamburg*, [1977] ECR 41.

[75] Cases 34/78 and 114/78, [1979] ECR 115 and 151.

[76] It may be recalled that before United Kingdom Accession, British Leyland established a plant in Belgium to assemble Minis for exactly the same reasons. It was closed after Accession.

[77] Case 162/83, *Cousin*, [1983] ECR 1101.

[78] Case C-26/88, [1989] ECR 4253.

duties would be imposed on direct importations of the finished product[79], laid down that anti-dumping duties might only be imposed if the value of the imported elements exceeded the rest by at least 50%. Putting it the other way round, the adding of 40% of its value within the Community prevented a product being treated as a dumped imported product. The 1994 version[80] starts from the premise that if the imported parts constitute 60% or more of the total value of the parts, circumvention will be considered to be taking place, unless the value added during assembly or completion is greater than 25% of the manufacturing costs. It remains to be seen if this is enough truly to confer origin.

Much more detailed rules on origin have been incorporated into arrangements made by the Community which give preferential treatment to imports from certain non-Member States, whether they be the free trade agreements with the EFTA Members, or the agreements with the developing countries under the Lomé Conventions, or under generalised tariff preferences. It has now clearly been held by the Court[81] that the Council does have power to adopt stricter rules on origin when granting preferential treatment to certain imports and that these more specific rules prevail over the general rules with regard to those imports to which they relate.

Conclusion

The Customs Union is long established, and the Uruguay Round will not make fundamental changes in its basic mechanisms. It will however lead to considerable changes in the system of agricultural trade, and there appears to be scope for conflict with caselaw doctrines such as Community preference – if the Court of Justice were to allow the provisions of GATT to be invoked in that context.

JOHN USHER

---

[79] Art 13(10) of the Council Regulation 2423/88, OJ 1988 L209/1.
[80] Council Regulation 3283/94 (OJ 1994 L 349/1).
[81] Case 385/85, *SR Industries* v *Administration des Douanes*, [1986] ECR 2929.

Chapter 9
Consolidation, Codification and Improving the Quality of Community Legislation – The Community Customs Code

Introduction

The Sutherland Report on "The Internal Market after 1992 – meeting the challenge"[1] emphasised the practical importance of consolidation and codification of Community legislation, particularly in the area of the internal market, a point which has also been taken on board by the Edinburgh European Council[2] among other fora.[3] Legislative consolidation is designed to make Community legislation at once more accessible, concise and comprehensible, while assuring legal certainty. Paralleling the transparency required by Community law of Member States in their legislation[4], it offers transparency which mere declaratory consolidation by the Commission published in the "C series" of the *Official Journal* cannot achieve, as such texts lack legislative force.[5] Previous attempts at legislative consolidation have, with the notable exceptions of the Community's Customs Code and public procurement, mostly met with slow success other than pious declarations of intent.[6] The principal reasons for this were twofold:

(i)   what should have been a technical exercise was often used as an excuse to reopen debate in the Council (but not normally in the European Parliament) on the substance of what had already been agreed in the legislation which it was proposed to consolidate;

(ii) in some cases the imminence of amending legislation was felt to be a reason to postpone consolidation pending the further amendments.

---

[1] SEC (92) 2277 final. The Report was also published in a non-standard citable form as a small (72 page) booklet with a foreword by Messrs Bangemann and van Miert.

[2] Bull. EC 12–1992, point 1.5.

[3] See the Commission's Communication *Follow-up to the Sutherland Report: Legislative consolidation to enhance the transparency of Community Law in the area of the internal market* COM (93) 361 final, p 1; the Commission's *Report on the Operation of the Treaty on European Union* adopted on 10 May 1995, Annex 12; see the Interinstitutional Agreement OJ 1995   C 293/2.

[4] See Case 167/73 *Commission v France* [1974] ECR 359 at 372–373.

[5] *e.g.* the informal consolidation of the Community social security co-ordination regulations in OJ 1992 C325. See also the Commission's publication of co-ordinated instruments relating to Foodstuffs (position on 30 April 1994), ISBN 92–826-8056–8. Texts concerning certain other areas of internal market legislation can now be consulted on the Commission's INFO 92 database.

[6] For a list of previous legislative consolidation proposals in the field of internal market legislation, see COM (94) 361 Final, Annex 1.

Given, however, the now universal commitment to legislative consolidation, the Commission has addressed its mind to areas of internal market legislation in which the need for transparency is most acute. Thus, for example, Community legislation on seeds comprises seven basic directives with 147 amendments; cosmetic products are dealt with by one basic directive with 21 amendments, and protective measures against the introduction of organisms harmful to plants and plant products are dealt with in one basic directive and 26 amendments.

In the course of its work to ensure consolidation, codification and increased transparency, the Commission has announced its intention to start work on the creation of a unified legislation on foodstuffs and to simplify specific foodstuffs legislation; to revise the existing pressure vessels legislation and to replace twelve basic metrology directives and their 31 amendments with a new proposal, in both cases based on the new approach to harmonisation.[7] In the field of freedom of establishment, much simplification is facilitated by the caselaw of the Court, although recent judgments have exposed certain weaknesses in the present approach which will necessitate legislative action.[8] A *conditio sine qua non* for success is, though, genuine commitment on the part of the Member States to the effectiveness of consolidation, codification and transparency. Thus the Commission will need to be confident that the threat of reopening tactics in the Council belong to the past; it will also undoubtedly revive its request to have delegated powers to consolidate legislation itself. If the Council is unwilling to trust the Commission this far, the systematic integration of amendments into new integral texts may be the answer in the long term, as a solution to the second problem relating to imminent amendments.

There are already two major areas, however, in which considerable success has been achieved in the consolidation and improvement of Community legislation, namely public procurement and the development of the Community Customs Code.[9] This discussion concentrates on the latter area, as sufficient attention has been paid to the Community's action in the former[10], although one or two points about the pressure for reform of public procurement harmonisation may usefully be made for comparison with the pressures for reform of Community customs legislation.

The internal pressure for adaptation of Community legislation on public procurement came principally as a result of the identification of that

---

[7] See, generally, COM (93) 361 final, Annex 2 and COM (94) 55 final p 15.

[8] See Case C-204/90 *Bachmann* v *Belgian State* [1992] ECR I-249 (with corrigendum, [1992] ECR Tables p 688) and Case C-112/91 *Werner* v *Finanzamt Aachen-Innenstadt* [1993] ECR I-429.

[9] Other examples of recent consolidation exercises include Directive 93/16 (OJ 1993 L165/1) relating to doctors and their qualifications; Directive 93/77 (OJ 1993 L244/23) on fruit juices and certain similar products.

[10] See Trepte, *Public Procurement in the EEC* (CCH, Bicester, 1993); Weiss, *Public Procurement in European Community Law* (Athlone Press, London, 1993); Wainwright (1990) 10 YBEL 133; Gormley in Uff and Lavers (eds), *Legal Obligations in Construction* (Centre of Construction Law and Management, London, 1992), and Cox, *The Single Market Rules and the Enforcement Regime after 1992* (Earlsgate Press, Winteringham, 1993).

field as a priority for action in the Commission's White Paper *Completing the Internal Market*[11] and the realisation that only with modernisation of the existing legislation and by ensuring the availability of remedies for failure to comply could the existing national preferences in a major sector of the Community's economy be broken down. The external pressure for adaptation of Community legislation in this field has been more periodic, reflecting successive GATT rounds, but the external importance of Community public procurement policy has acquired a new dimension with the introduction of Community preference in the absence of reciprocal market access ensured through bilateral or multilateral arrangements.[12]

In the field of Community customs legislation the pressure for change has also had internal and external facets. Thus the introduction of the Single Administrative Document[13], and first the introduction of common border posts[14] and then the abolition of systematic customs controls at the Community's internal frontiers necessitated the adaptation of all the Community's customs procedures – in particular (but not only) Community transit. It also means that Article 115 EC has effectively become a dead letter as it is now effectively impossible to enforce in a watertight manner any Commission decision authorising a Member State to refuse Community treatment to a particular product from a third country already in free circulation within a Member State.[15] The external pressure resulted in part from the improvement of the formalities and transit arrangements with neighbouring states[16] and later the creation of the European Economic Area; in part from international developments in the Customs field[17]

---

[11] COM (85) 310 final. See, generally, Bieber *et al* (eds), *1992: One European Market?* (Baden-Baden, 1988); Gormley (1989/1) LIEI 9, and Van Bael (1989/1) LIEI 21. On external aspects, see Usher (1986) 6 YBEL 159; Cremona (1990) 15 ELRev 283, and Eeckhout, *The European Internal Market and International Trade: A Legal Analysis* (OUP, 1994).

[12] See now Directive 93/38 (OJ 1993 L199/84), Art 37, replacing the earlier Directive 90/531 (OJ 1990 L297/1), Art 29 which was something of an opening gambit or invitation to treat. See also n 57, *post*.

[13] Originally by Regulation 678/85 (OJ 1985 L79/1), see also Regulations 679/85 (OJ 1985 L79/7) and 1900/85 (OJ 1985 L179/4), subsequently replaced by Regulation 717/91 (OJ 1991 L78/1) which was in turn repealed by the Community Customs Code.

[14] See Regulation 4283/88 (OJ 1988 L382/1), repealed by Regulation 3648/91 (OJ 1991 L 348/1) with effect from the entry into force on 1 January 1993 of Regulation 2726/90 on Community transit (OJ 1990 L 262/1), which latter Regulation has itself been replaced by the Community Customs Code (except for Art 3(3)(b) which deals with the remaining goods covered by the Act of Spanish and Portuguese Accession which do not as yet benefit from the abolition of customs duties or other measures provided for in that Act).

[15] As to the meaning of "in free circulation within a Member State", see Art 10(1) EC.

[16] See Decision 87/267 (OJ 1987 L134/1) approving the Convention on the simplification of formalities in trade in goods and Decision 87/415 (OJ 1987 L226/1) approving the Convention on a common transit procedure.

[17] Such as the International Convention on the Harmonized Commodity Description and Coding System, see Decision 87/369 (OJ 1987 L198/1) and the International Convention on the Simplification and Harmonization of Customs Procedures, see Decision 75/199. Various annexes to the latter measure have been accepted by the Community, sometimes with reservations, see *e.g.* Decisions 87/593 (OJ 1987 L362/1); 87/594 (OJ 1987 L362/8); 88/355 (OJ 1988 L161/3), and 88/356 (OJ 1988 L161/12), dealing respectively with Annexes E.5; F.3; B.2 and E.4.

and also – perhaps even primarily – from the desire to ensure a more watertight common commercial policy through the tightening of the Community rules on special procedures such as inward and outward processing, processing under customs control and free zones and free warehouses. This latter aspect had been identified some years before the grand consolidation in 1992 and 1993. Hence the initial replacement of earlier directives by regulations[18] – which are much stronger instruments of co-ordination than directives as they leave much less discretion in the hands of the Member States. These regulations have in turn been replaced by the provisions of the Community Customs Code and implementing measures which codify and further strengthen the Community's customs legislation, although far from rendering national provisions redundant the Code expressly envisages their continued existence. Accordingly, for example, customs authorities[19] may, in accordance with the conditions laid down by the provisions in force[20], carry out all the controls they deem necessary to ensure that customs legislation is correctly applied.

Background to the Community Customs Code

The decision to codify Community customs legislation is nothing new; its origins can be traced to the approach of establishing numerous instruments of customs legislation at the Community level, as opposed to taking the more gradual route of allowing the various national customs provisions to come gradually closer together as a result of recommendations from the Commission. The advantages of the more radical route were in particular the more certain and solid legal basis thereby afforded; the simplification through the application of a clear Community scheme; the enforceability of harmonisation through regulations or directives (as opposed to the non-binding nature of recommendations), and the clear role given to the Commission as the logical co-ordinator of the customs union and the (albeit then embryonic) common commercial policy. The ultimate goal of codification was already clearly identified by the Commission as long ago as 1971[21] and has been repeatedly restated.[22] Codification at

---

[18] *e.g.* Regulation 1999/85 (OJ 1985 L188/1) replaced the old Directive 69/73 (OJ (special ed) 1969 (I) p 75) with effect from 1 January 1987.

[19] *i.e.* the authorities responsible *inter alia* for applying customs rules, Regulation 2913/92 (OJ 1992 L302/1), Art 13. This definition differs from that previously used, *e.g.* in Regulation 1715/90, Art 1(2)(c) "any authority competent to apply customs rules, even if that authority is not part of the customs administration".

[20] *i.e.* Community or national provisions, Regulation 2913/92 (OJ 1992 L302/1), Art 13.

[21] In the *General Programme for harmonisation of Customs Legislation* SEC (71) 682 final (28 April 1971).

[22] See COM (75) 67 final; COM (77) 210 final, and COM (79) 8 final (OJ 1979 C84 and Bull. EC 3–1979, points 1.4.1.-1.4.5.).

Community level also reflects the approach in a number of Member States of ensuring that all dealings between the authorities, undertakings and citizens concerning customs matters are conducted on the basis of a single framework. In political circles there were also increasing calls for an end to the fragmentation of Community provisions in the customs field.

What made the presentation of the Community Customs Code timely and ensured its identification as a political priority was the happy conjunction of three key elements. First, the success of the more salami-tactic approach of ensuring that proposals in various sectors of customs legislation were approved, meant that modernisation of these sectors had been achieved.[23] The political risk of attempting a great leap was thus overcome by ensuring that the substantive leap to a Code was no longer a leap accompanied by major policy choices. Thus the transition, mentioned above, from the use of directives to the stronger instrument of regulations had already been achieved and the Member States had already consented to stricter co-ordination with fewer loopholes for the exercise of national discretion – a particularly sensitive point in view of the economic importance in various sectors of procedures such as inward and outward processing. Secondly, the effect of the progress in harmonisation at Community level, particularly of the increased use of regulations rather than directives which resulted in far less discretionary policy freedom at the national level, was to make the national customs codes ever more devoid of substance, thereby increasing the desirability of new and more appropriate structural arrangements. Finally, Article 8A EEC (as it then was, now Article 7A EC) makes express reference to, *inter alia*, Article 28 E(E)C, thereby emphasising the importance of the customs union in the external (common commercial policy) aspects of the single market. This point highlights part of the difference between the concepts of an internal market and a common market.[24] The codification of Community customs legislation became at once a means of clarifying and making more transparent commercial relations with third countries as well as a response to the requirement of Article 29(a) E(E)C that the Commission be guided by the need to promote trade between Member States and third countries.

---

[23] Only in respect of appeal procedures does the Community Customs Code introduce a wholly new element not previously the subject of individual legislation. The previous proposal in this field (COM (80) 860 final) was withdrawn on presentation of the proposal for the Community Customs Code (COM (90) 71 final).

[24] As to the difference between the concepts of a common market and an internal market, see Kapteyn and VerLoren van Themaat, *Introduction to the Law of the European Communities* (2nd ed, Deventer/London, 1989) 78–79. The remaining element of difference is that a common market requires no artificial distortions of competition.

The Community Customs Code

Council Regulation 2913/92[25] establishes the Community Customs Code and consists, like ancient Gaul, of three essential parts. Titles I-III set out the basic definitions and the factors on which duties and other measures are applied, such as the customs tariff, origin of goods and customs valuation; they also set out the provisions applicable to goods brought into the customs territory of the Community until they are assigned a customs-approved treatment or use. The heart of the Code is mostly contained in Title IV which deals with the Customs-approved treatment or use of goods. That concept is defined as the placing of goods under a customs procedure; the entry of goods into a free zone or warehouse; the re-exportation of goods from the customs territory of the Community; the destruction of goods, or their abandonment to the Exchequer.[26] A customs procedure means release for free circulation;[27] transit; customs warehousing; inward processing; processing under customs control; temporary admission; outward processing, or exportation. Title V deals in a single article with goods leaving the customs territory of the Community. Finally, Titles V-IX deal with privileged operations; the incurrence, recovery and extinction of a customs debt; appeals, and final provisions relating to delegated powers for the Commission to adopt implementing legislation, the legal effect in a Member State of measures taken, documents issued and findings made in another Member State, and repeals.

Regulation 2913/92 repeals 28 regulations or directives adopted by the Council between June 1968 and March 1991; Commission Regulation 2454/93[28] which implements Regulation 2913/92 repeals a further 77 regulations or directives. However, the simplification is not expressed simply in terms of the amount of legislation repealed. Thus the transfer from a sector-by-sector approach to a global approach for Community customs legislation means that much duplication is avoided and consistency is assured. For example, provisions common to authorisations for certain customs procedures[29] or customs procedures with economic im-

---

[25] OJ 1992 L302/1, implemented by Commission Regulation 2454/93 (OJ 1993 L253/1). For the Commission's proposal, see COM (90) 71 final; for the amended proposal, see COM (91) 98 final. For the revisions taking account of the Council's common position and the European Parliament's second reading, see COM (92) 423 final. For the most detailed commentary on Community customs legislation and the free movement of goods, see Vaughan (ed), *Law of the European Communities* Service (London, looseleaf since 1990, completely revised 1994–1995) Part 12 (in Vol 3). The present discussion highlights some points of particular interest in this consolidation exercise, but does not purport to repeat the author's detailed commentary in Vaughan.

[26] Regulation 2913/92, Art 4(15).

[27] *i.e.* in accordance with Art 10(1) EC.

[28] OJ 1993 L253/1.

[29] *i.e.* in the case of non-Community goods, external transit; customs warehousing; inward processing in the form of a suspension system; processing under customs control, or temporary importation, Regulation 2913/92, Art 84(1)(a).

pact[30] are set out only once[31], as is also the case with provisions relating to customs declarations[32] and decisions relating to the application of customs rules.[33] Artificial divisions are also terminated, for example the concepts of customs debt, a customs debtor and entry in the accounts were previously spread over three separate instruments and are now set out clearly in Title VII of Regulation 2913/92.

In deciding which provisions should properly be included in the Code and which provisions were more appropriate for inclusion in implementing legislation, account has generally been taken of the distinction between core provisions and implementing provisions[34], although this distinction has not necessarily led to a reallocation of competence between the Council and the Commission, given that many matters[35] are to a large extent governed by international agreements to which the Community is a party. As a result, any changes require negotiations with third countries which must in any case be approved by the Council. The ostensible intention to make Community customs legislation readily accessible to non-specialists must, though, be greeted with a certain amount of surprise, as any person who simply reads the Code with its 253 articles will still not master the whole picture without also tackling the implementing legislation running to 915 articles and (now) 116 annexes. The result is, though, undoubtedly a substantial improvement on the mass of previous legislation. A possible alternative would have been to split the Code into several regulations, in order to ensure that there were no complications about delegation of powers for implementing legislation. However, such an approach would have been inconsistent with the desire for unity which was an essential element in the transparency which the whole exercise sought to achieve.

The question of delegation of powers remained controversial to the end, with the Commission accepting an amendment to the common position on Article 249 proposed by the Parliament.[36] The Parliament,

---

[30] *i.e.* customs warehousing; inward processing; processing under customs control; temporary importation, or outward processing, *ibid*, Art 84(1)(b).

[31] *Ibid*, Arts 84–90.

[32] *Ibid*, Arts 59–78.

[33] *Ibid*, Arts 6–10.

[34] Although there are instances of implementing provisions being included in the Code itself, *e.g.* Art 33 which lays down the items not to be included in the customs value of goods, provided that they are shown separately from the price actually paid or payable.

[35] Such as customs valuation; Community transit and the Single Administrative Document.

[36] The Parliament also proposed an amendment relating to the fourth para of Art 253 which brought Art 183 into effect a year early. That article (the sole article in Title V) deals with goods leaving the customs territory of the Community. The Commission accepted this amendment too and the Council approved Art 253 as so amended. The point of the amendment was that with the completion of the internal market and the entry into force on 1 January 1993 of Regulation 2726/90 (OJ 1990 L262/1) goods could in certain circumstances (*e.g.* transit of Community goods from one Member State to another, by sea, land or air, other than via an EFTA country, partially outside the Community) leave the customs territory of the Community without being placed under a customs procedure. Accordingly, there had to be an appropriate Community-level mechanism for supervision to ensure that prohibited or restricted goods did not leave the customs territory of the Community without re-entering it.

insisting on the adoption of the Commission's original proposal, proposed an advisory committee structure for the Customs Code Committee rather than the management committee structure of the Nomenclature Committee dealing with the Common Customs Tariff[37] and regulatory committee structures proposed in the common position. The benefit of Parliament's and the Commission's proposal was twofold: first, it was consistent with the Declaration on the powers of implementation of the Commission annexed to the Final Act adopting the Single European Act;[38] secondly, it meant that only one procedure was necessary for the adoption of implementing measures in the customs field. The Council, however, insisted on maintaining its view as set out in the common position and those structures were approved.

A number of effects of this codification exercise can be highlighted, in particular relating to the time for ascertaining the applicable basis of assessment to duty and the restricted extent to which national provisions may supplement Community provisions. The general rule, replacing previous divergent approaches, now stated in Article 214(1), is that the amount of the import duty or export duty applicable to goods must be determined on the basis of the rules of assessment applicable at the time when the customs debt in respect of them is incurred. In relation to the role of national provisions, the Commission recognised that existing Community legislation was often the result of hard-fought compromises, but concluded that to perpetuate many of the possibilities for national provisions to deviate from Community provisions would be incompatible with a harmonious Community approach. Accordingly, the Customs Code does not permit national authorities to restrict the right of representation to those forms of representation allowed by their civil codes, although those authorities may restrict the right to make customs declarations by direct or indirect representation, so that the representative must be a customs agent carrying on his business in the territory of the country concerned. The Commission's proposal that this possibility should not apply to employees of the holder of the goods concerned, transporters and persons professionally involved in another Member State with inward and outward clearance of goods was, however, not accepted. Another example of the restrictive approach to national provisions is that there is no provision permitting national legislation to enlarge the scope of persons considered

---

[37] See Regulation 2658/87 (OJ 1987 L256/1), Art 10.

[38] The second para of that Declaration reads: "In this connection the Conference requests the Council to give the Advisory Committee procedure in particular a predominant place in the interests of speed and efficiency in the decision-making process, for the exercise of the powers of implementation conferred on the Commission within the field of Article 100a of the EEC Treaty." Three Treaty articles formed the legal base for the Customs Code: Arts 28, 100a & 113 EEC. Accordingly, the co-operation procedure (as required by Art 100a) was applicable, as the most democratic procedure (Arts 28 & 113 EEC made no provision for participation by the Parliament in the decision-making process). The central role of Art 100a was thus the logical justification for the Commission's preference for an Advisory Committee rather than a Management or Regulatory Committee to be involved in the preparation of delegated legislation.

to be customs debtors or to consider a person to be a customs debtor without taking account of that person's individual liability.

The remaining room for national measures is still considerable, however. They are still free, for example, to designate free zones or free warehouses, and the favourable treatment of processing operations in the old free port of Hamburg[39] and in the free zones of the Canary Islands, the Azores, Madeira and overseas departments continues. Thus it has not proved politically possible to restrict the Member States' freedom to use free zones as instruments of industrial policy; indeed the new definition of free zones and free warehouses specifically takes account of certain political aspects.[40] That much[41] is left to the customs authorities of the Member States is, though, inevitable, given that there is no Community customs administration as such. As is the case with agricultural legislation, the operation of the legislation and supervision of compliance is very much in the hands of national authorities, who are best placed to exercise control. However, when it appears necessary to strengthen defences against risks of fraud for certain categories of goods, or to resolve difficulties arising from the application by Member States of differing rules concerning the customs status of goods abandoned to the Exchequer, seized or confiscated, so as to ensure that the goods are not released into the Community's economic circuit without import duties being paid, the Commission is swift to ensure that the necessary delegated legislation can be adopted.[42] Another possible problem area is that certain elements of the exercise of national discretion in relation to inward processing operations may well give rise to competition between the Member States for such operations.[43]

Another area in which there is still considerable freedom of national action is appeals procedures. During the process leading to the adoption of the Customs Code, the Commission proposed that there should be three grounds of appeal: the absence of appropriate reasoning in a decision by the customs authorities; misuse of power, and infringement of the

---

[39] Subject to the reimposition of economic conditions for certain inward-processing operations if the Council, acting by a qualified majority on a proposal from the Commission, so decides, Regulation 2913/92, Art 173(c).

[40] COM (91) 98 final, p 1.

[41] *e.g.* discretion as to whether or not to require the payment of security for the payment of a customs debt; the right of customs authorities, in accordance with the conditions laid down by the (national or Community) provisions in force, to carry out all the controls they deem necessary to ensure that customs legislation is correctly applied, and the right of the Member States, in so far as Community legislation lays down no rules on the matter, to determine the competence of the various customs offices situated in their territory (*aficionados* will remember the French requirement that video recorders be cleared through Poitiers), account being taken, where applicable, of the nature of the goods and the customs procedure under which they are to be placed.

[42] *e.g.* Regulation 3665/93 (OJ 1993 L335/1) amending Regulation 2454/93 (OJ 1993 L253/1) before the latter came into force.

[43] *e.g.* competition in relation to the period within which compensating products must have been exported or re-exported (although specific time limits may be laid down by the Commission in accordance with the committee procedure (*i.e.* in accordance with Regulation 2913/92, Art 249) for certain import goods or certain processing operations).

provisions in force. These Community-level grounds proved unpalatable to the Member States, with the result that the actual grounds of appeal are determined in accordance with the normal national rules for appeals against decisions of the administration. Whilst standing to lodge an appeal is determined by the Customs Code – the criteria[44] are either that the decision relates to the application of customs legislation and concerns the applicant directly and individually[45], or that a requested ruling has not been given within the prescribed period[46] – the provisions for the implementation of the appeals procedure are left entirely in the hands of the Member States[47] and Title VIII of the Code (governing appeals) does not apply to appeals lodged with a view to the annulment or revocation of a decision taken by the customs authorities on the basis of criminal law.[48] Whilst the Commission rightly saw the adoption of a Community Customs Code as an essential element in the establishment of a European Legal Area[49], the inability to agree at least as developed a system of remedies in this sphere as has been agreed in relation to public procurement[50] is a reminder of just how far the Community still is from a genuine European Legal Area with equal enforcement of Community rules in all the Member States.

Conclusions

As an exercise in legislative codification, rather than merely consolidation, the Community Customs Code and its implementing legislation are undoubtedly masterpieces of relative simplification, although the absence of any table of correspondence between the old and the new provisions is scarcely conducive to an understanding of the principal changes which have taken place. Such tables have been issued before[51] and were indeed promised[52] on this occasion, although it appears that in view of the mammoth task of ensuring the accuracy of the implementing Regulation 2454/93 (which has subsequently been amended on a number of points) and certain inaccuracies in the informal table which was apparently used internally by the Commission's services, it was decided not to produce a table this time. An additional factor seems to have been that this particular exercise was not merely an exercise in consolidation but a global codification.

---

[44] *Ibid*, Art 243(1).

[45] Which presumably must be interpreted in a manner identical to the interpretation given to that phrase by the Court of Justice in relation to Art 173 EC.

[46] As to which, see Regulation 2913/92, Art 6(2).

[47] *Ibid*, Art 245.

[48] *Ibid*, Art 246.

[49] See COM (90) 71 final, p 8.

[50] See Directives 89/665 (OJ 1989 L395/33) and 92/13 (OJ 1992 L76/13).

[51] *e.g.* in Regulation 1214/92 (OJ 1992 L132/1), Annex XVI, relating to Community transit (that Regulation is repealed by Regulation 2454/93 (OJ 1993 L253/1), Art 913.

[52] COM (90) 71 final, p 9.

In the future, consolidation and codification exercises will have to bear in mind the standards required by the Council Resolution on the quality of drafting of Community legislation.[53] That Resolution contains 10 points, of which a number are of particular relevance for evaluation of the effectiveness of the Customs Code as a contributor to the transparency of Community legislation. Point 1 requires the legislation to be clear, simple, concise and unambiguous, avoiding unnecessary abbreviations, "Community jargon", and excessively long sentences. Point 3 requires the provisions of Community legislation to be consistent with each other and the same term to be used throughout to express a given concept. Finally, although this is not in fact a problem in relation to the Customs Code, Point 8 requires the avoidance of inconsistency with other existing legislation. For the most part, the Code satisfies all the requirements of Point 1, although the clarity of the implementing legislation is less satisfactory than the clarity of the Code itself. In relation to Point 3, the Code sometimes refers to "provisions in force" which is defined in Article 4(23) and sometimes to "customs legislation" which is not defined. The term "procedure" is defined in relation to Articles 85–90 of the Code in Article 84(1)(a), but it also occurs elsewhere.[54] These are, though, merely minor, even nit-picking points against the background of this impressive exercise.

The importance of legislative consolidation or codification in relation to the internal effectiveness of the single market within the Community has rightly been recognised[55] in the context of the transparency of Community law, but it is not only the Community's internal purposes which are well served. Consolidation and certainly codification also serve an external purpose in that the resulting instrument can form the basis for the negotiation of international agreements with the Community's major trading partners. In the field of customs co-operation such agreements are being sought, in particular with Canada, Hong Kong, Japan, Korea and the United States.[56] In the field of public procurement, new and then consolidated Community legislation has been a major weapon in negotiations in particular with the United States[57] and it may certainly be expected that

---

[53] OJ 1993 C166/1. See Barents (1994) 1 MJ 101 & Kellerman in Curtin & Heukels (eds.) *Institutional Dynamics of European Integration, Essays in Honour of H.G. Schermers* (Dordrecht, 1994) Vol 2, 251. This paper was written before the publication of the recommendations of the Molitor Group, COM(95)288 final on legislative and administrative simplification.

[54] *e.g.* in Arts 59(1) & 74(2), although it must be admitted that it becomes clear from Art 59(2) what some of those procedures are. There is, though, a difference, as Art 59(2) embraces wider procedures than those listed in Art 85(1)(a). There is also a difference between the term 'procedure' used in Art 84(1)(a) and the term 'customs procedure with economic impact' used in Art 84(1)(b). The point is, of course, that confusion arises about the meaning of the word 'procedure' which is different according to the specific context.

[55] For a list of single market legislation needing consolidation, see COM (93) 361 final.

[56] COM (94) 55 final, pp 21–22, on the basis of a Council Decision of 5 April, 1993, Bull. EC 4–1993, point 1.3.60.

[57] See Decision 93/323 on the Memorandum of Understanding between the EEC and the US on government procurement (OJ 1993 L125/1), Bull. EC 5–1993, point 1.2.23, and Regulation 1461/93 (OJ 1993 L146/1) in response to sanctions applicable outside the scope of the Memorandum of Understanding.

the Community will also take the opportunity afforded by consolidation or codification exercises in other fields to improve the effectiveness of its commercial policy at the same time as improving the effectiveness of the internal application of its legislation.

While as a result of the Uruguay Round some adaptation to the implementing Regulation 2454/93[58] will be required, in relation to the added protection for importers through the requirements that customs administrations must state in writing the reasons for doubting the declared value and that importers must have a right of reply[59], and in relation to procedural changes concerning information on origin[60], no amendments are necessary to the Code itself as a result of the Round, which is in line with current Community practice. Further major changes resulting from the conclusion of the Work Programme for harmonisation set up under Part IV of the Agreement on Rules of Origin in the Uruguay Round will not have to be introduced until 1998 at the earliest, as the work on that programme is at present planned to last three years.[61]

LAURENCE W GORMLEY

---

[58] OJ 1993 L253/1.

[59] This results from the Decision Regarding cases where Customs Administrations Have Reason to Doubt the Truth or Accuracy of the Declared Value, formally adopted at the ministerial meeting in Marrakesh on 15 April 1994 and incorporated into the Final Act embodying the results of the Uruguay Round. The papers from the College of Europe's Conference *The Uruguay Round Results: A European Lawyers' Perspective* (18–19 November 1994) will be published shortly.

[60] The implementing legislation will be brought into force in due course. For the proposal see OJ 1995 C 260/8 & COM(95)335 final.

[61] COM (94) 414 final, p 7.

Chapter 10
The European Community and the General Agreement on Trade in Services

Introduction

Over the decades since the Second World War, services have become an increasingly important part of national economies.[1] The GATT (1947) makes no specific provision for services, although certain of its rules do impinge on services.[2] It was not until the late 1970s that the development of international trade in services became a sufficiently high priority for attention to be focused on barriers to this trade.

At this time the European Court of Justice began to elaborate its jurisprudence relating to trade in services[3], and at about the same time the United States, in particular, became concerned about the obstacles to international trade in services that were affecting its own enterprises.[4] Financial services, transport and telecommunications are among the most controversial sectors, where developed nations, undercut in relation to their manufacturing operations, hope to make use of technical expertise to increase their share of world trade.

These considerations eventually led to the inclusion of services within the Uruguay Round discussions. The Agreement on Trade in Services had a difficult birth. Developing countries were suspicious of the motives of the developed world and reluctant to make commitments. Outside the United States, many developed countries were also reluctant to extend the GATT negotiations to new areas, preferring to consolidate the results of the Tokyo Round. Only slowly did they recognise the growing role of trade

---

[1] The United States has a particularly large service sector. About 79% of workers in the United States are employed in the service sector, which accounts for about 52% of GDP (President's Council of Advisers, *The Economic Report of the President* (1993), Tables B-41 and B-7)). In other Western countries the share of GDP and employment accounted for by the service sector has increased over the last 20 years and accounts for more than 50% of each (Grimwade, *International Trade: New Patterns of Trade, Production and Investment* (1989) p 411).

[2] *e.g.*, Art V which concerns freedom of transit.

[3] *e.g.*, Cases 110 and 111/78, *van Wesemael*, [1979] ECR 35; Case 279/80, *Webb*, [1981] ECR 3305; Case 205/84, *Commission v Germany*, [1986] ECR 3755; Cases C-154, C-180 and C-198/89, *Commission v France, Italy and Greece*, [1991] ECR I-709; Case C-76/90, *Säger v Dennemeyer & Co. Ltd* [1991] ECR I-4221. The wording of these decisions has increasingly paralleled that used in the recent and revolutionary *Cassis de Dijon* decision (Case 120/78, [1979] ECR 649).

[4] See Lazar, "Services and the GATT: US Motives and a Blueprint for Negotiations", (1990) 24 *Journal of World Trade* 135–145.

competitors. This has posed problems for the Community in its external trade relationships. It has not been prepared to allow service suppliers from non-EC states to establish themselves within the Community and compete with Community service suppliers in the liberalised sectors without seeing some corresponding market access opportunities being made available in the home markets of those service suppliers. For this reason, where Community secondary legislation does make provision for the external dimension of its internal policies, it has made use of the concept of reciprocity: access to the Community market can be denied to non-Community service suppliers if their home state does not provide similar access for Community service suppliers. However the concept of reciprocity is inherently ambiguous. A requirement that a foreign state provides reciprocal treatment for Community service suppliers could amount to a demand that Community service suppliers enjoy exactly the same market opportunities in the foreign state as suppliers from that state can enjoy in the Community. Since the European market is so open, this could equate to a requirement that the foreign state restructure its regulation of the service in question along the same lines as Community regulation. However, reciprocity may also be given a much less controversial meaning. It may, for example, be interpreted as simply a requirement that Community suppliers are not subjected to discriminatory treatment in the foreign state if suppliers from the foreign state are not discriminated against in their operations within the Community.[12] Because of this ambiguity, the inclusion of the concept of reciprocity in the draft of the Second Banking Directive[13] led to a clash with the United States which feared that an intrusive interpretation of reciprocity would be adopted. The United States argued that national treatment[14] rather than reciprocity should be sought for the purposes of regulating international trade in services. This exchange of views led to some modification of the Second Banking Directive, but more fundamentally the Community expressed the intention to deal with problems of access to non-EC markets by means of multilateral negotiations in the context of the Uruguay Round. A multilateral framework for achieving liberalisation of trade in services would obviate the need for a reciprocity clause in Community legislation. It was therefore a very clear objective of the European Community to ensure that the GATS included specific commitments by other Member States in service sectors of interest to the Community, which would ensure that Community service suppliers would have increased access to the markets of those states.

---

[12] The concept of reciprocity was anyway being used by individual Member States before the Community assumed its regulatory role: see Eeckhout, *ibid* at pp 52–53. For further elaboration of the different shades of meaning that may be attached to the concept of reciprocity see Wils, "The Concept of Reciprocity in EEC Law: An Exploration into these Realms", (1991) 28 CMLRev 245 and references cited therein.

[13] Council Directive 89/646, OJ 1989, L386/1.

[14] *i.e.*, the principle that foreign suppliers should be treated in the same way as domestic ones.

The scope of the GATS: the meaning of trade in services

The range and variety of services and the different ways in which they can be provided make it hard for analysts to establish categories wide enough to cover all services and precise enough to use as the basis for the construction of acceptable theories.[15] Three crucial differences between goods and services have been identified which have influenced the approach to regulation of trade in services. First, services cannot be stored, but require immediate consumption. Second, production and consumption must take place simultaneously.[16] These characteristics have brought into play the need to consider the right of establishment in the context of provision of services.[17] The third difference is the intangible nature of services.[18] They cannot be examined prior to consumption. This means that information about services is particularly important to enable the consumer to understand the "product". It also in part accounts for the high degree of regulation in this sector.[19]

Against this background the GATS attempts to provide a definition of "the supply of services"[20] which is based on four categories of operations. Article I defines trade in services as the supply of a service:

(i) "from the territory of one Member into the territory of any other Member." This first category covers "separated" services, where there is no need for either provider or consumer to move from their home states. Examples of such services include telecommunications, broadcasting and transport services.

(ii) "in the territory of one Member to the service consumer of any other Member." The second category involves the movement of the consumer to the territory in which the service provider is situated as will typically be the case with tourism. Other common services for which the consumer may go to the territory of the service supplier include education and medical services.

(iii) "by a service supplier of one Member, through commercial presence in the territory of any other Member." The third category

---

[15] See *e.g.*, Eeckhout, *supra*, n 11 at pp 7 *et seq*; Bhagwati, "Services", in Finger and Olechowski (eds), *The Uruguay Round: A Handbook on the Multilateral Trade Negotiations* (1987), p 208; Stern and Hoekman, "Negotiations on Services", (1987) 10 *The World Economy* 1; Grimwade, *International Trade: New Patterns of Trade, Production and Investment* (1989), pp 406–408 and 413–416. See also the different views on the services being provided in Case 352/85, *Bond van Adverteerders v The Netherlands*, [1988] ECR 2085.

[16] Stern and Hoekman, "Negotiations on Services" (1987) 10 *The World Economy* 1.

[17] See Messerlin, "Services", in *The European Community as a world trade partner* (1993), pp 129–156 at 138.

[18] Stern and Hoekman, *supra*, n 16.

[19] Messerlin, *supra*, n 17.

[20] Art XXVIII which provides that for the purpose of the Agreement "supply of a service" includes the production, distribution, marketing, sale and delivery of a service.

relation to legal services is that the service can only be provided ˌ
persons and not through commercial presence in the host state. Aˌ
common limitation is that where a service is supplied through a juridˌ
person, a particular form of organisation must be adopted.[24] For developing countries, restrictions on the amount of equity in a joint venture that
may be held by non-nationals are usual.

The general obligations accepted by the members in Part II of the
Agreement[25] give further substance to the members market access and
national treatment commitments.

The MFN principle in Article II introduces one of the most characteristic features of the GATT system to trade in services. It ensures that, subject
to permissible exemptions negotiated during the Uruguay round[26], and
special treatment arising out of the close proximity of two members[27], for
measures covered by the GATS, members must accord immediately and
unconditionally to services and service suppliers of any other member,
treatment no less favourable than it accords to like services and services
suppliers of any other country.

To assist in promoting transparency and enforceability of the GATS
rules, the members are required to administer measures which restrict
trade in services in a reasonable, objective and impartial manner. Decisions concerning authorisation to provide a service must be made promptly and there must be mechanisms for the review of the decisions of
authorities.[28]

The GATS also recognises that market access may be impeded by inappropriate rules of competition law.[29] Articles VIII and IX introduce the
need for members to have adequate competition laws to deal with anti-
competitive practices which may impede trade in services. Article VIII
deals with monopoly suppliers of services in a member. It requires members to ensure that any monopoly suppliers of services in its territory does
not, in the supply of the monopoly service in the relevant market, act in a
manner inconsistent with that member's obligations under Article II and
specific commitments. In addition members must ensure that a supplier
does not abuse its monopoly in one market in order to gain a competitive
advantage in another market which is subject to that member's specific

---

[24] In the European Community's Schedule of Specific Commitments, limitations on market
access and national treatment are in most cases registered on a country by country basis, not for
the Community as a whole – although occasionally Community law does entail that limitations are
introduced by all EC Member States.

[25] Arts II to XV.

[26] See Art XXIX, Annex on Article II Exemptions.

[27] Art II (3).

[28] Art IV. Under Art VII of the GATS a similarly objective and reasonable approach must be
adopted where members are prepared to recognise licences, certificates, education and experience gained in another country. However, Art VII does not impose on members any obligation to
recognise such licences etc.

[29] A further context in which the experience of the European Community can be clearly
identified. It should be noted that the GATS does not rule out in principle the possibility of states
authorising monopoly suppliers, but requires them to be strictly regulated.

qualifications, procedures, technical standards and licensing do not constitute unnecessary barriers to trade in services. These disciplines will aim
to ensure that any regulatory rules restricting market access are based on
objective criteria and are not more burdensome than necessary to ensure
the quality of the service.[32] Once again, however, the sectoral approach
of the GATS deprives this legislative role of the Council for Trade in
Services of much of its potential impact. Members have no obligation to
accept market access commitments in sectors that they do not wish to
liberalise.

Even where members do accept market access and national treatment
commitments in relation to particular service sectors, they can still limit
their measures of liberalisation to certain modes of supply, and may be
more willing to allow a service to be provided from an establishment
within their territory than from abroad. Messerlin[33] has provided a detailed examination of the differences between the Internal Market programme and the approach adopted by the GATS. He highlights the fact
that greater competition between services occurs where cross-border supply is permitted, than where there is insistence on commercial presence in
the host state. Service suppliers who establish a presence in the host state
are obliged to comply with its regulatory rules, and therefore add to the
number of suppliers, but cannot introduce new types or methods of supply. Where a supplier can operate the service from its home state, and
therefore under different regulatory rules, the consumer is presented with
different forms of regulation and has a wider choice. This may lead to
"competition among rules" such that the most popular or practical system of rules, from the consumer's point of view, will be adopted by other
states. Against this background it is evident that the GATS is a far less
dynamic instrument of trade regulation. Nevertheless, Messerlin suggests
that the experience of the European Community may attract other states
to adopt forms of regulation applied within the Community with a resulting liberalisation of trade.

These differences make it important to distinguish the respective
spheres of application of the Treaty of Rome and of the GATS. The GATS
applies when both supplier and consumer of the service in question have
specific links with a member. In the case of natural persons, the person
must be resident in, and a national of, a member.[34] Juridical persons can
benefit from the provisions of the GATS if they are constituted or otherwise organised under the law of a member and engaged in substantive
business operations in the territory of that or any other member.[35] Thus a
company incorporated in England but which conducts all its business in
Japan can benefit from the GATS provisions. Article 58 EC would appear

---

[32] *i.e.*, a principle of proportionality.
[33] *Supra*, n 17 at pp 143 *et seq.*
[34] Art XXVIII (k).
[35] Art XXVIII (m).

145

to suggest that such a company could also enjoy free movement under Community law, since it uses incorporation as a connecting factor – provided that the registered office[36] is also in an EC Member State. However in practice a real and continuous link with the economy of a Member State is required before free movement under Comunity law is permitted.[37] Other EC Member States could therefore rely on their individual limitations on market access set out in the Community's schedule of specific commitments in relation to such a company.

The impact of GATS on the external relations of the Community

The most important question for the Community must be how far it has achieved its negotiating goals. In order to participate in the GATS it is obliged to abandon reciprocity as a mechanism for encouraging trade liberalisation and to adopt the MFN principle.[38] However, the Community does not appear to have been particularly reluctant to do this – presumably because the demand for reciprocity is a very unwieldy instrument for obtaining its trade goals. Its inherent uncertainty and the indignation which its use arouses in the breasts of the Community's trading partners are not conducive to its use as part of a negotiating strategy.

The success of the GATS negotiations from the Community's point of view involves consideration of two different issues: first, the extent to which access to markets of interest to the Community has actually been improved, and second, the extent to which to the GATS, as part of the overall agreement on a World Trade Organization, creates an institutional environment in which market access can be progressively liberalised.

On the first of these issues, the Community has suffered a number of disappointments. An obvious example, to pursue an earlier theme, is the failure to achieve improved access to the United States financial services market.[39] The United States has refused to adopt the MFN principle in relation to financial services and in its schedule of specific commitments has not broadened its approach to market access in this sector. It has also been reluctant to increase market access in the fields of basic telecom-

---

[36] Or principal place of business or central administration.

[37] See the 1962 General Programme for the abolition of restrictions on freedom of establishment. This requirement is also emphasised in the Horizontal Commitments section of the European Community's schedule of specific commitments.

[38] With limited exceptions where emergency measures and safeguards are necessary.

[39] See the Resolution of the European Parliament on the results of the Uruguay Round, OJ 1994 C114.

munications and transport.[40] The European Community would also like to have seen improved access to the service sector, and particularly the financial sector, in Japan, but little progress has been made.

However, this lack of progress in specific sectors must be seen in a broader context. By participating in an international agreement on services, the European Community can exert pressure for continued liberalisation of international trade in a less confrontational manner than before. The WTO can act as broker to facilitate negotiations. The GATS specifically provides for new negotiating rounds and the gradual liberalisation of trade as experience highlights significant trade barriers. Highly regulated sectors of the economy will anyway be slow to change:[41] a process of mutual exchange of information and education is necessary. The obligation to provide information imposed by Article III will assist in this process, which should ultimately bear fruit in the form of new liberalising measures.

Furthermore, quite apart from the general obligation to have negotiating rounds under the GATS, there are also a number of specific commitments to further negotiations, within the main text itself, in annexes to the Agreement and in Ministerial Decisions adopted at the Marrakesh Conference. In each case the subject matter of these continuing negotiations is of considerable significance to the European Community[42], and securing a commitment to continuing negotiations was seen as an important achievement of the Round. Indeed, the commitments contained in the annexes to the GATS are described in the Commission's Proposal for a Council Decision on the conclusion of the results of the Uruguay Round of Multilateral Treaty Negotiations[43] as ''one of the most important results secured by the Community last December in Geneva''.

A further achievement from the point of view of the Community was the fact that, in spite of pressure from the United States, it managed to avoid

---

[40] These are of course sectors which are vitally important to the national economy and over which many states wish to preserve their domestic control. It is noteworthy that there are a number of annexes to the GATS in relation to these sectors, modifying or specifying in more detail the commitments required by the GATS or providing for further negotiations. Thus the annex on financial services ensures that the GATS does not undermine Member State prudential rules or affect government regulation of central banks. However, the United States' concern is that it is already a very open market, and does not wish to provide further opportunities for non-US service suppliers without obtaining some corresponding opening of foreign markets. Many countries made use of the sectoral approach of the GATS to restrict their liberalisation measures to a limited number of sectors and are considered to be ''free-riding'' on the generosity of the United States. An indication of the desire of the United States to use the importance of its market as leverage in future talks on financial services is its attempts to pass legislation which would use reciprocity as a test for allowing foreign service providers to enter that market: the Fair Trade in Financial Services Bill failed to obtain the approval of Congress; the National Treatment in Banking Bill has recently passed through Congress (see 140 Cong Rec H 10409).

[41] A point explicitly noted in the Resolution of the European Parliament on the results of the Uruguay Round, OJ 1994 C114.

[42] Negotiations are to continue in the fields of financial services, basic telecommunications, shipping, the movement of persons, civil aviation, government procurement (Art XIII), subsidies (Art XV) and emergency safeguards (Art X).

[43] COM (94) 143.

making any commitments in relation to the audio-visual sector that would undermine its policy of European quotas for works such as films.[44]

Looking to the impact of the GATS on other multilateral trading relationships, the new agreement will be significant for the European Community in its relations with ACP States. In Article 185 of the fourth Lomé Convention it committed itself to further negotiations on services to take account, and take advantage, of the outcome of the Uruguay Round.

The needs of developing countries were supposed to have been a major focus of the Uruguay Round as a whole, and were specifically identified as one of the considerations informing the framework of the GATS. However, in practice the GATS contains few concrete rules of assistance to these members. The principle that the increasing participation of developing countries should be fostered is taken into account by a call for the members to negotiate specific commitments that will strengthen the domestic services sector of developing countries and improve their access to technology and to export markets[45], while at the same time adopting a flexible attitude as to the degree of liberalisation demanded from developing countries in the schedules of specific commitments.[46] The only specific obligation imposed, however, is for developed country members to establish contact points within two years after the entry into force of the Agreement to enable suppliers in developing countries to get access to information relevant to their supply of services in those developed countries.[47]

Further progress in this area was impossible because so much energy during the negotiations was devoted to resolving the disputes between the Community and the United States. The renegotiation of Lomé will therefore be seen by the ACP states as an opportunity to flesh out the general commitments established during the GATS negotiations.

Conclusions

The GATS provides a useful framework within which the European Community can develop the external dimension of its trade in services. The approach of the Agreement reflects many of the ideas already developed within the Community which will facilitate co-ordination between external and internal trade issues. Although in concrete terms limited liberalisation of trade in services has been achieved, formal procedures for exchanging information and developing regulatory disciplines now exist. These will pave the way for renewed efforts to negotiate further liberalisation in the future.

WENDY KENNETT

---

[44] See *News of the Uruguay Round*, 069, for a note on the audio-visual sector.
[45] Art IV.
[46] Art XIX (2).
[47] Art IV (2).

Chapter 11
The External Dimension of Community Social Policy: the Ugly Duckling of External Relations

"the fact that European social policy is now emerging increasingly in the context of the external relations of the Union arises . . . from the reality that world competition is increasingly socio-economic in character".[1]

The Community competence in the field of external relations in the social field has always been uncertain. The tension and difficulties were highlighted by the Court of Justice in *Opinion 2/91*[2] and continue to provide a source of conflict between the Commission and the Member States. Nevertheless, the social dimension of international trade has important consequences for the economies of both developed and developing states.

This chapter will first consider the Community's own internal competence to enact labour standards and will then examine the rationale for the development of a Community social policy. It will suggest that the Community is motivated in part by the desire to avoid social dumping by the Southern states of the Community. However, concerns about social dumping within the Community pale in comparison with the risks of social dumping on a world scale. Consequently, the chapter will argue that the creation of enforceable international labour standards is important for the continued development of the Community's own social policy. Given the importance for the Community of international labour standards, the chapter will conclude with an examination of the Community's own competence to participate in negotiating and signing such international agreements.

The Community's internal competence in the social field and the development of a Community social policy

An element of ambiguity has always surrounded any discussion about the

---

[1] Commission White Paper, *European Social Policy: A Way Forward for the Union*, COM(94)333, p 59.
[2] Judgment of 19 March 1993, [1993] ECR I-00–00; [1994] IRLR 135.

existence of a Community social policy.[3] While the economic objectives of the EC Treaty have received the wholehearted endorsement of the Member States, this has not always been the case with the social dimension. This ambivalence was reflected in the Treaty of Rome itself where a disparate set of provisions, only some of which were legally binding, demonstrated a limited acknowledgement of the role of the social dimension in the Common Market.

The turning point came in October 1972 when, on the eve of the accession of the three new Member States, the heads of government meeting in Paris issued a communiqué emphasising "that vigorous action in the social sphere is to them just as important as achieving Economic and Monetary Union".[4] This change of approach can be explained in part by reference to the social unrest in Western Europe in 1968,[5] and in part by a realisation that the Community had to be seen as more than a device enabling business to exploit the common market. It was felt that the Community required a human face to persuade its citizens that the social consequences of growth were being effectively tackled.[6] Failure to do so might have jeopardised the whole process of economic integration.[7]

In response, the Commission drew up an Action Programme[8] which precipitated a phase of remarkable activity. Important directives combatting sex discrimination were adopted[9] and the whole field of sex equality assumed a new importance as a result of judgments by the Court of Justice in the *Defrenne* cases.[10] An action programme and a number of directives were adopted in the field of health and safety[11] and, in the face of rising unemployment, measures were taken to ease the impact of mass redundancies[12], the transfer of undertakings[13], and insolvent employers.[14]

---

[3] See, for more detail, Nielsen and Szyszczak, *The Social Dimension of the European Community* (Copenhagen, Handelshojskolens, 1993, 2nd ed), Chap 1; Collins, *The European Communities, The Social Policy of the First Phase* (London 1975, Shanks); *The European Social Policy Today and Tomorrow* (Pergamon, Oxford 1977); La Terza, *Diritto comunitario e Lavoro* (Pirola Editore, 1992), Chap 4, Teague, *The European Community, the Social Dimension, Labour Market Policies for 1992* (Kogan Page, 1989), especially Chap 4.

[4] EC Bulletin 10/1972, para 6, p 19.

[5] Wise and Gibb, *Single Market to Social Europe* (Longman, 1993), p 144.

[6] Shanks, *The European Social Policy Today and Tomorrow* (Pergamon, Oxford, 1977) p 378. This justification continues today – COM(94) 333, p 9.

[7] This section relies heavily on Barnard, *EC Employment Law* (Wiley, 1995) Chap 2.

[8] OJ 1974 C 13/1.

[9] Directive 75/117 on equal pay (OJ L45/75), Directive 76/207 on equal treatment (OJ L39/76) and Directive 79/7 on equal treatment in social security (OJ L6/79).

[10] Case 80/70 [1971] ECR 445, Case 43/75 [1976] ECR 455 and Case 149/77 [1978] ECR 1365.

[11] *e.g.*, Council Directive 77/576/EEC (OJ L76/35) on safety signs, Council Directive 78/610/EEC (OJ L197/12) on vinyl chloride monomers and Parent Directive 80/1107/EEC (OJ L327/8).

[12] Directive 75/129/EEC (OJ No L48/29).

[13] Directive 77/187/EEC (OJ No L61/27).

[14] Directive 80/987/EEC (OJ No L283/23).

The social dimension of the Community took more concrete form with the signing of the Community Charter of Fundamental Social Rights 1989[15] by 11 of the 12 Member States. Drawing extensively on the European Social Charter of 1961[16], the "pendant" of the European Convention on Human Rights[17], and International Labour Organization (ILO) Conventions, the Charter listed 12 "fundamental social rights of workers". The Commission's Action Programme[18], issued at the same time, contained 47 proposals concerning the implementation of the principles set out in the Social Charter.[19]

The legislation predating the Single European Act 1986 was proposed on the basis of Article 100 EEC (measures directly affecting the establishment or functioning of the common market) and/or Article 235 EEC (measures necessary to attain one of the objectives of the Community), both requiring a unanimous vote by the Council of Ministers.[20] Amendments to the Treaty of Rome introduced by the Single European Act 1986 extended the use of qualified majority voting. For example, Article 100a(1) permitted the use of qualified majority voting for measures having as their object the establishment and functioning of the internal market. However, according to Article 100a(2), "paragraph 1 shall not apply . . . to those [provisions] relating to the free movement of persons nor to those relating to the rights and interests of employed persons".

---

[15] For a full discussion on the Social Charter see Vogel-Polsky, "What future is there for a social Europe following the Strasbourg Summit", (1990) 19 ILJ 65; Bercusson, "The European Community's Charter of Fundamental Social Rights of Workers", (1990) 53 MLR 624; Hepple, "The Implementation of the Community Charter of Fundamental Social Rights", (1990) 53 MLR 643; Watson, "The Community Social Charter" (1991) 28 CMLRev 37; Wedderburn, "The Social Charter, European Company and Employment Rights: An Outline Agenda", (Institute of Employment Rights, 1990).

[16] The European Social Charter 1961 is, in some respects, more comprehensive than the Community Charter. For example, it guarantees the right to work and contains a wider definition of the right to bargain collectively and to strike. It has also established a system of supervision albeit weak, by the Committee of Experts – Hepple, "The Implementation of the Community Charter of Fundamental Social Rights" (1990) 53 MLR 643 p 645. See also Harris, *The European Social Charter* (Charlottesville: University Press, Virginia 1984); Betten (ed), *The Future of European Social Policy*, (Kluwer, Netherlands, 1991); 'The European Social Charter and International Standards I and II' (1961) 84 *International Labour Review* 354 and 462.

[17] Harris, "A Fresh Impetus for the Social Charter" (1992) 41 ICLQ 659.

[18] COM (89) 568 Brussels.

[19] Social Europe 1/90, Commission of the European Communities (Brussels, 1990) contains the full text of the Social Charter, the Action Programme, background material and comments. Reports on the progress of the implementation of the Action Programme can be found in COM (91) 511 final, summarised in ISEC/B1/92, and Szyszczak (1992) 21 ILJ 149, ISEC/B25/93 and COM(93)668 final.

[20] *e.g.*, Council Directive 75/117/EEC (OJ L45/19) on equal pay was adopted on the basis of Art 100 EEC, Council Directives 76/207/EEC (OJ L39/40) and 79/7/EEC (OJ L6/24) on equal treatment were adopted on the basis of Art 235 EEC and Council Directive 77/187/EEC on transfers of undertakings was adopted on the basis of Art 100 EEC.

By contrast, Article 118a(1) also introduced by the SEA 1986, provided that "Member States shall pay particular attention to encouraging improvements, *especially in the working environment*, as regards the health and safety of workers" (emphasis added). To help achieve this objective Article 118a(2) provided that the Council could adopt directives laying down minimum standards by a qualified majority vote (now the Article 189c procedure). Consequently, the Commission, adopting a very broad approach to Article 118a, proposed a wide variety of measures on this basis.[21] These ranged from health and safety measures, narrowly construed[22], to measures which more closely related to working conditions.[23] This approach has been criticised by the British Government which has challenged, under Article 173, the choice of Article 118a as the appropriate legal basis for the Working Time Directive.[24]

The Treaty on European Union, agreed at Maastricht in December 1991, offered a further choice of legal bases: Articles 2(2) and 2(3) of the Social Policy Agreement.[25] Any legislation adopted under these Treaty provisions is not binding on the United Kingdom[26] because the United Kingdom has not acceded to this part of the Treaty.[27]

The debate over the existence and shape of the Community's social policy

In its White Paper on Social Policy the Commission recognised that legislating for higher labour standards and employee rights has been an important part of the Union's achievements in the social field.[28] The key

---

[21] According to the White Paper, the Social Charter Action Programme "foresaw 21 proposals for directives, most of which were based on Article 118A" (COM (94) 333, p 29).

[22] *e.g.*, the framework Directive 89/391/EEC on the introduction of measures to encourage improvements in the safety and health of workers at work (OJ 1989 L183/1).

[23] See, *e.g.*, Council Directive 92/85/EEC (OJ 1992 1 348) on the protection of pregnant workers. However, Art 118a(3) does refer more generally to "working conditions".

[24] Council Directive 93/104/EC (OJ No.L 307/18).

[25] See generally Watson, "Social Policy after Maastricht" (1993) 31 CMLRev 481; Whiteford, "Social Policy After Maastricht" (1993) 18 ELRev 202; Barnard, "A Social Policy for Europe: Politicians 1 Lawyers 0" (1992) 8 IJCLLIR 15; Weiss, "The Significance of Maastricht for European Social Policy" (1992) 8 IJCLLIR 3; Bercusson, "The Dynamic of European Labour Law after Maastricht" (1994) 23 ILJ 1, Fitzpatrick, "Community Social Law After Maastricht" (1992) 21 ILJ 199.

[26] The European Works Council Directive was the first measure adopted under Art 2(2) of the Social Policy Agreement. However, despite the British opt-out there is evidence that British multinationals are applying the Directive to their British workforce. This has been the case with United Biscuits, *The Times*, 10 November 1994 and more generally, "Anger at Works Council Deals", *The Guardian*, 13 February 1995.

[27] See generally, Towers, "Two Speed Ahead: Social Europe and the UK after Maastricht" (1992) 23 IRJ 83.

[28] COM(94)333, 29.

objectives have been both to ensure that "the creation of a single market did not result in a downward pressure on labour standards or create a distortion of competition, and to ensure that working people also shared in the new prosperity".[29] In other words, the justification for Community measures included two elements: the welfare of the workers concerned and the creation of conditions for "undistorted competition".[30]

The welfare element of Community social policy can perhaps be most easily seen in the directives on health and safety. Article 1(1) of the framework Directive 89/391/EEC[31] makes clear that the aim of the Directive is to introduce measures to encourage improvements in the health and safety of workers at work. To help achieve that objective it contains "general principles concerning the prevention of occupational risks, the protection of health and safety, the elimination of risks and accident factors, the informing, consultation [and] balanced participation of workers and their representatives".[32] Article 5(1) goes on to provide that the employer has the duty to ensure the health and safety of workers in every aspect related to the work. However, while the emphasis of the Directive is on worker protection, it is also intended to ensure that all employers in all Member States bear the costs of this worker protection. There is no derogation for small and medium sized enterprises[33], nor does the Directive limit the employer's responsibility by providing that the employer should only take all reasonably practicable steps.

The desire to create conditions of undistorted competition has been caused by concern over social dumping – the phenomenon of standards of social protection being depressed, or at least prevented from rising, by increased competition after 1992 from states with substantially lower standards.[34] Community action to establish transnational standards may ensure the establishment of a level playing field between Member States by establishing parity of costs imposed by legislation on employers. More positively, Community action may be seen as providing a minimum floor of rights below which state regulation cannot fall.[35] This helps prevent

---

[29] *Ibid.*

[30] Kapteyn and Verloren Van Themaat suggest that this term, also used in the context of Arts 101 and 102 EC, applies to the situation where one group of undertakings in a Member State is subject to higher or lower charges than other groups of undertakings in the same Member State, in the other Member States there is not an equal deviation for the same group of undertakings as compared with other groups and the deviation must not be compensated by other charges or benefits, in Gormley (ed), *Introduction to the Law of the European Communities* (Kluwer, 1990, 2nd ed), 485. See also the Ohlin report (1956) 74 *International Labour Review* 99, 105.

[31] OJ L 183/1.

[32] Art 1(2).

[33] This is despite the requirement imposed by Art 118a(3) that such directives should avoid imposing administrative, financial and legal constraints in a way which would hold back the creation of small and medium-sized enterprises.

[34] Mosely, "The Social Dimension of European Integration" (1990) 29 *International Labour Review* 147, 160. See generally, Teague, "Constitution or Regime? The Social Dimension to the 1992 Project" (1990) 27 *British Journal of Industrial Relations* 310, 322, Barnard, *op cit*, n 7.

[35] Deakin and Wilkinson, "Rights vs Efficiency? The Economic case for Transnational Labour Standards" (1994) 23 ILJ 289, 305.

destructive competition caused by a liberalised and integrated internal market but a deregulated and decentralised European market. Indeed, some would argue that harmonisation of social standards should be seen as a dynamic process where standards are not just the result or output of economic growth but also an input into economic development[36] of a kind needed to ensure that strategic factors do not lead either corporations or states to adopt a low-wage route to competitive survival.[37]

There is, however, a school of thought which suggests that Community social legislation is detrimental to the Union's long-term interests and, in particular, to the development of the poorer, Southern states, which may ultimately have deleterious consequences for the development of the Union itself.[38] Given that labour costs in Greece and Portugal are significantly lower than in Germany[39], the incentive to invest in the Southern European countries would be lost if, as a result of Community legislation, employers were obliged to pay higher wages or greater social security contributions which would provide more generous welfare benefits.[40] This would have the effect of undermining Greece and Portugal's comparative advantage which in turn would hinder their economic development while at the same time reinforcing the position of strength enjoyed by countries such as Germany and Denmark.[41] In other words, Community social legislation represents an indirect form of social protectionism intended to favour the best placed, largely Northern European, countries at the expense of their poorer neighbours.

It has also been argued that "high social standards are undermining the Community's competitiveness in world markets".[42] When addressing the House of Commons in the Maastricht debates, John Major, the British Prime Minister, argued that "Europe must compete with the United States and Japan as well. All across Europe people know that Europe is losing its competitiveness at present. Twenty years ago unemployment across Europe was 60% of that of the United States. Today it is 60% above the United States".[43] In recent years the Commission has also recognised the threat posed by the Pacific rim countries to a comprehensive European

---

[36] This view is endorsed by the Commission in its White Paper on Social Policy where it says the "the pursuit of high social standards should not be seen as a cost but also as a key element in the competitive formula" – COM(94)333, 9.

[37] Deakin and Wilkinson, *op cit* n 35.

[38] See, generally, Kierman and Beim, "On the Economic Realities of the European Social Charter and the Social Dimension of EC 1992" [1992] 2 *Duke Journal of Comparative and International Labour Law 149–162.* See also Addison and Siebert, "The Social Charter: Whatever Next?" (1992) 30 *British Journal of Industrial Relations* 495 and "The Social Charter of the European Community: Evolution and Controversies" (1990–1) 44 *Industrial and Labour Relations Review* 597.

[39] In 1990 average labour costs in industry in Germany were 20.08 ECUs contrasted with 5.24 ECUs in Greece and 3.57 ECUs in Portugal – *Eurostat 1992.*

[40] See Due, Madsen and Jensen, "The Social Dimension: Convergence or Diversification of IR in the Single European Market" (1992) 23 IRJ 85, 92.

[41] For criticisms of this view see Barnard, *EC Employment Law* (Wiley, 1995), Chap 2.

[42] COM(93)552, p 33.

[43] *Hansard*, 23 July 1993, p 630.

social policy. Jacques Delors, when President of the European Commission, acknowledged that there was less difference between Germany and Ireland than between Europe and Korea. However, he argued that this did not mean that the internal market should lead to a reduction in social rights[44], but only a recognition that there was a need for "a more flexible and pragmatic policy".[45] In its White Paper on Social Policy the Commission said that discussion was now necessary about the social rules necessary to complement trade. It added that:

"The Union recognises that other regions may need to compete on the basis of lower labour costs, based on lower wages, longer hours and more difficult conditions[46], but it is not in the interests of international cooperation that the exploitation of workers should become an instrument of international competition".[47]

In the face of the strong political arguments about the Community's loss of competitiveness on the world stage, it is clear that the creation of international labour standards would assist the Community's commitment to maintaining workers' rights at European level by requiring higher standards of employers on a world-wide scale, imposing a greater financial burden on those employers and arguably, depriving them of their comparative advantage. This tends to suggest that the Community's desire for international labour standards represents in part a further form of social protectionism, this time intended to preserve Community industry in the face of world-wide competition. However, in the Presidency Memorandum of March 1995 on the social dimension of international trade, the President strongly denied such suggestions. He said that "the aim is neither to undermine the comparative advantages of developing countries nor to impose the social system of European countries on other countries".[48] Instead, he seemed to suggest that the Community is motivated only by a

---

[44] Quoted in Hirsch, "Un Volet Social pour le Grand Marché', [1988] *Revue du Marché Commun*, pp 371–372.

[45] Commission, "The Social Dimension of the Internal Market", *Social Europe*, 1988, p 62.

[46] The Commission's realism in respect of lower unit labour costs was explained in its explanatory memorandum accompanying the draft atypical workers' Directives (COM(90)228 final). In the Community context it said that differences between Member States in respect of wage levels, non-wage costs and rules on working conditions "do not hamper the operation of healthy competition in the Community. The differences in productivity levels attenuate the differences in unit labour costs to a considerable degree. Moreover, other production cost components tend to be higher in the less developed Member States where nominal costs are the lowest". Consequently, the Commission did not make any provision in the proposals for part-time and fixed-term workers to receive pro-rata rights to equal pay with those employed on a full-time basis. Despite this, it did propose standards in respect of indirect costs "resulting from different kinds of rules on different types of employment relationship, which may provide comparative advantages which constitute veritable distortions of competition", where cost differences are not offset by factors such as differences in productivity. Consequently, the Commission proposes that atypical workers be given, *vis-à-vis* full-time workers, social protection under statutory and occupational social security schemes and the same entitlements to annual holidays, dismissal allowances, and seniority allowances in proportion to the total hours worked.

[47] COM(94)333, p 60.

[48] Presidency Memorandum discussed at the Labour and Social Affairs Council, Brussels 27 March 1995, 5961/95 (Presse 94), President: Michel Giraud.

desire to secure the welfare of workers, recognising "the problems arising from inadequate working and social standards. Exploitation of the labour of children and prisoners cannot be tolerated".[49]

The need to create international labour standards

The desire to set international labour standards is by no means new. The establishment of the International Labour Organization in 1919 represented one of the earliest attempts to set up a body to create international standards. The long-term origins of the Organization lay in the inhumanity of the industrial revolution, and the resistance by employers, who feared international competition, to the reform of working conditions.[50] As one commentator observed at that time:

"The only answer was to try to find a way to dilute unrestricted international competition by establishing minimum living conditions throughout the world below which workers should not be allowed to fall yet leaving the theory of comparative advantage intact".[51]

Early efforts at setting international standards were frustrated by the reluctance of some states, particularly Britain, "to put their industrial laws at the discretion of a foreign power".[52] However, by the time of the signing of the Peace Treaty at Versailles in 1919, the British Government had lent its support to the inclusion of labour matters in the Treaty negotiations. This was attributed in part to political concerns that the impact of the Russian Revolution in 1917 would spread towards the West, and in part to economic concerns that once free competition was restored it "would be very difficult to raise the general standard of wages and conditions" unless "similar standards were applied in all competing markets". Consequently, it was clearly to the advantage of Britain, "a country that was among the most advanced in the regulation of conditions of employment" to encourage the movement towards the setting of international standards.[53] Social protectionism cloaked in a desire to improve labour standards for the benefit of workers clearly has a long history.

As a result, the Preamble to Part XIII of the Peace Treaty states that while the function of the League of Nations is the establishment of universal peace, this can be achieved "only if it is based upon social justice". Article 427 of the Treaty established nine guiding principles of the ILO, including the acknowledgement that labour is not a commodity or article

---

[49] *Ibid.*

[50] Ewing, *Britain and the ILO*, Institute of Employment Rights (2nd ed, 1994), p 2, citing Barnes, *History of the International Labour Organisation* (1926).

[51] Ewing, *op cit*, n 50 citing Alcock, *History of the International Labour Organisation* (1971), p 5.

[52] Ewing, *op cit*, n 50 citing Alcock, *op cit*, p 10.

[53] Alcock, *op cit*, n 50 p 19.

of commerce, and the recognition of the right of association for lawful purposes, the payment of a wage to maintain a reasonable standard of life, the adoption of an eight hour day or 48 hour week, the adoption of a weekly rest period of at least 24 hours to include Sunday where practicable, the abolition of child labour and equal remuneration for men and women for work of equal value.[54] The unique feature of the ILO is its tripartite structure where the representatives of workers and employers take part in all discussions and decision-making on an equal footing with governments. Each member of the ILO has four representatives at the annual conference: two government delegates and two people representing employers and employees respectively.[55] The Community, by contrast, has only observer status at the ILO. The governing body of the ILO has, however, accepted that the Community may participate in ILO negotiations but the Member States remain responsible for any failure to comply with ILO conventions.[56]

The annual conference of the ILO adopts either Conventions or Recommendations which together form the international labour code. At present there are 176 Conventions covering a wide range of subjects including those of general application such as the Freedom of Association and Protection of the Right to Organise Convention No. 87 1948, and those which apply to specific groups, such as the Paid Vacations (Seafarers) Convention 1949[57] and the Night Work (Women) Convention 1919, 1934 and 1948.[58] The Conference decides whether to adopt proposals either as Conventions or Recommendations.[59] In both cases the Member States undertake to bring the provisions of the Convention or Recommendation before the body competent to enact legislation. Finally, Article 19(8) of the ILO Constitution provides that ILO Conventions only lay down minimum standards which states, by "law, award, custom or agreement", are free to improve upon.

The ILO is by no means the international body prescribing international labour standards.[60] The aims of the United Nations include

---

[54] These principles were further defined by the Declaration of Philadelphia in 1944.

[55] Constitution, Art 3. According to Art 7 of the Constitution 28 of the 56 members of the governing body represent governments, 14 represent employers and 14 represent employees.

[56] See documents drawn up by the International Labour Office on 12 February 1981 and 31 May 1989.

[57] Convention 91.

[58] Convention 4, 41 and 89. In Case C-158/91 *Levy* [1994] IRLR 138 the Court recognised that while Art 5 of Directive 76/207/EEC on equal treatment requires national legislation prohibiting night work by women to be set aside, this rule does not apply according to Art 234(1) EEC/EC in cases where the national provision was introduced by virtue of an agreement concluded with a non-member country before the entry into force of the EC Treaty. None of the 12 Member States are now party to the Convention. A new non-discriminatory Convention has now been passed (No 171) which the ILO hopes all Member States will ratify. See EIRR 219, April 1992.

[59] In both cases a two-thirds majority of all votes cast is needed for adoption – Art 19 paras 5 and 6 of the Convention. Conventions are communicated to Member States for ratification while Recommendations are communicated with a view to being given effect by "national legislation or otherwise" – Constitution, Art 19, para 6(d).

[60] See Betten, *International Labour Law: Selected Issues* (Kluwer, 1993)

"solving international problems of an economic, social, cultural or humanitarian character".[61] One of the principal organs of the UN, the Social and Economic Council, conducts studies on social and economic matters from which it makes recommendations and prepares Conventions for adoption by the General Assembly. This includes the International Covenant on Economic, Social and Cultural Rights adopted by the General Assembly in 1966 which fleshes out the Universal Declaration of Human Rights. On a regional level the Council of Europe has adopted the European Convention for the Protection of Human Rights and Fundamental Freedoms 1950 which includes recognition of the right of freedom of association. The European Social Charter 1961 contains a more detailed exposition of employment rights protected by the Council of Europe. These include the right to just conditions of work, the right to safe and healthy working conditions, to fair remuneration, to freedom of association, and to bargain collectively. By November 1995 the European Convention has been signed by 36 European states and ratified by 31 and the Social Charter has been signed by 27 states and ratified by 20. Further afield, the Organization of American States has adopted the American Convention on Human Rights and its additional Protocol of San Salvador 1988 "in the area of economic, social and cultural rights"; the Organization of African Unity has adopted the African Charter on Human and People's Rights; and the Arab Labour Organization has been established whose principles are analogous with the ILO. The North American Free Trade Agreement (NAFTHA) also contains a commitment in the Preamble that the governments of the US, Canada and Mexico resolve to "create new employment opportunities and improve working conditions and living standards in their respective territories" and to "protect, enhance and enforce basic workers' rights", although little substance is given to these rights in the body of the text.

The most recent attempt at encouraging the establishment of international labour standards came with a call by the French, at the G-7 jobs summit in March 1994, for the inclusion of a "social clause" in the Uruguay Round of the GATT negotiations. The French argued that while competition from countries with low pay was a fact of international trade, this situation should not permit the violation of elementary labour standards.[62] France received support from countries such as Canada, Italy and Greece, as well as the European Commission, although these parties wanted to place some limits on a "social clause" to avoid upsetting the developing countries and newly industrialised countries of South-East Asia.[63] The United States also supported some form of social clause, albeit one couched as a general text on various fundamental workers' rights (such as a prohibition on forced labour and child labour), perhaps based

---

[61] Art 1 of the UN Charter.
[62] See EIRR 244, May 1994, p 24.
[63] *Ibid.*

on ILO standards. International trade union organizations, including the European Trade Union Confederation (ETUC), also argued that countries within GATT, when signing trade agreements, should have to guarantee minimum collective rights, such as the right to collective bargaining and the prohibition of forced labour and child labour. They argued that the failure to comply with such standards should result ultimately in higher tariffs on goods from the countries concerned.

Despite such high-level support, the final negotiations at the Ministerial meeting in Marrakesh did not result in the inclusion of a social clause in the Final Act text. However, in his concluding remarks, the Chairman of the Trade Negotiations Committee, Sergio Abreu Bonilla[64], indicated that matters including the examination of the relationship between the trading system and internationally recognised labour standards would be discussed by the Preparatory Committee for inclusion in the agenda of the World Trade Organization's (WTO) work programme.[65] In addition, the Corfu European Council concluded that the European Union would play an active role in efforts to ensure that the WTO could effectively carry out its task of ensuring observance of the rules drawn up jointly. It would also promote progress in combatting unfair trade conditions. Social issues are to be discussed in this context.[66] The new 10-year Generalised Tariff Preference (GSP) scheme does, however, include a social clause. It aims to ensure the promotion of quality development by helping developing countries to face the additional cost of more advanced social policies, in particular the right of association and of collective bargaining, and the abolition of child labour.[67]

At the Labour and Social Affairs Council meeting in March 1995 a consensus emerged on the need to promote core fundamental social rights in the context of multilateral trade relations, without intending "to promote some kind of protectionism which would penalise the economies of the most vulnerable countries". Consequently, the President suggested that the social dimension be confined to fundamental rights – the right to organise and to bargain collectively, abolition of forced labour and elimination of child labour, and the prohibition of discrimination in work – "respect for which can be guaranteed irrespective of the level of economic development of the states concerned".[68] The President talked of establishing a link between minimum social standards and the liberalisation of trade which should help to "promote the right to work and the consolidation of the liberalisation of trade". Any change should be gradual "with incentives and technical cooperation in the context of their necessary economic development".

---

[64] Minister for Foreign Affairs of the Eastern Republic of Uruguay.

[65] MTN.TNC/MIN(94)/6.

[66] COM (94) 333, p 61.

[67] *Ibid.*

[68] Presidency Memorandum on the Social Dimension of International Trade, 5961/95 (Presse 94).

The Community's involvement in creating international labour standards

If the Community is enthusiastic about developing a social dimension to external trade relations, this raises questions about its external competence, given the uncertainty in respect of its internal competence. Article 228(1) EC allows the Council to authorise the Commission to open the necessary negotiations of agreements between the Community and one or more Member States or international organizations "where this Treaty provides". Although, on its face, the EC Treaty adopts the model of "enumerated powers", the Court in its landmark judgment in the *ERTA*[69] case rejected this principle in favour of the principle of parallelism, where the Community Treaty power is co-extensive with its internal powers and so cuts across all areas of its internal competence listed in Article 3 EC.[70] However, despite this judgment, the precise nature of the Community's competence to conclude international agreements is far from clear, as was recently demonstrated in the context of the Uruguay Round of the GATT trade talks. Although the Uruguay negotiations were conducted on behalf of the European Community and the Member States by the Commission alone in order to ensure maximum consistency in the conduct of the negotiations[71], the WTO Agreement was signed by the President of the Council and Sir Leon Brittan, a European Commissioner, on behalf of the Council of the European Union, and by representatives of the Member States on behalf of their respective governments.[72] Shortly before the Ministerial meeting at Marrakesh the Commission submitted to the Court a request for an Opinion under Article 228(6) EC concerning the EC's competence to conclude all parts of the WTO Agreement.

The Court concluded that the Community had sole competence, pursuant to Article 113 EC, to conclude the Multilateral Agreements on Trade in Goods but that the Community and its Member States were jointly competent to conclude the General Agreement on Trade in Services (GATS). The Court refused to accept the Commission's arguments that Articles 100a and 235 EC gave it exclusive competence in respect of GATS. As regards Article 100a, the Court said that where harmonising powers

---

[69] Case 22/70 *Commission* v *Council* [1971] ECR 263.

[70] Emeliou, "Towards a clearer demarcation line? The division of external relations power between the Community and Member States" (1994) 19 ELRev 76, 78–79.

[71] The minutes of the meeting at which the Council approved the Punta del Este declaration, which launched the Uruguay negotiations, stated that "this decision (authorising the Commission to open the negotiations provided for in this declaration) does not prejudge the question of competence of the Community or the Member States" – cited in *Opinion 1/91* of 15 November 1994. Normally, an agreement concluded in an area where competence is shared between the Community and the Member States must be negotiated and implemented jointly – Cases 3, 4 and 6/76 *Kramer and others* [1976] ECR 1279, paras 39–45 and *Opinion 1/78* [1979] ECR 2871, para 60.

[72] This procedure was followed in pursuance of the decision taken by the Council and the representatives of the Member States at a meeting on 7 and 8 March 1994 – cited in *Opinion 1/94* of 15 November 1994.

have been exercised, the harmonisation measures adopted may limit, or even remove, the freedom of Member States to negotiate with non-Member countries. However, it said "an internal power to harmonise which has not been exercised in a specified field cannot confer exclusive competence in that field on the Community".

In respect of Article 235 EC, the Court said that this provision could not in itself vest exclusive competence in the Community at international level. It added:

"internal competence can give rise to exclusive external competence only if it is exercised. This applies *a fortiori* to Article 235".

Consequently, applying this ruling by analogy to the social field, the Community's competence to enter into international agreements in respect of, for example, the prohibition of forced labour and freedom of association, where no Community legislation has been adopted to date and no specific legal basis has been provided by the Treaty, would at the most be concurrent rather than exclusive.

This point was highlighted further by the Court's earlier ruling in *Opinion 2/91*[73] concerning ILO Convention No 170 relating to the safety in the use of chemicals at work. The purpose of this Convention was to prevent or reduce the incidence of chemically induced illnesses and injuries at work. This was to be achieved by ensuring that all chemicals are evaluated to determine their hazards by providing employers and workers with the information necessary for their protection and by establishing principles for protective programmes.[74]

During the negotiations leading up to the agreement of this Convention, the Commission argued that the subject matter of the Convention fell within the exclusive competence of the Community, a fact disputed by some Member States.[75] The Court concluded that the Community enjoys an internal legislative competence in the area of social policy and that Convention No 170, whose subject matter coincides with several directives adopted under Article 118a, fell within the Community's area of competence. The Court then distinguished between two situations to determine whether that competence was exclusive. The first concerned fields where the Community can establish minimum requirements, and the second concerned areas where the Community has harmonised legislation.

In respect of the first, the Court said that in areas where the Community could only lay down minimum requirements the Member States also had competence and were free to adopt more stringent measures.[76] Thus,

---

[73] Opinion of 19 March 1993, 93/C 109/01 [1994] IRLR 135.
[74] Preamble to Convention 170.
[75] For a background to the dispute, see the report for the hearing and Betten (1993) IJCLLIR 244.
[76] See also Council Directive 80/1107/EEC (OJ L327/8) on the protection of workers from the risks related to chemical, physical and biological agents at work, based on Art 100 EEC, and individual directives adopted pursuant to Art 8 of Directive 80/1107/EEC, all of which lay down minimum requirements.

while Article 118a(1) provides that "*Member States* shall pay particular attention to encouraging improvements, especially in the working environment, as regards health and safety of workers" (emphasis added), Article 118a(2) provides that *the Community* (the Council) is given powers to lay down *"minimum requirements"* by directive to help achieve the objective laid down in Article 118a(1) (emphasis added) and by Article 118a(3) Member States are entitled to "maintain or introduce more stringent measures for the protection of working conditions". Thus, the Court concluded the Community's competence was concurrent and not exclusive.

Second, in respect of those areas where the Community had not simply laid down minimum requirements but had harmonised rules, for example, rules relating to classification, packaging and labelling of dangerous substances and preparations[77], the Court ruled that the Community alone had competence and consequently Member States could not undertake such commitments outside the framework of the Community institutions.

The Court also suggested that co-operation between the two sides of industry was a matter for concurrent competence although account had to be taken of the objective pursued by such consultation. While recognising that "as Community law stands at present, social policy and in particular co-operation between the two sides of industry are matters which fall predominantly within the competence of the Member States" these matters have not been "withdrawn entirely from the competence of the Community". It pointed to Article 118b which provides that the Commission shall endeavour to develop a dialogue between management and labour at European level.[78] Finally, the Court concluded that the Community is also competent to undertake commitments to put the substantive provisions into effect.

Where, as in the case of ILO Convention No 170, the subject matter of an agreement falls within the joint competence of the Member States and the Community, the Court said that there must be a close association between the two, particularly in light of the fact that the Community has only observer status at the ILO and so cannot itself conclude an ILO Convention, which it must do through the medium of the Member States.

The EC Treaty itself provides that the Commission must ensure "the maintenance of all appropriate relations with the organs of the United Nations, of its specialised agencies[79] and of the General Agreement on

---

[77] Council Directive 67/548/EEC (OJ/SE 1967, p 234); Directive 79/831/EEC (OJ L259/10) and Directive 88/379/EEC (OJ No L 187, p 14).

[78] The question of the Community's competence under Art 118 was also at issue in Joined Cases 281, 283 and 287/85 *Germany and others v Commission* (migrant workers case) [1987] ECR 3203. The Court ruled that migration policy is capable of falling within the social field within the meaning of Art 118 in so far as it concerns the impact of third county migrant-workers on the Community employment market and on working conditions. It added that Art 118 conferred on the Commission the powers to arrange consultations but the subject matter of the notification and consultation falls within the competence of the Member States.

[79] The ILO became a specialist agency of the UN after the Second World War.

Tariffs and Trade".[80] It must also maintain "such relations as are appropriate with international organizations".[81] In addition, the Community must establish "all appropriate forms of co-operation with the Council of Europe"[82] and must also establish "close co-operation with the Organization for Economic Co-operation and Development".[83]

The Commission alluded to the problems caused by the Community's uncertain legal relationship, with the ILO in its White Paper on Social Policy. It referred to the importance of ensuring that "an acceptable solution is found to resolve in a constructive fashion the outstanding questions relating to the participation of the Union and the Member States at the International Labour Conference".[84] The biggest stumbling block relates to the tripartite structure of the ILO. If the Community were to act on behalf of the Member States, the national workers' and employers' organizations fear that their role within the ILO might be reduced. The Commission has now proposed a Council Decision on the exercise of the Community's external competence at International Labour Conferences in cases falling within the joint competence of the Community and its Member States.[85] This involves the Community and the Member States formulating joint replies to the ILO questionnaire sent out as a preliminary to the opening of a conference session, with the Member States consulting the two sides of industry on the proposed Community reply and Council authorisation for the Community to take part in the negotiations of a draft Convention and Recommendation at first and second reading, with close co-operation with the Member States. Where a convention or recommendation has been adopted Member States must notify the International Labour office that the competent authorities are the competent institutions of the Community and the Member States.

Finally, if international standards are successfully adopted, the Community must recognise that standards on their own are not sufficient: they need mechanisms through which they are implemented, monitored and enforced. At Community level, the Court of Justice has been instrumental in securing these objectives, through the development of the doctrine of supremacy of Community law[86], the doctrine of direct effect[87], and establishing that national courts must provide genuine and effective

---

[80] Art 229(1).

[81] Art 229(2).

[82] Art 230 EC.

[83] Art 231 EC. The OECD has initiated studies of possible links between trade and social standards.

[84] COM(94) 333, p 59.

[85] COM (94) 333, p 59.

[86] See, *e.g.*, Case 6164 *Costa* v *ENEL* [1964] ECR 585 and Case C-213/89 *Factortame (No 1)* [1990] ECR I-2433.

[87] See, *e.g.*, Case 26/62 *Van Gend en Loos* [1963] ECR 1 in respect of Treaty provisions, and most recently, Case C-91/92 *Faccini Dori* [1994] ECR I-3325 on the vertical direct effect of directives.

remedies to those seeking to enforce a Community law right.[88] While this has been possible within the framework of a "new legal order"[89] it is less easy to secure in the context of world trade. The UK's refusal to heed ILO criticism in 1989 about the British failure to comply with ILO Convention No 87[90] provides a salutary lesson of the impotence of international norms.

Conclusions

The feeling that the Community's desire to create international labour standards may be motivated in part by the wish to secure the welfare of workers and in part by fears of social dumping on the world stage demonstrates that the debate currently taking place in the Community about the desirability of setting standards at supra-national level is replicated and magnified at international level. Whatever the motivating force, it is clear that the creating of international labour standards is firmly on the Commission's – and probably the Community's – agenda. The ugly duckling of Community policy may yet emerge as a fully grown swan.

CATHERINE BARNARD

---

[88] See, *e.g.*, Case 14/83 *Von Colson* [1984] ECR 1891 and Case C-271/91 *Marshall (No 2)* [1993] 3 CMLR 293.

[89] Case 26/62 *Van Gend en Loos* [1963] ECR 1.

[90] This is well documented by Brown and McColgan, *op cit*, pp 270–276.

Chapter 12
Tragic Triumph: Agricultural Trade, the Common Agricultural Policy and the Uruguay Round

It has long been recognised that the Community enjoys exclusive competence in respect of its common commercial policy. Relying upon Articles 113 and employing a wide range of legal instruments, not least its capacity to enter into international agreements, the Community defines its role in the international trading order. In so doing it is guided and constrained by the legal norms laid down in the GATT and its associated instruments – rules which, in principle at least, constitute a binding and hierarchically superior part of Community law.[1] Yet, it would be misleading to conceive the external trade law of the Community as wholly premised upon those Treaty provisions conferring power in respect of commercial policy. Rather this body of law has its origins also in a wide range of domestic, apparently internal, Community policies. Few would deny the role of Community competition law in shaping the Community's relations with its trading partners. Likewise the capacity of industrial or regional development policy to influence global trading relations should not be overlooked. Yet, it is in respect of the operation of the Community's agricultural policy that the futility of seeking to conceive the external as distinct from the internal becomes most apparent. The impact of the Common Agricultural Policy (CAP) upon the external trade law of the Community is at times explicit. Hence, for example, the Lomé Convention provides for continuing Community flexibility with respect to import treatment for agricultural products, and directly attributes the need for such flexibility to the functioning of the CAP.[2] Similarly, the more recently concluded "Europe" Agreements emphasise the role of the CAP in the process of negotiating future import concessions.[3] More frequently, however, the external trade implications of this policy remain implicit, though of the utmost importance, and emerge as an apparently incidental "side-effect" of a contentious domestic policy.

---

[1] Cases 21–24/72, *International Fruit Company* v *Produckschap voor Goenten en Fruit,* [1972] ECR 1219. See, however, Opinion 1/94 [1994] I-ECR 5276, in which the European Court found that the competence to enter into the WTO Agreement was shared between the Community and the Member States. See Scott, "The GATT/WTO in 1994: Perspectives from the European Court of Justice" *1994 Butterworths Annual European Review* (1995), 25–45.

[2] Article 168(d) Lomé IV, OJ 1991 L229/3.

[3] See, *e.g.*, Chapter 2 of the agreement with Poland, OJ 1993 L348/2.

The purpose of this paper is to examine the operation of the CAP in an external setting, focusing upon those policy instruments which have caused and continue to cause such consternation outside of the Community – most visibly in the United States but also throughout much of the "developing" world. First, the paper will examine the implications of the principal CAP mechanisms from an international trade perspective and highlight the role and traditional limitations of the GATT in regulating their use. This is intended to facilitate an understanding of the challenges faced in the Uruguay Round negotiations and as such no account will be taken at this stage of the conclusions reached. The paper will then outline the substantive nature of the World Trade Organization Agreement in so far as it concerns agriculture and the changes this necessitates with respect to the Community's agricultural trade policy in the cereals sector. It will be argued that the conclusions of the Uruguay Round in respect of agriculture operate to legitimate, from an international trade perspective, the earlier 1992 reforms of the CAP and that, as such, they should be seen as a minimalist package which does little to address the fundamental underlying problems or to mitigate the widespread hardship caused by the CAP, notably in much of the "third world".

The GATT and agricultural trade before the Uruguay Round

Both legally and factually complex, research into even a single aspect of the CAP has been likened to chasing a moving target through thick fog.[4] Yet, notwithstanding its elaborate nature and the considerable variation between individual product markets and agricultural "regimes", it remains relatively straightforward to identify broad categories of measures inherent in, or ancillary to, the CAP which influence, and arguably distort, patterns of international trade. The decisions of various GATT Panels examining complaints against the Community attributable to the CAP are particularly useful in performing this task and will also be used to exemplify the traditional inadequacy of the GATT in regulating trade in agricultural products.

Central to many of the most important common market organizations instituted by the CAP is the payment of agricultural subsidies to a variety of parties in a myriad of forms. In this respect the provision of production subsidies to farmers which are available either directly or, more commonly, indirectly as a result of the "buying-in" of agricultural commodities by national intervention agencies established by Community law, is crucial. In general, the GATT does not prohibit the use of such subsidies, recognising as it does their legitimate role in promoting social and

---

[4] Usher, *Legal Aspects of Agriculture in the European Community* (1988) at p*vii*.

economic objectives. Article III.8 (b) which prohibits discrimination between domestic and imported products in respect of taxation and regulation exempts from its scope "the payment of subsidies exclusively to
domestic producers". Similarly Article VI.7 which regulates the use of
countervailing duties as a response to illicit subsidies recognises the prima
facie legitimacy of price and income stabilisation schemes in respect of
primary products, where these are not directly tied to export prices.

The traditional "hands-off" approach of the GATT to the payment of
domestic subsidies can be exemplified by reference to the decisions of the
GATT panel in the infamous "oilseeds" case.[5] The panel concluded that
the production subsidies payable by the Community were liable to condemnation due to their capacity to undermine and nullify specific tariff
concessions granted to the United States during the Dillon Round. It did
not demand the dismantling of the subsidies regime but rather accepted
that a renegotiation of its tariff concessions could similarly eliminate the
impairment in question. The capacity of such domestic subsidies to themselves disrupt international trade is a matter of continuing debate. As early
as 1960, however, it was recognised that "it is fair to assume that a subsidy
which provides an incentive to increased production will, in the absence of
offsetting measures, e.g. a consumption subsidy, either increase export or
reduces imports".[6] Similarly, Article 11 of the 1979 Subsidies code[7] acknowledges that such subsidies may cause or threaten injury to another
party or nullify the benefits of the GATT by affecting the competitive
relationship between parties. Nonetheless the code, like the GATT Agreement itself, does not seek to prohibit such subsidies, but rather invites
parties to seek to avoid such effects and to take into account any potential
adverse external effects in their formulation of domestic subsidy regimes.

Yet more clearly and unambiguously pernicious from an international
trade perspective is the utilisation of two additional forms of subsidy by the
CAP – processor and export. Indeed the "oilseeds" regime which has
been the source of considerable acrimony between the Community and
the United States was very largely premised upon the former. It has been
suggested that the subsidies payable by the Community in respect of
oilseeds have typically been four times as high as the equivalent payments
by the United States[8], resulting in an estimated loss of market share equal
to one billion US Dollars per year for the United States.[9] The "oilseeds"

---

[5] European Economic Community: Payments and Subsidies Paid to Processors and Producers
of Oilseeds and Related Animal-Feed Proteins, BISD 37, 86 (1991); Payments and Subsidies Paid
to Processors and Producers of Oilseeds and Related Animal-Fed Proteins – Follow-up on the
Panel Report, *GATT Activities 1991: An Annual Review of the Work of the GATT*, 69 (1992).

[6] *Review Pursuant to Article XVI:5*: BISD 9, 188 at 191 (1991).

[7] *The Agreement on Interpretation and Application of Articles VI, XVI, XXIII of the General Agreement on
Tariffs and Trade*, BISD 26, 56 (1980).

[8] Nordgren, "The GATT Panels During the Uruguay Round: A Joker in the Negotiating
Game" (1991) 25 *Journal of World Trade* (1991) 57–72 at 61.

[9] Arnold, "The Oilseeds Dispute and the Validity of Unilateralism in a Multilateral Context"
(1994) 30 *Stanford Journal of International Law* 187–220 at 189.

Panel was more emphatic in its condemnation of such subsidies in the light of GATT, Article III, which requires non-discriminatory treatment of national and imported products. Nevertheless, it is not possible to conclude that in general processor subsidies which compensate those who purchase goods of Community origin for the difference between the higher Community and world-market price will invariably fall foul of the GATT. Vital to the "oilseeds" regime was the tendency of such subsidies to "over-compensate" processors by awarding a subsidy which was higher than the actual price differential. It was because of this that the Panel concluded that this regime could be said to create a positive incentive to purchase domestic rather than imported products. As such it remains arguable whether subsidies which "merely" and accurately reflect the prevailing differences in price would constitute discrimination within the meaning of Article III.

It is, however, in relation to export subsidies that the inadequacy of the GATT has been most striking. It is well known that the "buying-in" system of the CAP has engendered substantial increases in production in respect of many agricultural commodities, notably cereals, sugar, dairy products, beef and veal. In an effort to mitigate the burden (financial, political and moral) of surplus production within the Community a system of export restitution was devised which essentially operates to compensate Community exporters for the difference between the market price in the Community and the lower world-market price. Such export subsidies which absorb more than half of the Community's agricultural budget, operate to facilitate Community penetration of external agricultural markets and to dispose of its surpluses, albeit at low prices, on the world market. Although economists continue to argue endlessly over the "true" costs of the CAP for third countries there can be little doubt that the consequences are devastating, notably though not exclusively for much of the "third world". One author exemplifies the multifarious costs by observing that:

"During 1986, at the height of the dumping hostilities, the United States and the European Community were selling wheat surpluses in West African countries such as Mali and Burkina Faso at prices as low as $60 a ton – around a third lower than equivalent production, transport and marketing costs for locally produced cereals like sorghum and millet. In order to do so they were using direct and indirect subsidies of $100 a ton to bridge the gap between domestic support and export prices. The inevitable result of this unequal competition between the Treasuries of Europe and North America and vulnerable peasant farmers was a fall in rural household incomes (as cheap food imports depressed locals staple prices, falling investment in agriculture, and in some cases, migration from the land."[10]

Add to this list: food dependence and insecurity, a decline in agricultural export earnings, budgetary imbalance and falling rural employment, and it is clear that the, at best, marginal success of the CAP in supporting

---

[10] Watkins, *Fixing the Rules: North–South Issues in International Trade and the GATT Uruguay Round* (1992), p 64. See also Roarty, "The Impact of the Common Agricultural Policy on Agricultural Trade and Development" (1987) *National Westminster Bank Quarterly Review*, 12–27.

agricultural communities inside the Community has been achieved at the expense of those situated outside. In seeking to offset the social, cultural and environmental costs of a declining agricultural economy the Community has in effect exported its problems to countries which will not or cannot engage effectively in the "subsidies race".

Yet neither the capacity of the GATT, nor the political will of certain contracting parties, to confront such flagrant inequities is great. While Article XVI acknowledges the disruptive effects of export subsidies and their capacity to threaten attainment of the objectives of the agreement, it does not prohibit their use in primary products except where these result in the subsidising party enjoying a more than equitable share of world trade in the relevant product market. The effectiveness of this restriction has been undermined by the diffidence of various GATT Panels. When in 1978 Australia lodged a complaint challenging the Community's export subsidies for sugar the panel acknowledged that the Community regime constituted "a threat of serious prejudice" within the meaning of Article XVI.1 and readily conceded the reality of continuous and substantial increases in the Community's exports of sugar.[11]

Nevertheless, it concluded that "there was not sufficient evidence to state that the increased Community exports in recent years had to a considerable extent directly displaced Australian exports from world markets" and that as such "it was not in a position to reach a definite conclusion that the increased share had resulted in the European Community's having more than an equitable share of world export trade in that product, in terms of Article XVI.3".[12]

Once again the subsidies code[13] does little to mitigate the inadequacy of the GATT in this respect. While its language is less compromising and while it clarifies certain technical questions such as the previous representative period to be used in assessing shifting patterns of international trade[14], the concept of "a more than equitable share of world trade" remains a loose cannon which has undermined the practical utility of the code. In the early 1980s the United States instituted a series of complaints under the GATT concerning the Community's agricultural policy. Among these complaints were those relating to export subsidies on poultry, sugar, pasta and wheat. In each of these cases the relevant GATT Panel emphasised the difficulties inherent in the notion of a more than equitable market share and found it impossible to establish any clearly defined causal relationship between the provision of export subsidies and the Community's enhanced export performance. Yet the evidence seems quite overwhelming. In, for example, the EC Export Subsidies on Wheat Flour case[15], the Community's share of the relevant market had increased,

---

[11] European Communities – Refunds on Exports of Sugar, BISD 26, 290 (1980).
[12] *Ibid* at p 308.
[13] *Supra*, n 7.
[14] *Ibid*, Art 10(2)(b).
[15] European Communities – Export Subsidies on Wheat Flour (subsidies code).

during the representative period, from 58% to 66% while United States exports had declined from 25% to 21%. After such decisions one commentator was able to conclude that:

"The special exemption of agriculture from the general prohibition against export subsidies in Article XVI of the GATT has been a major source of disputes in international agricultural trade for decades, a major source of distrust and contempt for the GATT dispute settlement process, and a major sticking point of US–EC negotiations in the last few rounds of trade negotiations."[16]

It is not, however, only the subsidies inherent in the CAP which render it contentious from an international trade law perspective. Implicit too in the CAP are a range of non-tariff barriers to trade which seek to protect domestic production from more competitively priced imports. Among the most important are the multitude of quotas, both quantitative and seasonal, and import licensing schemes which limit access to the Community's own market. Notwithstanding the general commitment in the GATT to eliminate non-tariff barriers to trade in Article XI, it contains a specific exception for agricultural import quotas and similar measures which operate, *inter alia*, to reinforce domestic supply control measures. Hence where the Community under the CAP seeks to limit domestic production (however halfheartedly) of a like or substitutable product, for example by way of set-aside, extensification, co-responsibility levies or domestic quotas, import quotas remain a legitimate tool of international trade. At any rate effective enforcement of the preconditions which attach to the Article XI exception, relating in particular to domestic supply control, remains difficult, not least due to the granting in 1955 of a waiver to the United States which releases it from its obligations under Article XI.2(c)(i).[17] It has been suggested that though the waiver applies only to the United States, it has resulted in a certain reluctance on the part of other contracting parties to comply faithfully with its terms.[18]

The variable import levy too is an integral part of the CAP. This involves the construction of a threshold price for imports set in relation to the Community's target price and the charging of a levy which represents the difference between this threshold price and the import price. As the threshold price is invariably higher than the prevailing Community

---

[16] Hathaway, "Agriculture", in Schott (ed), *Completing the Uruguay Round: A Results Orientated Approach to the GATT Trade Negotiations* (1990) 56–57. See also Coccia, "Settlement of Disputes in GATT under the Subsidies Code: Two Panel Reports on EEC Export Subsidies", (1986) 16 *Georgia Journal of International and Comparative Law* 1–44 and more generally for an excellent analysis, Montaña-Mora, "International Law and International Relations Cheek to Cheek: An International Law/International Relations Perspective on the US/EC Agricultural Export Subsidies Dispute", (1994) 19 *North Carolina Journal of International Law and Commercial Regulation* 1–60.

[17] This waiver was granted because of s 22 of the US Agricultural Adjustment Act 1935 which requires the President to impose restrictions on imports which may harm domestic farm support programmes. A 1951 amendment to this section provides that no trade agreement be applied in a manner which is inconsistent with this section.

[18] See Hillman, "Agriculture in the Uruguay Round" (1993) 28 *Tulsa Law Journal* 761–793.

market price, Community producers retain a clear competitive advantage. Notwithstanding the patently protectionist intention and nature of this instrument it is in general (except where it operates to nullify or impair previously negotiated tariff concessions) consistent with the GATT. After all Article 11 seeks to eliminate prohibitions or restrictions "other than duties, taxes or other charges".

In the wake of the Uruguay Round: towards "A GATT with teeth"?[19]

The Final Act Embodying the Results of the Uruguay Round of Multilateral Trade Negotiations imposes a dual obligation on participants: first, to adopt the ministerial declarations and decisions formulated during the course of the negotiations, and second, and more important, to submit for approval to the relevant authority, the so-called Agreement Establishing the World Trade Organization (the WTO Agreement), with a view to it entering into force no later than 1 July 1995. Integral to this WTO Agreement are the annexes attached thereto which include, in the sphere of agriculture, a separate and specific "Agreement on Agriculture" and the Uruguay Round Protocol to the GATT 1994 including the appended schedules of concession.[20]

Whereas the former provides a general framework for the liberalisation of trade in agricultural products, the latter records the specific commitments of the members to eliminate or reduce tariff and non-tariff barriers to trade in goods, including agricultural goods.[21] The status of the Agreement on Agriculture (as well as the other eleven agreements contained in Annex 1A) is clarified in a General Interpretive note which states that:

"In the event of conflict between a provision of the General Agreement on Tariffs and Trade 1994 and a provision of another agreement in Annex 1A, the provision of the other agreement shall take precedence to the extent of the conflict."

Hence this Agreement is not only legally binding and subject to the fortified dispute settlement mechanisms introduced by the WTO Agreement, but it is also hierarchically superior to the GATT 1994 itself.

The Agreement on Agriculture, together with the Uruguay Round Protocol, seeks to address the three principal issues highlighted in the first

---

[19] This quotation is borrowed from an article by Montaña-Mora, itself entitled "A GATT with Teeth: Law Wins Over Politics in the Resolution of International Trade Disputes" (1993) 31 *Columbia, Journal of International Law* 103–180.

[20] The scope of the GATT 1994 is defined in a "General Interpretative Note" which is itself contained in Annex 1A of the WTO Agreement. It consists of the GATT 1947 as amended and modified, legal instruments which have entered into force under the GATT 1947, "understandings" set out in Annex 1A which relate to the interpretation of specific GATT articles, explanatory notes contained in the annex, and the Uruguay Round Protocol.

[21] Appendix 1 relates to tariff concessions and tariff quotas on agricultural goods, while Appendix 5 relates to agricultural subsidies.

part of this chapter, that is, market access, domestic support and export competition. Before assessing the implications of these measures for the Community's external trade law as mediated by its agricultural policy, it is necessary to explore the nature of the commitments undertaken by the Community.

In the area of domestic support "developed" member countries are required to reduce their level of support by 20% over a six-year implementation period. Domestic support commitments are expressed in monetary terms on a product-specific basis as an "aggregate" or, where this is not practicable, an "equivalent" measurement of support, the rules for the calculation of which are laid down in Annexes 3 and 4 of the Agreement. To be excluded from such calculations are a range of domestic support measures which are perceived as essentially non- or only marginally trade distorting. Hence Article 6(4) of the Agreement introduces a *de minimis* rule whereby domestic support which does not exceed 5% of the total value of production of a specific product or in the case of non-product-specific support 5% of the value of total agricultural production, is not to be included.

Similarly, Article 6(5) exempts certain direct payments granted within the framework of a programme aimed at reducing domestic production. More important perhaps, and indicative of a significant Community "victory" during the negotiations, are the "Green Box" measures outlined in Annex 2 which are also to constitute "exempt" subsidies. Among the most crucial in this respect are (i) direct payments for producers provided through a publicly funded programme, not in the form of price support and which are not related either to volume of production or the factors of production employed; (ii) decoupled income support; (iii) investment aids; (iv) assistance provided for person or land retirement programmes; (v) payments under environmental programmes which do not exceed the extra costs or loss of income incurred in the course of complying with such a programme. Also of the utmost importance from a Community perspective is the decision to give "credit" for reductions in domestic support levels instituted since 1986. A newly established Committee on Agriculture will review the implementation of these and other commitments.[22]

In respect of export subsidies, "developed" member countries will be obliged to reduce their value by 36% over six years and the volume of subsidised exports by 21% over the same period. Whereas the years 1986–1990 are in general to constitute the base period for such reduction commitments, where subsidised exports have increased since then, the calculations will, in certain circumstances, be premised upon the 1991–1992 level. Whereas Article 9(1) defines the concept of an export subsidy, Article 10 incorporates an "anti-circumvention" clause which seeks to ensure that export subsidies other than those included in Article 9 will not be "applied in a manner which results in, or which threatens to lead to,

---

[22] See Arts 17 and 18 of the Agreement on Agriculture.

circumvention of export subsidy commitments". The Agreement also specifies that where the overall volume of exports in a given product market exceeds the level set out in a specific schedule of concession, it will be for the exporting state to establish that no export subsidy has been granted in respect of this additional volume. As such it shifts the burden of proof from the receiving to the exporting state.

"Due Restraint" or "peace" provisions in Article 13 of the Agreement establish an understanding between member countries that domestic support measures and export subsidies maintained in conformity with the Agreement and Uruguay Round Protocol will be largely non-actionable under the GATT 1994 and Annex 1A to the Subsidies Agreement and, where they remain actionable, due restraint will be shown in initiating any countervailing duty investigations. Hence although the new GATT regime to some extent mitigates the inadequacies highlighted above (particularly as a result of the Agreement on Subsidies and Countervailing Measures which for the first time unambiguously prohibits export subsidies and other subsidies contingent upon the use of domestic as opposed to imported goods), the Agreement on Agriculture denies the applicability of these more general rules in so far as they might operate to accelerate the pace of reform beyond that envisaged in the Agreement itself. The "peace" provisions are to apply for nine years.

As to market access, the Agreement is indicative of the more general preference within GATT for tariff as opposed to non-tariff barriers. Non-tariff barriers are to be replaced by tariff barriers which offer a largely equivalent level of protection. Such tariffs as well as existing tariffs are in turn to be reduced by "developed" country members by 36%, relative to the base period (1986–1988), over the six-year implementation period. Minimum reductions are to apply on individual tariff lines. Minimum access tariff quotas at reduced rates are to be maintained or established where imports constitute less than 3% of domestic production, rising to 5% by the end of the implementation period.

This commitment to transparency and predictability through tariffication is to some extent undermined by specific safeguard provisions in Article 5 and special treatment criteria in Annex 5. The former legitimises the imposition of additional duties in the event that the price of imported goods falls by more than 10% relative to the 1986–1988 reference level. The more substantial the drop in price the higher the additional rate of duty applied. Moreover, additional duties may further be charged in the event of a significant import "surge". The "trigger" level in this respect is variable according to the market share enjoyed by imported products relative to domestic consumption. The more substantial the market share in the three years preceding the action, the less substantial the increase required to "trigger" the imposition of such additional duties.

The special treatment provisions contained in Annex 5 constitute an exception to the general prohibition on non-tariff barriers in Article 4(2). Thus, import restrictions can be maintained until the end of the implementation period where: (i) the product in question enjoyed a market share of less than 3% during the period 1986–1988; (ii) no export subsidies have been paid in respect of such products since 1986; (iii) effective mechanisms designed to reduce domestic production of the product are in place; (iv) minimum access opportunities are provided equally – 4% in the first year of the implementation period, rising to 8% by the last year. The agreement of the members is required to extend such special treatment beyond the end of the implementation period and at any rate additional commitments are to be undertaken at this time.

Also of importance within the Agreement on Agriculture is Article 14 which notes that members agree to give effect to the Annex 1A Agreement on Sanitary and Phytosanitary Measures. This Agreement concerns food safety and animal and plant health protection measures. It accepts that members have a right to regulate such matters but stresses that they should not discriminate arbitrarily between members. It encourages members to base their regulations on international standards wherever possible although it accepts that higher levels of protection may be necessary where these can be justified on scientific grounds. It provides guidance concerning the assessment of risk and the intensity of regulation to be applied. The Agreement requires that such measures be applied in a transparent manner and establishes a committee which will constitute a forum for consultation and the monitoring of international harmonisation of standards. The Agreement is essentially hortatory in nature, no doubt a matter of considerable relief to those who have argued that at an international level it is the regulated who do the regulating.[23]

Towards a more equitable agricultural trading order?

The conclusion of the Uruguay Round marked the beginning of a new phase in the debate about agriculture in the Community. Confronted by the reality of what at one time seemed unattainable, the new focus for debate concerned the compatibility between the GATT package and the CAP, particularly after the latter's most recent reform.[24] Fuelled by vigorous Commission participation, which finally demonstrates that the Commission is more susceptible to pressures from the inside than from the outside, the debate has highlighted issues surrounding the implementation of the WTO Agreement in respect of agriculture, and uncertainties concerning the scope and nature of further CAP reforms which it may necessitate. Yet concealed by this intense and complex debate is a more fundamental, though not entirely unrelated, question which begs an analysis not only of means but of end. Is the Agreement the "single most

---

[23] See, *e.g.* Avery *et al*, *Cracking the Codex* (1993).
[24] See Swinbank, "CAP Reform, 1992" (1993) 31 *Journal of Common Market Studies* 359–372.

important trade deal the world has ever seen"?[25] or is it a "sham"[26] and a "licence for overproduction and dumping"?[27] In other words, if the Community's external trade law in the sphere of agriculture is largely mediated through the CAP, will the CAP in the wake of the Uruguay Round imply an external trade policy which is at once more equitable and less self-interested? Focusing on the important cereals sector this part will now examine the implications of this "deal", examining first its impact upon Community exports to third-country markets and, second, its capacity to liberalise third country access to the Community's own market.

The European Commission is confident that it can meet the demands of the GATT package in respect of export competition, even without further decisive reform of the Community's cereals "regime". Given that the reductions agreed in the GATT in respect of export subsidies are premised upon a reference period which predates the 1992 reforms of the CAP, the Commission is emphatic in its insistence that the Community has already taken the steps necessary to bring about an appropriate fall in both the value of subsidies paid and the volume of subsidised exports. After all, a central plank of the 1992 reforms was the agreement to reduce domestic support prices by 29% over three years, commencing at the start of the farming year on 1 July 1993. Such a cut not only more than satisfies the requirements of the Agreement in respect of domestic support, thereby paving the way for smaller reductions in other sectors under the principle of aggregation, but it also necessarily implies a narrowing of the gap between Community and world-market prices and a concomitant decline in the value of export subsidies payable. Moreover, as Jean Cloos (former Chef de Cabinet in DG XI) points out[28] such a dramatic cut in domestic prices is not necessarily production-neutral. He argues that the effect will be to discourage farmers from maximising output and to provide an incentive for them to maintain production at a level which is close to their 1992 output. When set-aside is added to the equation, which the Commission anticipates inducing a 9% fall in production[29], together with the anticipated increase in the consumption of domestic grain, Cloos concludes that productivity will increase by no more than 1% a year between now and the year 2000. Thus by the end of the GATT implementation period, total Community production will equal 175 million tonnes (mt), with domestic consumption absorbing around 153 mt, leaving an

---

[25] John Major quoted in Brock and Fletcher, "Farm Deal Lifts Trade War", *The Times*, 21 November 1992, at 1.

[26] Watkins, in "GATT Deal 'Better than Nothing' for Developing Nations", *Agra Europe*, 15 April 1994, E/5-E/6 at E/6.

[27] Jenkins, *Capping the GATT and Gatting the CAP* (1994).

[28] See "CAP Reform and the GATT: Alternative Views" *Agra Europe* 25 February 1994, P1-P2.

[29] "CAP Reform: The Dangers of Complacency" *Agra Europe* 7 January 1994, P/1-P/2. It is important to observe that the percentage of land to be set-aside has, for the marketing year 1996/7, been reduced to 10%. This reflects the effects of adverse weather conditions during 1995/6, together with a higher than anticipated world market price due, in part, to growing demand from the Chinese market. See Council Regulation 2336/95 OJ L 236/1.

exportable surplus of 25 mt which is within the Community's limit (which includes an allowance for food aid) of 25.9 mt.

Needless to say, the Commission's own assessment is arguably unduly optimistic. Researchers at Agra Europe anticipate an exportable surplus of at least 30 mt by the end of the implementation period.[30] While the arguments are complex and often highly subjective, there are a wide variety of factors which tend to support the less complacent forecasts issued by those outside of the Community. First, the rate of "slippage" inherent in set-aside is likely to be higher than anticipated by the Commission, perhaps as high or even higher than 50%.[31] This likelihood is increased by the decision to introduce, *inter alia*, a system of permanent, non-rotational set-aside and strengthened by the experiences of the Community during the first year following its reforms. Notwithstanding an overall fall in land area planted to cereals equal to 8.2%, the volume of production fell in 1993/94 by only 1.3% from the previous year.[32] Of equal significance is the assumption that farmers will in the future refrain from seeking to maximise output. This rests upon the premise that the new lower price is insufficiently high to provide an incentive to increased production over and above the reference yield which attracts additional compensatory payments. While this may indeed be accurate for the majority of Community farmers, for the 20% minority who produce 80% of output it is unlikely to be so. For many of these farmers whose per unit cost is around 75 ECU per tonne, the new price of around 100 ECU leaves substantial scope for a profitable increase in yield. This likelihood is further increased by the decision to suspend the application of previous "stabilizer" mechanisms, particularly co-responsibility levies which had in 1992/93 been charged at a basic rate of 5%. As such the Council has been accused of beginning its "new regime by nullifying the effect of the previous reform package agreed in 1988".[33]

If the estimates of those outside the Commission prove to be more realistic than those of the Commission itself, a fundamental question arises relating to the implications of this additional surplus from an international trade perspective. If it is assumed that the Community faithfully complies with its commitments under the Uruguay Round package relating to export subsidies, is it then fair to suppose that such a surplus, while presenting immense internal problems for the Community, will be neutral and, at worst, marginal in its capacity to distort patterns of international trade? Certainly the WTO Agreement concerning agricultural trade is premised upon such a supposition. While the Agreement on Agriculture does not prohibit exports at a level beyond that established in the schedules, it does require that the Community demonstrate that such exports

---

[30] *Supra*, n 29 at P/2.

[31] See *e.g.*, Herlihy & Madell, *The Effectiveness of the EC's New Set-Aside Programme: An Assessment Based on US Experience and Interviews with EC Farmers* (1993).

[32] "EU Cereals Harvest Fell by Only 1.3 Per Cent in 1993" *Agra Europe* 25 March 1994, M/11-M/13.

[33] See *Agra Europe* 22 May 1992, P/1.

are free from export subsidies. What it does not require, however, is that such production is independent of all subsidies, domestic as well as export. On the contrary, as has already been noted, the Agreement explicitly exempts a wide variety of domestic support measures such as those laid down in Annex 2, a series of exemptions which the Community intends vigorously to exploit, principally by way of compensatory payments designed to compensate farmers for lost income resulting from the price reduction implicit in the 1992 reforms. Such payments, like the compensation for set-aside and that offered under the agri-environmental and early retirement programmes, will be excluded from the calculation of the Community's AMS and will be able to rise and fall without incurring the wrath of the international legal community. For many it was this decision to exclude such a wide range of domestic support mechanisms from the parameters of the new agreement that constitutes the single most important deficiency inherent in the new GATT package. For others it was this aspect which made the package acceptable. It has been observed in this respect that:

"What both those Member States concerned about EC farm support spending and those third countries concerned about export competition from the EC now need to worry about is the "nightmare scenario"; where the EC's cereal production continues to increase, the Community cuts its support price to export without subsidies . . . and it increases its compensatory payments to cover the further reduction in EC producer price. In this way direct payments to farmers would replace export subsidies, but the effect would be the same. There is nothing in the Blair House Agreement [nor the final agreement] on compensatory subsidies to prevent the Community from doing this."[34]

Hence the fear is that the movement away from explicit export subsidies to compensatory payments in a variety of forms may imply little more than a shallow and convenient change of appearance. Such subsidies may in effect, if not in name, operate to promote Community exports at a lower than competitive price. As Watkins has observed, they may constitute *de facto* export subsidies.[35] This may pose a particularly serious threat to the capacity of the new regime to mitigate the worst excesses of the CAP on an international stage in that when Community support to the cereals sector is aggregated including such payments, total expenditure more than doubled from 1992 to 1994.[36] For farmers it is not the box into which the subsidy fits which is important but rather the overall level of subsidies payable, and ultimately it is for them, not the Community, to determine the use to which such subsidies will be put. For those "efficient"[37] Community farmers who currently produce at a unit cost which is lower than

---

[34] "EC Gains Time on Cereal Exports" *Agra Europe* 10 December 1993, P/1-P/2, at P/1.

[35] *Supra*, n 27.

[36] "Reform Increases Cereal Support Burden" *Agra Europe* 15 April, P/2-P/3 at P/1.

[37] "Efficient" in this sense does not of course account for the environmental costs associated with intensive production techniques employed in the Community. Environmental "dumping" is, however, a concept which, at present, has no place in international trade law.

the new support price, there is no reason to expect that "exempt" domestic support payments will not be employed to subsidise exports rather than to sustain profits at a level which ensures viability.

The flaws inherent in the GATT package are at once more visible and less contentious in the realm of market access. It is unlikely that the Agreement will lead to a significant reduction in the absolute level of protection enjoyed by Community producers in their home market. It would be surprising if it were otherwise, given the Commission's expectations of a rise in the consumption of domestic grain. This surely must imply the displacement of imported products, in particular oilseed meal and grain substitutes for animal feeds. The problem is not simply that the rate of tariff decline required is too low (36% over six years) and the starting point too high (1986–1988), but that a declining tariff equivalent will not increase the competitiveness of imported goods when such a decline is matched by an equivalent or greater decline in Community prices. Hence with the shrinking gap between Community and world market prices which flows from the Community's 1992 reforms, a substantially smaller tariff percentile will produce an equivalent level of price protection. The observation has been fairly made that:

"The tariffication and reduction of the "tariff equivalent" requirements can very easily be met through the changes already made by the EC Council, because the threshold price will have been reduced from 222 ECU/tonne to 155 ECU/tonne by 1996. An approximate calculation shows that by reducing the EC price for grain from 222 ECU/tonne to 155 ECU (1996) the EC is likely to have, on the basis of an average world price of 95 ECU/tonne, for example, reduced the necessary variable levy on imports from 127 ECU to 60 ECU, a reduction of 53 per cent."[38]

Indeed so relaxed was the Community during the final days of the negotiations over its ability to adequately protect Community farmers under the new tariff arrangements that it agreed to forgo some of the protection which the new tariff levels could afford, undertaking, in respect of wheat, rye, barley, maize and sorghum, ". . . to apply a duty at a level and in a manner so that the duty-paid import price . . . for cereals will be greater than [155% of] the effective intervention price . . .".[39] It is likely that the level of reduction applied by the Community in the cereals sector will be substantially more than the required 36% and that as a result proportionately smaller reductions (of at least 15%) in other product markets (*e.g.* sugar) will be introduced.

It should also be recalled in respect of market access that the safeguard clause contained in the Agreement on Agriculture affords the Community an additional degree of protection in the event of a substantial (more than 10%) decline in import prices, often the result of currency fluctuations.

---

[38] Gardner, *The GATT Uruguay Round: Implications for Exports from the Agricultural Superpowers* (1993), p 8.

[39] Tangermann, "The GATT and Community Preference for Cereals" *Agra Europe* 15 July 1994, E/8-E/10 at E/8.

To this extent even the predictability and transparency sought by the Agreement is to an extent undermined by what is effectively a reintroduction of the "variation" inherent in the Community's import levies.

The minimum access clause does little to offset these doubts. While minimum access of 3% is to be secured in 1995, rising to 5% of domestic consumption by the year 2000, this does not imply an absolute obligation but merely a commitment to encourage imports through the introduction of reduced tariff quotas of around one-third of the rate generally applicable in respect of the given quantitative limit. It is indeed "a strange use of the English language to refer to '*Minimum Access Commitments*', when there is no real obligation to ensure that the specified quantities are imported".[40]

Conclusion

It will have been observed that the premise which underlies this chapter is a critical one. Many in the Commission might well conclude that it is these very criticisms which show so clearly how eminently satisfactory from the Community's point of view the Uruguay Round finally turned out to be.

Furthermore, the new Agreement has been predominantly portrayed, at least in developed countries, as a move from GATT to GATTT – General Advantage to the Totality. The image is of an agreement from which everyone will benefit, and even the richer producers and exporters of primary produce have expressed approval for what they see as an improvement in the quantity of trade which they may anticipate. From a Commission perspective much was achieved and relatively little conceded. What then is the reason for the criticism of such an apparent triumph?

Essentially it arises from the recognition that the CAP (and similar US policies) have had, and may now be expected to have, implications for poor countries which must surely be unacceptable. This paper has argued that the CAP has operated to distort patterns of international trade and that such distortion can be expected to continue post-Uruguay. Distortion of trade however is a neutral phrase which does little to illuminate the profound hardship and loss of life quality for which the CAP has been responsible. Shrinking international and domestic markets, and falling agricultural prices, both staple and export, have undermined the viability of traditional agriculture in parts of the "third world" while rising developed country subsidies have ensured that even the most "efficient" third country producers can barely compete. Although such arguments have been alluded to only briefly they must surely be seen to raise issues which the Commission must address before declaring itself well

---

[40] "Unanswered Questions on GATT Implementation" *Agra Europe* 11 February 1994, E/8-E/10 at E/8-E/9.

satisfied with what has been achieved. Not only altruism demands such a conclusion. The effect upon the rich countries of both the environmental and human tragedies to which these policies necessarily lead are all too apparent while the model of agriculture upon which such policies are premised is neither environmentally nor financially sustainable.

JOANNE SCOTT[41]

---

[41] The author would like to thank Wade Mansell for his most helpful comments on a draft of this chapter.

Chapter 13
Balancing Trade Freedom with the Requirements of Sustainable Development

Introduction[1]

The integration of social, environmental, and economic concerns lies at the heart of the commitment to sustainable development to which the European Community, the Member States and many members of GATT are at least formally dedicated.[2] In purely legal terms the principle of sustainable development, while much talked about, defies precise definition and risks dismissal as a political aspiration rather than a legal concept. Nevertheless, inspirational provisions lie at the heart of many constitutional legal systems, motivating the interpretation of substantive and procedural rules and establishing general principles of law which have a substantial influence in practice. Integration forms the formal kingpin of the Community's sustainability strategy – the legal integration of the principles of free trade with those of environmental protection perhaps its most difficult task.[3] In the process of fulfilling the obligation to integrate it

[1] Martin Hession is a lawyer and senior research scientist at the Environmental Change Unit at Oxford University; Richard Macrory is IBM Director of the ECU and Professor of Environmental Law.

This article is derived from work undertaken for a research project funded by the European Commission (DG XII) entitled "Institutional Adjustment to Sustainable Development" co-ordinated by CSERGE at the University of East Anglia.

[2] While the fundamental task of the Community has always centred on free trade it has also always incorporated other social and political objectives. The question whether free trade is an objective in itself or the means of attaining a broader range of objectives is answered in Article 2, which makes clear that the market is a means to an end rather than an end in itself. Article 2 cwas amended to reflect the Community's interest in environment protection; "*Article 2* The Community shall have as its task by establishing a common market and an economic and monetary union and by implementing the common policies or activities, to promote throughout the Community a harmonious and balanced development of economic activities, sustainable and non-inflationary growth respecting the environment, a high degree of economic convergence of economic performance, a high level of employment and of social protection, the raising of the standard of living and quality of life, and economic an social cohesion and solidarity among the member states". The recently adopted WTO contains similar language: *Preamble to the WTO* "Recognising that their relations in the field of trade and economic endeavour should be conducted with a view to the raising of standards of living, ensuring full employment, and a large and steadily growing volume of real income and effective demand, and expanding the production and trade in goods and services, while allowing for the optimal use of the worlds' resource in accordance with the objective of sustainable development, seeking both to protect and preserve the environment and enhance the means of doing so".

[3] Art 130r(2) reinforced at Maastricht requires that environmental protection requirements be integrated in the definition and implementation of other policy. Integration has been adopt as a formal policy objective in the 5th Action Programme "Towards Sustainability" 1993.

will be demonstrated whether the interests of trade and the environment are ultimately reconcilable and by what institutional framework this may be achieved – if at all. The balance achieved at a community level displays some of the difficulties of integration adopted and implemented at a supranational level. Though reinforced by recent amendments to the Treaty, the process towards sustainability might be described as in its early stages, and there is already ample evidence in the eyes of some that the process cannot be completed while leaving protection afforded to both interests undiminished.

Historically, the Legal Order of the European Community has provided a framework within which provisions relating to the free market have been developed and applied in a manner unique between states.[4] Though in many instances the legal language is the same, the essential provisions of the Treaty relating to goods, services and capital go far beyond anything suggested by the Uruguay round of GATT. In particular the existence of an independent enforcement agency and the principles of superiority and direct effect of community law provide for a particular style and level of enforcement within the EC to which GATT may only distantly aspire. The recognition that individual provisions of the Treaty relating to free trade can have the effect of invalidating national law and that these provisions can be invoked even by individuals has had a profound effect on Member States, ability to regulate the national public interest in matters affecting trade.

Article 30 in particular has been broadly interpreted to invalidate measures which potentially indirectly hinder interstate trade – a test very little legislation appears to pass. Adopted by the Court in the interests of establishing an integrated market, this broad interpretation of Article 30 of the EC Treaty[5] has, in the absence of a formal division of powers between the Member States and the Community or an express bill of rights respecting individuals[6], lead to a commensurate expansion in recognised socially motivated justifications from the general prohibition. These justifications in the form of general principles and interests commonly recognised in the European legal system are interpreted by the European Court of Justice which therefore has a broad power to review national legislation adopted under them. In a similar manner, where the Community has regulated, the Court has allowed an extensive interpretation of the Treaty and Community tasks to justify Community legislation in

---

[4] See Petersmann "The EC And GATT on the Economic Functions of GATT Rules" 1984 Legal Issues of European Integration 37 who characterises the Community and GATT as incorporating the liberal market idea in legal constitutional form (see also Petersmann n25 below). But see Staker "Free Movement of Goods in the EEC and Australia: A Comparative Study" 1990 YBEL 10 on Art 92 of the Australian Constitution for a description of a similar federal provision guaranteeing free trade.

[5] Prohibiting quantitative restrictions and measures having equivalent effect which have been interpreted in the light of the objective of attaining a single market see note *infra*.

[6] 291/69 *Stauder* v *Ulm* 1969 ECR 419, 11/70 *International Handelsgesellschaft* 1970 ECR 1125, 4/73 *Nold II* 1974 ECR 491, 44/79 *Liselotte Hauer* v *Rheinlandpfalz* 1979 ECR 3752–3765.

respect of these concerns. In both cases the principles of legality and certainty have been undermined.

Essential competences relating to the harmonisation of domestic stand-ards and the Common Commercial Policy, both ostensibly directed at the establishment of a single market within the Community, have always neces-sarily encompassed other considerations for which trade is commonly regulated. But, ever broader interpretation of the legal bases for market action is, ultimately, an unsatisfactory legal foundation for Community measures which have had only a tenuous connection to the objectives. Even so, the express recognition provided by recent Treaty amendments of separate bases defined according to independent objectives demon-strates the limitations of a system of separate legal bases operated accord-ing to a teleological approach, where legitimate objectives and measures adopted to satisfy them increasingly overlap. Resulting tensions within the definition of each basis are reinforced both by the division between broadly unitary trade policy and concurrent policies representing other aspects of the public interest and the proliferation of legislative pro-cedures required for their adoption.

At an international level the increased interrelationship between trade and other issues has caused the Court of Justice to hesitate between an inclusive interpretation of Article 113 and the recognition of competence in the Member States.[7] Similarly within the Community while the concept of the market effect was used to justify particular environmental measures under Articles 100 and 235 in the absence of an alternative specific com-petence, the adoption of a separate legal basis (Article 130r-t), for the environment has outlined a conflict between the interests of competitive equality and market unity and the legally reinforced recognition of a decentralised pursuit of environmental protection.

Developing a Community framework

To date an holistic approach to the Treaty and judicial testing of legislative discretion according to developed principles of non-discrimination, neces-sity and proportionality[8] as well as the objective factors for review of legal bases have formed the geography of the Trade and Environment Division in Community law. The place and influence of the newer principles of

---

[7] Most recently the balance has come down in favour of a less monolithic Common Commer-cial policy than some have argued for, Opinion 1/94 *Re the Uruguay Round Treaties Commission* v *Council* 1995 Common Market Law Reports 205. For critique see Bourgeois "The EC in the WTO and Advisory Opinion 1/94: An Echternach Procession" (1995) 32 No 3 CMLRev 736–787.

[8] 138/79 *Isoglucose* 1980 ECR 333, 113/76 Skimmed Milk, Benuhle 1977 ECR 1211 and *Buitoni* 1979 ECR 677–686 for examples in practice. Generally De Búrca "The principle of Propor-tionality and its application in EC Law 1993 YEL 105".

integration and subsidiarity in the review of action pursued in the general interest remain to be determined according to a defined framework of Community constitutional law itself as yet in its early stages.[9]

The following is suggested as a possible framework within which the principles of free trade and environment might be reconciled or integrated at Community level. While nowhere defined in the Treaty, a broad outline can be gauged in the application of particular community rules.

Statements of pre-emptive norms

These are Treaty provisions and General Principles of Law given highest value by the Court, of a binding character invocable against and by the Community institutions, or the Member States, but also in some circumstances are also invocable by and against individuals (in that sense giving rise to what might be termed personal constitutional rights). Article 30 of the Treaty guaranteeing free trade, and fundamental rights recognised as general principles of law fall into this category.[10]

A duty to act or to respect particular interests

An obligation on the part of the Community to act in favour of a particular interest. Such a statement is suggestive of a pre-emptive norm, but may perhaps be distinguishable in that it is invocable only by the Community institutions and the Member States between each other. Such obligations may be found in many of the early Treaty articles establishing the common external tariff and the common market and have formed the basis for the courts' jurisprudence on exclusivity.[11] A duty on the Community to respect a particular interest forms a limitation on the exercise of power in judicial review but may not amount to the grant of a right. The integration requirement may fall into this category.[12] And perhaps even the duty to

---

[9] For the constitutional character of the Community Parti Ecologiste "*Les Verts* v *European Parliament*" 1986 ECR 1339, and see generally Lenearts "Fundamental Rights to be Included in a Community Catalogue" 1991 European Law Review 367.

[10] Confirmed in ADBHU 1985 ECR 531 at 549 See also Quinn and MacGowan "Could Article 30 Impose obligations on individuals" 12 ELR 163. It should be remembered that whereas the right to trade across frontiers recognised in ABHU applies to Community and national legislation alike, the court recognises the application of other "human" rights to Community provisions only (see John Temple Lang "The Sphere in which Member States are obliged to comply with General principles of Law and Community Fundamental Rights Principles" 1991/1 Legal Issues of European Integration 23.

[11] In particular duties to adopt particular measures by particular dates appear to have this effect see particularly *Commission* v *United Kingdom* 1980 ECR 1045.

[12] It appears that whether by sympathetic interpretation or by formal recognition of the duty to integrate contained in Article 130r(2) the proximity principle has been allowed to modify the application of a Community law rule (derogations to Article 30) in the Wallonia Waste Case 2/90 *Commission* v *Belgium* [1993] CMLR 365 (see below).

fulfil elements of the general action plan in Article 130s(3) falls into this category.[13]

General principles of law

General duties operate in the sphere of Community discretion. These principles are binding but operate in respect of the application of other interests and norms: their effect is therefore dependent on the operation of a norm or interest: Article 5 Duty of Solidarity[14], Article 7 Non-discrimination or Equality are examples.[15] Necessity, Proportionality and Subsidiarity (Article 3b) and perhaps at least some of the Principles of Environmental Action detailed in Article 130r(2), in particular proximity (see below) are similar principles though perhaps lower-order principles regulating the application of pre-emptive norms, duties and basic principles on recognised interests.[16]

Statement of Community interest

The Community's interest in a particular objective authorising the adoption of particular measures pursuant to the appropriate legal basis and forming the legal boundaries of a Community power: (Article 130r (Environment), Article 43 (Agriculture)). These interests justify an intrusion upon pre-emptive norms subject to the basic principles of non-discrimination, necessity and proportionality.[17]

Statement of Member States' interest

The Treaty also recognises Member States' interests which also justify limited exceptions to the pre-emptive norms of Community law subject to the principles of necessity, proportionality and equality: (Article 36, and the Mandatory requirements Cassis di Dijon).[18]

---

[13] Hession and Macrory "Legal Issues of a New Environment Policy" Chap 10 O'Keeffe and Twomey (eds) in *Legal Issues of the Maastricht Treaty* (Wiley 1994) 163–164.

[14] Giving rise to ERTA implied powers and pre-emption which derives ultimately from Art 5 but gives rise to other duties *Fisheries Commission* v *UK* 1980 ECR 1045 and *Opinion ILO Convention No 170* [1993] Common Market Law Reports 800 and Opinion 1/94 Uruguay Round Agreements 1995 CMLR 205.

[15] See discussion on non-discrimination below and for relevance of environmental principles on Wallonia Waste Case (n 12 *supra*) also below.

[16] Wallonia supra n 12.

[17] The existence of such an interest is a matter of interpretation and not limited to express policy statements, as the ADBHU case (*supra* n 10) concerning the environment demonstrated prior to the adoption of an express legal basis.

[18] While the Member States may be said to retain all powers not ceded to the Community the interpretation of the extent of Community power is difficult. Art 36 is one of the few places in the Treaty where state interests are indirectly recognised and listed. Until the formal identification of concurrent policies permanently preserving state rights to legislate under the subsidiarity principle (Art 3b) and more stringent measures powers provisions (Art 130t) these "police powers" remained subject to the possibility of permanent and absolute harmonisation in so far as this was possible through Art 100.

Statements of interpretative value

Principles which are suggestive but have no autonomous effect (but none-theless are likely to have some interpretative value in a legal framework): Subsidiarity may fall into this category.

Pre-emptive trade norms and the environmental interest

A fundamental assumption is made as to the effects of trade and environ-ment provisions, the reasons for which are rooted in politics and the nature of the interests themselves. Whereas Article 30 of the Treaty pres-ents a pre-emptive and directly effective provision establishing an area of individual protection equivalent to that of an individual right, Environ-mental Protection Provisions are defined as legislative interests in lan-guage which denies the possibility of such effects.[19] The traditional justification for this lies with the difficulty in determining the limits and standard of protection required by the latter. And yet the limits of what represents the common market are no more certain than those of environ-ment. Both definitions incorporate questions of scale and degree linked to social and political choices. Indeed the Community definition of the mar-ket (single, common and internal) is uncertain and finds an unsteady application in the substantive rules governing its establishment.[20] None-theless the current broad hierarchy of principles reflect a legal presump-tion in favour of trade freedom and economic growth over scientific uncertainty as to the environmental consequences of these choices. This presumption lies at the heart of a liberal economic and social order based on competition and risk.

One element of the distinction is traditional in that trade freedom reflects a classical individual right, falling within traditional notions of property, capable of objective legal protection to the holder of such

---

[19] The Constitutions of Portugal and Greece recognise a right which while not self-executory for these reasons has a certain legal/discretionary value in review. The Court's recognition of a constitutional right to be found in national constitutions would be one alternative approach to founding an environmental norm at Community level.

[20] The single market is implemented or enforced through several substantive rules. Arts 85 and 86 on Competition (Fair and Perfect Competition between undertakings); Art 12 (prohibiting the introduction of new duties on imports and charges of equivalent effect while further articles provide for the abolition of existing standards now achieved (Art 16); the central Art 30 prohibit-ing quantitative restrictions on imports and measures having equivalent effect interpreted to establish the principle of mutual recognition of product-related standards throughout the Com-munity. This mutual recognition principle is applied to a lesser but increasing extent in other areas notably Arts 52–62: Services prohibition on the introduction of new Arts 71 and 73b Capital (weaker provisions), Art 48: Free Movement of Workers (standstill plus): Arts 52–53: (standstill plus) Right of Establishment, (standstill plus) and Art 72 on Transport.

rights.[21] As a result, Free Movement of Goods in particular[22] has been interpreted to include a sufficiently substantive set of criteria to provide an adequate standard for the judicial review of Community and Member State legislation.[23] This character – one of individual right – derives from the special nature of the Community Treaty which acts increasingly as a constitutional charter. Member States are policed not only by themselves but by the Commission under Article 169 and by individuals in accordance with the doctrine of direct effect.[24] The Community itself is policed under the provisions of Article 173 by the Member States and its own institutions and individuals insofar as a Community decision is of "direct and individual concern".[25]

In contrast, environmental protection rather than embodying a freedom more commonly implies a restriction on individual activity mediated through the legislative activities of a state which is either duty bound to protect the environment or is recognised to have a discretionary interest in doing so.[26] As such a right to the environment is not easily associated with an individual for enforcement save in so far as some element of the environment amounts to an asset falling within traditional notions of private property or another more traditional right and is protected in this way.

One suggested method of achieving an individualisation of rights and responsibility over the environment is the internalisation or monetisation

---

[21] Rene Barents "The Community and the Unity of the Common Market: Some Reflections on the Economic Constitution of the Community" 33 (Dunker and Hamblot, 1990) German Yearbook of International Law 9–36.

[22] Art 8a provides that the internal market is based on four freedoms: Free movement of Goods, Workers, Services and Capital which are elaborated in individual provisions of several articles of the Treaty: Arts 12, 30, 59 etc.

[23] Nonetheless the concept of a "common market" is nowhere defined though it is mentioned in several provisions: Arts 9–102 assist in its definition through detailing aspects of public and private activity which is incompatible with the establishment and functioning of the market though these provisions. The Court has attempted to define the essential character of the market in several cases; 270/80 *Polydor* v *Harlequin* 1982 ECR 329 "The Treaty seeks to create a single market reproducing as closely as possible the conditions of a domestic market" and 15/81 *Schul* 1982 ECR 1409 "the elimination of all obstacles to intra-Community trade in order to merge the national markets to those of a genuine internal market". These cases themselves contain some margin for interpretation – see *supra* n 21 at p 10.

[24] Arts 12 (Customs Duties and Charges having equivalent effect) 26/62 *Van Gend en Loos* 1963 ECR 1 and Art 30 (Quantitative Restrictions and measures having equivalent effect) are directly effective: 13/68 [1968] *Salgoil* ECR 453. 74/76 *Ianelli* 1977 ECR 557 and *Pigs Marketing Board* v *Redmond* 1978 ECR 2347.

[25] As to the desirability of a trade norm and individual access to it see Petersmann "Limited Government and Unlimited Trade Powers. Why Effective Judicial Review of Foreign Trade Restrictions Depends on Individual Rights" in Hilf and Petersmann *National Constitutions and International Economic Law* (Kluwer 1993).

[26] The extension of the state's interest in the environment to include precautionary as well as preventive or protective measures implies an extension of public power without an appropriate mechanism for rational review of such policies against objectively determinable facts or reasons (see discussion on precaution and proportionality below). See McGarity *Reinventing Rationality The Role of Regulatory Analysis in the Federal Bureaucracy* (Cambridge University Press 1991) for a US discussion of the problem, (particularly Chap 9). This difficulty has led to warnings of a danger of an authoritarian ecological state see Michael Kloepfer "An Authoritarian Ecological State?" 1994 EELR 112.

of environmental costs.[27] Even if distribution of rights according to a market were desirable and could negate all the disadvantages of a more inflexible approach through central regulation it must be doubted whether all environmental problems can be given a value. Reference to such an approach demonstrates nonetheless that the extent to which a market incorporates environmental assets and liabilities may vary in different Member States and this is one way the application of trade rules to environmental problems is delimited.[28]

The central objection to the recognition of an environmental right remains the absence of an objective standard of protection and the judgement than any standard must be set through the legislative rather than the judicial method. The Treaty of Rome has endorsed though not defined a high level of protection but "normativity" of this statement is doubted or at least limited.[29] The objection is not consistently applied however as while it is used to deny the possibility of a norm against which legislation may be measured in terms of its environmental component, judicial testing of measures against an objectively determinable standard of protection has been suggested where it has been alleged it is trade restrictive. Inherent scientific uncertainty as to the effects of particular actions operating through a complex system of possible processes, interactions and cumulative effects makes an excessive reliance on science to determine an objective assessment of risk or harm of human activity.[30] This is not to deny that the conditions for a trade restriction nor indeed a test insuring protection is not judicially determinable even in conditions of uncertainty, but merely to state that science on its own cannot be relied upon to establish an objective standard against which particular measures may be judged in all cases.

In addition the philosophy of both interests is different. Whereas the single market is a human construction and of its nature requires a certain unity of conditions, the environment is not, and must be regulated according to a hierarchy of provision with regard to the global, regional and local levels according to different conditions and circumstances.[31] In contrast

---

[27] Nonetheless in conditions of uncertainty environmental risks themselves unquantifiable are still less capable of market valuation. The process of cost benefit analysis of environmental messages displays some of the problems of such an apples and oranges approach (McGarrity).

[28] *Vide* discussion whether waste is a good in *Wallonia*. The issues of patenting living organisms in the area of biotechnology and discussions on civil liability for environmental harm also come to mind.

[29] Lenaerts "Fundamental Rights to be Included in a Community Catalogue" 1991 European Law Review 367.

[30] John Stonehouse "Science Risk Analysis and Environmental Decisions" UNEP Trade and the Environment Series No 5. ISSN 1020–1610.

[31] A rather crude attempt to define what is appropriate can be made with reference to physical or trans-boundary nature of particular environmental problems:
Global Environmental Problems: Climate, Stratospheric Ozone, Highly Migratory Species, the High Seas.
Regional Environmental Problems: More limited trans-boundary problems, Sulphur Dioxide, NOX, migratory species, Rivers, Regional Seas.
Local Environmental Problems: Suspended Particulates, Waste Disposal, other localised pollution.

Non-discrimination and universally applicable uniform standards are the foundation of Community trade policy, while Subsidiarity[32] and Minimum Standards[33] provision reinforce the non-unitary nature of the environment policy.

Different physical and social conditions logically suggest local regulation. Hence restrictions on trade in environmentally hazardous material are justifiable to protect the local environment (though perhaps invidious to the market). Regulation in the interest of the environment, at a Community level must be justified as being more effective than that at local level suggesting some trans-boundary element. This is supported by criterion of effectiveness – the use of national trade instruments to protect the local environment from external sources of pollution is indirect enforcement of local standards at the best of times. It is also apparently unjustified on environmental grounds given that the definition of environmental interest seems to be restricted to state boundaries.[34] Regulation to achieve conditions of competitive equality or the application of Article 30 to achieve this have no such limitation however and the consequent harmonisation need not reflect local conditions allowing an equalisation of standards.[35]

Article 30 and the extent of the free market in goods[36]

The Common Market created by the European Community is far more ambitious than anything attempted in the GATT Agreements. The substantive elements of the market defined by the Treaty are a free trade area

---

[32] Community action is permissible only if *and* only in so far as the objectives of the proposed action cannot be sufficiently achieved by the Member States and can therefore by reason of the scale and effects of the proposed action be better achieved by the Community (Art 3b).

[33] Art 130t authorising the introduction of more stringent protective measures *compatible with the treaty* and Art 100a(4) authorising the *maintenance* of more stringent environmental protective measure in limited circumstances.

[34] The argument whether an interest in environmental protection justifies unilateral regulation of trade in respect of the external environment (process standards) for Member States or the Community remains untested. *Dassonville* Case 1974 ECR 837 at 840 suggests that Art 36 justifies measures for the protection a state's own interests and not for the protection of interests of other states. The *Scottish Grouse* Case (169/89 *Goumeterrie van den burg* 1990 ECR. 2143) suggests a similar analysis. See also Krämer "Environmental Protection and Article 30 of EEC Treaty" 30 Common Market Law Review 1990 111–143 at 119–120 for a contrary view.

[35] For discussion of unilateral trade restrictions at an international level see Schoenbaum "Trade Sanctions Domestic, Enforcement of Agreement, Anti-Competitive Factors", AJIL Vol. 86 1992 701. Principle 12 of Rio Declaration, differentiates between direct and indirect regulation.

[36] A subject on which much has been written: see *supra* n 21; Wils "The Search for a Rule in Article 30, Much Ado about Nothing" Vol. 18 No. 6 ELR 475; J Steiner "Drawing the Line: Uses and Abuses of Article 30 EEC" 1992 (29) Common Market Law Review p 754; Mortelmans "Article 30 of EEC Treaty and Legislation Relating to Market Circumstances; Time to Consider a New Definition" 28 Common Market Law Review; White "In Search of the Limits of Article 30 of the EEC Treaty" 26 Common Market Law Review 235–280.

established in accordance with Articles 12–17 which provide that all customs duties and charges of equivalent effect be progressively abolished between the Member States and a customs union established under Articles 18–28a providing for a common tariff to apply with respect to third states. Much of the effective bite of the internal market in goods has been established by Article 30 which provides that quantitative restrictions and measures having equivalent effect are prohibited.[37] The Treaty as amended provides that the Community may adopt measures to harmonise provisions which directly affect the establishment or functioning of the Common Market,[38] or measures which have as their object or effect the establishment of the internal market[39] – the latter defined as an area without internal frontiers in which free movement of goods, persons, services and capital is ensured.[40] Both the concept of Common Market and Internal Market are difficult to define further. Even so, on the basis of these provisions and particularly Article 30 the Court has confirmed that "the principle of Free Movement of Goods and Freedom of Competition, together with freedom of trade as a fundamental right are general principles of law of which the Court ensures observance" [ADBHU *supra* n 10]. These fundamental principles define a pre-emptive norm of free trade applicable to the Community[41] and the Member States alike, and are invocable as individual rights in the national legal systems, rendering contrary measures inapplicable.[42]

Defining the extent of this putative human right has proved fraught and while it is clear that the prohibition incorporates elements of non-discrimination and distortion of intra-community trade the latter element in particular has caused some difficulty in application leaving the law in a state of confusion.[43]

---

[37] One of the shorter treaty articles: Art 30: Quantitative Restrictions on Imports and on all measures having equivalent effect shall without prejudice to the following provisions be prohibited between the Member States.

[38] The formula of Art 100.

[39] The formula of Art 100a.

[40] Art 7a.

[41] 80 & 81/77 *Societe les Reunis Sarl et al v Receveur des Dounes* 1978 ECR 927 at 946–947 (provision authorising charge having equivalent effect to custom duty in Art 31(2) of Reg. 816/70)and 61/86 *United Kingdom v Commission* 1988 ECR i 37/83 *Rewe Zentral* 1984 ECR 1229 and 15/83 *Denkavit* 1984 ECR 2171 (disparities ruled justifiable or inevitable).

[42] *Salgoil* 13/68 ELR. 453, *Ianelli v Mer* 74/76 1977 ECR 557, *Pigs Marketing Board v Redmond* 1978 ECR 2347 (direct effect of Art 30).

[43] To quote Advocate General Jacobs "The European Court of Justice: Some Thoughts on its Past and its Future" in The European Advocate Winter 1994–95 (Bar European Group UK) ISSN 1351–4172.

(1) Non-discrimination or equality[44]

The presence or absence of discrimination cannot be established in the absence of other substantive criteria applicable in one situation and not in another in which it is claimed there is discrimination. Here we are concerned with a general freedom to trade across frontiers attaching to goods. Equality of treatment, according to an Aristotelian conception requires consistency in some circumstances and differentiation in others.[45] Discrimination therefore consists in treating either similar situations differently or different situations identically.[46] The basic requirement in Community law is that there be no discrimination on grounds of origin.[47] This requirement is essentially a negative and rather limited requirement which states grounds which are insufficient to justify different treatment but fails to address justifiable grounds upon which products may be differentiated.

The distinction between similar and dissimilar situations can be presented in two ways.

The first involves searching for a physical difference inherent in the object of the freedom (in the case of goods a like products approach). The second alternative involves searching for an objective justification for the distinction made between products (which may be broader than differences in the physical nature of the goods themselves).[48] It is suggested that elements of the general interests recognised by Community law are grounds which justify distinction and render it non-discriminatory.[49] The second alternative allows a greater range of distinguishing features than the former including distinctions justified according to environmental

---

[44] Art 6 "Within the scope of application of this Treaty . . . any discrimination on grounds of nationality shall be prohibited" – Non-discrimination is a general principle not limited to free movement of goods but can mean different things in different places (see standstill prohibition on discriminatory treatment under the transport title Case 195/90 *Commission* v *Germany* and the case confirms that pre-existing inequality forms no justification for the adoption of more discriminatory measures with respect to charges for heavy goods vehicles).

[45] Nicomedean Ethics Aristotle.

[46] (Art 36, 13/63 ECR *Italy* v *Commission* 1963 ECR 165 "The different treatment of non-comparable situations does not lead automatically to the conclusion that there is discrimination. An appearance of discrimination in form may therefore in fact correspond to an absence of discrimination in substance. Discrimination in substance would consist in treating either similar situations differently or different situations identically".

[47] Art 6 above and the final sentence of Art 36 "such prohibitions shall not constitute a means of arbitrary discrimination . . .".

[48] In this sense discrimination is not "arbitrary discrimination" (final sentence para 36) and see 13/63 *Italy* v *EEC Commission* ECR 165.

[49] See *Servinde* 1984 ECR 4209 para 28: difference in treatment is objectively justified inter alia in the light of particular provisions of Community law. The question whether the process by which a good is produced is a valid ground for distinction is obviously related to the question whether the decision to restrict access of goods on this ground is justifiable on criteria of effectiveness (it is necessarily indirect regulation after the event). If discrimination were the only criteria upon which a measure might be found trade restrictive the question whether Art 36 applies with respect to the external environment becomes irrelevant. As this is patently not the case the legitimacy of a process standard must be related to on this question. See n 34 *supra*.

effects of production as well as those inherent in the goods themselves or indeed the objective general principles of environmental policy.[50]

In addition the Court recognises that there may be natural advantages and disadvantages which do not amount to discrimination and are allowed to lie where they fall. These might be said to form the basis of the comparative advantage the internal market is intended to exploit.[51]

Distortion or restriction of intra-Community trade

National treatment of imported goods-regulated by a provision on non-discrimination may still have the effect of partitioning the Single Market as goods marketable in one state may not be marketable in another state because of different applicable standards. It is clear that what is prohibited by Article 30 goes beyond simply discriminatory measures as the limited exceptions to the rule provided for are still stated to be the subject of a requirement of non-discrimination. It is equally clear that Article 30 could not have been envisaged to invalidate all measures adversely affecting the operation of the market as the Treaty affords a legal basis for the harmonisation of national measures which do so.

The central problem is determining what is restrictive of *intra-community trade* without some even indirect discriminatory element. Indistinctly applicable measures may have discriminatory effects when applied to products from different countries.[52] Here the question becomes one of assessing the probity of the distinction adopted: essentially whether the justification provided is objectively justified when compared with its discriminatory effects.[53]

The Court in the Dassonville Case has drawn a very wide circle about Article 30 ruling that "all trading rules which are capable of hindering directly or indirectly, actually or potentially, intra-Community trade must be considered measures having an effect equivalent to quantitative restrictions". Such measures may even include measures which show no discrimination on their face and even measures which do not have a heavier

---

[50] Such as precaution; prevention at source and polluter pays. See *Wallonia Waste* Case *infra*. The discrimination must necessarily be proportionate to the legitimate differences recognised by the Treaty – which in the case of environment can be difficult to assess and enforce. The principle that damage ought as a priority be prevented at source for instance might work both ways, to encourage process standards dealing with pollution arising at source, or to preclude them, if use of such indirect sanctions rather than direct regulation of the source were considered to breach the principle.

[51] The burdens of natural differences such as physical location and transport costs are allowed to rest where they lie (Case 52/79 *Procureur du roi* v *Marc JVC Debarre & Others* 1980 ECR 833) and Case 63–69/72 *Wilhelm Werhahn Hansmulne & Oth* v *Council* 1973 ECR 1229). Art 130r(3) itself seems to confirm this as a general principle in environmental legislation requiring that differences in physical factors be taken into account in Community legislation.

[52] Amount to "disguised restrictions on trade" (final sentence of Art 36).

[53] In this way the question whether indistinctly applicable measures are trade retraction and whether they may be justified are intimately interlinked, though the Treaty itself requires these questions are treated separately (Arts 30 and 36).

impact on foreign goods per se.[54] In essence indistinctly applicable measures which have a general restrictive effect on trade are technically within the ambit of Article 30. For a time it appeared that there were few areas of market regulation where Article 30 would not apply.[55]

It has been suggested that there has been an attempt by the Court to make the trade rules applicable to states coextensive with those applicable to undertakings under the competition policy.[56] The result has been that the broad *Dassonville* definition "of measures having equivalent effect" means that Article 30 operates as a quasi-presumption against rules regulating trade rather than a substantive rule invalidating measures restrictive of intra-community trade.[57] In the absence of a clear standard of competition and trade freedom applicable to trade in a single market[58] the formula is ultimately unsatisfactory.

This test is therefore very broad indeed as the *Cassis di Dijon* Case confirmed. Here the Court found that any product legally marketable in the country of origin (and by analogy in free circulation within the Community) must be admitted to the national market in the absence of justification provided for by the Treaty. The presumption becomes one that products legally on the market in one Member State must be admitted without restriction to the domestic market.[59]

Under this test it is difficult to overcome the presumption that any legislation with only a potential and indirect effect on trade is not prohibited. Measures found to fall within the prohibition have included such diverse regulation as limits on production[60], checks and inspections on goods[61], packaging requirements[62], national goods buy-only policies[63] or even restriction on video rentals.[64]

In recent years the full consequences of *Dassonville* and *Cassis de Dijon* has lead the Court into difficulties and the Court has found certain restrictions (on working hours or sales outlets for spirits and limitations on

---

[54] Interestingly a recurring argument is that not all measures impinging on trade may be considered restrictive the Advocate General even suggested that veterinary inspection in the general Community interest assisted rather than interfered with trade 46/76 *Bauhuis* 1977 ECR 5 Opinion of Advocate General para 7.

[55] This is particularly important in environmental terms as regulation of use and disposal of goods even if indistinctly applicable and factually non-discriminatory are still plainly capable of causing an indirect trade restriction – as *Danish Bottles* demonstrates.

[56] See this consequence made explicit *Cassis di Dijon Rewe-Zentrale AG v Bundesmonopoloverwaltung fur Branntwein* 1979 ECR 649.

[57] Kapteyn and van Themaat *Introduction to the Law of the European Community*, 2nd ed (Kluwer, 1992) p 380–381.

[58] See three connotations in Kapteyn and van Themaat p356.

[59] *Cassis di Dijon: Rewe-Zentrale AG v Bundesmonopoloverwaltung fur Branntwein* 1979 ECR 649.

[60] Quotas on milling wheat 190/73 *Van Haaster* [1974] ECR 1123.

[61] 251/78 *Denkavit* [1979] ECR 3369.

[62] *Prantl* [1984] ECR 1299 *Rau* v *Smedt* 1982 ECR 3901.

[63] 249/81 *Commission* v *Ireland* [1982] ECR 4005.

[64] Ban on release within one year to protect Cinema viewing *Cinetheque* v *FNCF* 1985 ECR 2605.

Sunday trading[65] etc) to fall outside the scope of Article 30. The ground upon which certain indistinctly applicable measures have been found to fall outside the prohibition remain confused despite an attempt to clarify the Court's policy in the recent *Keck and Mithouard* Case.[66] Here the Court expressly recognised that its policy of regulating all potentially restrictive legislation through granting exceptions has its limits and that there are indeed areas of legislative policy the effect of which on intra-Community trade is not sufficient to bring them within the ambit of Article 30.[67]

The recognition of general interests of the Community and the Member States

A narrow interpretation of Article 30 which is applicable to the Community and the Member States alike would create a Single Market based on competition of regulatory orders in which Member States wishing to preserve higher standards would be in the position of having to pay for them through a commensurate loss in comparative advantage.[68] Alternatively a broad interpretation brings into question the need for a legislative basis for harmonisation of standards where Article 30 appears to achieve a dismantling of trade barriers in the absence of formal harmonisation. The former has the disadvantage of leading to a downward pressure on standards in a race to match the lowest common denominator as to cost, and the latter to a great deal of legal uncertainty.

The broad interpretation favoured in the *Cassis* formula has enabled the review of national regulation of markets and ultimately derives from the Court's dissatisfaction with the pace of harmonisation through legislation. Judicial harmonisation of national standards is effected through the application of Community principles through an extended list of justifications-mandatory requirements. *Keck and Mithouard* notwithstanding, the basic formula of broad prohibition and regulated exception continues. The process initiated by *Dassonville* by which a greater number of trading rules have been caught by an extensive definition of the pre-emptive norm

---

[65] 155/80 *Oebel* 1981 ECR 3147 and 75/81 *Blesgen* 1982 ECR 11211, 69/93 and C-258/93. *Punto Cas Spa.* ECR. 1994.C-23/89 *Quietlynn* v *Southend Borough Council* [1990] ECR 3059.

[66] C-267 And C-268/91 *Keck And Mithouard* [1993] ECR I-6097, para 16 and 17 in particular. Comment Roth 31 (1995) Common Market Law Review 845.

[67] See also Chalmers "Repackaging the Internal Market – Ramifications of the *Keck* Judgment" 19 (1994) European Law Review 385. This is again important in environmetal terms as common use restrictions based on planning or licensing of activities are just the sort of measures the *Keck* Case appears to exempt from the full rigours of the *Dassonville* formula. Measures restricting traffic or the local use of non-biodegradable materials appear to have escaped application of the principle in two cases: *R* v *London Boroughs Transport Committee ex. P. Freight Association Ltd* 63 CMLR p 5 and *Enichem Base spa and others* v *Comune di Cinisello Balsamo* 989 ECR 2491.

[68] Norbert Reich "Competition between Legal Orders a New Paradigm for Community Law" 29 (1992) Common Market Law Review 861–896.

but have been saved by an ever-growing legion of mandatory requirements may be criticised if only because legal certainty has been compromised.

The Community interests: objectives in the general interest

In the *ADBHU* Case[69] the Court confirmed that Article 30 is generally binding on the Community as well as the Member States, but recognised that the Community may adopt measures in pursuit of objects in the general interest which include environment protection: "the principle of freedom of trade is subject to certain limits justified by the objectives of general interest pursued by the Community provided the rights in question are not substantially impaired". Here certain provisions of a Community Directive derogating from absolute free movement with respect to waste oil were confirmed by the Court.[70] Judicial review of Community legislation is difficult to effect and the Community has a broad discretion to regulate trade in accordance with the provisions of the legal powers it is granted in pursuit of Community objectives.[71] Nonetheless restrictions on trade adopted by the Community are clearly subject to the requirement that they be non-discriminatory and that they are necessary and proportionate to the end in view, as well as a general obligation not to infringe individual human rights.[72] The discretion afforded to the Community is clearly broad: the Court in ADBHU stated that Community measures were reviewable only if they were manifestly inappropriate having regard to the objective being pursued.[73]

The Member States' interests: Article 36 and mandatory requirements

Similarly Member State restrictions can be justified according to a list of interests exhaustively listed in Article 36.[74] The extension of Article 30

---

[69] *ADBHU* 1985 ECR 531 at 549.

[70] 75/439 Directive on Waste Oils see p 549 of the *ADBHU* judgment.

[71] *Supra* n 21.

[72] This is confirmed by Art 3b of the Treaty "Any action by the Community shall not go beyond what is necessary to achieve the objectives of this Treaty".

[73] 331/88 *The Queen* v *Ministry of Agriculture ex. P. FEDESA & Others* 1990 ECR 4032.

[74] Art 36 "The provisions of Arts 30–34 shall not preclude prohibitions or restrictions on imports, exports or goods in transit justified on grounds of public morality, public policy or public security: the protection of health and the life of humans, animals or plants; the protection of national treasures possessing artistic, historic or archaeological value; or the protection of industrial or commercial property. *Such prohibitions shall not however constitute a means of arbitrary discrimination or a disguised restriction on trade between Member States.*"

implied in *Dassonville* lead the Court to establish a further non-exhaustive list of mandatory requirements which might also justify unilateral action.[75] The *Danish Bottles Case*[76] has confirmed that the protection of the environment is a mandatory requirement. It is clear that measures taken in pursuit of Article 36 or the mandatory requirements may not be discriminatory.[77] Nonetheless in certain circumstances different treatment of imported products may be justified according to objective criteria provided equivalent measures are taken with respect to domestically produced products.[78]

In contrast with the position internally, in the external sphere the right of Member States to take independent protective action is uncertain. The Treaty appears to provide that the Member States are at once required not to agree external trade measures outside the Community framework, but may introduce independent trade restrictions in respect of internal trade. In practice power is delegated to the states acting as trustees of the Community interest; Regulation 288/82[79] provides that Member States may introduce restrictions on grounds similar to those listed in Article 36 but nonetheless there is some uncertainty as to whether this includes environment protection.[80]

Community harmonisation retains as a purpose the harmonisation of national standards justified by Article 36 and mandatory requirements at a Community level, and once this legislation has been adopted it appears to restrict or extinguish recourse to Article 36 in so far as it is exhaustive.[81] The adoption of general provisions authorising the retention or adoption of more stringent measures apparently precludes this restriction in

---

[75] In *Cassis di Dijon supra* n 59. But, the interests listed are justifications not reserved powers and are therefore amenable to review by the Court 35/76 *Simmenthal* 1976 ECR 1871.

[76] 302/86 *Commission* v *Denmark* 1986 ECR 4607.

[77] Second sentence of Art 36 and for example *Gilli and Andres* 1980 ECR 2071 confirms the same limitation on action taken in pursuance of a mandatory requirement; "it is only where rules which apply without discrimination to both domestic and imported products may be justified as necessary in order to satisfy imperative requirements that they may constitute an exception to the requirements arising under Article 30".

[78] 4/75 *Rewe Zentralfinanz-LandwirtschaftsKammer* 1975 ECR 843 "different treatment of imported and domestic products based on the need to prevent the spread of harmful organisms could not be regarded as arbitrary discrimination if effective measures are taken in order to prevent the distribution of contaminated domestic products and if there is reason to believe in particular on the basis of previous experience that there is a risk of the harmful organism spreading if no inspection is held on importation".

[79] See the replacement of national with Community quotas see Kapteyn and van Themaat at p803 *supra* n 57. Regulations 288/82, 1765/82 and 2603/69 include national safeguard clauses similar to Art 36.

[80] Demeret, "Environmental Policy and Commercial Policy: The Emergence of Trade Related Environmental Measures (TREMS) in the External Relations of the European Community" in Maresceu (ed) *The European Community's Commercial Policy After 1992: The Legal Dimension* (Martinus Nijhoff, 1993) 315–319 at p346–347.

[81] 29/87 *Denkavit* v *Danish Minister for Agriculture* [1988] ECR 2965, 169/89 *Gourmeterrie van den Burg BV* 1990 ECR 2143 para 8, 2/90 *Wallonia* [1993] CMLR 365 itself, (vide the rather restrictive interpretation of Art 14 of Dir in *Scottish Grouse Case* 169/89), as the ability to adopt more stringent standards is confirmed in the Treaty text which is superior to secondary legislation adopted under it (Art 130t). More stringent standards are still required to be consistent with the treaty (Art 130t and 100a(4)).

certain circumstances but the Community cannot add to the discretion afforded to the Member States under Article 36 or the Mandatory Requirements.[82]

Discrimination and the principles of environmental action

It has been assumed that the principles of environmental action detailed in Article 130r(2) had a limited, if any, legal effect. The *Wallonia* case[83] provides an interesting precedent for the use of one of these principles to modify the operation of the general non-discrimination requirement relating to measures restrictive of trade.[84] Though no express reference is made to the integration requirement the case appears to mark the first positive integration of environmental protection requirements into the definition and implementation of the Community's other policies.

In the *Wallonia* Case a blanket ban on import of non-hazardous waste into the province of Wallonia was upheld by the Court. Much of the judgment was concerned with whether waste amounted to a "good" subject to the provisions of Article 30. The Court determined that it was and gave little consideration to necessity and proportionally, merely noting that the influx of waste into Wallonia was a serious problem. Most controversially the non-discrimination requirement was held inapplicable on the grounds that waste originating outside Wallonia was legally distinguishable from waste originating within Wallonia by reference to the proximity principle recognised in Article 130r(2) of the Treaty.

The Court failed to deal with Advocate-General Jacob's observation that proximity had not been expressly incorporated in the Wallonian legislation giving grounds to his opinion that the regional ban was not sufficient to claim the benefit of the principle.[85] The argument appears to be that either proximity was not the interest actually pursued by the legislation or, alternatively, that the regional ban was not proximate enough to satisfy such a justification. It appears to be conceded that if proximity is relevant to justification for a restriction of trade it would be difficult to rule a measure unjustified simply because it is not sufficiently restrictive of

---

[82] *De Peijper* 1976 ECR 613–640 para 31 see *infra* [Oliver].

[83] *(Wallonia Waste) Commission* v *Belgium* 1993 Common Market Law Reports 365.

[84] For a comparable case in the United States where a waste import ban was ruled discriminatory see *Philadelphia* v *New Jersey* 437 US 617 1978.

[85] Citing perhaps the requirement that there should be equivalent treatment of domestic products having the same harmful effects *Rewe ZentralFinanz* v *Landwirtshaftskammer* 1975 843–863. The important point was proximity allowed discrimination on grounds of origin and not the environmentally deleterious character of the waste per se.

trade.[86] A rule as to the appropriate geographic scope of a waste transport ban might ultimately encourage greater environmental protection but imply a harmonisation of the size and authority of local and regional authorities dealing with waste and invalidate many imperfect measures along the way.

In the same judgment the Court ruled that national legislation might not be applied against provisions of a directive which provided an exhaustive regime for inter-state trade in hazardous waste. A breach *by the Community* of the proximity principle in this case was neither argued nor considered. As a result, and a matter of some criticism, the more hazardous waste remained subject to a more liberal trade regime.

Necessity and proportionality: relating the restriction to the interest

Two principles directed towards the relationship between the objective authorising a restriction and the means adopted to do so and a test comparing objectives are often rolled into one.[87] In fact proportionality encompasses at least three separate tests factors.[88]

– *Effectiveness:* that the measure is sufficient to achieve the stated objective (and in that sense is necessary to achieve it).[89]
– *Minimum Restrictiveness:* requires that the least restrictive effective option is adopted to achieve the stated objective.
– *Proportionality in the strict sense:* which balances not the means to the ends but two ends, where the means adopted to enforce one objective are considered against the seriousness of the infringement of an alternative objective of equal or other value.

It is apparent that measures must show a reasoned relationship to the interest pursued. Establishing this is a matter of some complexity. Both an objective test, based on the actual effects of a supposed restriction, and a subjective test, which looks only to the interest pursued by the legislator, have their attractions.[90] However, the Court is extremely restricted in its

---

[86] It might be argued that a ban at city level would affect intra-Community trade less directly than one effected at state or regional borders and it is not clear whether a ban at national level say in Luxembourg could be supported by the principle expounded in the judgment.

[87] 122/78 *Buitoni* (1979) ECR 677 defines a proportionate measure as "what is appropriate and necessary to attain the objective sought".

[88] Schwarz, *European Administrative Law* (Sweet and Maxwell 1992).

[89] *Cassis di Dijon op cit* "Obstacles to movement within the Community must be accepted insofar as those provisions may be recognised as necessary in order to satisfy mandatory requirements".

[90] *Commission v UK Poultry* 40/82 1982 E.C.R 2793 the real purpose was not to protect health but domestic production.

capacity to examine factual evidence and relies for the most part on the formal reasoning for a particular measure supplied by the Community or the Member State.[91] The objective test is theoretically the more verifiable but requires the greatest factual input. The subjective test requires that the Court look into the "mind" of the legislature but even where there is a duty to give reasons for a measure these may be disguised. The real motivation behind the subjective approach is the detection of some failure underlying the reasoning supplied. It is suggested that the terms arbitrary and disguised restriction ought to be interpreted in this light.

The difficulties encountered in establishing an objective standard of environmental protection recur in this context, as assessing the formal necessity of a particular action to achieve the interest requires some appraisal of the standard implied by the interest itself. As already commented upon an objective standard is difficult to come by. It is submitted that whether a particular standard is justified or not in the interests of environmental protection ultimately must be within the discretion of the legislator to determine. If it is inappropriate to substitute the judgment of the Court for that of the political authorities in one context it must be so in another.[92] If not, environmental protection is as capable of becoming a pre-emptive and directly effective norm as any other.

Nevertheless statements in *ADBHU* that the Community "cannot go beyond the inevitable restrictions which are justified by the pursuit of an objective standard of protection"[93] seem to suggest that an objective standard is available. In more recent cases the Court has manage to avoid the problem directly and has given contradictory signals. The judgment in *Danish Bottles* seems to suggest that there is a reasonable standard of protection to which the Member States will be held. In the *Wallonia* case[94] the objective justification of a trade ban and its relative justification when compared with possible less restrictive measures was accepted by the Court without discussion.[95]

Generally speaking, Community law recognises some discretion whereby Member States may choose to apply standards in pursuit of recognised interests. However as "such standards cannot be determined unilaterally by the Member States"[96], this discretion is reviewable according to Community law. The level of discretion appears to vary according to the interest pursued.[97]

---

[91] Art 190 requires that Community measures be reasoned.

[92] Kramer "Environmental Protection and Article 30", 30 CMLR 111 1993 at 123 is of the opinion that Member States are free to choose the level of protection.

[93] Para 15 of judgment.

[94] *Re Imports of Waste: EC Commission v Belgium* 1993 CMLR 365 Vol. 66(8) see Hancier & Sevenster (1993) 30 CMLRev 351.

[95] Such as a licensing system as applied in the case of hazardous waste.

[96] 41/74 *Van Duyn v Home Office* [1974] ECR. 1337.

[97] *De Búrca supra, Sedemund* and 121/85 *Conegate* 1986 ECR 1007 and 34/79 *Henn and Darby* 1979 ECR 3795.

For example with regard to human health (an objective of environmental protection) Member States have a wide margin of discretion. In particular the "health and the life of humans rank first among their property or interests protected by Article 36 and it is for the Member States within the limits imposed by the Treaty – to decide on the degree of protection they intend to pursue and in particular how strict the checks to be carried out are"[98] but even here the Court has suggested the discretion is limited according to objective factors by the requirement that measures may be adopted only in so far as necessary "for the effective protection of health and life of humans".[99]

If the guarantee of free movement afforded by the Treaty is viewed as a presumption rather than an absolute standard of protection the problem can be approached as one relating to the onus and standard of proof necessary to rebut this presumption. It is clear in this sense that while the Community must raise evidence establishing the presumption, the onus of justifying trade-restrictive measures lies with the Member States.[100]

It is clear that scientific evidence alone may not be sufficient to discharge the standard required. While a measure may be shown to be discriminatory if scientific evidence clearly establishes that there is no difference between products justifying discrimination on health grounds[101] establishing the positive and objective necessity of particular restrictions through scientific evidence can be extremely difficult in many cases.[102] Innumerable factors militate against complete reliance on scientific evidence for environmental protection. The development of new processes and substances far outpaces adequate testing, even where testing the results cannot be reliably extrapolated to conditions in the field etc. The precautionary principle designed to meet these limitations seems to demand at least a certain discretion for Member States where a scientific assessment of effects and risks result in uncertainty. In consequence the application of precaution to the necessity test would provide that uncertainty is in itself a justification for action in restraint of trade.

Several cases in the area of product standards appear to confirm this approach – a recognition of uncertainty as a factor in establishing the Member State discretion to apply trade restrictive measures. Indeed the application of proportionality to test measures adopted on this justication

---

[98] Case 174/82 *Sandoz BV* 1983 ECR 2445 at para 19.

[99] Sedemund p 31–32 and 104/75 De Peijper 1976 ECR 613 : liberal interpretation of risk which was ruled genuine if claimed one life over 20 years.

[100] The onus on the Member State to prove justification of necessity 227/82 *Van Bennekom* 1983 ECR 3883 para 40. "It is for the national authorities to demonstrate in each case that the marketing of the product in question creates a serious risk to health".

[101] 124/81 *Commission* v *UK* 1983 ECR 205 Retreatment of UHT milk was not justified as the technical data showed retreatment made no difference to the milk.

[102] Sedemund "Statement on the Concept of Free Movement of Goods and the respect for National Action under Article 36 of the EEC Treaty" in Schwarze *Discretionary Powers of the Member States in the Field of Economic Policies* (Baden-Baden 1988).

risks becoming meaningless.[103] Nevertheless other cases imply that states must at least take steps to establish the uncertainty upon which they rely before a precautionary approach may be relied upon.[104] The adoption of a duty on individuals to establish that there are no harmful effects prior to release of a new substance into the environment is therefore precluded.[105]

The concept of technical need for a particular additive in a foodstuff may reduce still further the importing state's discretion.[106] In *German Beer* Advocate General Slynn adopted a broad interpretation of this concept.[107] The test in *German Beer* points to a case-by-case assessment of particular substances to establish the legality of a ban or restriction in use. Sedemund points out that contrary to a common understanding of precaution the solution adopted in a case-by-case assessment of risk still ignores the possible cumulative effects of chemicals and disallows a policy based on reducing an overall risk to the public by a limitation on the amount of chemicals in the food supply.[108]

Given the reality of these factors a full integration of the precautionary principle suggests less reliance on a scientific assessment of risk to justify restrictive measures in the absence of evidence establishing that no harm may result not only from the substance in question but a clearer recognition that the presence or absence of a scientific assessments of risk cannot on its own be relied upon to establish the legality or otherwise of Member State action.[109] The development of a comprehensive framework through which the law may deal with scientific uncertainty and avoid an over-

---

[103] See generally Sedemund but particularly Case 53/80 *Kaasfabriek Eyssen* 1981 ECR 409 paras 13 and 14 and *Heijn* 1984 ECR 3280, 97/83 *Melkunie* 1984 ECR 2367 at 2385.

[104] 178/84 *Van Bennekom* 1988 para 35 CMLR 1 *Muller* 1980 ECR 1511 *German Beer* 1987 ECR 1227 "it is for the national authorities to demonstrate in each case that the marketing of the product in question creates a serious risk to public health".

[105] Case 174/82 *Sandoz BV* 1983 ECR 2445 "in so far as there are uncertainties at the present state of scientific research it is for the Member States, in the absence of harmonisation, to decide what degree of protection of the health and life of humans they intend to assure, having regard however to the requirements of the free movement of goods within the Community", and their limits under the EEC Treaty: here a requirement that manufacturers supply proof that a particular additive was safe was found unlawful (para 24) but in Case 251/78 *Denkavit Futtermittell* 1979 ECR 3369 the Court failed to decide whether a blanket assumption that additives were harmful unless the contrary was proved amounted to a unjustified restriction on trade.

[106] Sandoz *supra* at para 19.

[107] *Commission* v *Germany* (Beer) 1987 ECR 1227. The case involved additives in beer, where the chemical was authorised in another state for use in imported products, the importing state must authorise the chemical in question; (1) provided international scientific data shows it to be harmless to individuals with dietary habits of its population, or otherwise, if it meets a genuine technical need and there is a procedure for authorisation, the state has taken steps to establish whether it is harmful and action is available for refusal of authorisation. Technical need is to be determined with reference to the imported.

[108] At p 30.

[109] In the context of Art 100a(4) and the Court's approval of national standards under that provision. The recent *Pentachlorophenol* Case 41/93 *French Republic* v *Commission of the European Communities.* 1994 ECR 1829 appears to confirm the requirement that measures must be legally if not scientifically justified or reasoned. As the reasons given by the Commission for confirmation in this case were ruled insufficient the judgment does not in itself rule out a precautionary approach.

reliance on mechanistic quantitative assessments of risks remains a matter of some controversy world-wide.

Acting in the Community interest and finding an appropriate legal basis[110]

In contrast with the GATT system the pre-emptive provisions of the Treaty concerning the customs union and the internal market are supplemented by provisions creating an interest in measures which supplement and support the basic scheme. The Community is expressly provided with the power to adopt measures for the establishment and functioning of the Market and the regulation of international trade. The interaction between trade provisions and environmental principles is therefore not limited merely to that of pre-emptive norm and public interest (at whatever level) described above.

The definition of the Community task detailed in Article 2 of the Treaty is supplemented by particular provisions which confirm the Community's powers to adopt measures which will ultimately contribute to its attainment.[111] The interpretative value of Article 2 may modify or reinforce these provisions in the ultimate attempt to ensure a holistic interpretation of the whole Treaty, but the difficulty in reconciling individual policies suggests that the final balance of measures adopted in fulfilment of Article 2 remain political choices open to the Community institutions to investigate.[112] Nonetheless the Court maintains a policing role even in the balance of legislative choice through its insistence that an express choice of legal basis is necessary and that this choice must be exercised according to objective factors amenable to judicial review

The diversification of legal bases for Community action with the adoption of the Single European Act and reinforced at Maastricht has presented the Court with a clear choice between legislative models and little guidance on the factors relevant to their respective application (see table on page 217). Initially at least the Court has hesitated in response to the

---

[110] Bradley "The European Court and the Legal Basis of Community Legislation" Vol. 13 (1988) Common Market Law Review p379. Barents "The Internal Market and some Observations on the Legal Basis of Community Legislation" (1993) 30 Common Market Law Review 85; Geradin "Trade and Environment: The Community Framework and National Environmental Standards" 1993 YEL 151; Lenearts "Some Reflections on the Seperation of Powers in the European Community" 28 Common Market Law Review 1991; Emiliou "Opening Pandora's Box: The Legal Basis of Community Measures before the Court of Justice" (1994) 19 ELR 488.

[111] In addition (III) Art 43 (Agriculture), and (IV) 76 (Transport) may be mentioned as regulatory bases designed to promote integration in particular sectors (V) Art 130s in common with (VI) Art 118 and others are bases which are dedicated towards social, political or perhaps ethical interests and do not directly promote integration.

[112] See Art 3 listing the Community policies "for the purposes set out in Article 2 the Communities activities shall include . . .".

increased complexity of the system and encountered considerable difficulty in the identification and application of objective factors for the review of the selection of particular bases. Caselaw suggests that the addition of new legal bases to the Treaty have initiated a process of adaptation by the Court.

As already mentioned, in addition to the interposition of additional legal bases the Community's task has recently been recast by Maastricht to reflect a more equal balancing of economic and environmental considerations.[113] The approach taken is closely mirrored in the preamble to the agreement establishing the World Trade Organisation.[114] The Treaty is therefore ambiguous as to the model whereby a sustainable balance of interests may be achieved. It recognises both a system of separate bases dedicated to ostensibly distinct interests and the necessity of integration through the obligation to integrate environmental protection requirements into all policies. The following sections are intended to show both the inherent complexity of operating a series of distinct bases and the particular difficulties arising from the interposition of an obligation to integrate on an already difficult system.

Procedural and substantive consequences of the choice of legal basis

The question of choice of legal basis for Community measures is fundamental for two basic reasons concerned with preserving the legitimacy and coherence of Community action; each elements of the rule of law.

Firstly, the requirement of legitimacy and rationality, derived from Article 3b[115] and Article 190[116] of the Treaty, relies on establishing the appropriate Treaty basis which both delimits Community competence (at least theoretically) and determines the division of powers through the procedures according to which measures designed for particular ends may be adopted – unanimously or by qualified majority vote, with parliamentary consultation, co-operation[117] or co-decision.[118] The exercise of a choice between bases is therefore politically charged and constitutionally important, and the courts review the principle method of policing the Communities division of powers.

Secondly, the choice of legal basis has substantive consequences with relation to the nature of the legal order thereby created and effects the

---

[113] Art 2 *supra.*
[114] Preamble to WTO Agreement see *supra.*
[115] "The Community shall act within the limits of the powers conferred upon it by this treaty and of the objectives assigned to it therein".
[116] [Measures] "adopted . . . shall state the reasons on which they are based . . .".
[117] A procedure detailed in Art 189c.
[118] Detailed in Art 189b.

coherence of Community law. There are several modes of policy: according to one framework there are those which are exclusive and unitary *per se*, such force being derived from the Treaty itself[119], and those which are concurrent allowing Member State action, in accordance with the doctrine of pre-emption, only in so far as Community measures have not yet been adopted.[120] Recent amendments to the Treaty system have added another suggesting that the old assumption that many areas of concurrent policy would ultimately become exclusive by reason of legislative pre-emption has been abandoned.

Firstly, several of the newer areas of policy expressly preserve the ability of Member States to adopt more stringent measures, a factor which the Court has ruled has a fundamental effect on the pre-emptive effect of measures adopted by the Community within the context of these policies.[121] Secondly, Article 3b provides that in non-exclusive areas the principle of subsidiarity applies, which would tend to entrench the concurrent nature of policies deemed not exclusive (though what exclusive means in this sense has yet to be interpreted).

Balancing pre-emptive norms interests and the trade environment relationship

In the ebb and flow of interpretative relationships between various elements of the Treaty system three principle tensions may be described.

Pre-emptive norm and interest

Firstly, a tension between "negative harmonisation", through the disapplication of national rules, and positive harmonisation, through the adoption of Community measures, rests in the relative interpretation of Article 30, and the pre-emptive norm of free trade it contains, and, the Community power to establish the market through legislation detailed in Article 100 and 100a.[122] There is a direct relationship between the extent to which national measures are rendered inapplicable by Article 30 and saved by Article 36 or mandatory requirements and the extent to which measures may be adopted which have as their object the establishment of the internal market. Article 100–100c must be necessary only to the extent that the measures it is proposed to harmonise are not already invalidated automatically. Thus the legislative space for the Community and the Member States in environmental matters is as has been described in the first

---

[119] *e.g.* the common commercial policy or aspects of marine fisheries conservation.
[120] Such as the Environment Policy.
[121] Opinion 2/91 ILO No 170[1993] Common Market Law Reports 800.
[122] Vide the extension implied by Cassis de Dijon *supra*.

section limited by the extent of Article 30 and recognised interests justifying departure from this rule.[123]

Exclusive and concurrent policies

Secondly, the tension between two models of harmonisation within the Community system. The first is a system of progressive adaptation of national rules to conditions of absolute uniformity necessary to ensure non-discrimination and competitive equality between states in a single market upon which the trade policy is based. The second is a system of minimum standards with a concurrent freedom on the part of Member States to adopt more stringent standards with regard to a particular interest where diverse situations are recognised to require a diversity of solutions.

Regulatory and deregulatory interests

The third tension lies in implicit regulatory and deregulatory elements of the Treaty system: Harmonisation of Law on whatever basis necessarily includes both deregulatory and regulatory elements. Nonetheless the Court has attempted to draw a distinction between harmonisation pursuing the establishment and functioning of the market which is deregulatory, and harmonisation directed at environmental protection which is necessarily regulatory or restrictive of trade.[124] Whether this can be properly justified given that the trade basis (100a) expressly recognised that harmonisation may have regulatory effects, and more generally it is submitted that even liberalising measures leave intact a degree of market restriction justified in terms of some public interest.

These modes of legal order attributed to the interests represented in the several Community policies reflect not only the division of powers between the Community institutions and between the Community and the Member States, but also fundamental conceptions as to the nature of the policies themselves which repeat and reflect the interaction of the trade norm and the environmental interest discussed above. Of course each individual policy is subject to general requirements as to necessity and proportionality as well as the operation of general principles of law recognised by the Community as embodying fundamental rights, but in addition, the interaction and formal integration of principles governing these policies also present possible limitations on their scope and effect. The Court of Justice in refining its approach to Article 30 and establishing a

---

[123] Remembering always that Art 30 is pre-eminent but still only one of the Market rules which might invalidate state or individual action with an environmental motivation. See particularly Reto Jacobs "EC Competition Policy and the Protection of the environment" 1993 Legal Issues of European Integration 1993 37.

[124] Case 155/91 *Commission* v *Council* [Waste Framework Directive Case] 1991 ECR 2867.

caselaw on the choice of legal basis has fluctuated in its approach to all of these relationships.[125]

The legal bases available

The key legal bases relevant to environmental policy can, in summary, be seen to fall into 3 groups:

(i) The trade bases

These are divided into two bases of general application dedicated to external and internal trade respectively and several internal bases covering sectoral markets.

- Article 113: the Common Commercial Policy dedicated to measures regulating the Community's external trade. Member States are precluded from adopting such measures unilateraterally (it is formally exclusive) and must rely on the Community to adopt measures falling within the scope of this policy. The Community may adopt these by qualified majority voting in the Council and there is only limited parliamentary involvement.
- Article 100–100c: in effect several bases dedicated to the establishment and continued functioning of the common or internal market. The Community may adopt harmonisation measures affecting the market by co-decision of parliament and the council (the later acting by qualified majority voting)

Already the system provides scope for difficulty in determining the basis applicable to measures which affect external and internal trade simultaneously.

(ii) Sectoral markets

The market is recognised to have several components, some of which serve certain social or economic ends requiring a separate definition and set of objectives principles. Among these are Agriculture (Article 43), Transport (Article 78) and Taxation (Article 99). These sectoral bases are recognised to be *lex specialis* to Article 100–100c, incorporating measures which though dedicated to establishing a functioning market, affect or are directed at objectives prescribed in these policies. Here again there is

---

[125] Han Somsen on C155/91 1993 Common Market Law Review 121 and 29 (1992) p140–151, *Titanium Dioxide Commission* v *Council* 1991 ECR 2867, Barents, "The Internal Market Unlimited: Some Observations on the Legal Basis of Community Legislation" 20 Common Market Law Review 85 (see p 92) problems of delimitation.

potential ground for dispute as each basis is subject to a different procedural regime.[126]

(iii) General non-market bases

Including Harmonisation of Social Policy (Article 118) and Fiscal Measures (Article 99).

The Environmental Basis

(Article 130r) provides an alternative focus for regulation and formally
encompasses measures directed at four objectives. The distinction between the basis and some but not all of the market-oriented bases is that
measures adopted under the policy are formally, as a requirement of the
Treaty, minimum stringency measures and cannot pre-empt more stringent measures consistent with the Treaty. The policy is also subject to a
subsidiarity requirement (indeed between the SEA and Maastricht it was
the only policy subject to this requirement). Environmental policy specifies no less than four possible procedures for the adoption of measures.
Unanimity is preserved for some ill-defined policy areas, though the Council may agree to ordinary qualified majority voting for these, co-decision is
prescribed for the adoption of action programmes, co-operation for all
other measures.

Finding objective factors for review

The central difficulty with a system of functionally defined legal bases that
are procedurally distinct is that many measures formally dedicated to one
function in fact effect several. The statement that the choice of legal basis
must be made according to objective factors amenable to judicial review[127], while an essential element of the rule of law, results in considerable difficulty given the way in which the scope of individual bases is
defined. An approach based on ascertaining legislative intention or determining the primary objective according to the content or effects of particular provisions will only rarely provide objective factors upon which the
choice of legal basis can be exercised or reviewed. A centre of gravity or
primary purpose test has been applied under the fiction that in most cases
a most important objective may be identified. Even if this were true, this
rule remains open to legislative manipulation as legislation might be

---

[126] Community rules on competition, state aids and free movement of services, capital and
persons should not be forgotten, each of which prescribe a particular freedom or substantive rule
and recognise the possibility of derogation to various extents.

[127] *Re Generalised Tariff Preferences EC Commission* v *Council* 1987 ECR 1483.

drafted not according to the needs of different situations but according to which mix of provisions might reasonably be adopted pursuant to a favourable legal basis. As a result, the Commission, the Council, the Member States, and latterly the Parliament have been provided with ample room for argument before the Court. The Court's search for a definition has resulted in controversy and uncertainty. Arguably the Court has not yet managed to define these factors with sufficient certainty, leading in particular to a rather confused division between the different environmental and unitary trade modes of regulation.

The effect of the integration principle

Attempts by the Treaty draftsmen to rationalise the system have perhaps ultimately served only to muddy the waters. The integration principle[128], the legal effects of which have yet to be examined by the Court, at once promotes environment protection and yet has undermined at least initially the separate legal basis for environment of which it forms a part.[129] The general requirement that environmental protection requirements be integrated into the definition and implementation of other policies has allowed other bases to be used for this purpose. Article 100a (the basis for internal market harmonisation) expressly refers to environmental objectives and preserves the ability of Member States to maintain more stringent measures even after harmonisation.[130] On the other hand the environment policy is not entirely removed from taking economic factors into account. General integration can work both ways, as Article 130r(3) suggests[131] and the broad freedom granted to Member States to adopt more stringent measures under Article 130 t is more specifically limited by the words "not incompatible with this Treaty", generally accepted to refer to trade requirements.

The meandering balance of interpretations

Three distinct phases or approaches can be discerned in the Court's approach to striking the balance between legal bases, each of which displays not only the difficulties arising from an attempt to impose rational grounds for review on a system of functional bases but a degree of political activism on the part of the Court in the Community's interest.

---

[128] Art 130r(2) states that environmental protection requirements must be integrated into the definition and implementation of other policies.

[129] *Titanium Dioxide Commission* v *Council* 1991 E.C.R. 2867 *infra.*

[130] Art 100a(4) and Case 41/93 *French Republic* v *Commission* 17 May 1994 Commission decision confirming provisions annulled. See Hans Somsen "Applying More National Environmental Laws after Harmonisation" European Environmental Law Review Aug./Sept. 1994 238.

[131] In preparing its policy on the environment, the Community shall take account of; " – environmental conditions in the various regions of the Community; – the economic and social development of the Community as a whole and the balanced development of its regions".

An expansive interpretation of trade objectives

There are two factors driving an inclusive interpretation of the legal basis governing trade. Firstly the Court has always been reluctant to find particular measures ultra vires the Community and has consequently adopted a broad interpretation of Community powers generally. Secondly, the imperative to preserve a unity of conditions in the market and particularly external trade relations has supported an expansive interpretation of the scope of the trade bases in particular, the consequences of which have been to preclude unilateral action by the Member States externally.

Article 113 and the inclusive interpretation[132]

There are several statements by the Court that the legal basis for international commercial policy incorporates the power to adopt measures regulating international trade in other interests.[133] The definition of the common commercial policy established to regulate external trade expressly includes the qualification that it should be "harmoniously achieved". One might ask harmonious with what? Though the phrase may be adequately explained in terms of preserving some internal harmony in the move towards a liberalisation of external trade, the fact that the conditions of trade are to be regulated expressly recognises that the external trade policy at least has a regulatory as well as a deregulatory focus.[134]

In any event the Court of Justice has ruled that while pursuing the objectives of external trade the Community might also pursue objectives not simply promoting the deregulation of world trade. The *International Rubber* opinion confirmed that the establishment of a regulatory system for commodities trading under UNCTAD fell within the Community's Common Commercial Policy even though the instruments adopted did not form part of the traditional armoury of trade instruments.[135] In effect

---

[132] See generally Bourgeois "The EC in the WTO and Advisory Opinion 1/94: An Echternach Procession" 1994 Common Market Law Review 736.

[133] Demeret in Maresceu (ed) *The European Community's Commercial Policy After 1992: The Legal Dimension* 315–319 p355 and the instrumental character of Art 113.

[134] *Article 110* By establishing a customs union between themselves, Member States aim to contribute, in the common interest, to the harmonious development of world trade, the progressive abolition of restrictions on international trade and the lowering of customs barriers.

[135] Opinion 1/78 *International Rubber:* [45] Art 113 empowers the Community to formulate a commercial policy based on uniform principles, thus showing that the question of external trade must be governed from a wide point of view and not only having regard to the administration of precise systems such as customs and quantitative restrictions. The same conclusion may be deduced from the fact that the enumeration in Art 113 of the subjects covered by commercial policy . . . is conceived as a non-exhaustive enumeration which must not, as such, close the door to the application in the Community context of any other process intended to regulate external trade. And at p 2917 a measure . . . "Must be assessed having regard to its essential objective rather than in terms of individual clauses of an altogether subsidiary or ancillary nature".

the instrumental theory of legal basis was displaced in favour of a teleological theory of legal basis.[136]

In the Generalised Tariff Preferences (Preferential Treatment itself is not GATT compatible but nonetheless agreed to by the parties) the Court confirmed that development objectives might indeed fall within the CCP. In this case the Council argued that the aims of the measure were developmental and as such went beyond the aims of the Commercial Policy.[137] The Court, expressly noting that the Community's aims included the harmonious development of world trade[138] and developments in international law[139], suggested that such objectives must be incorporated into trade objectives. If this were not the case the CCP would become nugatory over time as trade instruments developed.[140] It must be noted that development co-operation has since achieved an independent status with the adoption of further provisions in 1992 at Maastricht.[141]

Even after the adoption of a separate environmental basis including the competence to conclude international agreements the Court continued the trend by confirming that measures touching on aspects of environment protection may also be adopted on the basis of Article 113.[142] In the Chernobyl Case[143] the Greek Government (in a minority on a vote to adopt restrictions on the import of certain agricultural products) challenged the ability of the Community to adopt such a measure on the basis of Article 113. As the matter concerned the protection of public heath (an objective of the environment policy) the Greek Government argued that such a measure should have been on the basis of 130s (which incidentally required a unanimous decision). Nonetheless the Court found the measure rightly adopted on the basis that (1) the measure was intended to regulate trade between the EC and not member countries (2) the regulation established uniform import rules (3) Article 130r(2) established that

---

[136] See Advocate General Lenz (1987 ECR 1493) para 57 and 58 objective and subjective tests: is it a measure which aims to influence and at the same time alter the form of world trade? Is trade objectively influenced?

[137] Generalised Tariff Preferences 45/86 *Commission* v *Council* [1987] "reflects a new concept of international trade relations in which development aims to play a major role" [18].

[138] Para 17.

[139] Para 17. The Link between trade and development has become progressively stronger in modern international relations. It has been recognised in the context of the United Nations, notably by UNCTAD and in the context of GATT in particular through the incorporation in the GATT of Part IV entitled trade and development.

[140] Para 20.

[141] Art 130u. The Community policy in the sphere of development co-operation which shall be complementary to the policies pursued by the Member States, shall foster the sustainable economic and social development of developing countries, and more particularly the most disadvantaged of them; the smooth and gradual integration of developing countries into the world economy; the Community and the Member States shall comply with the Commitments and take account of the objectives they have approved in the context of the United Nations and other competent international organisations. Art 130v The Community shall take into account the objectives referred to in 130u in the policies that it implements which are likely to affect developing countries.

[142] 62/88 *Chernobyl* Case 1990 ECR I 3743.

[143] *Op cit.*

environment protection might be part of other policies; (4) and Article 130r-t left intact existing powers to adopt under other bases including this one.

In the environmental sphere there has been a marked reluctance to accept that environmentally related trade measures fall within the Common Commercial Policy. Member States have feared recognition that essential elements of an environmental policy should fall within the ambit of an exclusive policy precluding Member State action. Equally trade policy specialists within the Commission have feared that in recognising an exception the unity of the trade policy has been undermined. Though there have been no cases expressly covering the point, all international environmental agreements have been adopted on a basis other than Article 113.[144]

In addition the Community has adopted unilateral trade restrictions despite concerns as to the legality of some provisions under GATT. Trade measures unilaterally adopted by the Community include; measures to protect whale and cetacean products[145], seal pups[146], animals trapped by inhumane methods.[147] In each case there was some argument over the appropriate legal basis and in each, save the last, it was concluded that Article 113 was inappropriate. The Whales and Cetacean Products Directive was proposed using 113 as a basis, but German and Danish arguments that the restrictions were moral rather than environmental prevailed[148]. The Directive was adopted under Article 235 in the days before Article 130s.[149] Britain had pressed for the introduction of the ban partly on the ground of the uncertain legality of its earlier unilateral ban. The Seals Directive was also proposed using Article 113 as a basis but eventually was adopted on the basis of Article 235. The Leghold Trap Directive is the latest in this series of measures and was again proposed on the basis of 113 but interestingly was finally adopted on a dual legal basis thus preserving a non-exclusive element.[150]

---

[144] International Agreements with a trade character adopted under Art 130s: – 88/540 OJ l297 31.10.88 Vienna Convention for the Protection of the Ozone Layer and the Montreal Protocol Adopted under Art 130s – 81/69 OJ l252 5.9.81 Washington Convention on International Trade in Endangered Species (note the preamble) Art 235 – 82/461 EEC OJ L210 18.7.82 Convention on the Conservation of Migratory Species of Wild animals: with Art 235 as a basis, – 93/98/EEC OJ L39 16.12.93 Basle Convention on Transboundary Movements of Waste, with Art 130s as a basis – only one has been adopted on the basis of Art 113 – International Tropical Timber Agreement L313 22.11.85 p9 85/424 OJ L236 3.9.85 p8.

[145] 348/81 OJ L39 12.2.81 Council regulations on common rules for imports of whales or other cetacean products, and, 3786/81 OJ l377 31.12.81 Commission regulation laying down provisions for the implementation of common rules. These rules were subsumed in CITES Regulation 3626/82.

[146] Directives 83/129, 85/444, 89/370 Directives concerning the importation into Member States of Skins of certain seal pups and products derived therefrom.

[147] Leg hold Traps 3254/91 OJ l308, 9.11.91 adopted on a dual basis Art 113 and 130s.

[148] See Haigh *Manual of European Environmental Policy* (Longman/IEEP, 1992) Looseleaf Service at p 9.3–3.

[149] See Haigh 9.4–3.

[150] 3254/91 OJ L. 308 9/11/91 p 1.

Article 100 and 100a – an inclusive interpretation of the market

Internally, in the absence of an express power to regulate for environmental protection, those provisions designed to authorise harmonisation regulations affecting trade in the Member States, became the subject of an expansive interpretation so as to include the power to regulate trade in pursuit of a rather broader range of objectives. In a sense the shift in emphasis (or more properly definition) was inevitable as the process of replacing national measures with Community harmonisation measures inevitably involved the implicit adoption by the Community through its harmonisation measures of the policy underlying the national regulations it sought to replace. Arguably it was legally justifiable in the treaty's requirement that the essentially economic objectives of the Treaty be harmoniously achieved.[151]

Of particular relevance to the current discussion, in the absence of an express basis for environmental measures, such measures were adopted under Article 100 and under Article 235. Arguably certain environmental measures "directly affect the establishment or functioning of the common market" therefore satisfying the objectives prescribed in the former, and in so far as this was not so they were "measures necessary to attain one of the objectives" where a power did not already exist. This latter proposition is based on a development of language in Article 2 defining the core task of the Community to include the promotion of a "harmonious development of economic activities" and to achieve "a better standard of living".

In a sense the recognition of the environmental interest as one of the elements required in such a harmonious development was also reflected in the recognition of additional mandatory requirements authorising trade restrictive measures following a broader interpretation of Article 30. The objective of the general interest authorising a modification to the operation of Article 30 in ABHU both legitimised Community environmental policy and led inevitably to recognition of the interest at national level through a mandatory requirement.

Again by analogy with external trade, even after the adoption of an express basis for environmental regulation, the Court took the view that environmental measures adopted at least partially with the aim of harmonising competitive distinctions in the Member States, ought in preference to be adopted under Article 100a.[152] In *Titanium Dioxide*[153] the

---

[151] Art 2 before Maastricht amendments "the harmonious development of economic activities throughout the Community , a continuous and balanced expansion, an increase in stability, an accelerated raising of the standard of living, and closer relations between the states belonging to the Community".

[152] A burden on undertakings justifies harmonisation of national provisions – *Re Detergents: EC Commission* v *Italy* 9/79 1980 E.C.R 1089, *Re Fuel Directive: EC Commission* v *Italy* 92/79 1980 ECR 1115.

[153] *Commission* v *Council* (Titanium Dioxide) 1993 CMLR 359 Vol. 68.

Commission argued that the Directive concerned was more properly adopted under Article 130s than under 100a. The Court, while it agreed that the Directive pursued two interests simultaneously decided that where two relevant bases were available, though a measure ordinarily should be adopted pursuant to all relevant bases[154], where the procedures were different and mutually incompatible, one basis had to be chosen. The Court settled on Article 100a and the co-operation procedure, as to adopt the measure under 130s alone would undermine the very substance of the guarantees afforded to Parliament in Article 100a under 100a. The Court took express comfort in the integration requirement which recognised that measures with an environmental component might be adopted pursuant to other bases.[155] The decision was much criticised as it appears to undermine the operation of 130s.

Recognising the place of a separate basis

Nonetheless in *151/91 Commission* v *Council*[156] the Waste Framework Directive was confirmed to fall under Article 130s rather than 100a and the internal market. The Court based its finding on the reasoning that the Directive restricted rather than promoted free movement and while it affected the operation of the market, these effects were ancillary to the main objective.

In common with the recent tendency to recognise that trade restrictive measures may be adopted under Article 130s where environmental protection is the primary purpose of the measure it appears to be accepted that 130s is also the basis for external environmentally motivated trade restrictions In *European Parliament* v *Council.*[157] While Parliament's right to challenge a waste regulation was denied on procedural grounds the Court confirmed the regulatory/facilitatory approach.

The place of the sectoral markets and the relationship between internal and external regulation

The recognition of particular interests or objectives pertaining to particular sectoral markets has also raised questions as to legal basis. The scope of operation of these policies has been determined on the basis that they form exceptions to the generality of the trade provisions. In the *Hormones* Case[158] a prohibition on growth promoters for fattening purposes was ruled to fall within Article 43, which could be interpreted to

---

[154] Paras [17]-[18].

[155] At para 22.

[156] 155/91 *Commission* v *Council* (Waste Framework) [1993] ECR 939, noted Nicolas de Sadeleer in Journal of Environmental Law 1992.

[157] Case 187/93 *E.P.* v *Council* Regulation of Waste Shipments 1994 ECR 2857.

[158] 68/86 *United Kingdom* v *Council* 1988 ECR p 855 and see Rene Barents "Some Reflections on the Hormones Judgement" 1988 Legal Issues of European Integration 1–19.

include aspects of the public interest as *lex specialis* to Article 100.[159] If a measure contributes to the objectives of Article 43 then this basis is sufficient.

As a result, so an argument goes, not only do these bases form a derogation to Article 100–100c (the general provisions) but also to Article 113. This is controversial not least because an assumption had arisen that the Common Commercial Policy represented the external face of all the community's economic competences at least. The ERTA confirmed that implied external competence was available with respect to all internal competences where this was necessary to fulfil the objectives of individual policies. In the *Veterinary Inspection* Case[160] the question whether Article 43, Article 100 or Article 113 was the appropriate basis was resolved in favour of Article 43.[161] It appears that Article 43 can be used for external trade rules as well as harmonisation of production and marketing agricultural products. In essence these measures served a dual purpose both the removal of distortions and public health.[162]

Trade-related environmental measures and the Uruguay Round opinion

Demeret has argued that in consequence of *Chernobyl* and the *Titanium Dioxide* judgments, Trade Related Environmental Measures (TREMS) ought to be adopted on the basis of 113.[163] On the other hand Volker[164] suggests that *Chernobyl* was a special case. Here the fact that there are two bases for the adoption of trade measures – one dealing with the internal the other with its external face – created a particular problem. He argues that in *Chernobyl* internal measures had been adopted under Article 31 of the Euratom Treaty which had no external equivalent requiring that Article 113 be chosen as a basis. Otherwise where measures govern internal and external trade simultaneously these are not matters falling within the ambit of Article 113 but fall to be adopted according to the internal basis.

However the recent Opinion 1/94 concerning the Uruguay Round of GATT seems to contradict even this. Here the EEC Court rejected Article 43 as the appropriate bases for provisions on phytosanitary measures. It

---

[159] P855,896 of Völker *infra* n 164.

[160] 131/87 *United Kingdom* v *Council Health and Veterinary Inspections* 1989 ECR 3743.

[161] See also 11/88 *Commission* v *Council* 1989 ECR 3799.

[162] See paras 26, 27 and 28 of the judgment.

[163] Demeret in Maresceu (ed) *The European Community's Commercial Policy After 1992: The Legal Dimension* 315–319 at 356–357. Nevertheless he does recognise that the direct regulation of trade was not an element of *Titanium Dioxide* which reduces its significance for the trade policy.

[164] Volker *Barriers to External and Internal Community Trade* (Europa Institute 1993) at 187–189.

ruled that such measures should be adopted under Article 113 on the grounds that in the case of this particular agreement the objectives it fulfilled were not of the Community's agriculture policy but that of the trade policy, namely a liberalisation in trade in Agricultural products.

Despite this the general approach of adopting an inclusive interpretation to Article 113 suffers a general reverse, if not in principle then in practice.[165] Given the concentration on a teleological rather than an instrumental method of ascertaining the legal basis the classic problem looks set to continue. The practise of adopting trade measures with an environmental object pursuant to an environmental basis seems to remain legitimate, as does the adoption of measures intended to liberalise trade which have environmental consequences on the basis of Article 113. While the integration requirement formally requires that environmental protection requirements be incorporated into Article 113 as much as any other basis, the practical effect of the requirement to date must be doubted.

Conclusion

The growing jurisprudence of the Court of Justice concerning the choice of legal basis for environmentally related instruments can hardly be said to have brought clarity to the analysis, and, as we have argued, is unlikely to do so in that it is rooted in a classical functional model of separate policies in competition which fails to reflect current and future environmental reality. The concept of sustainable development, if it is to move beyond a mere political commitment, implies in the longer term a far more fundamental integration of an environmental perspective into economic and resource policies than has hitherto been proposed or imagined. We question whether the current constitutional and legal structure of the Treaty adequately reflects these challenges.

It might be argued – and no doubt will be at the forthcoming Inter-Governmental Conference – that if the procedures for adopting Community legislation were harmonised, the political arguments concerning the correct legal basis of instruments would be largely removed. Yet, as we have tried to demonstrate, this in itself will not provide the answer. There remain substantive distinctions between exclusive and non-exclusive policies, which reflect differing principles and hierarchies of norms, and which will continue to give rise to tension. Nor does the mere expression of an overall goal of sustainable development (as, post Maastricht already appears in the Treaty, albeit in rather garbled form) or the legal requirement to integrate environmental dimensions into other policy areas (as

---

[165] *e.g.* paras 40 and 41 concerning GATS and para 54 et seq. On TRIPs and generally Bourgeois *op cit supra.*

appears in Art 130R) satisfactorily deal with the problem, but glosses over underlying and more insidious distinctions in philosophy.

We have shown how certain aspects of trade-related principles within the Treaty, and especially Article 30, have been given pre-emptive legal status. One way forward would be to attribute to environmental protection requirements an enhanced status quite independent of specific Community environmental legislation and based on the development of principles of environmental protection and sustainable development.

Ultimately, these principles would provide a basis for the legal review of Community action, but also support the legal justification of national measures where these fall within the scope of Article 30. This process is not perhaps as controversial as might first appear, and can be said to have already begun in the recognition of the proximity and precautionary principles in recent caselaw on trade-restrictive measures.

This sort of development, however, still implies tensions and balancing acts. A more fundamental restructuring would recognise that the "rational and prudent use of natural resources", one of the principles of Community environmental policy and inherent in the concept of sustainable development, is also or should be one of the aims of the market system which an economist would support. If such a principle were fully locked into the goals of the market, one could envisage a situation where, say, both Community and national restrictions or measures which interfere with the attainment by the market of these objectives, could be legally challenged, both by individuals and governments. The true power of the Community legal structure would then be harnessed towards sustainable development. Such a vision may be too much to stomach for many involved in the process of Treaty development and change. Yet the fundamental philosophical differences between those promoting free trade and those promoting political union (who at the 1992 Intergovernmental Conference operated as separate committees) cannot be disguised by the fact that their handiwork appears in a single document. The compromise between the philosophy of market freedom and that of sustainable development fails to disguise a fault line in the Community structure between the centralist and the federalist, free marketeers and environmentalists, exclusive and non-exclusive competences, absolute and minimum standards, majority and unanimous decision-making. Ultimately, tinkering at the edges may produce only confusion and a misplaced reassurance.

MARTIN HESSION
RICHARD MACRORY

Some Legal Bases relevant to the Environment

Co-decision	Article 130r(3) **ENVIRONMENT**	General Action Programmes setting out priority objectives to be attained
	Article 100a **Approximation of Laws (by way of derogation from Article 100)**	Harmonisation with the aim of establishing functioning of the internal market
Co-operation	Article 130s(1) **ENVIRONMENT** as a contribution to preserving, protecting and improving the quality of the environment; protecting human health; the prudent and rational utilisation of natural resources and promoting measures at an international level to deal with worldwide environmental problems	Action to achieve the objectives referred to in Article 130r
	Article 75 **TRANSPORT** the objectives of the Treaty in matters governed by the transport title	Common rules on international transport across the territory of one or more Member States etc
Qualified Majority Voting	Article 130r(2) **ENVIRONMENT**	
	Article 113 **COMMON COMMERCIAL** to contribute in the common interest to the harmonious development of world trade, the progressive abolition of restrictions on international trade and the lowering of customs barriers	Measures to implement the Common Commercial Policy
	Article 43 **AGRICULTURAL** increased agricultural productivity, a fair standard of living for the agricultural community, the stabilisation of markets, the availability of suppliers and that supplies reach consumers at reasonable prices	Measures for the Common Organisation of the market in Agriculture
Unanimous Voting	Article 130s(2) **ENVIRONMENT**	– provisions primarily of a fiscal nature – measures concerning town and country planning, land use with the exception of waste management and measures of a general nature, and management of water resources – measures significantly affecting a member states choice between different energy sources and the general structure of its energy supply
	Article 100 **Approximation of Laws** the approximation of laws which directly effect the establishment or functioning of the common market	directives for the approximation of laws which directly affect the establishment or functioning of the common market
	Article 75(3) **TRANSPORT (by way of derogation from Article 75(2)**	Transport policy: where would have a serious effect on the standard of living and on employment in certain areas
	Article 99 **HARMONIZATION OF INDIRECT TAXATION** as article 100a	Provisions for the harmonisation of legislation concerning turnover taxes, excise duties and other forms of indirect taxation necessary to ensure the establishment and functioning of the internal market
Budgetary Procedure	Article 130d **STRUCTURAL FUNDS** to promote overall harmonious development . . . leading to the strengthening of . . . economic and social cohesion	The tasks priority objectives and organisation and general rules to ensure the effectiveness of the Structural and Cohesion funds

217

Chapter 14

Recent Developments in EC Anti-Dumping Practice and the GATT

Introduction

This chapter examines a number of recent developments in EC anti-dumping law and practice. In three main sections it covers: certain international aspects including the Uruguay Round results and the European Economic Area Agreement ("the EEA"); the new EC substantive anti-dumping rules adopted in the context of the new GATT Anti-Dumping Agreement and the World Trade Organisation ("the WTO"); and the new EC procedural rules.

The completion of the Uruguay Round after seven years of negotiation and the establishment on 1 January 1995 of the new WTO have created a framework in which anti-dumping rules should be applied for the foreseeable future. Accordingly, attention is directed primarily at the way the Council, following proposals from the Commission, has replaced the 1988 basic anti-dumping regulation in the light of the new GATT Anti-Dumping Agreement.

Finally, consideration is given to whether the new EC rules are likely to provide effective protection to EC industry in a global economy and whether that protection is lawful in the context of the new WTO and the new dispute resolution body's jurisdiction.

International aspects

The World Trade Organization agreements

The GATT

The General Agreement on Tariffs and Trade ("the GATT"), Article VI of which covers anti-dumping measures, was originally conceived as an agreement on trade policy to be adopted by an international institution which would have been called the International Trade Organisation ("the ITO"). The creation of the ITO appeared imminent in 1947. When it did not materialise, the GATT itself acquired a *de facto* status as an international institution. Despite the weakness and incompleteness of its institutional framework, the GATT has consistently acted, and been treated, as a legal entity separate from its contracting parties. It has been permitted to perform in part the function which it was intended that the ITO should perform, as a third institutional pillar, standing alongside the World Bank and the International Monetary Fund, supporting the post-war global economic order.

The WTO

The Uruguay Round of Multilateral Trade Negotiations under the GATT took place from 1986 to 1993 and the results replace the multi-tier multilateral trade order which emerged from the Tokyo Round in 1979. The 1994 Marrakesh Agreement Establishing the World Trade Organization ("the WTO Agreement")[1] combines the main agreements negotiated in the Uruguay Round into a single treaty. It is intended eventually to replace the 1947 GATT and create the WTO with a mandate to provide "the common institutional framework for the conduct of trade relations among its Members".

The new order

After the Tokyo Round of GATT trade negotiations, each contracting party to the GATT could choose to which of the resulting agreements it would become party. In contrast, the results of the Uruguay Round form part of the multilateral trade agreements that must be accepted in their entirety under the WTO agreement.[2] The WTO Agreement will in principle establish for the first time an order under which all countries assume the same obligations.[3]

The WTO Agreement prevails over any inconsistent multilateral trade agreement annexed to it, among which the GATT[4] is subordinate. It encompasses not only a new GATT Anti-Dumping Agreement but also a Dispute Settlement Understanding which sets down new rules and procedures that will govern the resolution of any dispute between members of the WTO concerning any of the agreements covered in the WTO Agreement.

---

[1] See GATT, *The Results of the Uruguay Round of Multilateral Trade Negotiations: The Legal Texts* (1994).

[2] Article II.1 of the WTO Agreement provides that: "The agreements and associated legal instruments included in Annexes 1, 2 and 3 (hereinafter referred to as the "Multilateral Trade Agreements") are integral parts of this Agreement, binding on all Members".

[3] The WTO stipulates that: "Each Member shall ensure that conformity of its laws, regulations and administrative procedures with its obligations as provided for in the annexed Agreements".

[4] The legal regime of the GATT following the Uruguay Round has been incorporated into the WTO Agreement by reference in Annex 1A. This, together with the six understandings interpreting GATT provisions and the Uruguay Round Protocol on market access and other concessions for trade in goods, is defined as the GATT 1994.

The new GATT Anti-Dumping Agreement

The 1979 Anti-Dumping Code

The Agreement on Implementation of Article VI of the General Agreement on Tariffs and Trade 1994 ("the 1994 Anti-Dumping Agreement") resulting from the recent Uruguay Round and included in Annex 1A of the WTO Agreement, revises the rules governing the application of anti-dumping measures contained in the 1979 Anti-Dumping Code.[5]

Although it leaves the basic foundations intact, the 18 articles of the new Agreement substantially amend most of the 16 articles of the 1979 Anti-Dumping Code, and there are two new annexes dealing with verification procedures and the use of best information available in cases of non-co-operation. Only those articles[6] dealing with developing countries, anti-dumping measures taken on behalf of a third country and the Committee on Anti-Dumping Practices escaped revision. Certain unilateral practices of parties to the 1979 Code (in particular the EC) have been developed into multilateral rules while others have been outlawed by the new instrument.

Different viewpoints

Different governments took fundamentally different views of the adequacy of the multilateral rules on anti-dumping measures and their proper role in the international trade system. Countries subjected to the application of anti-dumping measures[7] questioned the procedures for the initiation and conduct of anti-dumping investigations, the substantive methodology for determining the existence of dumping and material injury, and the nature and duration of anti-dumping measures adopted by certain countries in what was conceived by them to be a biased and protectionist manner. Although reconsideration of the economic rationale justifying anti-dumping measures and the consistency of proposals with the basic principles of Article VI of GATT was invited, it remains unaddressed in the new GATT Anti-Dumping Agreement.

The major users of anti-dumping measures[8], in particular the EC and the United States, take the view that effective and workable anti-dumping rules are essential to maintain an open and liberal trading system. During the negotiations, these countries were concerned to improve the legal certainty and effective enforcement of anti-dumping measures. They sought new remedies to prevent anti-dumping measures from being

---

[5] The Agreement on the Implementation of Article VI of the General Agreement on Tariffs and Trade concluded in 1979 at the end of the Tokyo Round of Multilateral Trade Negotiations. The first Anti-Dumping Code was negotiated during the Kennedy Round of GATT trade negotiations (1962–1967).

[6] Articles 14, 15 and 16 of the new Agreement.

[7] Particularly Hong Kong, Japan, Korea, the Nordic and ASEAN countries.

[8] The EC, the United States, Canada, Australia and New Zealand.

undermined by recent practices such as circumvention of duties through the export of parts and assembly operations conducted within importing countries.

The Dunkel Draft

Notwithstanding the lack of any significant progress in negotiations throughout 1991, Arthur Dunkel, the then Director-General of GATT, presented a compromise text of a new anti-dumping agreement as part of the Draft Final Act issued on 20 December 1991 ("the Dunkel Draft").[9]

Late American amendments

Although the result of arbitration rather than direct negotiation between the parties, the text of the Dunkel Draft would have been acceptable to most interested participants, and a general reluctance to re-open discussions was apparent. In November 1993, however, prompted by strong domestic criticism, the United States submitted a list of proposed changes to the text. The United States' insistence coupled with the crucial role it played in relation to other aspects of the negotiations and the pressure of an imminent deadline for the conclusion of the Uruguay Round combined to produce a final agreement on anti-dumping on 12 December 1993 in which many of their proposals were included.

Deletion of anti-circumvention provisions

The most significant omission from the 1994 Anti-Dumping Agreement was anti-circumvention measures. The Dunkel Draft made provision for duties to be applied to parts and components of a finished product assembled in an importing country, or in a third country, but the provisions were not comprehensive enough to satisfy the United States which insisted that duties should also be applicable where parts or components originated from a third country supplier.

When it became apparent that no agreement could be reached on their proposals to strengthen the provisions, the United States requested that both the anti-circumvention provisions and the country-hopping provisions be deleted in their entirety from the Dunkel Draft. The issue of circumvention has been referred by Ministerial Decision to the new WTO Committee on Anti-Dumping Practices.[10] Despite silence in the 1994 Anti-Dumping Agreement, provisions relating to anti-circumvention appear in the new EC 1994 anti-dumping regulation.

---

[9] Document MTN: TNC/W/FA, 20 December 1991.

[10] No time frame has been fixed within which this matter must be resolved (and no parameters confining the substantive matters for the Committee's consideration have been fixed).

The final text

The 1994 Anti-Dumping Agreement only applies prospectively, *i.e.* to investigations and reviews of existing measures initiated pursuant to applications which had been made on or after the date it entered into force for any particular Party to the WTO Agreement, and provisions are made for the transitional period.[11]

The need to compromise on some of the major issues has resulted in certain ambiguities, and some of the later amendments are not drafted as clearly as they might have been. There is also no compulsory uniformity when applying certain of the new rules. For example, WTO members may, if they choose, subject anti-dumping measures to a "public interest" test.[12] They may continue to impose anti-dumping duties corresponding to the full amount of the dumping margin even if a smaller amount is all that is necessary to remove the threat of injury to a domestic industry.[13] There is still no uniform system for the assessment and collection of duties. WTO members remain free to elect between anti-dumping duties and price undertakings.

Dispute resolution

Article 17: consultation and dispute settlement

The resolution of anti-dumping issues will be facilitated by the streamlined procedures of the Uruguay Round Dispute Settlement Understanding (the "DSU")[14] which, except as otherwise provided by Article 17 of the 1994 Anti-Dumping Agreement, applies to the settlement of disputes under the 1994 Agreement. A strict timetable with deadlines is to govern all the important steps in the process, including the establishment of panels, the completion of panel proceedings, the interim review stage, the appeal procedure and the adoption of panel reports.

Under the GATT each code was a separate treaty with its now non-compulsory dispute settlement mechanism. Once a panel under GATT was set up, it could only concern itself with matters covered by the particular treaty under which it was established. This was clearly an invitation to the contracting parties to go forum shopping. By contrast the DSU will create a compulsory integrated system of resolving disputes between

---

[11] See Article 18(3).

[12] The EU has applied a "Community interest" test under which the overall interests of the Community are taken into account in deciding whether or not to apply anti-dumping measures. In para 2.1.2.(a) of its 11th Report on The Community's Anti-Dumping and Anti-Subsidy Activities (1992), the Commission stated that "over the last five years this has become an increasingly important aspect in the implementation of the Community's anti-dumping policy".

[13] The Community applies a "lesser duty" rule under which care is taken to ensure that the level of the measure applied is the minimum necessary to remove the injury. In the five years comprising 1988 to 1992, the average measure imposed was only half of the average dumping margin which was 40%. See para 2.1.2.(a) of the Commission's 11th *Report on the Community's Anti-Dumping and Anti-Subsidy Activities* (1992).

[14] Contained in Annex 2 to the WTO Agreement.

members of the WTO concerning any of the agreements covered by it. However, while the GATT 1947 and the WTO co-exist[15], it may be possible to apply the dispute-settlement procedures of both regimes to the same measure.

By-passing of intermediate conciliation process

Consistent with the Dunkel Draft, Article 17 no longer contains the intermediate conciliation procedure provided for in Article 15.3 of the 1979 Anti-Dumping Code. As soon as consultations have failed to resolve a dispute over an anti-dumping action, a member can make a request to the Dispute Settlement Body[16] to establish a panel, provided at least that a provisional measure has been taken which is considered to have a significant impact by the member affected.

Together with the guideline in Article 12.8 of the DSU to the effect that the panel should take no longer than six months to produce a final report once its terms of reference have been established, this by-passing of a possibly lengthy period of attempted conciliation will no doubt expedite the dispute-resolution process.

The new procedure is one aspect of an overall "legalisation" of a process which has so far tended to be highly political and calls for a change of approach by the EC, which, unlike the United States, has viewed the GATT dispute settlement as a process of negotiation rather than adjudication.

Scope and standard of review

The Dunkel Draft did not include any of the United States' proposals for rules defining the scope and standard of review in panel decisions. Late additions resulted in Article 17.6 which addressed these issues, albeit not in complete accord with the US proposals. A bias in favour of the validity of the measure under review is incorporated. In relation to issues of fact, the panel need only be satisfied that the authorities' establishment of the facts was "proper" and that the evaluation of those facts was "unbiased and objective". These terms are inherently ambiguous allowing the exercise of a certain amount of discretion. If so satisfied, the evaluation may not be overturned even though the panel itself might have reached a different conclusion; the panel has no *de novo* jurisdiction.

Where the Agreement admits of more than one permissible interpretation, the panel must find the measure adopted by the authorities to be in

---

[15] The WTO Agreement provides that the GATT 1994 is legally distinct from, and may co-exist with, the existing GATT 1947.

[16] Dispute settlement will no longer take place under the auspices of the Committee on Anti-Dumping Practices.

conformity with the Agreement if it rests upon any one of those interpretations.[17]

More frequent resort to multilateral dispute settlement proceedings in the area of anti-dumping can be expected in line with the trend which began around 1990, especially since more countries will be bound by the 1994 Anti-dumping Agreement than were bound by the 1979 Code and test cases on the application of the new rules can be expected. The ambiguity and scope for interpretation of some of the provisions of the Agreement leave ample opportunity for the application of the standard of review formulated in Article 17.6 to be tested.

Article 17 does nothing to clarify the nature of the recommendations which can be made by panels in such disputes in the event that a measure taken is considered to be inconsistent with the obligations of the Member responsible; a highly controversial issue has been whether it is appropriate for panels to recommend the revocation or reimbursement of anti-dumping duties or to recommend that the Member reconsider specific aspects of a determination on which the measure is based.

Under the 1994 Anti-Dumping Agreement, an appeals body, able to review panel reports, will be created and the final rulings and recommendations, whether rendered by a panel or by an appellate body, will be binding on the parties.[18] Only a consensus to reject the panel or appellate report will prevent the latter from becoming operative.[19] It is no longer possible for the losing party to block the adoption of panel and appellate reports, even if it can rally support from a majority of the members.

The EEA

Following the entry into force on 1 January 1994 of the European Economic Area (EEA) Agreement, Council Regulation 5/94 was adopted.[20] It suspended all anti-dumping measures against the then EEA countries in accordance with Article 26 and Protocol 13 of the Agreement. In short, the suspension was to last as long as the EEA countries implemented the "acquis communautaire" of internal market legislation, and complied with the competition and state aid rules, annexed to the EEA Agreement.

Since Austria, Finland and Sweden joined the Community on 1 January 1995, Regulation 5/94 was of limited relevance. However, the EEA Agreement still applies to the other EEA countries Iceland, Norway and Liechtenstein (Switzerland decided not to become a member).

---

[17] A Ministerial Decision on review of Article 17.6 of the 1994 Anti-Dumping Agreement provides for a review of that Article after a period of three years with a view to considering the question whether the standard of review in this provision is capable of general application. See GATT *The Results of the Uruguay Round of Multilateral Trade Negotiations: The Legal Texts* (1994), p. 453.

[18] Article 17.14 DSU provides that the appellate reports shall be "unconditionally accepted" by the parties to the dispute. Whether this provision will influence the European Courts to revise their present reluctance to accept the direct effect of GATT rules remains to be seen.

[19] Articles 16(4) and 17(4) DSU.

[20] OJ 1994 L.

Regulation of anti-dumping measures within the EC

General framework of the 1994 anti-dumping Regulation

The new EC anti-dumping rules are to be found in Council Regulation 3283/94 of 22 December 1994 on protection against dumped imports from countries not members of the European Community ("EC")[21], as amended by Council Regulation 355/95.[22]

The main purpose of the new EC Regulation ("the 1994 Regulation") is to amend the previous rules in the light of the 1994 Agreement.[23]

Protection against dumped or subsidised imports from countries not members of the EC was previously provided by a single regulation: Council Regulation 2423/88[24], as amended by Regulations 521/94 and 522/94.[25]

For the first time, a separate Regulation has been adopted on subsidies and countervailing measures[26] in line with the 1994 GATT Subsidies Agreement.[27] The 1994 Regulation has repealed Regulation 2423/88 as amended. However, the streamlining of the decision-making process and the time limits introduced by Regulations 521/94 and 522/94 have also been incorporated into the new anti-dumping regime.

The 1994 Regulation generally came into force on 1 January 1995. It applies to proceedings and interim review investigations initiated after 1 September 1994. It also applies to expiry review investigations for which the notice of impending expiry is published after 1 September 1994.[28] By an amendment to the 1994 Regulation[29], Regulation 2423/88, although repealed, will continue to apply to such proceedings and review investigations pending on 1 September 1994 and not concluded by 1 January 1995 until 1 September 1995 when the new EC timetable came into force (see below).

Outline

The 1994 Regulation follows closely the text of the 1994 Agreement. This new approach is intended to ensure the transparent implementation of the new rules despite the extent of the changes.[30]

As the Commission stated in the Explanatory Memorandum to its proposal for the regulation, the EC approach is:

"to transpose the language of the 1994 Agreement into Community legislation to the extent possible and for this purpose the Agreement, rather than the existing

---

[21] OJ1994 L 349/1.
[22] OJ 1995 L 41/2.
[23] See recital 3 of the preamble to Regulation 3283/94.
[24] OJ 1988 L 209/1.
[25] OJ 1994 L 66, pp 7–10.
[26] Council Regulation 3284/94, OJ 1994 L 349/22.
[27] The Agreement is contained in Council Decision 94/800 , OJ 1994 L 336/156.
[28] See Article 24.
[29] Council Regulation 355/95, OJ 1995 L 41/2.
[30] See recital 5.

Community legislation ... has been taken as the basis for the proposed legislation".[31]

The 1994 Agreement contains new and detailed rules on almost every aspect of anti-dumping. In particular, this is true with regard to:

"the calculation of dumping, procedures for initiation and the subsequent investigation, including the establishment and treatment of the facts, the imposition of provisional measures, the imposition and collection of anti-dumping duties, the duration and review of anti-dumping measures and the public disclosure of information relating to anti-dumping investigations".[32]

Limited amendments also are made to the injury rules.

However, the Commission's Explanatory Memorandum describes only the main areas where the transposition of the 1994 Agreement involved changes or clarifications to its text to meet EC policy demands. According to the Commission:

"Additions to the Agreement are few and they have, for the most part, been restricted to: clarifications where the Agreement is unclear; incorporation of existing provisions on EU's rather unique procedures and decision making, amended to take account of Court judgments; and the amendment or incorporation of EU specific rules on issues such as negligible import volumes, absorption, circumvention and Community interest, on which the Agreement is silent, imprecise or where it merely gives an indication of minima".[33]

The other issues subjected to this treatment are: start-up costs; non-market economy countries' normal value; fair comparison; conclusions of investigations; violation or withdrawal of undertakings; retroactivity; refunds; suspension and registration of imports.

The EC's objective in adopting the 1994 Regulation, as in negotiating the 1994 Agreement, was to improve the transparency, legal certainty and effective enforcement of anti-dumping rules and to increase the rights of parties concerned.[34]

The main changes in the new anti-dumping regulations can be considered under three headings:

(a) Determining the existence of dumping and injury;
(b) Procedural aspects of anti-dumping investigations;
(c) Anti-dumping measures and remedies.

The substantive issues are discussed below. Procedural issues are examined in the next section. The final section deals with anti-dumping measures and remedies.

---

[31] See COM (94) 414 final.
[32] See recital 5.
[33] See COM (94) 414 final.
[34] See COM (94) 414 final, Explanatory Memorandum, p 2.

The new EC substantive anti-dumping provisions

Determining the existence of dumping and injury

This section identifies the main substantive changes introduced by the 1994 Regulation. These concern the determination of dumping (Article 2) and injury (Article 3). Specific changes affect:

(a) the conditions determining when domestic sales at below cost prices may be disregarded for normal value purposes as not being "in the ordinary course of trade";

(b) the calculation and allocation of costs for the purposes of normal value, and in particular start-up costs;

(c) the methods available for constructing normal value;

(d) the fair comparison rules;

(e) the calculation of normal value for imports from non-market economy countries;

(f) the injury rules, and in particular cumulation, the role of the dumping margin, other factors and the list of factors relevant to a threat of material injury.

Article 2: determination of dumping

The basic definition of what constitutes dumping is unchanged in Article 1.2 which states that:

"A product is to be considered as being dumped if its export price to the Community is less than a comparable price [the normal value] for the like product, in the ordinary course of trade, as established for the exporting country".[35]

The dumping margin is the amount by which the normal value exceeds the export price.[36]

Normal value

Similarly, the general rule remains that normal value should be calculated on the basis of actual prices paid or payable in the ordinary course of trade in the exporting country.[37] The exceptions arise when either domestic sales are not "in the ordinary course of trade" or "do not permit a proper comparison".[38]

---

[35] For a similar definition see Article 2.1 of both the 1979 Code and the 1994 Agreement.
[36] See 1994 Regulations, Article 2(12).
[37] *Ibid*, Article 2(1).
[38] *Ibid*, Article 2(3), and 1994 Agreement, Article 2.2.

227

The exceptions apply, for example, to domestic sales where the volumes are insufficient to be representative[39], are made between associated parties[40] or made in non-market economy countries.[41]

The EC rules have permitted two alternative methods of calculating normal value when the actual price is precluded, in addition to the specific non-market economy rules. The first involves normal value being constructed from production costs (materials and manufacturing overheads), selling, general and administrative expenses together with an amount for profit. The second, which is rarely used, is based on the export price to third countries.

Sales below cost

Among the exceptions to normal value based on actual domestic prices are sales made at a loss. The 1994 Regulation defines the circumstances in which domestic and third country export sales at prices below per unit (fixed and variable) costs of production plus selling, general and administrative costs may be treated as not being "in the ordinary course of trade". The conditions specified are that the sales must be made within an "extended period of time" in "substantial quantities" at prices which do not provide for recovery of all costs within a "reasonable period of time".[42]

The main change is the definition of the notions of "extended period of time", "substantial quantities" and prices which do not provide for the recovery of all costs within a "reasonable period of time".

The "extended period of time" should normally be one year but must not be less than six months. "Substantial quantities' of sales below cost will exist within such a period when it is established that the weighted average selling price is below the weighted average unit cost, or that the volume of sales below unit cost is not less than 20% of sales being used to determine normal value.[43]

It appears that the relevant period of time for establishing whether sales are below costs may still be the investigation period in accordance with previous EC practice (*i.e.* not less than six months immediately prior to the initiation of the proceedings). In particular, prices which are below cost at the time of sale but above weighted average costs for the investigation period must be considered to provide for recovery of costs within a "reasonable period of time".[44]

---

[39] See 1994 Regulation, Article 2(2), first included in 1994 although the 5% of exports test as a practice was introduced in 1985. See also, 1994 Agreement, Article 2.2 and footnote 2.
[40] See 1994 Regulation, Article 2(1)(b).
[41] *Ibid*, Article 2(7).
[42] *Ibid*, Article 2(4), and 1994 Agreement, Article 2.2.1.
[43] *Ibid*, Article 2(4)(b), and 1994 Agreement, Article 2.2.1 and footnotes 4 and 5.
[44] *Ibid*, Article 2(4) (a), and 1994 Agreement, Article 2.2.1 last sentence.

Start-up costs

The 1994 Regulation specifies the rules on the calculation and allocation of costs in the context of normal value generally, including the special situation of start-up costs often relevant to sales at a loss, and in particular the definition of start-up and the extent and method of allocation.[45]

Accordingly, the 1994 Regulation requires a special cost adjustment for start-up costs when calculating the cost of production for the purpose of constructing normal value or determining whether sales are below cost.

Since no precise definition of the terms "costs affected by start-up operations" or the length of "the start-up period" are given by the 1994 Agreement, the 1994 Regulation seeks to remedy the situation.[46] The former are defined as costs "affected by the use of new production facilities requiring substantial additional investment and by low capacity utilisation rates" which could cover both new products and new factories. The latter is defined flexibly by reference to "the circumstances of the producer or exporter concerned, but shall not exceed an appropriate initial portion of the period for cost recovery".[47] Since the period for cost recovery is defined as normally one year, the start-up period should logically be less than one year.[48]

Costs must normally be calculated on the basis of records kept by the exporter or producer under investigation and must be properly allocated with preference given to the turnover basis.

However, for the purpose of the start-up costs adjustment, the average costs for the start-up phase are those applicable at the end of the start-up period which takes place within or during part of the investigation period. They also must be treated as the weighted average costs for the investigation period when determining if prices provide for recovery of costs within a reasonable time (under the sales below cost rules). Moreover, "information relating to a start-up phase which extends beyond that period shall be taken into account in so far as it is submitted prior to verification visits and within three months from the initiation of the investigation".[49]

Constructed normal value

The 1994 Regulation does not alter the different methods permitted for constructing normal value but is more specific, like the 1994 Agreement, as to the methodology to be applied to determine amounts for selling, general and administrative (SG&A) costs and profit.[50]

Article 2.2.2 of the 1994 Agreement requires the amounts for SG&A and profit to be calculated by reference to "actual data" pertaining to

---

[45] *Ibid*, Article 2(5)(b), and 1994 Agreement, Article 2.2.1.1.
[46] *Ibid*, recital 6, and COM (94) 414 final, p 3 para 1.
[47] *Ibid*, Article 2(5) (b).
[48] See Commission's reasoning in COM (94) 414 final, p 3 para 1.
[49] *Ibid*, Article 2(5) (b) last sentence, and 1994 Agreement, Article 2.2.1.1.
[50] See recital 6, Regulation 3283/94.

production and sales in the ordinary course of trade of the like product by the exporter or producer under investigation. It lists without any hierarchy the alternative methods of calculation to be used where no such data exists, among which members are free to select at their discretion:

"(i) the actual amounts incurred and realised by the exporter or producer in question in respect of production and sales in the domestic market of the country of origin of the same general category of products;

(ii) the weighted average of the actual amounts incurred and realised by other exporters or producers subject to investigation in respect of production and sales of the like product in the domestic market of the country of origin;

(iii) any other reasonable method, provided that the amount for profit so established shall not exceed the profit normally realised by other exporters or producers on sales of products of the same general category in the domestic market of the country of origin."

The 1994 Regulation has reversed the order of the first two options while following the text closely.[51] One significant addition has been made to the first option under the 1994 Agreement, which is the second in the 1994 Regulation. The EC text contains the words "in the ordinary course of trade" which are only found in the opening paragraph of the Agreement text.[52]

This accords with EC practice of only taking into account profitable sales when calculating profit for the purposes of constructed normal value.[53]

Fair comparison

A number of major changes have been made by the 1994 Regulation in the context of a fair comparison between export price and normal value:

– the introduction of "fair comparison" as a separate principle from the requirement that normal value and export price must be compared at the same level of trade and in respect of sales made as nearly as possible at the same time and that due allowance or adjustments be made for differences affecting price comparability;[54]
– the clarification and extension of the adjustments permitted to allow for differences in price comparability;[55]
– the relationship between fair comparison and constructed export prices, and in particular the requirement to establish normal value at a level of trade equivalent to that of the export price, or to make due allowance, where price comparability (in comparing constructed export

---

[51] See 1994 Regulation, Article 2(6).
[52] *Ibid*, Article 2(6) (ii).
[53] See *e.g.*, Drams originating in Japan, OJ 1990 L 20/5, para 46.
[54] See 1994 Agreement, Article 2.4 (first three sentences) and Article 2.10 (first two sentences).
[55] See 1994 Agreement, Article 2.4 (third sentence); 1994 Regulation, Article 2(10) (second sentence and Article 2(10) (a) and (i).

price with normal value) is affected by the cost adjustments made in constructing the export price when sales are made through a related sales company (asymmetry);[56]
– the introduction of exchange rate rules which apply when the fair comparison requires currency conversion;[57]
– the introduction of new averaging techniques applicable when a fair comparison between normal value and export price are made, to avoid a bias in favour of finding dumping through zeroing of negative dumping margins.[58]

These changes reflect to a large extent the changes to the fair comparison rules introduced by the 1994 Agreement.

Article 2.4 of the 1994 Agreement, now specifically provides for a fair comparison as a separate principle in its own right.[59] The rest of Article 2.4 is far more specific and detailed than its counterpart (Article 2.6) in the 1979 Code. In accordance with the fair-comparison principle, due allowance must be made for differences affecting price comparability, including "differences in conditions and terms of sale, taxation, levels of trade, quantities, physical characteristics, and any other differences which are also demonstrated to affect price comparability".[60]

This reflects EC practice but the 1994 Regulation now expressly refers to all standard direct selling expenses: transport, insurance, handling, loading and ancillary costs as well as packing, credit, after-sales costs and commissions.[61]

In addition, the 1994 Regulation includes discounts and rebates together with quantities in the list of adjustments for fair comparison whereas previously they were dealt with when calculating the basic net price.[62] In theory, level of trade adjustments were also made in the context of establishing prices. For this reason, the Commission has indicated that "it is no longer rational to grant an adjustment for a fixed overhead like salesmen salaries outside the context of a level of trade adjustment".[63] It intends only to give such an adjustment where justified under level of trade which means that the previous adjustment for differences in salesmen salaries when determining prices will disappear.

These changes appear to be influenced by the new requirement in the 1994 Agreement[64] not to duplicate adjustments, since the 1994 Regulation states:

---

[56] *Ibid*, Article 2.4 (fourth and fifth sentences); 1994 Regulation, Article 2(10) (third sentence and Article 2(10) (d)).
[57] *Ibid*, Article 2.4.1; 1994 Regulation, Article 2(10) (j).
[58] *Ibid*, Article 2.4.2; 1994 Regulation Article 2(11).
[59] Article 2.6 of the 1979 Code referred to a fair comparison only obliquely.
[60] Emphasis added to reflect the changes to Article 2.6 of the 1979 Code which provided simply that due allowance should be made "for the differences in conditions and terms of sale, for the differences in taxation, and for the other differences affecting price comparability".
[61] See 1994 Regulation, Article 2(10) (e)–(i).
[62] See Regulation 2423/88, Article 2(3).
[63] See COM (94) 414 final, p 4, para 3.
[64] See 1994 Agreement, Article 2.4 footnote 7.

"Any duplication when making adjustments shall be avoided, in particular in relation to discounts, rebates, quantities and level of trade".[65]

Asymmetry

In situations where a foreign exporter sells both on its home market and in the importing state through a related sales company, the method of comparison adopted by the EC had given rise to what is known as the "asymmetry" problem. When netting back the export price and normal value to an ex-factory level, it has been the EC's practice to subtract all costs (including overheads) and profits from the export price (as part of the process of establishing the export price at the Community frontier level) while only deducting "directly related selling expenses" from normal value. The asymmetry occurs because these "directly related selling expenses" do not include overheads, and profits are not taken into account.

Article 2.4 of the 1994 Agreement provides that, in relation to constructed export prices:

"allowances for costs, including duties and taxes incurred between importation and resale, and for profits accruing, should also be made. If in these cases price comparability has been affected, the authorities shall establish the normal value at a level of trade equivalent to the level of trade of the constructed export price, or shall make due allowance as warranted under this paragraph."

This provision is reflected in two separate EC rules. The first sentence of Article 2.4 is taken up by the rule on constructing export prices at the Community frontier level.[66] The rest is covered by the level of trade adjustment rule which expressly applies to "a constructed export price"[67] and by the fair comparison principle itself.[68]

Averaging techniques and negative dumping margins

The EC practice of comparing a normal value calculated on the basis of a weighted average for the whole of the investigation period with an export price determined on a transaction-by-transaction basis has tended to inflate the dumping margins found. The main objection to this practice is that no credit is given for negative dumping margins resulting from other transactions during the period being made at prices above normal value. Nevertheless, the United States and the EC argued that such a comparison was necessary to counter "targeted dumping" – isolated dumping which might otherwise be unpunished.

---

[65] See 1994 Regulation, Article 2(10).
[66] *Ibid*, Article 2(9) (a).
[67] *Ibid*, Article 2(10) (d).
[68] *Ibid*, Article 2(10) first two sentences.

The 1994 Regulation now provides for comparison on a "like with like" basis. The existence of dumping margins:

"shall normally be established on the basis of a comparison of a weighted average normal value with a weighted average of prices of all export transactions to the Community or by a comparison of individual normal values and individual export prices to the Community on a transaction-by-transaction basis".[69]

Exceptionally, the 1994 Agreement says a weighted-average normal value may be compared to the price in an individual export transaction provided that:

"the authorities find a pattern of export prices which differs significantly among different purchasers, regions or time periods and an explanation is provided why such differences cannot be taken into account appropriately by the use of a weighted, average-to-weighted, average or transaction-to-transaction comparison."[70]

This exception was incorporated in the 1994 Regulation subject to a condition that the general rule "would not reflect the full degree of dumping being practised".[71] Accordingly, the exception can only be applied if an adequate explanation is given as to why it reflects the full degree of dumping better than the general averaging rule. Presumably, the EC will continue to zero negative margins when it applies the exception.

Exchange rates

The new provision on exchange rates provides that where it is necessary to convert currencies when effecting a comparison, the conversion should ordinarily be based on the rate of exchange on the date of sale, and that fluctuations in exchange rates should be ignored.[72] Further detailed rules deal with forward sales and defining the date of sale.

Non-market economy countries

The 1994 Regulation also has introduced detailed rules codifying the existing practice concerning the procedure for selecting analogue countries when imports come from non-market economy countries.[73] This is unaffected by the 1994 Agreement.

Article 3: determination of injury

The 1994 Regulation contains new and amended injury rules which closely follow changes introduced by the 1994 Agreement. These affect in

---

[69] *Ibid*, Article 2(11) first sentence, and 1994 Agreement, Article 2.4.2.
[70] See 1994 Agreement, Article 2.4.2.
[71] See 1994 Regulation, Article 2(11) second sentence.
[72] *Ibid*, Article 2(10) (j), and 1994 Agreement, Article 2.4.1 and footnote 8.
[73] *Ibid*, Article 2(7).

particular cumulation[74], the role of the dumping margin[75], other factors[76] and the list of factors relevant to a threat of material injury.[77]

The 1994 Agreement contains a new provision in Article 3.3 for the evaluation, where appropriate, of the cumulative effects of simultaneous imports from more than one country if the dumping margin is more than *de minimis* and the volume imported from each country is not negligible.[78] This was a late addition to the text insisted on by the United States.

Article 5.8 sets quantitative standards for determining whether an investigation is to be terminated on the ground that the margin of dumping is *de minimis, i.e.* less than 2% of the export price[79], or on the ground that the volume of imports is negligible, *i.e.* dumped goods from a particular country account for less than 3% of imports of the like product.[80] Imports are not to be considered negligible if the "countries which individually account for less than 3% . . . collectively account for more than 7% of such imports". These rules apply to imports from any country; no exception is made for imports from WTO members which are developing countries.[81]

The 1994 Agreement, Article 3.4, permits "the magnitude of the margin of dumping" to be taken into account as a relevant economic factor in assessing the impact of dumped imports on the domestic market.[82]

Under Article 3.5, other possible causes of injury to the domestic market must also be taken into account during the investigation and not attributed to dumping.[83]

Article 3.7 introduces a list of factors for determining a threat of material injury largely taken from a 1985 Recommendation of the Committee on Anti-dumping Practices.[84]

The new EC procedural anti-dumping provisions

The new EC procedural rules affect the provisions governing initiation and subsequent investigation, including the establishment and treatment

---

[74] Article 3(4).

[75] Article 3(5).

[76] Article 3(7).

[77] Article 3(9).

[78] See 1994 Regulation, Article 3(4).

[79] *Ibid*, Article 9(3).

[80] *Ibid*, Article 5(7) which refers respectively to 1% and 3% (collectively) of market share and consumption. These provisions in the Dunkel Draft were amended as a result of the last-minute proposals of the United States. The provision on *de minimis* margins of dumping was amended to make reference to the export price rather than normal value. In relation to the determination of a negligible import volume, the Dunkel Draft had referred to a criterion based on market share which was the EC practice – see COM (94) 414 final, p 5, para 6.

[81] Articles 27.10–12 of the Agreement on Subsidies and Countervailing Measures resulting from the Uruguay Round contain special rules on minimal amounts of subsidies and minimal levels of import volume requiring termination of investigations of imports from developing country members.

[82] See 1994 Regulation, Article 3(5).

[83] *Ibid*, Article 3(7).

[84] *Ibid*, Article 3(9) (a) and (b).

of the facts, the imposition of provisional measures, the imposition and collection of anti-dumping duties, the duration and review of anti-dumping measures and the public disclosure of information relating to anti-dumping investigations.[85]

In addition to the new rules implementing the 1994 Agreement, this section deals with the reforms to the EC decision-making process, timetables and guarantees of fairness to the parties involved and interested third parties such as consumers. Particular attention is drawn to the transfer of jurisdiction from the Court of Justice of the European Communities ("the ECJ") to the Court of First Instance ("the CFI") in trade protection cases. Inevitably, these procedural changes will require an improvement in the standards of procedural safeguards and reasoning if Community measures are to avoid judicial review and provide watertight assistance to Community industry.

The new procedural rules and the 1994 Agreement

The new EC procedural rules are derived closely from the 1994 Agreement, just as is the case for the new substantive rules. In particular, the rules for the initiation of anti-dumping investigations and the rights of parties during such investigations have changed. Special provisions have been made for the publication and explanation of determinations made in anti-dumping proceedings. There are also new rules on domestic judicial review.

However, the new rules are to a large extent a consolidation of existing EC rules and practice or reflect EC proposals for reform during the Uruguay Round.

Timetable

The new Regulations set down a detailed timetable which is to be rigidly applied.[86] In particular, interested parties have to make themselves known, present their views and submit information within specified time limits, if such views and information are to be taken into account. The new timetable applies to proceedings to which the old EC anti-dumping legislation does not apply – *i.e.* to proceedings in relation to which an investigation pending on 1 September 1994 had not been concluded by 1 January 1995 or in relation to which an expiry review investigation is initiated following the publication before 1 September 1994 of a notice of impending expiry.[87] But the time limits for responding to complaints and the

---

[85] See 1994 Regulation, *op cit*, recital 5 of the preamble.
[86] These changes were first set out in Council Regulation 521/94, *op cit*.
[87] See Council Regulation 355/95, *op cit*, Article 1 which amends Articles 23 and 24 of the 1994 Regulation.

duration of proceedings and the imposition of provisional duties only apply from 1 September 1995, the date specified by the Council.[88]

Submission of complaint

A complaint may be submitted by any natural or legal person, or any association not having legal personality[89] to the Commission directly or via a Member State. It will be deemed to have been lodged on the first working day following its delivery to the Commission by registered mail or on the issuing of an acknowledgment of receipt by the Commission. A copy of the complaint is sent by the Commission to the Member States at this stage.[90] The minimum contents of a complaint must contain information relating to (a) the identity of the complainant and a description by the complainant of the volume and value of the domestic production of the like product; (b) a complete description of the product alleged to have been dumped, the identity of its country of origin or export, its exporter of foreign producer and importers; (c) prices and (d) the volume of imports and its impact on the domestic market.[91]

Consultation – initial decision

The decision to initiate proceedings following the lodging of a complaint may only be taken after consultation with the Advisory Committee.[92] The Committee consists of representatives of each Member State, chaired by a representative of the Commission.[93]

After such consultation and within 45 days of the lodging of the complaint[94], the Commission must either:

(a) initiate proceedings if there is sufficient evidence to justify doing so, and publish a notice to that effect in the Official Journal, or
(b) inform the complainant that insufficient evidence has been presented to justify the initiation of proceedings.

Before an investigation may be initiated, the Commission must be satisfied that the complaint has been made "on behalf of the Community

---

[88] See the amended text of the 1994 Regulation *op cit*, which provides: "[This Regulation] shall apply to proceedings to which Regulation (EEC) No 2423/88 does not apply. The time limits prescribed by Articles 5(9), 6(9) and 7(1) shall apply in respect of complaints lodged on or after 1 September 1995 and investigations initiated pursuant to such complaints", as amended by Council Regulations (EC) 355/95 and (EC) 1251/95.

[89] 1994 Regulation, Article 5(1).

[90] *Ibid*, Article 5(1) (a).

[91] *Ibid*, Article 5(2) (i), (ii), (iii) and (iv).

[92] *Ibid*, Article 5(9).

[93] *Ibid*, Article 15. Where necessary, consultation may be in writing only – Article 15(3).

[94] *Ibid*, Article 5(9).

industry".[95] Provided the Commission has examined whether 50% of producers in the Community within the definition of "Community industry", expressing a view on the complaint, are in favour, an investigation may be initiated even if only 25% of the Community industry expressly support the complaint.[96] On receipt of a complaint, the Commission is under an express duty to examine the accuracy and adequacy of the evidence provided in the complaint in order to determine whether there is sufficient evidence to justify the initiation of an investigation.[97]

Notice setting time limits

If the Commission initiates proceedings, it must publish a notice in the Official Journal (Article 5(9)). The published notice must state the periods within which interested parties must make themselves known, present their views in writing and submit information, if such views and information are to be taken into account during the investigation.[98] The notice must also state the period within which interested parties may apply to be heard orally by the Commission.[99] Until a decision is made to initiate an investigation, there should be no publicity relating to the complaint. However, the government of the exporters' country concerned must be notified of a properly documented complaint before an investigation is initiated.[100] After initiation, a non-confidential version of the complaint must be provided to the known exporters and authorities of the exporters' country. It must also be made available, upon request, to other interested parties involved.[101]

---

[95] *Ibid*, Article 4; 1994 Agreement, Article 4. The definition of "domestic producer" remains substantially the same. It has been said that in the light of the increasing globalisation of the economy, it is surprising that the term did not receive renewed consideration. The only significant addition is footnote 2 which defines the circumstances in which producers will be deemed to be "related" to exporters or importers. Footnote 8 to the 1979 Code had simply provided that "[a]n understanding among Parties should be developed defining the word 'related' ".

[96] 1994 Regulation, Article 5(4).

[97] 1994 Agreement, Article 5.3 and 1994 Regulation, Article 5(3).

[98] *Ibid*, Article 6.1 and 1994 Regulation, Article 5(10).

[99] 1994 Regulation, Article 5(10); see also Article 6(5) for the requirement that interested parties may within the period prescribed in the notice make a written request for a hearing, showing that they are an interested party likely to be affected by the result of the proceedings and that there are particular reasons why they should be heard. See also 1994 Agreement, Article 6.3. However, one difference between the two legislative measures is that Article 6.3 of the 1994 Agreement makes it clear that oral information must only be taken into account by the authorities if it is subsequently reproduced in writing and made available to other interested parties.

[100] 1994 Regulation, Article 5(5).

[101] *Ibid*, Article 5(11).

Replies to questionnaires

Article 6(2) provides that parties receiving questionnaires used in an anti-dumping investigation shall be given at least 30 days for a reply.[102] An extension to this period may be granted, taking due account of the time limits of the investigation and provided that the party gives a good reason, in terms of its particular circumstances, for such extension. Since this provision reflects current practice, there is no reason to believe that extensions of time beyond 14 days will normally be allowed.[103] The new time limits will increase the pressures under which the Commission officials operate and may discourage them from granting extensions of time for interested parties. However, when the increases in staff at the Commission dealing with anti-dumping matters take effect, this may change. It will depend on the extent to which Community industry takes advantage of the increased opportunities to gain competitive advantages through reliance on the new anti-dumping rules.

Imposition of provisional duties

Following the initiation of proceedings and their public notification, provisional anti-dumping duties may be imposed, but no sooner than 60 days, or later than nine months, from the initiation of the proceedings.[104]

Duration of provisional duties

Under Article 7(7) of the 1994 Regulation, provisional duties may be imposed for a period of six months, which may be extended for a further three months, or for nine months from the outset.[105]

Conclusion of investigations

Article 6(9) of the 1994 Regulation states that, except in special circumstances, investigations must be concluded, with or without measures being

---

[102] The time-limit for exporters is counted from the date of receipt of the questionnaire, which is deemed to have been received one week from the day on which it was sent to the exporter or transmitted to the appropriate diplomatic representative of the exporting country. See also 1994 Agreement, Article 6.1.

[103] In a recent notice of initiation concerning imports of computer disks from Canada, Indonesia, Macau and Thailand (OJ 1995 C 84/4), the Commission stipulated that exporters and importers had 37 days from the third day following publication in the *Official Journal, i.e.,* 40 days. The Commission has also given those who requested an extension of time an additional 14 days, namely a total of 54 days. Fourteen-days extension seems to be standard practice which will be unlikely to be exceeded once the new time limits are applied by the Commission.

[104] 1994 Regulation, Article 7(1). Although the 1994 Agreement, Article 7.3 provides for the ''not less than sixty days'' rule, the deadline of nine months is not set down.

[105] Whether the nine month time limit is imposed at the outset or the six month period is extended, provisional measures may only be imposed for nine months where exporters representing a significant percentage of the trade involved so request or do not object upon notification by the Commission. See also 1994 Agreement, Article 7.4.

imposed, within one year, and in no case more than 15 months after their initiation.[106]

If undertakings are accepted at the conclusion of an investigation, the investigation of dumping and injury may be terminated under Article 8 of the 1994 Regulation. But, in practice, the investigation will be continued, either at the request of the party giving the undertaking or by the Commission on its own initiative.

Requests for refunds

Within six months of the date on which the amount of a definitive duty is determined, a request for a refund of anti-dumping duties may be submitted by an importer to the Commission via the Member State in which the product in question was released into circulation.[107] Under Article 11(8)(C), refunds of duties must normally take place within twelve months, and in no case more than 18 months, after the date on which a request for a refund, duly supported by evidence, has been made.[108] The payment of any refund authorised should normally be made by Member States within 90 days of the decision to refund.[109]

As to the criteria to be used by the Commission in assessing whether refunds should be made, regard should be had to the 1994 Agreement and in particular Article 9.3.3 thereof. In the preamble to the 1994 Regulation and at Article 11(10) thereof, it is made clear that in calculating whether refunds are due or not, the Commission shall not, where export prices have been constructed, treat existing anti-dumping duties as a cost incurred between importation and resale when the duty is shown to be reflected in the prices of the products subject to measures in the Community. This is a change from the previous position taken by the Community, when duties were always treated as a cost.[110]

Interim reviews

Interim reviews of definitive anti-dumping measures can be initiated at any time by the Commission or at the request of a Member State. Additionally, any exporter, importer or Community producer may, by a request supported by sufficient evidence of need, seek interim review

---

[106] This deadline is one of the few differences between the EC legislation and the 1994 Agreement which sets the maximum time period for the conclusion of anti-dumping investigations at 18 months. See also, the Commission Explanatory Memorandum relating to the proposal for the 1994 Regulation.

[107] See 1994 Regulation, Article 11(8) (a).

[108] See 1994 Agreement, Article 9.3.1.

[109] *Ibid.*

[110] See *e.g.*, Case C-188/88, *NMB (Deutschland)* v *Commission*, [1992] ECR I-1689. An action has recently been brought before the Court of First Instance by various NMB subsidiaries, which seeks to overrule the previous NMB decision of the Court of Justice – see Case T-78/95, *NMB* v *Commission*, OJ 1995 C 119/27.

provided a reasonable period of at least one year has elapsed since the imposition of the definitive measure sought to be reviewed.[111]

Any review must be conducted expeditiously and Article 11(5) of the 1994 Regulation states that it must normally be concluded within 12 months of the date of initiation.[112]

Expiry of definitive measures

Unless it is determined in a review that the expiry of an anti-dumping measure would be likely to lead to a continuation or recurrence of the dumping and injury, a definitive anti-dumping measure must expire five years from its imposition or five years from the date of the conclusion of the most recent review covering both dumping and injury.[113] A notice of impending expiry must be published in the Official Journal at an appropriate time within the final year of the period of application of the measure. After publication, and no later than three months before the end of the five-year period, the Community producers are entitled to lodge a review request.

Guarantees of fairness to the parties involved and interested third parties

The new Regulation recognises that the interests of product users and consumer organisations should also be taken into account[114], along with the interests of exporters, importers, foreign producers and complainants. In previous anti-dumping proceedings, the Commission has refused the European Consumers' Organisation access to the non-confidential file and in 1991, the ECJ refused to hear a complaint made on its behalf.[115] The right to information for importers, exporters and complainants has already been upheld in the *Al-Jubail* case.[116]

In the preamble to the new Regulation, it is recognised that it is necessary to lay down how interested parties should be given notice of the information which the authorities require, ample opportunity to present all relevant evidence and a full opportunity for the defence of their interests, and that it is also appropriate to set out the conditions under which an interested party may have access to, and comment on, information presented by other interested parties.[117] It is also recognised that provision should be made for the treatment of confidential information so that business secrets are not divulged.[118]

---

[111] See 1994 Regulation, Article 11(3).
[112] See also 1994 Agreement, Article 11.4.
[113] See 1994 Regulation, Article 11(2) and 1994 Agreement, Article 11.3.
[114] See for example 1994 Regulation, Article 6(7) on access to the Commission's file and 1994 Agreement, Articles 6.4 and 6.5.
[115] Case C-170/89, *BEUC* v *Commission*, [1991] ECR I-5709.
[116] Case C-49/88, [1991] ECR I-3187.
[117] 1994 Regulation, Recital 13; see also 1994 Agreement, Articles 6.2, 6.3 and 6.4.
[118] 1994 Regulation, Recital 28 and Article 19.

Access to information

With due regard to the protection of confidential information, the Commission will provide the full text of the written complaint to both the known exporters and the authorities of the exporting country – unless the known exporters are particularly numerous, in which case the full text will be supplied only to the authorities or the relevant trade association. The full text of the written complaint will be made available to the other interested parties involved upon request.[119]

Article 6(7) provides that all information which is relevant to the presentation of their cases and which has been made available by any party to an investigation[120], may be inspected, on request, by the complainants, importers, exporters, users and consumer organisations which have made themselves known in accordance with Article 5(10), provided it is used in the investigation and is not confidential.[121]

Parties which offer an undertaking will be required to provide a non-confidential version of the undertaking, so that it may be made available to interested parties to the investigation.[122]

Article 20 of the 1994 Regulation deals with disclosure. Article 20(1) provides that the complainants, importers, exporters and representatives of the exporting country may request disclosure of the details underlying the essential facts and considerations on the basis of which provisional measures have been imposed. Article 20(2) covers final disclosure of the essential facts and considerations on the basis of which the Commission intends to recommend the imposition of definitive measures, or the termination of an investigation or proceedings without the imposition of measures. Disclosure of these matters under Article 20 must be given in writing, as soon as possible.

Opportunity to be heard

The right to a fair hearing has already been recognised in the context of anti-dumping proceedings. In *Al-Jubail Fertilizer Company* v *Council*[123], the ECJ annulled provisions imposing anti-dumping duties on the grounds of procedural defects.

An interested party may be heard under Article 6(5) of the 1994 Regulation if, within the time period prescribed, it has requested a

---

[119] *Ibid*, Article 5(11).

[120] Other than in internal documents prepared by the authorities of the Community or its Member States. This distinction is not made in the 1994 Agreement, but reflects EC practice in anti-dumping and competition proceedings.

[121] 1994 Regulation, Article 6(7) is a particularly bad example of the typing errors in the English language text. It is understood that the Regulation will be republished to remove such errors in all language versions affected.

[122] 1994 Regulation, Article 8(4).

[123] *Op cit.*

hearing in writing showing that it is in fact an interested party likely to be affected by the result of the proceedings and that there are particular reasons why it should be heard orally.

Provisional measures may not be imposed until after notice of the initiation of proceedings has been published and interested parties have been given adequate opportunities to submit information and make comments in accordance with Article 5(10) of the 1994 Regulation.[124]

Provided they have made themselves known in accordance with Article 5(10), importers, exporters and representatives of the government of the exporting country and the complainants must be given the opportunity, on request, to meet those parties with adverse interests, so that opposing views may be presented and rebuttal arguments offered.[125] Again, the need to preserve confidentiality and also the convenience of the parties will be taken into account. Attendance at confrontation meetings is not obligatory and a party's failure to attend will not be prejudicial to that party's case.

Following inspection of the file under Article 6(7), an opportunity will be given to comment on the information inspected and those comments which are properly substantiated in the response should be taken into consideration by the authorities.

Confidentiality

Confidentiality is dealt with throughout the Regulation in the context of other matters but is specifically addressed in Article 19(1) of which provides that any information which is by nature confidential[126] or which is provided on a confidential basis by parties to an investigation[127] must, upon good cause shown[128], be treated as such by the authorities.

Article 19(2) requires interested parties providing confidential information to furnish summaries of the information provided.[129] While these summaries will not be confidential themselves, they must be sufficiently detailed to permit a reasonable understanding of the substance of the

---

[124] 1994 Regulation, Article 7(1); see also 1994 Agreement, Article 7.1.

[125] *Ibid*, Article 6(6); see also 1994 Agreement, Article 6.2.

[126] The same paragraph suggests that information might be confidential by nature for example "because its disclosure would be of significant competitive advantage to a competitor or because its disclosure would have a significantly adverse effect upon a person supplying the information or upon a person from whom he acquired the information"; see to the same effect Article 6.5 of the 1994 Agreement.

[127] Under Article 19(5), the Council, the Commission and Member States, or the officials of any of these shall not reveal any information received pursuant to the Regulation for which confidential treatment has been requested by its supplier, without specific permission from the supplier.

[128] Article 19(3) provides that requests for confidentiality should not be arbitrarily rejected and that information which is not capable of verification from appropriate, presumably independent, sources must be disregarded if insistence on confidentiality is unwarranted. See also Article 6.5.2 of the 1994 Agreement.

[129] See also Article 6.5.1 of the 1994 Agreement.

information submitted in confidence. Where this is not possible, the provider of confidential information must furnish a statement explaining why such summary was not possible.

Judicial review

Article 13 of the 1994 Agreement requires each country which is party to the multilateral agreements and whose legislation contains provisions on anti-dumping measures, to maintain judicial, arbitral or administrative tribunals or procedures for the purposes of the prompt review of administrative actions, final determinations and reviews thereof. It requires further that such tribunals or procedures be independent of the authorities responsible for the determination or review in question. This provision is new, but its effect may well be far-reaching in terms of the present strict rules concerning *locus standi* for bringing applications for judicial review before the Community courts.

Transfer of jurisdiction

The Council finally agreed in 1994 to transfer jurisdiction in anti-dumping and subsidy cases from the Court of Justice to the Court of First Instance.[130] This should assist Community industry adversely affected by unfair trade practices as well as defendants in Commission proceedings since the CFI can be expected to insist on much higher standards of reasoning in EC measures and in decision-making procedures. There will be greater need for complainants to co-operate with the Commission in the supply of evidence and legal arguments and to ensure that the Commission uses them properly. At the same time, defendants will be in a position to expose the weaknesses of the Community's regulations if reasoning is inadequate or evidence lacking.

In a recent paper[131], Advocate General Francis Jacobs has suggested that while it will be bound by the caselaw of the ECJ, the CFI may be expected to continue progressively to expand the test of "standing" applied to judicial review under Article 173 following the approach adopted by the ECJ.[132]

---

[130] Council Decision 93/350, OJ 1994, L 66/29. Appeals on a point of law may be made to the ECJ from the CFI.

[131] See Jacobs, "Judicial Review of Commercial Policy Measures After the Uruguay Round", *supra.*

[132] The position of the ECJ on standing in anti-dumping cases has evolved from allowing exporters named in a Council Regulation to challenge the regulations to allowing unnamed exporters, complainants, related and in certain cases unrelated importers the right to challenge EC dumping measures recognised as being of direct and individual concern to them. See for example Case C-358/89, *Extramet Industrie* v *Council,* [1991] ECR I-2501.

He also notes that the CFI may be expected to scrutinise more closely the Council and Commission anti-dumping measures.[133] Increased scrutiny has been evident in recent competition cases.[134] The first anti-dumping decision of the CFI[135] indicates that this is indeed so, with the Court showing itself willing to enter into the details of injury determinations by the institutions. In the particular case in question, the CFI annulled the regulation, in so far as it imposed anti-dumping duties on the applicant companies, on the grounds that the injury determination was flawed by errors of fact and law.

Jacobs questions whether an undertaking which could have challenged a regulation in the CFI directly under Article 173 will, having failed to do so, be able to challenge it in the national courts instead, and obtain a reference to the ECJ under Article 177. He suggests that, in the light of the recent state aid decision in *TWD*[136], it might be argued that such a course is not available because the more appropriate procedure of a direct action would thereby be circumvented and the appropriate forum avoided. However, he warns against the extension of the reasoning in *TWD* to anti-dumping cases on the ground that the standing of an undertaking affected by anti-dumping regulations is often uncertain whereas the recipient of an individual state aid undoubtedly has standing to challenge directly the decision of the Commission declaring that aid to be unlawful.[137]

Politics and the EC decision-making process

Under the original EC provisions, regulations imposing definitive duties could only be adopted by the Council acting by qualified majority. This gave interested parties considerable scope for lobbying the different Member States to vote in accordance with national, rather than Community interests. Now, under the new provisions, which follow the amendments laid down in Council Regulation 522/94, the Council only has to act by a simple majority, making lobbying more difficult.[138] The vote change resulted from a compromise in the inter-institutional negotiations. The Commission had proposed originally that it should take over responsibility for imposing definitive duties in order to supplement its existing power to impose provisional duties. This proposal was not acceptable to the

---

[133] The preamble to Council Decision 88/591/ECSC, EEC, Euratom, establishing a Court of First Instance of the European Communities recites that "in respect of actions requiring close examination of complex facts, the establishment of a second court will improve the judicial protection of individual interests".

[134] See *e.g.*, the decisions in Cases T-68/89, 77/89, *Flat Glass*, [1992] ECR II-1403 and Cases T-78/89, 84–86/89, etc, *PVC*, [1992] ECR II-315.

[135] Cases T-163/94 and T-165/94, *NTN Corporation and Koyo Seiko Co. Ltd v Council*, judgment of 2 May 1995.

[136] Case C-188/92, *Textilwerke Deggendorf v Germany*, [1994] ECR I-833.

[137] On this point, see further Advocate General Jacobs' opinion in the *TWD* case, particularly paragraph 14 thereof.

[138] See 1994 Regulation, Article 9(4). However, the recent photocopier review case was decided by a majority of 8 to 7.

Council, which had no desire to relinquish political control over dumping and other trade policy instruments. The move to voting by simple majority may not streamline the EC decision-making process as intended. In fact, it may lead to the proliferation of ill-considered anti-dumping measures which will in turn lead to more frequent challenges before the Community courts. Conflicts of interest between different producers or importers in the different Member States will be less open to political compromise in the general interest of the Community. Disappointed Community importers and producers may be forced to challenge Council measures in the CFI just as much as the condemned exporters from outside the Community. However, a blocking minority of Member States continues to be able to prevent the termination of an anti-dumping proceeding when proposed by the Commission, since the Council must act by a qualified majority to terminate proceedings.[139]

Application of anti-dumping measures

Anti-dumping measures and remedies

The main changes introduced by the 1994 Regulation in the context of anti-dumping measures and remedies are designed to implement the 1994 GATT Agreement. The changes affect the time limits for imposition of provisional and definitive duties (see previous section), the rules applicable to undertakings, refunds and reviews, retroactive duties and import registration as well as related rules on the lesser duty rule, Community interest and five-year automatic termination of duties (already discussed).

However, there are notable exceptions such as anti-absorption, circumvention and suspension introduced or modified to meet purely Community policy objectives.

Key aspects of the changes are examined in this section. The important role of judicial review by both the CFI and, on further appeal, the ECJ, as well as that of the new WTO dispute settlement body have been referred to above.

Article 7: provisional measures

Article 7 of the 1994 Agreement clarifies the substance of Article 10.1 of the 1979 Code. Provisional anti-dumping measures can be applied only after a preliminary determination of dumping and injury and no sooner than 60 days after an investigation has been properly initiated during which interested parties have been provided adequate opportunity to participate in the procedure. Following a proposal by the EC, provision has been made for the extension by 50% of the ordinary period (four or six months) during which preliminary measures may be applied when

---

139 *Ibid*, Article 9(2).

"the authorities, in the course of an investigation, examine whether a duty lower than the margin of dumping would be sufficient to remove the injury".

Accordingly, Article 7(7) of the 1994 Regulation provides that provisional duties may be imposed for six or nine months at the outset or be extended to a total of nine months where exporters representing a significant percentage of the trade involved so request, or do not object on notification by the Commission.

Article 8: price undertakings

Article 8 of the new Agreement covers price undertakings. The amendments introduced relate to the timing of the acceptance of price undertakings, the discretion of investigating authorities in deciding whether or not to accept price undertakings and the procedures for continuation of investigations after undertakings have been accepted.

Whereas Article 7.1 of the 1979 Code provided that price increases shall not be higher than necessary to eliminate the margin of dumping, the last sentence of Article 8.1 in the new Agreement states, "It is desirable that the price increases be less than the margin of dumping if such increases would be adequate to remove the injury to the domestic industry".

Article 8.2 provides that price undertakings may not be sought or accepted from exporters without first making a preliminary affirmative determination of dumping and injury. (Article 7.2 of the 1979 Code required only that an investigation should have been initiated.)

In response to pressure by the United States, under Article 8.3, "reasons of general policy" are the only justification necessary for declining to accept an offer of undertakings, thus allowing Members to exercise a considerable degree of discretion. Under Article 7 of the 1979 Code, price undertakings offered had to be considered impractical before they could be refused.

Where practicable, authorities of an importing member should now give the exporter reasons for considering the acceptance of a price undertaking to be inappropriate, and allow him to comment: Article 8.3. Where price undertakings are accepted, Article 8.4 requires the continuation of the investigation in relation to both dumping and injury if either the exporter wishes it to continue or the authorities unilaterally decide to continue.

Article 8 of the 1994 Regulation has incorporated these changes. However, a modification to past practice has been introduced by Article 8(9) to permit the imposition of definitive duties in cases where violation or withdrawal of undertakings is proven and by Article 8(10) to permit provisional duties when such violation is suspected.

Article 9: imposition and collection of anti-dumping duties

Article 9 of the new Agreement governs the imposition and collection of anti-dumping duties. It amends Article 8 of the 1979 Code by introducing new provisions on time limits for refund procedures[140], rules for determining when anti-dumping duties can be treated as a cost for the purposes of refund procedures[141], regulation of the imposition of anti-dumping duties on imports when the exporter has not been examined individually[142], and treatment of "new exporters".[143] It no longer contains a provision on the use of basic price systems in anti-dumping proceedings.

Bases of assessment

Articles 9.3.1 and 9.3.2 govern the assessment of anti-dumping duties on a "retrospective" basis and on a "prospective" basis respectively. The United States adopts the former method and the EC the latter. No harmonisation of the various assessment procedures in use being possible, the Agreement recognises that the use of different methods is equally permissible.

Refund calculation

The EC's practice in determining anti-dumping duty refunds has been criticised since, unless the product is sold on a duty unpaid basis, the duty paid is treated as a cost incurred between importation and first resale to an independent buyer which is deducted from the first resale price. Only if the resale price is increased by an amount at least equivalent to the sum of the dumping margin and the anti-dumping duty combined[144], will a refund be granted.

Article 9.3.3 of the new Agreement addresses the calculation of refunds where the export price is constructed in accordance with Article 2.3 and specifically provides that "authorities . . . should calculate the export price with no deduction for the amount of anti-dumping duties paid . . . in certain circumstances".[145]

Article 11(10) of the 1994 Regulation incorporates the EC's interpretation of the Agreement's restriction of the application of the "duty as a cost" principle. Such restrictions are extended thereby to all cases where export prices are constructed, including expiry and interim review procedures as well as refunds.

---

[140] Articles 9.3.1 and 9.3.2.

[141] Article 9.3.3.

[142] Article 9.4.

[143] Article 9.5.

[144] Known as the "double jump".

[145] The full text of Article 9.3.3 reads: "In determining whether and to what extent a reimbursement should be made when the export price is constructed in accordance with paragraph 3 of Article 2, authorities should take into account any change in normal value, any change of costs incurred between importation and resale, and any movement in the resale price which is duly reflected in subsequent selling prices, and should calculate the export price with no deduction for the amount of anti-dumping duties paid when conclusive evidence of the above is provided".

Exporters not examined individually

Under Article 9.4, where duties are imposed on imports from exporters who have not been examined individually, they may not exceed the weighted average margin of dumping established in respect of exporters or producers who have been examined individually[146] but margins which do not exceed the *de minimis* threshold shall not be taken into account. Article 6.10 introduces new rules on sampling techniques. However, where the absence of individual examination is the result of non-co-operation, the sampling rules give way to the non-co-operation rules in Article 18.

New exporters

Exporters who begin to export a product which is already subject to an anti-dumping duty but who did not export such a product within the investigation period, and who are not related to any exporters or producers subject to the existing anti-dumping duty, may benefit from Article 9.5 which requires that an expedited review be conducted to determine individual margins of dumping for the new exporters. No anti-dumping duties may be levied on imports during the review stage but anti-dumping duties may eventually be imposed retroactively and the authorities are permitted to withhold customs appraisement (see below) and/or request guarantees to ensure that this is possible.[147]

Article 11 of the 1994 Regulations introduces new rules on the three types of review: expiry, interim and newcomer.

Article 10: retroactivity and import registration

Article 11 of the 1979 Code permitted the imposition of anti-dumping duties retroactively to imports entered for consumption not more than 90 days prior to the date of the application of provisional measures, provided that injury was caused by "sporadic dumping" (massive dumping of imports in a relatively short period) and that either there was a history of dumping causing injury or the importer was, or should have been, aware that the exporter practised dumping and that such dumping would cause injury. The justification for the imposition of retroactive duties used to be that it should appear necessary in order to preclude the recurrence of such sporadic dumping.

Article 10.6 of the new Agreement removes the reference to "sporadic dumping" and rather than relying on the need to prevent recurrence, emphasises the likely undermining effect which massive dumped imports

---

[146] Provision is made for the situation where a prospective normal value is used as the basis for the assessment of anti-dumping duties. In such a case, the differences between the weighted average normal value of the selected exporters or producers and the export prices of exporters or producers are not individually examined.

[147] See Articles 9.5 and 10.7.

may have on the remedial effect of the definitive anti-dumping duty to be applied. A proposal of the EC resulted in the addition to Article 10.6(ii) of a proviso to the effect that the importers concerned should be given an opportunity to comment. Article 10.8 prohibits the retroactive application of anti-dumping duties under Article 10.6 to products entered for consumption prior to the date when an investigation was initiated.

Article 10(4) of the 1994 Regulation defines the terminology used by the Agreement. It makes it clear that a "history of dumping" will be established when dumping takes place over an extended period, "awareness" by the importer when the margins found are high and that dumping will be "massive" when, in addition to the level of dumped imports during the investigation period, there is a further substantial increase in imports just prior to the imposition of provisional duties (Article 10(4)(ii)).

The Commission's only proposal for the imposition of retroactive duties was not adopted by the Council.[148] However, this hesitance may disappear with the introduction of "withholding of appraisal" called "import registration" by Article 14(5) of the 1994 Regulation.

Import registration is a mechanism whereby the Commission requires national customs authorities to register imports until a decision is taken regarding them in the investigation concerned, for example investigations for new exporters, retroactivity or circumvention. The procedure would be identical to that used for provisional duties save that importers would not have to pay cash or give guarantees, but duties could be imposed retroactively to the date of registration. For example, under Article 10(4) definitive duties may be imposed on products which were entered for consumption not more than 90 days prior to provisional duties provided the imports were registered and that the period is not prior to the initiation of investigation.

The purpose of the import registration mechanism is to facilitate imposition of retroactive provisional, newcomer, circumvention and anti-absorption duties.

Article 11: duration and review of anti-dumping measures and price undertakings

The introduction of a "sunset" clause in Article 11.3 provides for the termination of any definitive anti-dumping duty no later than five years after its imposition or the most recent review of it under Article 11.3. The Dunkel Draft permitted the extension of the period of application of a particular anti-dumping duty only where that was considered "necesary" to prevent the continuance or recurrence of injury by dumped imports. As a result of late pressure by the United States the final text of the new Agreement allows prolongation where "the expiry of the duty would be

---

[148] See proceedings concerning urea originating in Czechoslovakia, GDR, Kuwait *et al*, OJ 1987 L 317/1.

likely to lead to continuance or recurrence of dumping and injury". This has been incorporated in Article 11 of the 1994 Regulations.

Under Article 18.3.2, members are allowed a transition period of five years from the date on which the WTO Agreement enters into force for them within which the "sunset" clause must be applied to existing measures (unless, as is the case in the EC, those measures are already subject to a "sunset" clause contained in the relevant members' national legislation).

Other EC changes

Additional changes have been made by modifying the anti-absorption rules in Article 12, the anti-circumvention provisions in Article 13 and by introducing a new suspension procedure in Article 14(4) of the 1994 Regulation.

Anti-absorption

The main change to the anti-absorption provisions in Article 12 is that they now specifically require a re-assessment of export prices and a new calculation of dumping margins where measures have had no impact on the prices of the goods subject to duty. An investigation to take account of changes in normal values is also permitted where evidence is produced by the exporter. Previously, the old rule (Article 13(11)) had been criticised as being incompatible with the GATT since there was no new dumping calculation made.

Anti-circumvention

The EC anti-circumvention rules were condemned by a GATT panel which the EC said it accepted only on condition that there was a satisfactory solution reached in the Uruguay Round. As noted already, the 1994 Agreement is silent on the subject which was left to further negotiation by a Ministerial Declaration at Marrakesh. The Commission has interpreted this lacuna as appearing to permit, for the first time, individual WTO members to deal with the problem unilaterally, pending a multilateral solution via the WTO Anti-dumping Committee.

As a result, Article 13 of the 1994 Regulation provides for the imposition of duties to imports of like products or parts thereof in the case of what is described as "classic" circumvention when assembly takes place in the EC or a third country other than that subject to the circumvented proceedings or in general, for example, through false origin declarations or through loss of origin under the EC Customs rules as a result of "country hopping".

Under these rules, three conditions must be satisfied:

– the assembly operation must have started or substantially increased since, or just prior to, the initiation of the anti-dumping investigation and the parts concerned must be from the country subject to measures; and
– the parts must constitute 60% or more of the total value of the parts of the assembled product except that in no case may circumvention be considered to be taking place where the value added to the parts brought in, during the assembly or completion operation, is greater than 25% of the manufacturing cost; and
– the remedial effects of the duty are being undermined in terms of the prices and/or quantities of the assembled like product and there is evidence of dumping in relation to the normal values previously established for the like or similar products.

It is difficult to predict how the EC will apply Article 13 which is a compromise between the 1987 rule's 60/40 parts test and the Dunkel paper's 25% added value test. It may well be simply a negotiating stance for future WTO discussions. However, the first case has been initiated in respect of computer disks.

Suspension

Article 14(4) of the 1994 Regulation introduces a new provision to enable the temporary suspension for a period of nine months of anti-dumping measures, when market conditions indicate that such measures are temporarily inappropriate. Previously, the measures had to be terminated altogether.

Conclusion

The 1994 Agreement and Regulation may be considered as milestones in the development of multilateral and EC trade regulation. In particular, greater precision has been introduced with regard to the substantive rules as well as greater legal certainty and fairness introduced in the context of procedural safeguards and anti-dumping measures for exporters and importers. However, the true test of the value of the changes must await the practice of the Commission and Council.

The new time limits applicable in EC investigations from 1 September 1995 will impose a new and unfamiliar pressure on the Community institutions.

The increased substantive and procedural standards will confront Community industry with a new challenge when resort is made to the unfair trade rules. Unless complaints and investigations comply with the new rules, any consequent anti-dumping duties will be vulnerable to attack before the CFI and, on appeal, the ECJ as well as the new WTO DSB.

A new era of EC anti-dumping practice can be anticipated. Sir Leon Brittan, the Commissioner responsible for introducing the streamlined procedures and time-limits, can be expected to require full compliance with the 1994 Agreement and Regulation. Exporters and importers can expect much greater attention to be paid to their procedural rights than in the past. Community industry must meet the challenges of the new "legalisation" or "judicialisation" of anti-dumping regulation if trade protection measures are to be effective. This will bring a much heavier burden on EC business since the Community institutions cannot satisfy the new stricter standards accepted in the new rules without fuller support and co-operation from Community industry than in some past cases.

MARK CLOUGH
FERGUS RANDOLPH

Chapter 15

The GATT Dispute Settlement System as an Instrument of the Foreign Trade Policy of the EC

GATT Article XXIII Dispute Settlement Procedures: Kinds of Complaints and Remedies

Six different kinds of complaints under GATT Article XXIII:1

The GATT regulates the settlement of trade disputes both at the national and at the international level. Article X:3(b) requires, *inter alia*, that:

"Each contracting party shall maintain, or institute as soon as practicable, judicial, arbitral or administrative tribunals or procedures for the purpose, *inter alia*, of the prompt review and correction of administrative action relating to customs matters. Such tribunals or procedures shall be independent of the agencies entrusted with administrative enforcement and their decisions shall be implemented by, and shall govern the practice of, such agencies unless an appeal is lodged with a court or tribunal of superior jurisdiction within the time prescribed for appeals to be lodged by importers. . . ."

Accordingly, tariffs and non-tariff trade barriers can be reviewed by domestic courts in most GATT contracting countries. Such court decisions, for instance United States court decisions in the field of anti-dumping law and Court of Justice decisions relating to the customs union law of the EC, may also influence GATT practice. In the past, they have also given rise to international GATT dispute settlement proceedings over the consistency of such judgments with the GATT obligations of the countries concerned.

International procedures for the settlement of disputes among GATT contracting parties are set out in Articles XXII, XXIII and in a few special GATT provisions, such as Article XVIII:12 (disputes over balance-of-payments restrictions) and Article XXIV:7 (disputes over the GATT consistency of interim agreements for a customs union or free trade area), which do not exclude recourse to the general GATT dispute settlement procedures in Article XXIII. Article XXII provides for bilateral and multilateral consultations "regarding such representations as may be made by

This contribution was written in 1994 and does not deal with the new dispute settlement system in the 1994 Agreement Establishing the World Trade Organization, which entered into force on 1 January 1995 and considerably modified the previous dispute settlement system of the "GATT 1947" analyzed in this paper. Cf. E.U. Petersmann, The Dispute Settlement System of the World Trade Organization (1994), CMLRev 1157–1244.

another contracting party with respect to any matter affecting the operation of this Agreement". Article XXIII:1 specifies six different kinds of "violation complaints" (Article XXIII:1(a)), "non-violation complaints" (Article XXIII:1(b)) and "situation complaints" (Article XXIII:1(c)).[1] The focus in Article XXIII:1 on the unusual notions of "nullification or impairment of any benefit accruing directly or indirectly under this Agreement" and on "the attainment of any objective of the Agreement being impeded", rather than on the traditional legal concepts of "legality of acts"[2] and "state responsibility" for "internationally wrongful acts", was inspired by earlier international trade agreements. Notably the pre-war bilateral trade agreements of the United States had attempted to protect the competitive benefits from reciprocal tariff liberalisation from being undermined by non-tariff measures, even if the latter were not prohibited (such as production subsidies). There was also a widely felt need among the drafters of the GATT in 1947 for a sort of "equity law jurisdiction"[3] which would enable collective decisions to deal with the impairment of Treaty benefits resulting from trade restrictions due to unforeseen new situations, such as a world-wide monetary crisis or a depression with widespread unemployment.

In GATT practice, only two of the six kinds of complaints under Article XXIII have been actively used by GATT contracting parties. Over 90% of the altogether more than two hundred disputes under Article XXIII have been "violation complaints" over "nullification or impairment of benefits accruing under the GATT".[4] Fifteen complaints have been "non-violation complaints" over "nullification or impairment of benefits accruing under the GATT". Only four disputes under Article XXIII involved "situation complaints" referring to "other situations" in terms of Articles XXIII:1(c). Moreover, in only three complaints did the complainant contend that "the attainment of any objective of the Agreement" was being impeded. Contrary to the expectations of some of the drafters of Article XXIII, the post-war economic crises – such as the breakdown of the fixed exchange rate system, the quadrupling of oil prices and the widespread "stagflation" during the 1970s – prompted increased efforts at trade liberalisation (*e.g.* in the 'Tokyo Round' from 1973–1979) rather than increased recourse to GATT Article XXIII. Beyond the rights GATT law explicitly confers, the only other "benefits accruing under the General Agreement" recognised by the contracting parties under Article XXIII:1, were the protection of reasonable expectations – based on reciprocal tariff negotiations – as to the maintenance of the conditions of competition prevailing at the time of the negotiations, or as to the agreed balance of reciprocal tariff concessions.

---

[1] For an analysis of these different kinds of complaints see: Petersmann, 'Violation-Complaints and Non-Violation Complaints in Public International Trade Law', (1991) 34 *German Yearbook of International Law* 175–229.

[2] *cf.* Article 173 EC.

[3] See Article XXIII:1, b and c GATT.

[4] For a chronological list of 195 disputes under Article XXIII from 1948–1993 see: Analytical Index, *Guide to GATT Law and Practice* (GATT 1994), pp 719–734.

So far, no GATT panel and no GATT dispute settlement ruling has ever based its legal findings on Article XXIII:1(c) or on the impeding of "the attainment of any objective of the Agreement". In view of the vague language and criteria for such "situation complaints" and complaints over "impeding of GATT objectives", it is to be welcomed that these unpredictable types of complaints have fallen into disuse.

Rulings and recommendations under Article XXIII:2

GATT Article XXIII:2 provides for three kinds of remedies: rulings, recommendations and suspension of obligations. Paragraph 2 states, *inter alia*:

"If no satisfactory adjustment is effected between the contracting parties concerned within a reasonable period of time, or if the difficulty is of the type described in paragraph 1 (c) of this Article, the matter may be referred to the CONTRACTING PARTIES. The CONTRACTING PARTIES shall promptly investigate any matter so referred to them and shall make appropriate recommendations to the contracting parties which they consider to be concerned, or give a ruling on the matter, as appropriate. . . . If the CONTRACTING PARTIES consider that the circumstances are serious enough to justify such action, they may authorize a contracting party or parties to suspend the application to any other contracting party or parties of such concessions or other obligations under this Agreement as they determine to be appropriate in the circumstances."[5]

"Prompt investigations" and "appropriate recommendations" or, where there is a point of contention on law or fact, "appropriate rulings" are obligatory. The authorisation of countermeasures is optional and admissible only "if . . . the circumstances are serious enough to justify such action" and the suspension of concessions or other obligations are "appropriate in the circumstances".[6] The power to "give a ruling" includes the power to decide on the GATT-consistency of disputed trade measures and, in this context, to decide on the interpretation and application of GATT provisions that are relevant for the dispute settlement. It also includes the power to determine the legal responsibilities and "secondary obligations" of a contracting party that has been found to have violated GATT law.

The adoption by the CONTRACTING PARTIES (usually acting through the GATT Council) of a dispute settlement report (prepared by a "panel" of three or five independent experts) is regarded in GATT practice as a

---

[5] With regard to the use of the term CONTRACTING PARTIES in capital letters, see GATT Article XXV:1: "Representatives of the contracting parties shall meet from time to time for the purpose of giving effect to those provisions of this Agreement which involve joint action and, generally, with a view to facilitating the operation and furthering the objectives of this Agreement. Wherever reference is made in this Agreement to the contracting parties acting jointly they are designated as the CONTRACTING PARTIES".

[6] See Article XXIII:2. Article 22:6 of the Dispute Settlement Understanding of the 1994 Agreement Establishing the World Trade Organization (WTO) introduces, however, a legal obligation and corresponding right to the suspension of concessions if the specified conditions are met.

"ruling" and authoritative determination of the existing GATT rights and obligations of the disputants in the instant case. Arguably, it also constitutes "subsequent practice in the application of the treaty which establishes the agreement of the parties regarding its interpretation" in terms of Article 31 of the 1969 Vienna Convention on the Law of Treaties, and has to be taken into account in the interpretation of GATT law. This is borne out by the fact that GATT dispute settlement practice often refers to interpretations adopted in earlier panel reports. However, GATT dispute settlement practice also confirms that – in accordance with the general international law practice that judicial and other dispute settlement decisions do not have legally binding "precedent effects" for future disputes – the GATT CONTRACTING PARTIES and dispute settlement bodies remain free to decide to depart from the GATT interpretations of prior panel reports. Unlike generally binding authoritative interpretations of GATT rules adopted by the CONTRACTING PARTIES pursuant to Article XXV, the legally binding effect of dispute settlement rulings under Article XXIII:2 is thus limited to the disputing parties, their concrete dispute and the specific legal findings adopted by the CONTRACTING PARTIES.

"Recommendations" relate to the implementation of "rulings" and differ from "rulings" by their legally non-binding character. In order to be "appropriate", recommendations must be consistent with GATT law and with applicable general international law. For instance, in case of a discriminatory tax on imported products in violation of Article III:2 or an import quota violating Article XI:1, the recommendation must respect the range of legal options which GATT law grants to the defaulting country to remove the GATT-inconsistency (*e.g.*, reduction of the higher tax on imports, increase in the lower tax on domestic products, abolition of the tax, recourse to Article XIX as legal justification of temporary safeguard measures). In such cases, the dispute settlement body will only request the defendant to bring the inconsistent measure into conformity with GATT law by appropriate means of the country's own choice. More specific requests to take specified actions are only permissible under Article XXIII:2 if the illegal measures concerned cannot be legalised through invocation of other GATT provisions and the requested action (*e.g.*, withdrawal of an illegal anti-dumping duty) is the only way of bringing the contested measure into conformity with GATT law (*e.g.*, because there is no possibility of correcting *ex post* the infringement of a procedural or substantive rule).

Remedies under GATT law

Like most other international agreements, neither the GATT nor the 1979 Tokyo Round Agreements define the legal responsibilities of a contracting party that has violated its obligations. But it has long been recognised in GATT dispute settlement practice and in "secondary GATT law" that "the first objective of the CONTRACTING PARTIES is usually to secure the withdrawal of the measures concerned if these are found to be inconsistent with the General Agreement. The provision of compensation should be resorted to only if the immediate withdrawal of the measure is impracticable and as a temporary measure pending the withdrawal of the measures which are inconsistent with the General Agreement."[7]

GATT law thus conforms with the general international law principle that the breach of an obligation entails the responsibility of the defaulting state and gives rise to "secondary obligations". But the different types of substantive consequences ("remedies") recognised under general international law in respect of internationally wrongful acts – cessation of illegal acts, restitution in kind, reparation by equivalent, satisfaction and guarantees of non-repetition – are applicable in the context of GATT law only to the extent that GATT law does not provide otherwise.[8]

Cessation of illegal measures

The withdrawal of illegal measures has long been recognised as the first objective of dispute settlement procedures under Article XXIII. This is in line with the general international law obligations to perform international treaties in good faith, to withdraw illegal measures and to wipe out all the consequences of the illegal act. As the illegality of a trade measure may be removed not only by the withdrawal of the measure concerned but also by its justification through invocation of one of GATT's safeguard clauses, the standard recommendation of panel reports is to request the defaulting country to bring its measure into conformity with the General Agreement. Specific recommendations to remove a particular illegal act have been made if the defendant country had no other legal option because, for instance, an illegal anti-dumping or countervailing duty could not be legalised retroactively and revocation of the illegal duty was the only way of acting in conformity with GATT law.

Restitution in kind

In the "Trondheim Panel Report" adopted by the Government Procurement Committee in May 1992, the Panel concluded that Norway had not complied with its obligations under the Agreement on Government Procurement in its single tendering procedure for certain government procurement for the city of Trondheim.[9] In examining the request by the United States that the Panel recommend that Norway take the necessary

---

[7] Understanding Regarding Notification, Consultation, Dispute Settlement and Surveillance, adopted on 28 November 1979, Annex para 4, BISD 26 S/216.

[8] For a detailed comparison of the general international law of state responsibility and of its substantive consequences with remedies under GATT law see Petersmann, *supra*, n 2.

[9] See BISD 39 S/400 and GATT document GPR.DS2/R of 28 April 1992. For an analysis of the remedies issue in this case see Mavroidis, "Government Procurement Agreement: The Trondheim Case", (1993) 48 *Aussenwirtschaft*, 77–94.

measures to bring its practices into compliance with the Agreement with regard to the Trondheim procurement, the Panel noted:

". . . that all the acts of non-compliance . . . were acts that had taken place in the past. The only way mentioned during the Panel's proceedings that Norway could bring the Trondheim procurement into line with its obligations under the Agreement would be by annulling the contract and recommencing the procurement process. The Panel did not consider it appropriate to make such a recommendation. Recommendations of this nature had not been within customary practice in dispute settlement under the GATT system and the drafters of the Agreement on Government Procurement had not made specific provision that such recommendations be within the task assigned to panels under standard terms of reference. Moreover, the Panel considered that in the case under examination such a recommendation might be disproportionate, involving waste of resources and possible damage to the interests of third parties." (paragraph 4.17).

Thus, notwithstanding the United States' request for effective remedies because standard GATT recommendations would not constitute a sufficient remedy, the Panel considered restitution in kind by means of annulling the contract given to the Norwegian firm and by recommencing the procurement process as "disproportionate". It only requested Norway *pro futuro* "to take the measures necessary to ensure that the entities listed in the Norwegian Annex to the Agreement conduct government procurement in accordance with the above findings" (paragraph 5.2). The Panel noted in this respect that "Panel findings, once adopted by the Committee, would constitute guidance for future implementation of the Agreement by the Parties" (paragraph 4.24). It referred to the then ongoing political renegotiations on a new Government Procurement Agreement which, in the meantime, introduced new "challenge procedures" into the Agreement enabling suppliers to challenge alleged breaches of the Agreement arising in the context of public procurement.

The Trondheim Panel finding seems to be in accordance with past dispute settlement practice in GATT and with the recognition also in general international law that restitution in kind may not be required if it is materially or legally impossible or excessively onerous for the country which has violated its obligations. In GATT dispute settlement proceedings under Article XXIII, the claimant states have regularly requested only withdrawal of the illegal act *ex nunc* without demanding re-establishment of the *status quo ante* or of the situation that would have existed in the absence of the illegal act. The reason for this is that GATT rules (*e.g.*, Articles I, III, XIII) prescribe minimum standards for the non-discriminatory treatment of traded goods and, in GATT jurisprudence, have been construed to protect "expectations on the competitive relationship between imported and domestic products" rather than "expectations on export volumes".[10] It is therefore often impossible to recreate

---

[10] See *e.g.*, *US Taxes on Petroleum and Certain Imported Substances*, Panel Report adopted on 17 June 1987, BISD 34 S/136, at 158.

retroactively the "lost trade opportunities" or to calculate, and make good for, the "lost trade volumes". Even the reimbursement of illegal customs duties or illegal internal taxes has never been requested in GATT dispute settlement practice since, *inter alia*, their repayment to individual importers would not re-establish the competitive conditions to which exporting countries had been entitled in the past under GATT law.

It is only in the field of anti-dumping and countervailing duty law that five panel reports have recommended not only the revocation of illegal anti-dumping or countervailing duties but also their reimbursement. When the 1985 GATT Panel report on New Zealand's anti-dumping duties on imports of electrical transformers from Finland was adopted by the GATT Council in July 1985, New Zealand stated that it had already complied with the request to reimburse the illegal anti-dumping duties. In a subsequent dispute over US anti-dumping duties on Swedish stainless steel products, a similar recommendation to reimburse illegal anti-dumping duties was, however, opposed by the defendant; the United States has so far "blocked" the adoption of this 1990 Panel report and refused to reimburse the illegal anti-dumping duties in view of the lack of a specific legal basis for such reimbursement in current US trade legislation.[11] The 1991 Panel report on US countervailing duties on Canadian pork, which was adopted in July 1991, found that the US subsidy determination had not been made in conformity with Article VI:3. However, the Panel recognised that the infringement of this procedural requirement could be rectified retroactively, and that there was therefore no legal basis for a specific finding that countervailing duties should not have been levied at all and had to be reimbursed. Thus the Panel:

"decided to recommend that the CONTRACTING PARTIES give the United States the option of either reimbursing the amount of the countervailing duties designed to offset the subsidies . . . or making a subsidy determination which meets the requirements of Article VI:3 and reimbursing the duties to the extent that they exceed an amount equal to the subsidy so determined to have been granted to the production of pork."[12]

In conclusion it may be said that, even though many national legal systems and EC law recognise a right to restitution of illegal duties and charges and GATT Article X:3 explicitly requires national "judicial . . .procedures for the . . . prompt review and correction of administrative action relating to customs matters", GATT law seems to recognise only a limited legal basis for an international right to reimbursement of certain illegal duties. The exact scope of restitution in kind in GATT law depends on the legal context of the illegal measures concerned. In the 1992 Panel

---

[11] For a discussion of these disputes and of the legal remedies in GATT dispute settlement proceedings in the field of anti-dumping law see Petersmann, "Current Legal Problems in GATT Dispute Settlement Proceedings in the Field of Antidumping Law", in Friedmann and Mestmäcker (eds), *Conflict Resolution in International Trade* (1993) 167–200.

[12] BISD 38 S/30, 46, 47.

report on US anti-dumping duties on cement clinker from Mexico[13], the Panel relied on the four provisions in the 1979 Anti-dumping Agreement explicitly requiring reimbursement of anti-dumping duties[14] in concluding that:

"the existence of the obligation to reimburse duties imposed consistently with the Agreement strongly suggested that the responsibility of a Party having imposed a duty inconsistently with the Agreement comprised the reimbursement of such duties."

However, the Panel report recognised "that there might be situations in which such reimbursement would be excessively onerous for the Party concerned and should therefore not be requested of it."

Reparation by equivalent

Reimbursement of illegal anti-dumping or countervailing duties is a form of restitution designed to wipe out the consequences of the illegal measure. Reparation by equivalent refers to monetary or other compensation through alternative trade benefits. It has long since been recognised in GATT practice that compensation is voluntary under GATT law. Article XXIII does not authorise the CONTRACTING PARTIES to make legally binding recommendations on compensation. In the 1989 Chilean apple case, for instance, the GATT panel "noted that there was no provision in the General Agreement obliging contracting parties to provide compensation", and rejected a request by Chile that the panel recommend that the EC accord compensatory trade benefits to Chile.[15] Proposals to introduce into the GATT system an obligation to grant monetary or other compensation were discussed and rejected in 1966 and, again, during the Uruguay Round negotiations. Compensation may, however, be voluntarily agreed so as to forestall a request for an authorisation to suspend reciprocal trade concessions under Articles XXIII:2 or XXVIII. Such compensation must be granted on a most-favoured-nation basis consistently with GATT Articles I and XIII.

In GATT dispute settlement practice, the issue of compensation has been raised in the GATT Council only at the request of the complaining country. Panels have consistently construed GATT rules as competition rules protecting competitive conditions, and have regularly not addressed issues of "trade damage" and compensation. In a case involving a discriminatory tax in violation of Article III, the Panel concluded that it was "logically not possible to determine the difference in trade impact between the present tax and one consistent with Article III:2, and hence to determine the trade impact resulting from the non-observance of that

---

[13] See BISD 39 S/391 and GATT document ADP/82.

[14] cf. Articles 8:3, 8:4, 11:1, 11:3 of the 1979 Anti-dumping Agreement.

[15] See EEC Restrictions on Imports of Dessert Apples from Chile, Report of the Panel adopted on 22 June 1989, BISD 36 S/93, 134, 135.

provision".[16] In the "Trondheim Panel Report"[17], the Panel likewise saw no legal basis in the Agreement for a panel finding, requested by the United States, that Norway negotiate a mutually satisfactory compensation for the lost opportunities of US companies in government procurement or, if such negotiation did not yield a mutually satisfactory result, that the Government Procurement Committee should authorise the United States to withdraw benefits under the Agreement from Norway with respect to opportunities to bid of equal value to the Trondheim contract given to a Norwegian firm.

Satisfaction and guarantees of non-repetition

Under general international law, it is recognised that a judicial determination of the wrongfulness of a foreign measure may constitute in itself an appropriate remedy and form of satisfaction. The above-mentioned Trondheim Panel Report requested, for instance, that its interpretation of Norway's obligations under the Government Procurement Agreement be taken into account in future tendering procedures by Norwegian authorities. Remedies of satisfaction have been accorded in GATT dispute settlement practice also through a number of rulings on disputed trade measures which had already been withdrawn at the time of the dispute settlement proceeding. In the dispute over Canada's complaint against a US prohibition of imports of tuna, for instance, this remedy was requested by Canada so as to obtain assurances against a repetition of similar import prohibitions from the United States. The dispute settlement ruling accordingly confirmed the GATT inconsistency of the already eliminated import prohibition.[18] In the second Panel report on EC restrictions on imports of dessert apples, adopted in June 1989, the Panel again determined the GATT-inconsistency of trade restrictions which had already been eliminated, and justified this with "the questions of great practical interest raised by both parties"[19] and with the risk of similar future import restrictions by the EC.

Suspension of obligations and retaliation under GATT Article XXIII:2

According to Article XXIII:2:

"If the CONTRACTING PARTIES consider that the circumstances are serious enough to justify such action, they may authorize a contracting party or parties to

---

[16] Panel Report on US Tax on Petroleum, *supra*, n 10 at 158–159.
[17] *Supra*, n 9.
[18] See BISD 29 S/91, 108.
[19] BISD 36 S/93, at 130.

suspend the application to any other contracting party or parties of such concessions or other obligations under this Agreement as they determine to be appropriate in the circumstances. If the application to any contracting party of any concession or other obligation is in fact suspended, that contracting party shall then be free, not later than sixty days after such action is taken, to give written notice to the Director-General to the CONTRACTING PARTIES of its intention to withdraw from this Agreement and such withdrawal shall take effect upon the sixtieth day following the day on which such notice is received by him.''

The "customary" GATT dispute settlement practice in this respect was described in the 1979 "Agreed Description of the Customary Practice of the GATT in the Field of Dispute Settlement" in the following way:

"The last resort which Article XXIII provides to the country invoking this procedure is the possibility of suspending the application of concessions or other obligations on a discriminatory basis *vis-à-vis* the other contracting party, subject to authorization by the CONTRACTING PARTIES. Such action has only rarely been contemplated and cases taken under Article XXIII:2 have led to such action in only one case.''[20]

The drafting history of Article XXIII:2 confirms that it was designed to limit the customary law right of unilateral reprisals, whose exercise had contributed so much to the "law of the jungle" in international economic affairs during the 1930s, and to introduce, as stated by one of the drafters:

"a new principle in international economic relations. We have asked the nations of the world to confer upon an international organization the right to limit their power to retaliate. We have sought to tame retaliation, to discipline it, to keep it within bounds. By subjecting it to the restraints of international control, we have endeavoured to check its spread and growth, to convert it from a weapon of economic warfare to an instrument of international order.''[21]

Whereas, under general international treaty law as codified in Article 60 of the Vienna Convention on the Law of Treaties, a material breach of a multilateral treaty entitles other contracting parties to suspend, in whole or in part, the application of the treaty to the offending country, Article XXIII:2 excludes such a right of unilateral suspension of GATT obligations unless it is authorised by the CONTRACTING PARTIES. Lawful majority decisions under Article XXIII:2 and GATT-consistent political pressures are the legitimate means of settling disputes in a legal system based on third party adjudication. This is confirmed by the fact that the very broad "suspension power" and discretion of the CONTRACTING PARTIES under Article XXIII:2 to authorise the non-application of obligations to "any other contracting party or parties" as they determine to be "appropriate", has been used only once over the past 45 years.[22] Underlying this rare use of the "suspension power" is the widely shared insight

---

[20] BISD 26 S/216.
[21] UN document EPCT/A/PV/6 (1947), at 4.
[22] For a case study of this dispute and of the GATT experience with "economic sanctions" see Hudec, *The GATT Legal System and World Trade Diplomacy* (1975), pp 165–184.

that trade restrictions are mutually welfare reducing and, as already stated by the American delegate in 1952 during the GATT discussions on the Netherlands' request for retaliatory action, "the withdrawal of concessions can hardly be called a remedy when the objective of the Agreement is to hold down restrictions which conflict with the expansion of trade".[23] Contrary to a widespread misperception, the GATT dispute settlement system "is not a legal system which relies on the economic sanction as a coercive force".[24]

The GATT dispute settlement system as an instrument of the foreign trade policy of the EC: a success story

The EC as a GATT contracting party *sui generis*

At the time of entry into force of the Treaty establishing the European Coal and Steel Community (ECSC) on 23 July 1952, its six Member States had already become contracting parties to the GATT. The Convention on the Transitional Provisions, concluded between the ECSC members simultaneously with the ECSC Treaty on 18 April 1951, recognised the GATT obligations of the ECSC Member States, and Article 71 of the ECSC Treaty limited the commercial policy powers of the ECSC accordingly:

"The powers conferred on the Community by this Treaty in matters of commercial policy towards third countries may not exceed those accorded to Member States under international agreements to which they are parties. . . ."

As the ECSC Treaty establishes a "common market for coal and steel"[25] without aiming at a customs union in terms of GATT Article XXIV "with respect to substantially all the trade between the constituent territories of the union or at least with respect to substantially all the trade in products originating in such territories"[26], the ECSC states requested a "waiver" from certain GATT obligations under Article XXV:5. The waiver was granted in a Decision of 10 November 1952, which also included an undertaking by the High Authority of the ECSC

"that, in the exercise of the powers which the Treaty confers upon it and to the extent that such powers permit, it will act in accordance with the obligations which would apply if the Community were a single contracting party consisting of the European territories of the Member States, . . . [and] that, whenever a question arises as to the consistency of any action of the Community or of the Member States . . . with the obligations . . . to other contracting parties under the General

---

[23] *Ibid* at 175.
[24] *Ibid* at 184.
[25] Article 4 ECSC.
[26] Article XXIV:8.

Agreement, any recommendation, finding or decision by the CONTRACTING PARTIES with respect to such action . . . of the Community or the Member States shall have the same force and effect as it would have if the recommendation, finding or decision were made in respect of such action . . . of any other contracting party under the General Agreement."[27]

The EC Treaty explicitly provides for "the maintenance of all appropriate relations with the organs . . . of the General Agreement on Tariffs and Trade"[28] and for the full respect of pre-existing agreements of the Member States including GATT.[29] When the EEC Treaty was notified to GATT in 1957 pursuant to Article XXIV:7(a), the representative of the EEC stressed the consistency of the Treaty with the GATT and gave "the firm assurance . . . that as long as the Six would remain contracting parties to the General Agreement they would scrupulously observe their obligations under this Agreement".[30] The GATT Working Party, which examined the EEC Treaty, never reached agreement on its GATT-consistency.[31] But, since the "Dillon Round" (1960/61), the EC Commission was accepted in GATT negotiations and in GATT bodies as representative of the EC member countries and exercised almost all GATT rights (except voting rights) and GATT obligations (except the budgetary contributions) in the name of the Community like a GATT contracting party *sui generis*. Also GATT dispute settlement proceedings by third GATT contracting parties were initiated against the EC rather than against individual EC Member States. Since 1970, most trade agreements negotiated within GATT – except for protocols of accession and the 1979 Tokyo Round Agreements on Technical Barriers to Trade and on Trade in Civil Aircraft – were concluded on behalf of the EC as "Community agreements" without additional direct acceptance by individual EC Member States.

Even though the EC never formally accepted the "GATT 1947" (as distinguished from the "GATT 1994" as an integral part of the 1994 WTO Agreement) or its Protocol of Provisional Application, its initially only *de facto* GATT membership has long since evolved into a *de iure* GATT membership *sui generis* in addition to the continuing GATT membership of the individual EC Member States.[32] The recognition by the GATT contracting parties of this "double GATT membership" is illustrated by the following example. In the GATT Council meeting in June 1988, the EC representative agreed, on behalf of the Community, to an American request to establish a dispute settlement panel on the EC subsidies paid to processors

---

[27] BISD 1 S/18,19. For a detailed analysis of the "GATT status" of the ECSC see Petersmann, "Participation of the European Communities in the GATT: International Law and Community Law Aspects", in O'Keeffe and Schermers (eds), *Mixed Agreements* (1983) 167–198 at 175 *et seq.*
[28] Article 229.
[29] Article 234.
[30] GATT document IC/SR (1957) 39.
[31] See BISD 6S/68 *et seq* and Petersmann, "The EEC as a GATT Member – Legal Conflicts between GATT Law and European Community Law", in Jacobs, Hilf and Petersmann (eds), *The European Community and GATT* (1986), 23–71 at 35 *et seq.*
[32] For a detailed analysis see Berrisch, *Der völkerrechtliche Status der EWG im GATT* (1992).

and producers of oilseeds, and disregarded the declared opposition by the French delegate, who emphasised "that there was no consensus among the CONTRACTING PARTIES at this stage with regard to the US request".[33] In response to concerns whether the GATT Council chairman could determine a "consensus" in spite of the French objections, the EC representative declared:

"It was quite clear that France was a contracting party, but it was equally clear that France no longer had competence on matters of trade policy. That was the exclusive competence of the Community, which he represented in the Council as the representative of the Commission of the European Communities . . . If one were to follow any other type of reasoning, a large part of the GATT's achievements would in fact collapse, since agreements had been entered into by the Community, particularly in the negotiating rounds, past, present and future . . . To take the French views into consideration would put into question all the current Community's obligations and rights. For these reasons, even when France spoke as a contracting party, its views as to trade policies were null and void and could not be taken into account."

The GATT Council "agreed to establish a panel".[34] The following day, after the EC Commission had threatened to initiate an infringement proceeding against France pursuant to Article 169, the French Prime Minister formally apologised for the disregard of the EC's commercial policy powers by the French representative in the GATT Council meeting on 16 June 1988.

From a "power-oriented" towards a "rule-oriented" GATT policy of the EC

Between 1958 and 1980, the EC availed itself of the possibility of initiating Article XXIII GATT dispute settlement proceedings in only two cases.[35] During the same period, 11 complaints under Article XXIII had been directed against the EC and, between 1958 and 1973, 10 complaints against individual EC Member States.[36] It was only after the termination of the Tokyo Round negotiations that the EC began, since 1981, to use the GATT dispute settlement procedures more actively. From 1980 to 1992, the EC was the target of 30 complaints and the initiator of 25 complaints raised under Article XXIII of GATT.[37] The United States launched 11 of these complaints against the EC and was the object of 14 of the EC's complaints during this period. Japan was the target of four EC complaints,

---

[33] GATT document C/M/222, at 11.

[34] C/M/222, at 15.

[35] The 1973 complaint against the US tax legislation (DISC) led to the adoption of a panel report (BISD 23 S/98–114, 28 S/114) which found that the DISC legislation had resulted in export subsidies inconsistent with Article XVI:4. The 1976 complaint against Canada gave rise to a panel report (BISD 25 S/42–49) which found, *inter alia*, that the withdrawal by Canada of tariff concessions under Article XXVIII:3 had been excessive.

[36] For a list of GATT Article XXIII complaints against the EC and its Member States 1960–1990 see *Trade Policy Review: The European Communities* (GATT 1991), vol. I at 291 *et seq.*

[37] See the lists of cases *ibid* at 291 *et seq,* 296 *et seq; Trade Policy Review: European Communities* (GATT 1993) at 214 *et seq.*

two of which led to dispute settlement rulings in favour of the EC. A majority of all these disputes revolved around agricultural products. From 1980 to 1992, the EC was also involved in 29 dispute settlement proceedings under the 1979 Tokyo Round Agreements.[38] In 17 of these cases, complaints were brought against the EC under the Subsidies Code, the Anti-dumping Code, the Agreement on Technical Barriers to Trade, the Agreement on Government Procurement, the Agreement on Trade in Civil Aircraft, the International Dairy Arrangement and the Arrangement Regarding Bovine Meat; in the remaining 12 cases, complaints were initiated by the EC under the Subsidies Code, the Anti-dumping Code, the Agreement on Government Procurement, the Agreement on Technical Barriers to Trade and the International Dairy Arrangement.

Except for two complaints against Finland and Switzerland which were not further pursued by the EC, the EC never invoked Article XXIII against parties to its regional free trade, association or co-operation agreements; and none of these countries ever raised such a complaint against the EC. Each of these free trade or association agreements concluded by the EC provide for their own dispute settlement procedures, ranging from binding arbitration (under the Lomé Convention) and referral of disputes to the Court of Justice or to another tribunal (under the Association Agreement with Turkey) to common decision making and, in the absence of agreement, to unilateral interpretations and safeguard measures (under the bilateral free trade agreements with EFTA countries). But these court and arbitration procedures appear to have never been used. Notwithstanding bilateral consultations on several cases under the free trade area agreements with EFTA countries, unilateral safeguard measures have never been applied so far.

Why is it that the EC resorted so rarely to GATT Article XXIII until 1981? And why did the EC become an active user of Article XXIII complaints since 1981 and, during the Uruguay Round negotiations, an active supporter of "judicialising" the GATT dispute settlement system?[39] Jackson has distinguished between "power-oriented" and "rule-oriented" diplomacy, and has explained the preference of large countries for "negotiated dispute settlements" with their relative power in bilateral negotiations, and the preference of small countries for "rule-oriented dispute settlements" with the protection they derive from general rules and from third-party adjudication.[40] This analysis explains why less-developed GATT contracting parties have long since called for "legalising" and "judicialising" GATT dispute settlement procedures. But this

---

[38] See the lists in *supra* n 36 at 221 *et seq.*

[39] On the "judicialisation" of GATT dispute settlement procedures through the "Dispute Settlement Understanding" in the 1994 Agreement establishing the World Trade Organization see Petersmann, "The Dispute Settlement System of the World Trade Organization and the Evolution of the GATT Dispute Settlement System Since 1948" (1994) 31 CMLRev 1157–1244.

[40] Jackson, "Governmental Disputes in International Trade Relations: A Proposal in the Context of GATT" (1979) *Journal of World Trade Law* 1–21.

does not account for the different positions of the Unites States, which (*e.g.*, in the Tokyo Round negotiations) likewise attempted to make the GATT dispute settlement process less dependent on the consent of the parties to the dispute, and of the EC, which – until the mid-1980s – categorically opposed proposals, *inter alia*, for a "right to the establishment of a panel" and adoption of panel reports on the basis of "consensus minus two" (*i.e.*, without participation of the parties to the dispute).

Roessler has offered an alternative explanation of the divergent attitudes of the EC and the United States *vis-à-vis* the GATT dispute settlement system[41] and the EC's long-standing view that "GATT is a consensus body, one cannot transform it into a Court of Justice".[42] In his view, the differing policies of the EC and of the United States towards the substantive law of GATT account for their differing views on the GATT dispute settlement procedures. On the insistence of the United States, the basic GATT provisions (*e.g.*, for safeguard measures and agricultural restrictions) were drafted to suit the requirements of US legislation, and several GATT "waivers" were requested and granted so as to bring, for example, the 1955 amendment to the US Agricultural Adjustment Act, the 1965 Canada–USA Agreement on automotive products, or the 1983 Caribbean Basin Economic Recovery Act of the United States into conformity with GATT law. By contrast, as the EC neither participated in the drafting of the General Agreement nor – unlike the ECSC – requested "waivers" from its GATT obligations, the EC's agricultural and preferential trade regulations were challenged in numerous GATT panel reports. Thus, while the United States succeeded in adjusting its initial GATT obligations to its specific policy constraints, the EC took over the GATT rights and obligations of its Member States without formally acceding to GATT and without seeking "waivers" from its GATT obligations.

As a consequence, the EC emphasised GATT's function as a framework for "pragmatic negotiations" and downplayed the legally binding force of GATT law. As Roessler put it, the EC's efforts:

"were generally limited to achieving the *de facto* toleration of its policies, usually by making it clear how pointless it would be to attempt to pursue legal claims to victory and by offering at the same time to discuss the practical consequences of its policies."

Typical manifestations of this "anti-legal pragmatism" were, for example:

– the 1958 decision of the GATT CONTRACTING PARTIES, after futile debates on the legal consistency of the EC Treaty with GATT law and under pressure from the EC, "that it would be more fruitful if attention could be directed to specific and practical problems, leaving aside for

---

[41] Roessler, "L'attitude des Etats-Unis et de la CEE devant le droit du GATT", in Bourrinet (ed), *Les Relations Communauté Européenne – Etats Unis* (1987), 43–52.

[42] EC Commissioner DeClerq, quoted in *Agence Europe* No. 4243, 22 January 1986, at 9.

the time being questions of law and debates about the compatibility of the Rome Treaty with the General Agrement'';[43]

– a similar "GATT pragmatism" in the examinations of the compatibility with Article XXIV of the EC's preferential trade arrangements with the Mediterranean countries, EFTA countries and the less-developed member countries of the Yaundé and Lomé Conventions, whose compatibility with GATT law was each time left undecided in view of the diverging view of, on the one side, the EC Member States and their preferential trading partners, which account for the majority in the GATT Council, and, on the other side, adversely affected third GATT member countries;

– the "blocking" by the EC of GATT Panel findings against central elements of the EC's discriminatory agricultural and preferential trade policy – such as the GATT Panel findings against the EC's production aids on agricultural products[44], the EC's agricultural export subsidies[45], and the EC's non-reciprocal trade preferences[46], – and the negotiation of "pragmatic" solutions to the trade policy aspects of these disputes;

– the strong opposition by the EC to the establishment of a Legal Office in the GATT Secretariat until 1983, when the EC agreed to its establishment on the condition that the Director of the GATT Legal Office be an experienced trade diplomat; and

– the EC's long-standing opposition to a "legalistic" use of the GATT dispute settlement system because, as stated by the EC representative in a GATT Council meeting, the GATT dispute settlement procedure should not be expected to help resolve conflicts in which "vital national interests" were at stake.[47]

But is it really true that the EC – the world's largest single market, importer, exporter and "financier" of the GATT budget – cannot pursue its "vital interests" in conformity with its self-imposed GATT obligations for the use of transparent, non-discriminatory and welfare-increasing trade policy instruments? A systematic analysis of the past GATT dispute settlement proceedings against the EC[48] confirms that the GATT dispute settlement rulings related to discriminatory import restrictions and agricultural export subsidies which, from an economic perspective, reduce the welfare of EC consumers and redistribute income for the benefit of "rent-seeking" producer interests in a non-transparent and wasteful manner. Since GATT law does not limit the pursuit of any policy objectives, but

---

[43] BISD 7 S/70.

[44] See the Panel Report of 20 February 1985 on "EEC Production Aids Granted on Canned Peaches, Canned Pears, Canned Fruit Cocktail and Dried Grapes" L/5778.

[45] See the Panel Report of 19 May 1983 on "EEC – Subsidies on Export of Pasta Products" SCM/43.

[46] See the Panel Report of 7 February 1985 on "EC – Tariff Treatment on Imports of Citrus Products from Certain Countries in the Mediterranean Region" L/5776.

[47] C/M/198, 14.

[48] See Petersmann, "International and European Foreign Trade Law: GATT Dispute Settlement Proceedings against the EEC" (1985) 22 CMLRev 441–487.

only the use of non-transparent and welfare-reducing policy instruments, the large number of GATT dispute settlement proceedings against the EC can be seen as a sign of "government failures" in the EC's complex policy-making processes, for example, in the Council of Agricultural Ministers, which has been described by a former member of the EC Commission as an "institutionalised price cartel of protectionists".[49]

The EEC's changing attitude in favour of a more "rule-oriented" GATT policy and active use of the GATT dispute settlement system, especially since the beginning of the Uruguay Round negotiations in which the EC assumed a key role in strengthening international and European foreign trade law, can be seen as a turning point in the foreign trade policy of the EC.

The EC's "New Trade Policy Instrument" and the active use of the GATT dispute settlement system

Since 1982, the EC launched a large number of Article XXIII dispute settlement proceedings against trade measures of other GATT contracting parties which, in most cases, led to dispute settlement rulings in favour of the EC. These cases included, *inter alia*:

– The 1982 complaint by the EC against the "manufacturing clause" in the US copyright legislation, which led to a Panel report, adopted in May 1984, finding "that the Manufacturing Clause was inconsistent with Article XI of the General Agreement" and "the extension of the Manufacturing Clause beyond 1 July 1982 consequently had to be considered prima facie to nullify or impair benefits accruing to the European Communities under the GATT".[50]
– The 1985 complaint by the EC against import, distribution and sales restrictions by Canadian provincial agencies, which led to a Panel report, adopted in March 1988, recommending "that the CONTRACT-ING PARTIES request Canada to take such reasonable measures as may be available to it to ensure observance of the provisions of Articles II and XI of the General Agreement by the provincial liquor boards in Canada" and "to report to the CONTRACTING PARTIES on the action taken before the end of 1988, to permit the CONTRACTING PARTIES to decide on any further action that might be necessary".[51]
– The 1986 complaint by the EC against Japan's customs duties, taxes and labelling practices on imported wines and alcoholic beverages, which led to a Panel report, adopted in November 1987, finding "that whiskies, brandies, other distilled spirits, liqueurs, still wines and sparkling wines imported into Japan were subject to discriminatory or protective Japanese taxes contrary to Article III:2" and "had to be presumed to

---

[49] von der Groeben, *Aufbaujahre der EG* (1982), pp 152 *et seq.*
[50] BISD 31S/74, 91.
[51] BISD 35S/37, 92.

cause nullification or impairment of benefits accruing to the European Community under the General Agreement".[52]

- The 1987 complaint by the EC against US taxes on petroleum and certain imported substances, which led to a Panel report, adopted in June 1987, finding "that the tax on petroleum was inconsistent with Article III:2, first sentence and consequently constituted a prima facie case of nullification and impairment, and that an evaluation of the trade impact of the tax was not relevant for this finding".[53]
- The 1987 complaint by the EC against the United States' "customs user fee", which led to a Panel report, adopted in February 1988, finding that the "United States merchandise processing fee was inconsistent with the obligations of Articles II:2(c) and VIII:1(a)".[54]
- The 1987 complaint by the EC against Japan's export restrictions taken in the context of its agreement with the United States on trade in semi-conductors, which led to a Panel report, adopted in May 1988, finding that Japan's "coherent system restricting the sale for export of monitored semi-conductors at prices below company-specific costs to markets other than the United States [was] inconsistent with Article XI:1".[55]
- The 1987 complaint by the EC against section 337 of the US Tariff Act of 1930, which led to a Panel report, adopted in November 1989, finding "that Section 337 of the United States Tariff Act of 1930 is inconsistent with Article III:4, in that it accords to imported products challenged as infringing United States patents treatment less favourable than the treatment accorded to products of United States origin similarly challenged, and that these inconsistencies cannot be justified in all respects under Article XX(d)".[56]

In analysing this "success story" of the EC's active use of Article XXIII dispute settlement procedures, the following three aspects should be taken into account: first, the speed and legal quality of some of these panel reports illustrated that the GATT dispute settlement system offers an attractive alternative to protracted political negotiations with other trading powers. For instance, even though the Panel report on the US taxes on petroleum had to examine simultaneously three complaints by Canada, the EC and Mexico, was supported by six other GATT contracting parties intervening in support of these complaints, and was directed against one of the most important environmental laws of the US Congress, the Panel report was adopted by the GATT Council within less than four months after the establishment of the Panel. In the dispute over Japan's discriminatory liquor taxes, the EC had likewise attempted in vain to settle the

---

[52] BISD 34S/83, 126.
[53] BISD 34S/136, 159.
[54] BISD 35S/245, 290.
[55] BISD 35S/116, 162.
[56] BISD 36S/345, 396.

dispute through a long series of bilateral negotiations. Even the Japanese Government's own proposals for amending the protectionist liquor tax legislation had been rejected by the powerful "liquor lobbies" in the Japanese Diet. Given the complexity of the tax legislation (which, for example, classified liquors into 23 different categories and grades discriminating against foreign liquors), the GATT Council's adoption of the Panel report within nine months after the establishment of the Panel demonstrated once again that recourse to the GATT dispute settlement system enabled speedy and legally binding solutions even to highly politicised disputes among "super-powers", after bilateral consultations had failed to settle the dispute.

Second, the adoption of Council Regulation 2641/84 on the "Strengthening of the Common Commercial Policy with Regard in Particular to Protection Against Illicit Commercial Practices",[57] which was essentially a response to section 301 in the US Trade Act of 1974 (as amended), contributed to the changing attitude of the EEC *vis-à-vis* the GATT dispute settlement system. Both section 301 and Regulation 2641/84 (known as the "new instrument") provide for the Admissibility, and examination by the Executive of private complaints about illegal, unreasonable or illicit trade practices of other countries, which may then be pursued by the government at the international level and lead to the initiation of GATT dispute settlement proceedings.[58] Until 1993, EC producers launched six complaints under the "new instrument" against (i) section 337 of the US Tariff Act; (ii) Argentina's "dual taxation" on exports of soya beans and soya oil; (iii) Indonesia's alleged failure to provide adequate protection to the EC's record producers; (iv) Jordan's patent law; (v) Japanese harbour charges; and (vi) the allegedly discriminatory application of Thailand's copyright law.[59] In cases (i), (ii) and (v), the complainants contended that GATT rules had been violated by the countries concerned. While two complaints were rejected by the EC Commission, the complaint against section 337 led to the above-mentioned GATT Panel report. Three other complaints were settled through international negotiations with the countries concerned. Contrary to some initial fears, the "new instrument" seems to have operated as a legal restraint on protectionist pressures and as a means of promoting recourse to the GATT dispute settlement procedures for settling international trade disputes. The fact that four of the complaints related to intellectual property rights suggests that, under the new dispute settlement system of the (WTO) and the Agreement on

---

[57] OJ 1984 L252/1.

[58] On the important differences between Section 301 and the "new instrument" see *e.g.*, the comparative analyses by Bello, Bronckers and Davey in Part III of Demaret, Bourgeois and van Bael (eds), *Trade Laws of the European Community and the United States* in a Comparative Perspective (1992).

[59] For a survey of these complaints and EC actions see Castillo de la Torre, 'The EEC New Instrument of Trade Policy: Some Comments in the Light of the Latest Developments' (1993) 30 CMLRev 687–719.

-Related Intellectual Property Rights (TRIPS), the "new instru-
." might in future trigger many more invocations of the GATT–WTO
ate settlement procedures by the EC.

Third, in the context of the Uruguay Round negotiations on the
strengthening of the GATT–WTO dispute settlement system[60], the EC
strongly supported the proposals for further "legalising" and "judicialising" the GATT–WTO dispute settlement system and for making the
admissibility of trade sanctions conditional on their authorisation by the
WTO Dispute Settlement Body.

The GATT Dispute Settlement System as an instrument of the EC's domestic policy? Perspectives from the Court of Justice's 1994 "Banana Judgment"

The active use of GATT dispute settlement procedures against third countries is politically driven by the interest of domestic export industries in
access to foreign markets. However, the GATT prohibitions of tariffs, non-
tariff trade restrictions and of trade distorting subsidies are designed to
protect freedom of trade, non-discrimination, undistorted competition
and rule of law not only abroad but also at home for the benefit of
domestic consumers and other domestic citizens. Since GATT law prohibits only the use of welfare-reducing policy instruments without limiting
the "sovereignty" of countries to pursue whatever policy objectives they
want to pursue and to intervene into their economies in order to correct
"market failures", the GATT requirements to use transparent, non-
discriminatory and welfare-increasing policy instruments have a "constitutional function" enhancing the liberty and economic welfare of the citizens. As most GATT disputes are "secondary international conflicts",
which "spill over" to the intergovernmental level only after the "primary
domestic conflicts" between the consumer interests in liberal trade and
the "rent-seeking interests" of import-competing producers in trade protection are not resolved in a welfare-improving manner, enforcing GATT
rules for the benefit of domestic consumers, tax-payers and competitors is
even more important at home than abroad. Does the EC use GATT law
and the GATT dispute settlement system for fending-off, and disciplining,
protectionist pressures also at home?

The "domestic policy function" of GATT rules can be observed in many
GATT dispute settlement proceedings. In the EC's complaint against the
discriminatory US taxes on petroleum[61], for instance, the US Government

---

[60] See Petersmann, "The Uruguay Round Negotiations 1986–1991", in Petersmann and Hilf
(eds), *The New GATT Round of Multilateral Trade Negotiations* (1991, 2nd ed), pp 501–577 at 507 *et
seq.*
[61] *Supra*, n 10.

had pointed out – in the congressional legislative process leading to the enactment of this law – the incompatibility with the GATT of the tax discriminations and, in the GATT dispute settlement proceeding, did not contest the inconsistency of this tax discrimination with Article III. Yet, the EC's zeal to enforce the GATT legal disciplines *vis-à-vis* third countries is often not matched by equal efforts at enforcing the GATT legal disciplines and dispute settlement rulings also at home within the EC. The recent "banana dispute" between various Latin American banana exporting countries and the EC, and the Court of Justice's "banana judgment" of 5 October 1994 against Germany's application for the annulment of Title IV of the EC's Council Regulation 404/93 on the common organisation of the market in bananas[62], are illustrative of the interrelationship between international and domestic dispute settlement proceedings in the field of GATT law and of the often one-sided use of the GATT dispute settlement system by the EC.

In response to a 1993 complaint under Article XXIII by Colombia, Costa Rica, Guatemala, Nicaragua and Venezuela against import restrictions on fresh bananas by certain EC Member States, a GATT Panel report of 3 June 1993 found, *inter alia*, "that the quantitative restrictions maintained by France, Italy, Portugal, Spain and the United Kingdom on imports of bananas were inconsistent with Article XI:1" and "that the tariff preference accorded by the EEC to imports of bananas originating in ACP countries was inconsistent with Article I". According to the Panel report:

"a legal justification for the preference could not emerge from an application of Article XXIV to the type of agreement described by the EEC in the Panel's proceedings, but only from an action of the CONTRACTING PARTIES under Article XXV."[63]

Following the adoption of the Council Regulation 404/93 on the common organisation of the market in bananas, the five complainants requested the establishment of another GATT Panel under Article XXIII which, in a Panel report of 11 February 1994[64] found, *inter alia*, that:

- "the specific tariffs applied by the EEC on imports of bananas since 1 July 1993 accord treatment to imports of bananas less favourable than that provided for in the EEC's Schedule of Concessions and were, therefore inconsistent with the EEC's obligations under Article II:1";[65]
- "the preferred allocation of part of the tariff quota to importers who purchase EEC bananas was inconsistent with Article III:4", and "the preferred allocation of licenses to operators who purchase bananas from ACP countries was inconsistent with the EEC's obligations under Article I:1";[66]

---

[62] Case C-280/93, *Germany* v *Council* [1994] ECR I-4973.
[63] GATT document DS 32/R of 3 June 1993, at 83.
[64] GATT document DS 38/R of 11 February 1994.
[65] *Ibid* at 40.
[66] *Ibid* at 43.

EC's preferential tariff treatment of imports of bananas was incon
~t with Article I:1''[67], and "Article XXIV. . . could not justify the
~nsistency with Article I of the tariff preferences for bananas acco1ded by the EEC to the ACP countries".[68]

The Panel also emphasised in its concluding remarks that:

"nothing in its report would prevent the parties to the Lomé Convention from
achieving their treaty objectives, including the objective of promoting the production and commercialization of bananas from ACP countries, through the use of
policy instruments consistent with the General Agreement".

Parallel to these international GATT dispute settlement proceedings in
1993, Germany, supported by Belgium and the Netherlands, brought an
action under Article 173(1) for a declaration by the Court of Justice that
the import restrictions provided for in Title IV and Article 21(2) of Council Regulation 404/93 were void. In support of its position, Germany argued, *inter alia*:

– that compliance with GATT law was a condition of the lawfulness of
  Community acts, regardless of any question concerning the direct effect
  of GATT; and
– that the Regulation, whose preamble explicitly confirmed the intention to
  respect the Community's "various international obligations", infringed certain basic provisions of GATT to the detriment of EC Member States with
  traditionally liberal import regimes for bananas, as well as to the detriment
  of the freedoms, property rights, economic interests and legitimate expectations of EC importers and consumers of third country bananas.

In addition to Germany's action under Article 173(1), a significant
number of private banana trading companies requested the Court under
Article 173(2) to annul certain provisions of Council Regulation 404/93
and to order the EC, pursuant to Articles 178 and 215(2), to make good
any damage caused by the adoption of that regulation. These actions
before the Court of Justice illustrated the primarily "domestic nature" of
this "banana dispute", for example in terms of:

– the conflict between, on the one side, the interests of EC consumers and
  EC traders in a liberal, GATT-consistent trade regime for the less expensive, high-quality third country bananas and, on the other side, the
  "rent-seeking" interests of the few EC producers of expensive, low-
  quality bananas in trade protection; or
– the conflict between, on the one side, the interest in rule of law (including GATT law) by those Member States who had liberal import regimes
  for bananas and had voted against adoption of Regulation 404/93, and,
  on the other side, the "rent-seeking" interests of those Member States

---

[67] *Ibid* at 45.
[68] *Ibid* at 49.

who had long since restricted imports of third country bananas and had voted in favour of the adoption of the Regulation in order to continue their protection of the more expensive Community bananas and ACP bananas.

In its judgment, the Court of Justice concluded from the existence of GATT's safeguard clause[69] and GATT's dispute settlement procedures[70] "that the GATT rules are not unconditional" and "preclude the Court from taking provisions of GATT into consideration to assess the lawfulness of a regulation in an action brought by a Member State under the first paragraph of Article 173 of the Treaty".[71] Unfortunately, the Court failed to take into account that:

– many GATT rules (such as Articles III and XI:1) are more precise and unconditional than the often vague and conditional rules of the EC Treaty (such as Articles 30 and 92); and that
– the GATT dispute settlement rules explicitly require – contrary to the contention by Advocate General Gulmann that, in GATT law "it is to a large extent left to the contracting parties to solve their disputes by negotiation"[72] – that "all solutions to matters formally raised under the GATT dispute settlement system under Articles XXII, XXIII . . . shall be consistent with the General Agreement".[73]

Worse than the Court's failure to take GATT law into account and its frequent "judicial protectionism" in the field of trade policy is its disregard for some of the constitutional problems raised by the EC's banana regulations. The Court failed to mention that GATT law is binding on the institutions of the Community and on Member States not only in terms of GATT law, but also in terms of primary EC law.[74] Nor does the Court mention the obligation under Article 234 that the GATT obligations of the EC Member States "shall not be affected by the provisions of this Treaty". The Court further ignored that the preamble to the Council Regulation 404/93 explicitly referred to its declared objective "that the Community can respect . . . its various international obligations", and that this explicit reference could justify a judicial review of the lawfulness of Council Regulation 404/93 in the light of the EC's GATT obligations as determined in two GATT dispute settlement reports.[75]

---

[69] Article XIX.
[70] Article XXIII.
[71] Case C-280/93, *supra*, n 62 at 5073.
[72] *Ibid* at 5024–5025 per Advocate General Gulmann.
[73] Section A.2 of the Decision of the GATT CONTRACTING PARTIES on "Improvements to the GATT Dispute Settlement Rules and Procedures," 12 April 1989, BISD 36 S/59.
[74] Article 228(7).
[75] According to paragraph 111 of the judgment: . . . "it is only if the Community intended to implement a particular obligation entered into within the framework of GATT, or if the Community act expressly refers to specific provisions of GATT, that the Court can review the lawfulness of the Community act in question from the point of view of the GATT rules (see Case 70/87 *Fediol* v *Commission*, 1989 ECR 1781, and Case C-69/89, *Nakajima* v *Council*, 1991 ECR I-2069)."

,ourt, which in other disputes referred to the EC Treaty as a
 ,ational charter'', continues to shun some of the crucial problems
 C's "foreign policy constitution". For instance:

- Does the EC's treaty constitution, notably its principles of "limited Community powers"[76] and "primacy of international law"[77], not call for a
  principle similar to the one explicitly laid down in Article 71 ECSC,
  namely that "the powers conferred on the Community by this Treaty in
  matters of commercial policy towards third countries may not exceed
  those accorded to Member States under international agreements to
  which they are parties"?
- Can the EC Council, by majority decision, freely violate international
  guarantees of freedom and non-discrimination, which are binding on
  the Council under GATT law and under primary EC law, even if these
  international guarantees have been ratified also by national parliaments
  and their violation entails the international state responsibility also of
  those EC Member States (such as Germany) who wish to meet their
  international treaty obligations but were outvoted in the Council?
- What is the logic of the Court's statement in its "banana judgment" that
  "the Community institutions cannot disregard the international obligations entered into by the Community under the Lomé Convention"[78],
  but are free to disregard the worldwide GATT obligations of the EC and
  its Member States as determined by two GATT dispute settlement
  reports?
- Why were the primary Community law principles of freedom, non-
  discrimination and rule of law not construed in compliance with the EC's
  self-imposed international GATT obligations to protect freedom, non-
  discrimination and rule of law also in the transnational trade transactions
  of EC citizens? How could the Court justify its assertion that even obvious
  violations of GATT's guarantees of freedom and non-discrimination, confirmed in two GATT Panel reports, "correspond to objectives of general
  interest pursued by the Community and do not constitute a disproportionate . . . interference . . . (with) the rights guaranteed" under Community law?[79] Why can EC citizens not "claim an acquired right or even a
  legitimate expectation"[80] that the EC will respect the rule of law also in
  the field of GATT law, whenever the EC restricts the freedom of EC
  citizens to buy or sell goods in the best markets?

As mentioned above, the declared objective of the founders of GATT
law was to convert the foreign trade policy powers of governments "from a
weapon of economic warfare to an instrument of international order".[81] It

---

[76] *cf.* Article 3b.
[77] *cf.* Articles 228 to 234.
[78] *Supra*, n 62 at 5060.
[79] *Ibid* at 5065.
[80] *Ibid* at 5065–5066.
[81] *Supra*, n 21.

is regrettable that, almost half a century later, the handling of the "banana dispute" by the EC political institutions and the Court of Justice continues to reveal a preference for power politics and a disregard for the rule of law to the detriment of EC citizens. The EC has succeeded in limiting the national foreign trade policy powers of EC Member States by EC guarantees of freedom of trade and non-discrimination in intra-Community trade. But the EC's "domestic policy constitution" still needs to be supplemented by a "foreign policy constitution" limiting the foreign trade policy powers of the EC and protecting the freedom of trade of EC citizens in trade relations with third countries. The principle of "primacy of international law" over secondary EC law, which underlies the EC Treaty provisions in Articles 228 to 234[82], suggests that the worldwide GATT obligations of the EC should serve as the "uniform principles" on which the EC's common commercial policy "shall be based" according to Article 113. Respect for its legal obligations under GATT law and under primary Community law should prompt the EC Council to use GATT law and the GATT dispute settlement system not only as a means to promote freedom and non-discrimination abroad for the benefit of EC exporters, but also at home for the benefit of EC consumers, traders, competitors, tax-payers and for the general interest of EC citizens in the rule of law.

ERNST-ULRICH PETERSMANN[83]

---

[82] See: Petersmann's commentary on Article 234 of the EEC Treaty, in Groeben, Thiesing and Ehlermann (ed), *EWG-Vertrag Kommentar* (1991, 3rd ed), vol. III, at 5726.

[83] The author served as legal counsel in the GATT Secretariat from 1981–1990 and in the Uruguay Round Negotiating Groups on Dispute Settlement and Institutional Issues from 1987–1993.

Chapter 16

"Grey Area" Measures, the Uruguay Round, and the EC/Japan Commercial Census on Cars

"The European automobile industry is a key industry in the EU directly employing more than 1.8 million people in the supply and manufacturing chain. An additional 1.8 million people are employed in the distribution and repair sector. The livelihood of many more citizens depends indirectly on the success of the industry. The industry accounts for nearly 2% of total GDP in the EU."[1]

The European Commission's communication to the Council and European Parliament on the automobile industry underlines the economic and social importance of the automobile industry for the EU. Although its added valued is not very high, it creates demand in the rest of the economy, covering probably as much as 15% of the Community's industrial employment.[2] Naturally, the interests of the automobile industry are closely connected with public policy issues and various aspects of trade policy including diverse forms of protection. Trade relations among large

Evolution of import/export balance of passenger cars

	FRG	France	UK	Italy	Sweden	Japan	USA
1965	1145	405	568	204	–114	88	–458
1970	1299	1084	532	240	66	706	–1728
1975	706	956	67	283	–35	1782	–1434
1980	847	846	–504	–396	16	4199	–2499
1985	1484	551	–864	–396	18	5099	–3694
1986	1298	562	–884	–199	29	5465	–4018
1988	1255	680	–1143	–303	n.d.	4281	–3782
1989	1396	1111	–1148	–583	n.d.	2197	n.d.

The author is grateful to Marco Bronckers for his comments.

[1] COM (94) 49 final, 23 February 1994.

[2] Vigier, "La politique communautaire de l'automobile" (1992) *Revue du marché unique européen*, parts 3 and 4.

trading powers, *i.e.* Europe, the United States and Japan, became increasingly strained during the 1980s when Japan's automobile exports suddenly increased from a very low level.[3]

The history of the automobile industry in Europe and Japan has been characterised by decades of tariff protection against the export drive of the American motor industry, which used to be by far the world's most competitive. Until multilateral tariff reduction was achieved within the GATT, the weaker manufacturing countries maintained high tariff barriers.[4]

Tariffs on cars (in percentage terms)

	USA	Japan	France	Sweden	Italy	UK	FRG
1913	45	n.d.	9–14	n.d.	4–6	0	3
1929	10*	50	45	n.d.	6–11	33.3	20
1932	10	70**	47–74	n.d.	101–111	33.3	40
1950	10	40	35	n.d.	3.5	33.3	35
1960	8.5	35–40	30	13/15	31.4–40.5	30	13–16
1968	5.5	30	0/17.6	0/15	0/17.6	0/17.6	0/17.6
1973	3	6.4	0/10.9	10/8/0***	0/10.9	10.9	0/10.9
1978	3	0	0/10.9	10/0	0/10.9	0/10.9	0/10.9
1983	2.8	0	0/10.5	8.5/0	0/10.5	0/10.5	0/10.5
1987	2.5	0	0/10	6.2/0	0/10	0/10	0/10

* 1930   ** 1940 *** The first percentage indicates tariffs on vehicles originating in non-EFTA and non-EC countries, the second tariffs applicable to EC countries (which later became identical to EFTA rates), and the third, to EFTA countries.

An unexpected export surge from Japan in the 1970s radically changed trade relations. In the post-Tokyo Round context, where tariffs were drastically reduced but new safeguard rules were yet to be agreed upon, both the United States and car-producing EC countries negotiated various national measures to restrict imports. Japanese car imports, for example, were limited to 3% of the French market, mainly through administrative procedures relating to registration. In the United Kingdom, imports of Japanese cars were restricted to approximately 11% of the market through the industry-to-industry agreement between the British Society of Motor Manufacturers and Traders (SMMT) and the Association of Japanese

---

[3] Source: Chambre syndicale des constructeurs automobiles (France).

[4] See Sachwald, "De la libéralisation au néo-protectionnisme: le cas de l'industrie automobile", (1989) 4 *Politique étrangère*, 173.

Automobile Manufacturers (JAMA). Italy continued its quantitative restrictions which had been agreed as a condition for Japan's membership to the GATT, and were later listed in Annex II of Council Regulation 288/82 on common rules for imports.[5] The Benelux countries and the Federal Republic of Germany negotiated voluntary export restraints (VERs) with Japan in 1981.[6] Since 31 July 1991, however, the Commission has successfully established an EC-wide monitoring mechanism for motor vehicles in co-operation with the Japanese Ministry of International Trade and Industry (MITI). This VER arrangement, which is often called "commercial consensus", was notified to the GATT.[7]

In the subsequent Uruguay Round Agreement on Safeguards, it was agreed that:

"a Member shall not seek, take or maintain any VERs, orderly marketing arrangements or any other similar measures on the export or the import side. . . . Any such measure in effect on the date of entry into force of the WTO Agreement shall be brought into conformity with this Agreement or phased out in accordance with paragraph 2."[8]

According to Article 11(2), these special measures should be phased out within four years after the date of entry into force of the WTO Agreement. However, one exception is allowed for each importing member, although any such exception must be mutually agreed between the members concerned and notified to the Committee on Safeguards. This exception, to which the European Community is entitled until 31 December 1999, namely the "commercial consensus" on passenger cars, off-road vehicles and light commercial vehicle imports from Japan, is provided for by the Annex to the Agreement.

Thus, the EC/Japan commercial consensus has developed into a transparent form of VER, exempt until 31 December 1999 from the substantive rules contained in the Uruguay Round Agreement on Safeguards. In reality, the period during which the commercial consensus is an exception is not much longer than the four-year phasing-out period for other existing VERs. Now it is also relatively transparent under EC law, whereas in the past national VERs operated without Community authorisation. However, a VER would not be a "grey area" measure if it were completely transparent. The EC/Japan consensus, which was meant to be "grey", is bound to contain certain aspects which are unclear. This paper explores the

---

[5] OJ 1982 L31/1. Title IV of Regulation 288/82 concerns national trade policy-related measures, including administrative procedures regarding the national quantitative restrictions listed in Annex I. Regulation 288/82 was amended recently by Regulation 518/94.

[6] Bronckers, *Selective Safeguard Measures in Multilateral Trade Relations* (1985), pp 124–127.

[7] GATT Document L/6922, 16 October 1991. Germany communicated separately its reservations to the consensus, noting that its approval was on condition that (i) all restrictive measures would expire on 31 December 1999; (ii) EC-wide monitoring would take only the form of a statistical record with regard to those Member States not currently subject to restrictions; (iii) Japanese investment in the relevant areas would not be discriminated against; and (iv) car imports from third countries would remain unaffected (GATT document L/6924, 22 October 1991). See GATT, *Trade Policy Review: European Communities 1993*, vol. I, 170.

[8] Article 11, para 1(b).

status of this "consensus" under the GATT and European Community law in the post-Uruguay Round context.

"Grey area" measures and the Uruguay Round

Negotiating history

In 1987, during the Uruguay Round negotiations, the GATT Secretariat carried out an informal study of grey-area measures in order to facilitate the discussions within the Negotiating Group on Safeguards. This study identified some common characteristics based on a list of special measures relating to trade in footwear, steel, tableware, jute products, automobiles, beef, lamb, apples, motorcycles, TV receivers and silk fabrics. Grey area measures have as common characteristics: bilateral restraint arrangements of quantitative restrictions, surveillance systems or price undertakings; unilateral actions affecting imports for a period ranging from one to five years; unclear government involvement.[9]

The reasons for taking these measures are often related to disadvantages connected with the application of Article XIX GATT concerning anti-dumping or anti-subsidy actions. In many instances, grey area measures are used where it would not be possible for the importing country to justify an Article XIX action or where it would be too risky for exporters to follow that course of action. Countries can negotiate various measures outside the GATT rules, although these measures may be challenged under Articles I (MFN clause), XI(1) (prohibition of any restriction other than taxes and tariffs *i.e.*, the prohibition of measures such as quotas and import/export licences) and XIII (1) (the principle of non-discrimination in the application of quotas in pursuance of Article XII). In contrast to Article XIX actions which require injury to be established, the period to be limited and structural adjustment measures to be applied, grey area measures can be imposed without the occurrence of any of those conditions and without fear of retaliation. Most importantly, they have escaped the principle of non-selectivity, *i.e.* the application of the same restrictions on the product in the market from all exporting countries. Negotiating these measures on a selective basis seemed politically and commercially more convenient than Article XIX actions which is based on the most-favoured-nation (MFN) treatment.[10] Other trade instruments such as anti-dumping

---

9 MTN. GNG/NG9/W/6.

10 Article I GATT states *in fine*: ". . . any advantage, favour, privilege or immunity granted by a contracting party to any product originating in or destined for any other country shall be accorded immediately and unconditionally to the like product originating in or destined for the territories of all other contracting parties". The non-discrimination application of Article XIX is based on the interpretative note on GATT Article XIX that was incorporated into the Havana ITO Article 40, and a Panel decision (Textiles from Norway, vol. 27, BISD, 1981). The legal force of the interpretative note has been contested. See Bronckers, *supra*, n 6 at 18–19.

and anti-subsidy actions are often more unpredictable than grey area measures.

Some reasons for the exporting countries' acceptance of these measures may be the perceived threat that the alternative would be unilateral action with more severe effects on exports; economic reasons such as quota rents or stable market access; and the recognition of the importing countries' need for more time for structural adjustment. Whether exporting countries enter into these agreements or not depends largely on the bargaining relationships between the countries concerned. Industry-to-industry arrangements, in particular, lacked transparency and distorted competition but few actions were taken against them, often for political reasons.

In as much as recourse to grey area measures is related to the disadvantages of Article XIX actions, the new rules on multilateral safeguards negotiated during the Uruguay Round[11] are crucial for the future of grey area measures. The question of selectivity is one of the most hotly debated subjects.

Some countries and the EC advocated the introduction of selectivity to allow grey area measures to enter further into the realms of GATT legality. The idea of "consensual selectivity", permitting selective safeguard actions, was put forward on the condition that the prior agreement of the exporting country was obtained. However, this approach was rejected because it obviously favoured the most powerful governments. The introduction of a notification system was also proposed, but concern was voiced that notification without multilateral surveillance would result in the legitimisation of such measures.

As of 1991, only 24 Article XIX actions were instituted, compared to 284 alleged grey area agreements, of which the EC, the United States and Canada accounted for nearly 80%.[12] Developing countries advocated tougher rules on safeguards based on the MFN principle and the prohibition of grey area measures. Japan's position was to some extent similar to that of the developing countries, without however coinciding completely with them. Japan, for example, was not supportive of the idea of adjustment assistance.[13] The EC favoured maximum flexibility, particularly with regard to the notion of selectivity. It also advocated a long phase-out period (as long as eight years at one point in the negotiations) and restriction of compensation and retaliation.[14]

Implications of the Agreement on Safeguards

Compared to Article XIX, the new Agreement on Safeguards is clearer, particularly on the following points: criteria establishing injury (Article 4);

---

[11] During the Tokyo Round (1973–1979), negotiations on safeguards did not result in an agreement.

[12] Stewart (ed), *The GATT Uruguay Round: A Negotiating History (1986–1992)* (1993), vol. II, p 1726.

[13] *Ibid* at 1762–1763.

[14] *Ibid* at 1786–1787.

conditions for the application of safeguard measures (Articles 2, 5); transparency (Articles 11, 12); methods of investigation and the treatment of confidential data during the investigation (Article 3); prior consultations with exporters concerned (Article 12(3)); ceiling of quantitative restrictions (Article 5(1)); and maximum duration of safeguard measures, their extension and prohibition period (Article 7).

The implications of the new Agreement on Safeguards for grey area measures are far-reaching. The Uruguay Round negotiations resulted in the general prohibition of grey area measures[15], as well as the agreement that all these measures will be phased out no later than four years after the date of entry into force of the WTO Agreement, with one exception offered to each member.[16] Moreover, Article 11(3) prohibits members from encouraging or supporting the adoption or maintenance by public and private enterprises of non-governmental measures having equivalent effect to measures mentioned in Article 11(1). This means that government intervention or policy can no longer make companies immune to court actions under competition law.

However, the mere prohibition of these measures would have been only theoretical if the pressure to resort to VERs had remained unchanged, and the application of Article XIX had continued to be disadvantageous. The drawbacks of Article XIX actions were, therefore, remedied in two ways. First, through the introduction of a certain degree of selectivity on the part of the importing countries with regard to the sources of supply of the products to be restricted;[17] and secondly, by means of less rigid conditions for the application of the right to retaliation on the part of the exporting countries.

Uncertainties as to whether Article XIX actions should be applied on a non-discriminatory basis were settled by Article 2(2) of the new Agreement on Safeguards which provides that safeguard measures will be applied to a product being imported irrespective of its source. However, in cases where quantitative restrictions are applied – on the basis of a prior agreement with all exporting countries regarding the allocation of shares in the quota[18] – exceptions are allowed on certain conditions.[19] If imports from certain countries have increased and represent a disproportionate percentage of the total increase of imports of the product concerned in the representative period, and where serious injury has actually been caused (and not merely the threat of serious injury), selectivity of sources is possible in the allocation of quotas. Such a departure from the principle

---

[15] Article 11(1)(b) and its footnote 4 enumerate examples of these measures such as VERs, marketing arrangements, export moderation, export-price or import price monitoring systems, export or import surveillance, compulsory import cartels and discretionary export or import licensing schemes.

[16] Article 11(2).

[17] Selectivity on the part of developing countries is provided for by Article 9.

[18] Article 5(2)(a).

[19] Article 5(2)(b).

of non-selectivity is possible only through consultation among the parties concerned at the Committee on Safeguards, and on condition that such a modulation of quotas is made equitably with respect to all supplying countries. An investigation of injury is also required for the application of selectivity.

Another device contained in the new Agreement on Safeguards restricting the advantages of "grey area" measures for the importing countries is the softening of the terms of retaliation and compensation. Article XIX (3)(a) allowed the country affected by the safeguard measures to suspend GATT concessions after 30 days following the notice, if such measures were not agreed upon in prior consultations. Article 8(3) of the new Agreement stipulates that the right to retaliate should not be exercised for the first three years, provided that the safeguard measures are taken as a result of an absolute increase in imports, that is, not in the case of a relative increase.

In the light of the above mentioned provisions of the new Agreement on Safeguards, it will be difficult for governments to encourage actively "grey area" measures under the WTO, although for the countries accepting these measures, the incentive not to do so will not weaken significantly. Effectively, this may lead to the decrease of government-arranged VERs but to the increase of industry-to-industry arrangements.

EC/Japan commercial consensus under EC law

The so-called "consensus" on the import of motor vehicles reached on 31 July 1991 between the European Commission and Japan was expressed in the form of two parallel statements made by Mr Andriessen, then Vice-President of the Commission, and Mr Nakao, then Minister of International Trade and Industry.[20] The stated objective of the consensus is to take co-operative measures so as to avoid disruption in the Community market as a whole and the five "restricted" markets until 31 December 1999.[21] The EC proposed to abolish national import restrictions, not to apply Article 115 and to accept the Community-type approval from

---

[20] See *Agence Europe*, 2 August 1991. The notification to the GATT refers to the objectives of the co-operation as: "the progressive and full liberalization of the EC import regime on motor vehicles with avoidance of market disruption and, through an appropriate transitional period, to facilitate structural adjustments that may be required of EC manufacturers to achieve adequate levels of international competitiveness".

[21] Estimated 1999 export levels to the five "restricted" markets are: France, 150,000 units (5.3% of the market); Italy, 138,000 (5.3%); Spain, 79,000 (5.4%); Portugal, 23,000 (8.4%); and the United Kingdom, 190,000 (7% – less than the previous national restriction at 11% probably due to the important transplant production). The share of the remaining EC market allotted to exports from Japan would be 12.5%. The consensus covers assembled vehicles and sets of car parts (ckd-sets) containing more than 60% of the value of the components of a car.

Japanese car importers.[22] Japan in turn agreed to carry out dual monitoring.[23] It was confirmed that inward Japanese investment would continue to be free of restrictions and that the products of such enterprises could circulate freely within the EC. Bi-annual, bilateral consultations were to be held regarding current export trends, forecasts and adjustment of allocations. The EC and Japan would make appropriate notification to the GATT and jointly defend the monitoring system as a GATT-consistent measure. In addition, Mr Andriessen declared that the necessary measures would be taken to ensure that the operation of competition law would not constitute an obstacle to the operation of the arrangement. Although this issue was not covered by the consensus, it seems that the existing selective distribution system under the present Regulation 123/85 was conceived as one of the means to implement the "consensus". The selective distribution system would prevent massive indirect exports of Japanese cars to "restricted" markets.[24]

The Commission's representative in the *BEUC* case[25] stated in reply to a question raised by the Court of First Instance that the commercial consensus "was not recorded in writing and that it was not an official agreement for the purpose of Article 113 of the EEC Treaty, but rather a political commitment".

Nature of the agreement

The "arrangement", as described by the Commission, was approved by the COREPER meeting of 24 July 1991[26], but not signed by the Council. If the "consensus" had been an agreement within the meaning of Article 228, it should have been signed by the Council. In the Commission's view, the procedures set out in Article 228 for the conclusion of treaties were not applicable to the "consensus".

The obvious question to be asked is whether the "consensus" operates as an agreement. In Opinion 1/75[27], the Court said that the term "agreement" contained in Article 228 is to be interpreted widely and covers any undertakings entered into by entities subject to international law which have binding force, whatever their formal designation. The Commission, in various statements, pointed out that the "commercial consensus" is merely a forecast and not a binding understanding. If the consensus was

---

[22] This is an important advantage for Japanese car importers because this allows them to avoid protracted procedures for registration. See Case C-428/93, *Monin Automobiles*, [1994] ECR I-1707.

[23] *i.e.*, exports to the EC as a whole and to the five restricted markets, on the assumption that its exports would reach 1.23 million units in 1999 in a total EC market forecast of 15.1 million units.

[24] The Commission's communication to the Council and European Parliament entitled "European Motor Vehicle Industry: Situation, Issues at Stake and Proposals for Actions," COM (92) 166 final, stated that the selective distribution system under Regulation 123/85 would help the implementation of the commercial consensus during the transitional period.

[25] Case T-37/92, [1994] ECR II-285, at 316, para 59 *per curiam*.

[26] See Vigier, *supra*, n 2 at 99 (March 1992).

[27] [1975] ECR 1355.

considered as binding, it can be subject to judicial review by the Court of Justice. The legal effect of the "consensus" has not been tested before the Court, mainly because of market forces. Demand in the "restricted" markets since the implementation date of the "consensus" has been so weak, particularly in 1993, that Japanese car exports did not reach the forecasted level. Moreover, the strength of the yen has also adversely affected the competitiveness of Japanese cars.

The way in which the "consensus" is to be implemented is not entirely clear. However, there are some indications that it may not be binding. MITI has taken full responsibility for limiting Japanese car exports and distributes export quotas to each of the exporters by means of administrative "guidance".[28] Adherence to the "guidance" is ensured by reports on car exports collected from each company by MITI. Compared to the United States/ Japan Auto VER[29], however, the enforcement measures seem, for the moment, to be less stringent. Neither the United States/Japan nor the EC/ Japan Auto VERs have made cars subject to export licensing (namely by amending the Export Trade Control Order). Instead, they have been implemented through written and/or oral administrative "guidance". Under the United States/Japan Auto VER, the Japanese Government was prepared to make car exports to the United States subject to export licensing based on the Foreign Exchange and Foreign Trade Control Law and to proceed against the relevant company/exporter if it threatened to exceed the limits set down by MITI.[30] By contrast, MITI seems to be less determined to act in the case of excess exports to the EC markets and to be firm about putting an end to the arrangement in 1999.

The diversity of texts and interpretations of EC/Japan "commercial consensus" that exist among car industries and distributors is another indication that this arrangement may be difficult to enforce under certain circumstances. The most significant divergence in the interpretation seems

---

[28] The oft-cited definition of administrative guidance was made in a 1970 statement by the Japanese Government before the House of Councillors Commerce and Industry Committee. Administrative guidance does not involve legal authority for enforcement, as would the case of a restriction on civil rights or the imposition of a duty on the public. Administrative guidance refers to the function of an administrative agency – acting within the scope of its duty under the laws establishing the agency or within the scope of its jurisdiction – to persuade and guide a party to conduct its business in a certain way, in order to realise an administrative goal through the party's co-operation.

[29] The United States/Japan VER on cars was announced for the first time on 1 May 1981. It was in force until March 1994, when the transplants in the United States became the major source of supply of Japanese cars in the American market.

[30] In a letter, dated 7 May 1981, to the US Attorney General, the then Ambassador of Japan in the United States stated that: ". . . Further, if any firm should fail to make a report or should make a false report in violation of the provisions of Article Sixty-seven (67) of the Foreign Exchange and Foreign Trade Control Law, that firm will be proceeded against for punishment under Articles Seventy-two (72) and Seventy-three (73) of the Law.

If on the basis of the above reports it becomes clear that any company threatens to exceed the limits set forth by MITI, the Government of Japan will promptly make car exports to the US subject to export licensing, by amending the Export Trade Control Order (Cabinet Order No. 378 of 1949) in accordance with Article Forty-eight (48) of the Foreign Exchange and Foreign Trade Control Law. MITI would then enforce the export maximums it had established for each company by refusing to license exports in excess of those maximums . . ."

to exist between the Commission and French car industry, on the question of whether European transplant production is included in the scope of monitoring. Many in the French industry affirm that it is implicitly included.

What will happen if demand for Japanese cars rises beyond the agreed quota and cars are imported in excess of the forecast? This would indeed be a test as to whether the EC/Japan consensus is binding or not. This test, however, is unlikely to happen due to the high value of the yen which discourages Japanese exports. Another test for the legal status of the consensus is how the new EU members, such as Austria and Finland (where the market share of Japanese cars is very high)[31], will cope with restrictions. The accession Treaty for these countries does not include the commercial consensus as l'acquis communautaire, but the three new members later agreed to be part of the commercial consensus by the exchange of letters. It remains to be seen how the free circulation of Japanese cars in the rest of the EC will be limited since Article 115 has been declared to be redundant and anti-dumping measures cannot be used within the EC.

Competence of the Commission

The Court stated in the *Donckerwolcke* case[32] that, as full responsibility for commercial policy was transferred to the Community by means of Article 113(1), national commercial policy measures would only be permissible at the end of the transitional period by virtue of a specific Community authorisation. The Commission has already negotiated VERs with a large number of countries on numerous products. The Commission has described VERs as unilateral measures taken by the exporting country. Bronckers has pointed out that the Commission justified its power to impose quotas unilaterally on the ground that it has to safeguard Community industries against increasing import competition under the Community's import regime.[33] The Commission has also taken the position that its authority to impose quotas unilaterally includes the authority to negotiate VERs with third countries.[34] Some of the different VERs may be described as "settlements", following anti-dumping complaints by Community industries. The EC/Japan consensus has also been defended from an industrial policy viewpoint.

The Court of Justice does not necessarily consider that restrictive measures contradict the principles underlying the common commercial

---

[31] Japanese automobile share in the EFTA car market in 1992 was as follows: Norway 43.1%; Finland 42.2%; Austria 30.1%; Switzerland 30.1%; Sweden 29.75%. See GATT, *Trade Policy Review: European Communities 1993*, p 169. The Commission is, however, of the opinion that these figures are too high. Austria, Finland and Sweden reached an agreement in March 1995 and are now considered as "non-restricted" and included in the quote of 1 105 000 vehicles (average 21.5%).

[32] Case 41/76, [1976] ECR 1921.

[33] Bronckers, "A Legal Analysis of Protectionist Measures Affecting Japanese Imports into the European Community Revisited", in Völker (ed), *Protectionism and the European Community* (1987, 2nd ed), p 70.

[34] *Ibid.*

policy.[35] The Court has stressed that obtaining the agreement of supplier countries to voluntary restrictions of their exports to the Community prior to adopting coercive measures cannot be regarded as being unacceptable from the point of Community law. Such VERs illustrate the Community's effort to refrain from adopting coercive measures unless everything else fails.[36] The Court affirmed that it is legitimate for the Commission to take account of whether or not an exporter country is ready to accept a VER.[37] In the Court's view, the Commission has the power to negotiate VERs, which constitute a lesser evil than coercive import restrictions. The Court has also repeatedly stated that GATT commitments (particularly Articles XIX, XXII and XXIII) are couched in general terms and, therefore, cannot be treated as provisions which may serve as a yardstick in judging whether a Community measure is valid or not. Most importantly, neither Article II (schedule of concessions) nor Article XI (prohibition of quantitative restrictions) have been recognised by the Court as having direct effect. Thus, they confer no rights on natural or legal persons (or even Member States) to contest the validity of Community acts on this basis.[38]

The Court, however, has put limits to the Commission's powers in negotiating VERs. First, the Commission must observe the principle of proportionality.[39] Secondly, it should make a diligent inquiry and assess the facts as required by the relevant provisions of the EC Treaty. Thirdly, it should also take into consideration the exporters' legitimate expectations, such as, for example, the maintenance of traditional trade relations.[40] Finally, the Court has recognised that Community institutions enjoy wide discretionary powers in the sphere of commercial policy and have no obligation in their external relations to accord equal treatment in all respects to non-member countries.[41] The Commission's competence to agree VERs has, therefore, been confirmed by the Court. However, the prohibition of VERs contained in the Safeguard Agreement will have to be taken into consideration by the EC.

Uncertainties remain as to the objectives of the EC/Japan "commercial consensus". On the one hand, the consensus was a significant step towards the establishment of the single market since it led to the abolition of

---

[35] See *e.g.*, Case 112/80, *Dürbeck v Hauptzollampt Frankfurt-am-Main – Flughafen*, [1981] ECR 1095, at 1119–1120, para 44: "Article 110, which sets out the abolition of restrictions on international trade as a principle underlying the common commercial policy, cannot be interpreted as prohibiting the Community from enacting, upon pain of committing an infringement of the Treaty, any measure against the risk of a serious market disturbance."

[36] See *e.g.*, Case 112/80, *ibid*; Case 41/76, *supra*, n 32 at 1938; Case 245/81, *Edeka*, [1982] ECR 2745, at 2757.

[37] Case 245/81, *ibid.*

[38] Cases 21–24/72, *International Fruit Company*, [1972] ECR 1219; Case 9/73, *Schlüter*, [1973] ECR 1135; Case C-280/93, *Germany v Council* [1994] ECR I-4973.

[39] An attempt to agree on a VER is all the more legitimate since Article 3(2) of Regulation 2707/72 provides that any protective measures decided upon by the Commission may be adopted only "in so far, and for as long, as they are strictly necessary." This implies that when the Commission believes that the conditions requisite for the application of such measures are fulfilled, it must observe the principle of proportionality underlying the Community legal order. See Case 110/80, *supra*, n 35 at 1118 and Case 245/81, *supra*, n 36 at 2757.

[40] Case 245/81, *ibid* at 2758.

[41] See Case 55/75, *Balkan-Import-Export v Hauptzollamt Berlin-Packhof*, [1976] ECR 19.

commercial measures affecting the EC Member States individually, although it left intra-community restrictions by preserving five restricted markets.[42] A key objective of the "consensus", as stated above, is the progressive and full liberalisation of the EC import regime, thereby avoiding market disruption and the introduction of structural adjustments for EC manufacturers in order to achieve international competitiveness. The "consensus" can be classified as both a common commercial policy and an industrial policy measure. According to the Commission, however, the EC/Japan commercial consensus is outside Article 113. The objective of the "consensus" appears to be rather confusing to different parties.

Implications for competition

The Auto-VER between the United States and Japan concluded in May 1981 gave rise to abundant scholarly comment on its legality, not only in the light of the GATT but also under United States antitrust laws. However, no significant antitrust lawsuits were lodged concerning this VER which ended in March 1994. With regard to the EC/Japan VER, it is too early to say whether the "consensus" will survive intact or not under EC competition law. In the announcement concerning the EC/Japan "consensus", Commissioner Andriessen stated that measures will be taken to ensure that competition law does not constitute an obstacle to its operation.[43] For obvious reasons, it is unlikely that EC competition law will be applied to the practices of Japanese car manufacturers. MITI has also been most careful not to encourage horizontal agreements between exporters. It has dealt with each car manufacturer through administrative guidance, although the legal status of written administrative guidance in Japanese antitrust laws has not been very firmly established.[44] Japanese car manufacturers can probably escape antitrust liability under sovereign compulsion defence, in that the Japanese Government initiated the VER and now monitors exports. However, after 31 December 1999, the sovereign compulsion defence will no longer be valid in respect of VERs by virtue of Article 11(3) of the new GATT Agreement on Safeguards which prohibits governments from encouraging such measures.

Competition policy implications of the EC/Japan consensus in the EC market seem to be a rather more complicated issue. The Court of Justice and the Court of First Instance have dealt with cases which are more or less related to this question.[45] Most of these cases concern the legality of the

---

[42] Points 35 and 36 of the Commission's White Paper, "Completing the Internal Market", COM(85) 310, emphasised the importance of this step.

[43] *Agence Europe*, no. 5547 (n.s.), 2 August 1991.

[44] In the *Petroleum Cartel* case (Tokyo High Court, 29 September 1980), the Tokyo High Court implied that administration guidance as a standard practice to achieve regulatory goals, probably made the parties acting under such a guidance immune from liability under Japanese antitrust law.

[45] Case T-37/92, *BEUC* v *Commission*, [1994] ECR II-285; Case T-9/92, *Automobiles Peugeot SA* v *Commission*, judgment of 22 April 93, nyr; C-322/93P, *Peugeot SA* v *Commission*, [1994] ECR I-2727; Case C-28/90, *Asia Motors*, [1990] ECR I-2181; Case T-7/92, *Asia Motors*, judgment of 29 June 1993, nyr; Case C-386/92, *Monin Automobiles*, judgment of 26 April 1993, nyr; Case C-428/93, *Monin Automobiles*, [1994] ECR I-1707.

Commission's handling of complaints and some to importers' claims for compensation.

The *Peugeot* case concerned the role of an intermediary acting on behalf of ultimate consumers under the selective distribution system provided by a block exemption Regulation 123/85.[46] This case was not directly related to the "consensus". In as much as the selective distribution system is considered by the Commission as a means to implement the "consensus", and because the judgment indicates the extent to which the refusal to sell is justified under EC competition law, these cases also help to explore the implications of the Community trade policy for competition. The starting point for the Court of First Instance and the Court of Justice in the *Peugeot* cases is that "any derogation from the prohibition of agreements and decisions for concerted practices such as that provided by Regulation 123/85, ought to be narrowly interpreted".[47] In other words, the exemption to manufacturers and dealers from the obligation to supply and the conditions under which intermediaries can operate should not be extended more than necessary to protect their legitimate interests under Article 85(3). By its interpretation of the conditions laid down in Article 3(11) of Regulation 123/85, the Court indicated how much scope remained for parallel importers of motor vehicles. By clarifying the conditions imposed on the intermediaries (*i.e.*, only a direct contractual link between the intermediary and the final consumer) and distinguishing that case from *Binon*[48], the Court left a wide scope for parallel imports. If the argument is pushed to the extreme, it amounts to the Court's recognition of the manufacturer's or the dealer's duty to supply.

The *Peugeot* ruling was perhaps a confirmation of the Court's position that exemption from Article 85(1) cannot be granted for practices which would be in violation of some overriding Community principle, *e.g.*, maintaining the unity of the common market.[49] In its judgment in *Ford*[50], the Court affirmed that:

"the Commission is not obliged to carry out a detailed examination of all the advantages and disadvantages likely to flow from a selective distribution system when it has good reason to believe that a manufacturer has used such a system to prevent parallel imports and thus artificially to partition the common market."

The Commission's suggestion to use the selective distribution system under Regulation 123/85 as a means of preventing the flow of Japanese cars in certain "restricted" markets could also possibly be considered as a misuse.

---

[46] Commission Regulation 123/85 on the application of Article 83(3) of the Treaty to certain categories of motor vehicle distribution and servicing arrangements, OJ 1985 L15. On 16 October 1994, the Commission adopted a new text relating to the selective distribution of motor vehicles for 1995 when Regulation 123/85 expired.

[47] Case C-322/93P, *supra*, n 45 at 2747.

[48] Case 243/83, [1985] ECR 2015. In this case, a commercial agent acting under the mandate of a large number of consumers was held to be a reseller and not an intermediary.

[49] Cases 25–26/84, *Ford* v *Commission*, [1985] ECR 2725, per A.G. Slynn.

[50] *Ibid.*

In *BEUC*[51], the Court of First Instance indicated that it was not clear whether national restrictions such as the SMMT-JAMA agreement were valid after the adoption of the EC/Japan consensus, unless the issue was investigated. The Court of First Instance left this question unanswered since the Commission itself asserted that the "consensus" constituted a political act. The Commission's discretion in deciding whether or not to investigate was another issue discussed in connection with the notion of "Community interest" following *Automec II*.[52] While in *Automec II* the Court of First Instance recognised the Commission's discretion in deciding the Community interest, it appears to have limited its scope in *BEUC*. In the aftermath of this judgment, BEUC has requested the Commission to investigate the matter.[53]

After a series of unfruitful attempts, Asia Motors and other firms importing lesser-known Japanese and Korean cars[54] persuaded the Court of First Instance to annul the Commission's decision of 5 December 1991. This decision had rejected their complaint against importers of five well-known Japanese makes[55] who had allegedly reached a concerted agreement to share the 3% quota of the French market reserved for Japanese cars in the 1980s.

The Court of First Instance stated that the Commission's decision was not supported by sufficient and conclusive evidence that a concerted agreement did not exist between the five manufacturers to share among themselves the full quota of Japanese imports into France. Despite the French Government's argument that the five importers had no margin to manoeuvre because their actions formed an integral part of French public policy[56], the documents which were presented to the Court of First Instance revealed that these companies enjoyed a certain degree of autonomy of decision. The Court of First Instance reiterated its position that the fact that the anti-competitive behaviour of accredited importers was "favoured or encouraged" by public authorities, did not in itself render Article 85 inapplicable.[57]

The *Monin Automobiles* case[58] illustrates how the method of implementation of the EC/Japan "consensus" in France can put the imports of other foreign cars (*e.g.*, Korean cars) into disadvantage. Monin claimed that while the French authorities accepted type-approval of Japanese cars they delayed the approval of other foreign cars, thus causing injury to the applicant. The substance of the case was not discussed by the Court because the "*commisseur-priseur*" who referred the question to the European Court was not considered as a "court or tribunal" for the purposes of

---

[51] Case T-37/92, *supra*, n 45.

[52] Case T-64/89, [1990] ECR II-367.

[53] In the United States, indirect purchasers affected only by higher prices resulting from a restraint of trade did not have standing to challenge the restraint. *Illinois Brick Co.* v *Illinois*, 431 US, 720 (1977).

[54] Isuzu, Daihatsu, Suzuki, Subaru and Hyundai.

[55] Toyota, Honda, Nissan, Mazda and Mitsubishi.

[56] *e.g.*, Article 106 of *le code de la route français*.

[57] See Case 229/83, *Leclerc*, [1985] ECR 1.

[58] Case C-428/93, *supra*, n 45.

Article 177. Compared to the BEUC complaint which will probably only result in a judicial inquiry into the nature and validity of Community acts, *Asia Motors* and *Monin* represent private actions brought by injured parties which constitute a significant proportion of those whose interests are perceptibly affected. Depending on the way in which the French authorities handle future cases, these complaints may lead to further scrutiny of the anti-competitive behaviour of firms. Another potential class of complainants would be EC importers and dealers in Japanese automobiles who purchase directly from Japanese manufacturers. Their incentive to take action against the French authorities will depend on whether the benefits they derive from high prices due to the restriction on imports is greater than the marginal loss they experience from their decreased or limited market share.

The post-Uruguay Round context

This paper presented an overview of some of the key questions surrounding the EC/Japan commercial consensus reached in July 1991. Various trade instruments used to deal with international competitive conditions among large trading nations ranged from tariffs and quantitative restrictions to VERs. Increasing efforts have been made on the part of the EC to cope with Japan and other Asian countries whose export capacity is backed by a society particularly well adapted to mass production of consumer goods. In coping with the export surge through VERs, a wide range of problems arose as to the conformity regarding GATT and competition laws.

The Uruguay Round Agreement on Safeguards offers increased possibilities for the EC to use safeguard actions, while holding "grey area" measures to be illegal. It is difficult to predict how competitive the EC car industry will become and what types of trade instruments will be used in the year 2000. Northern car manufacturers will probably increase their competitiveness and advocate free trade, whereas southern manufacturers may still need protection. What instruments should then be used? Differences within the EC on this issue will be exacerbated, so that Community-wide protection may prove difficult. Given the new safeguard rules which prohibit governments from taking "grey area" measures, industries themselves may devise means of protection giving rise to more complicated competition problems. Anti-dumping measures may be another option.

Some "grey area" measures may still be inevitable despite their prohibition under the WTO. The GATT does not give EC citizens rights on which they can rely when challenging the validity of a measure adopted by a Community institution, and exporting countries may not be able to refuse what may satisfy their trading partners, particularly when these arrangements bring in quota rents.

HIROKO YAMANE

Chapter 17
Public Procurement and EC External Relations: A Legal Framework

Introduction

Market opportunities for public procurement in the European Union and third countries after completion of the Uruguay Round are about to increase ten-fold to well over 350bn ECUs annually[1] once the new multilateral Government Procurement Agreement (GPA) comes into force on 1 January 1996.[2] Even so this projected increase is tempered by two factors. First, the GPA is currently limited in its participation to just ten signatories[3], although collectively they account for the lion's share of an estimated US$1,000bn annually in global procurement, and thus it does not take account of procurement activities where no special agreement exists between the Community[4] and the third countries based on other, autonomous measures. Second, despite the virtual completion of the internal market during the course of which the Community has adopted specific legislation aimed at opening up public procurement through Community-wide advertising of contracts above defined thresholds, the establishment of non-discriminatory criteria for contract awards and eradication of discriminatory "national"

---

[1] European Commission Press Release, MEMO/94/29, *EU-US Negotiations on Public Procurement*, 21 April 1994.

[2] GPR/74, text also at Cmnd 2575 (Miscellaneous No. 13 (1994)), approved by Council Decision 94/800/EC of 22 December 1994, OJ 1994 L 336/1 (the GPA text is attached thereto). The new Agreement, although formally signed on 15 April 1994 at the Marrakesh Conference, which concluded the Uruguay Round, was not included in the negotiating mandate of 20 September 1986 at Punta del Este (GATT *Basic Instruments and Selected Documents* (BISD) 33S/19 (1987)). Instead it is taken up as one of the Plurilateral Trade Agreements in Annex 4 to the Agreement Establishing the World Trade Organisation (WTO Agreement); the WTO Agreement (but not Annex 4) is published in *Results of the Uruguay Round of Multilateral Trade Negotiations: The Legal Texts* (GATT Secretariat, 1994).

[3] Canada, the European Union, Hong Kong, Israel, Japan, the Republic of Korea, Norway, Singapore, Switzerland and the United States. Hong Kong and Singapore, although parties to the current 1988 GPA, have decided not to join the new agreement. Aruba is considering acceding to the new GPA and the People's Republic of China has observer status to the current Agreement.

[4] Within the context of the Uruguay Round, the term European Community is used, rather than European Union, since the Community is the named party to the new WTO under Article XI of the WTO Agreement; as of 1 January 1995 the Member States of the European Union, and thus the European Community, are: Austria, Belgium, Denmark, Finland, France, Germany, Greece, Ireland, Italy, Luxembourg, the Netherlands, Portugal, Spain, Sweden and the United Kingdom.

technical standards[5], recent research suggests that the overall outcome of Community's internal market policy in procurement has been "symbolic rather than substantive".[6] Many Member States have continued to flout Community law, for example by providing for a diversity of mechanisms which allow purchasers to evade rules or influence the choice of suppliers during the evaluation of bids.[7] Similar inconsistencies appear on the external plane where the exclusion and preference rules of Article 29 of the Utilities Directive (Article 36 under the consolidated directive)[8] potentially allow for the exclusion of tenders comprising products of third country origin which are in free circulation. The consequences of this policy with respect to the Community's trading partners, notably the United States, is discussed below.

It has also been suggested that the extent to which governments continue to favour domestic undertakings and thereby discriminate against import penetration from neighbouring Member States and third countries, may arise due to other, less traditional non-tariff barriers of a logistical, informational or cultural character.[9] Surveys of various Member States[10] in the late 1980s reveals that large parts of public sector purchases are dependant on relative proximity of the supplier with a propensity for "national" suppliers wherever possible, to the detriment of suppliers from further afield, in other words the distance aspect can act as a major logistical barrier to procurement supply.

---

[5] Directive 88/295 amending Directive 77/62 relating to co-ordination of procedures for the award of public supply contracts, OJ 1989 L127/1, now consolidated in Directive 93/36, OJ 1993 L199/1 (Supplies Directive); Directive 89/440 amending Directive 71/305 concerning co-ordination of procedures for the award of public works contracts, OJ 1989, L210/1, now consolidated in Directive 93/37, OJ 1993 L199/54 (Works Directive); Directive 89/665 on the co-ordination of the laws, regulations and administrative provisions relating to the application of review procedures to the award of public supply and public works contracts, OJ 1989 L395/33 (Remedies Directive); Directive 90/531 on the procurement procedures of entities operating in the water, energy, transport and telecommunications sectors, OJ 1990 L297/1 (Utilities Directive); Directive 92/50 relating to the co-ordination of procedures for the award of public service contracts, OJ 1992 L 209/1 (Services Directive) (*both* the Utilities and Services Directives have now been replaced by a consolidated version, Directive 93/38 co-ordinating the procurement procedures of entities operating in the water, energy, transport and telecommunications sectors, OJ 1993 L199/84)); Directive 92/13 co-ordinating the laws, regulations and administrative provisions relating to the application of Community rules on the procurement procedures of entities operating in the water, energy, transport and telecommunications sectors, OJ 1992 L76/14 (Utilities Remedies Directive).

[6] Swann (ed), *The Single European Market and Beyond* (Routledge, 1992), p 62; European Commission *The Opening-Up of Public Procurement* (Commission of the European Communities, 1993), pp 4–5; see also "Public Procurement in the Excluded Sectors" Supplement 6/88 – Bull. EC and for Community-wide discrimination in the provision of judicial and administrative remedies to aggrieved bidders, COM (88) 733 Final, para 14.

[7] Cecchini *The European Challenge 1992: The Benefits of a Single Market* (Wildwood House Ltd.), p 19.

[8] *Supra*, n 5.

[9] Madsen, "Is Culture a Major Barrier to a Single European Market? The Case of Public Purchasing" in Zetterholm (ed), *National Cultures and European Integration: Exploratory Essays on Cultural Diversity and Common Policies* (Berg Publishers, 1994), pp 149–157.

[10] Atkins Management Consultants "The 'Cost of Non-Europe' in Public Sector Procurement", vol 5, parts A and B in *Research on the Cost of Non-Europe* (Luxembourg, 1988), p. 12.

Likewise, despite Community attempts at improving transparency in public procurement through requirements such as compulsory publication of all tender offers above certain thresholds and the results of the awards in the *Official Journal of the European Community* as of 1 January 1993, the fact remains that some markets remain impenetrable where national suppliers have greater familiarity with the needs of the purchaser.[11]

Finally, there may be certain cultural barriers to procurement reflected in differing national attitudes, national preferences (including country-specific design), language barriers, or simply different ways of doing business, the latter to some extent reinforced by the principle of subsidiarity, all of which may affect purchasing. Likewise, any or all these factors may enhance national competitive processes but do little to further competition within the internal market or to encourage third country access to Community procurement markets.[12]

What follows is an analysis of the legal framework of the Community's public procurement activities on the external plane after completion of the Uruguay Round. It includes a review of the autonomous and conventional measures at the disposal of the Community in dealing with products, services and firms from third countries seeking access to Community procurement markets and equally access for Community products, services and firms to the procurement markets of third countries.

In assessing these measures attention will be drawn to the Community's policy in the field of procurement in the context of the Common Commercial Policy, the scope of that policy and the extent to which measures have been adopted under it. The autonomous and conventional measures are either of a trade-restricting or trade-liberalising character, dependant upon the chosen trade instrument although at times they may be interwoven.[13]

Scope of the Common Commercial Policy in public procurement

As with other aspects of the Common Commercial Policy (CCP), Article 113 EC forms the starting point for a review of the division of competences between the Community and the Member States in the field of public procurement. Under Article 113 EC, the Community is expressly empowered to make CCP, including "changes in tariff rates, the conclusion of tariff and trade agreements, the achievement of uniformity in measures of liberalisation, export policy and measures to protect rules such as those

---

[11] *Supra*, Madsen, n 9, pp 150 and 152.
[12] *Ibid*, pp 153–157.
[13] Arrowsmith, "Third Country Access to E.C. Public Procurement: An Analysis of the Legal Framework" (1994) 4 PPLR 1 at p 4.

to be taken in cases of dumping or subsidies". In Opinion 1/78[14] the Court considered that the Community's competence should not be interpreted restrictively since "the enumeration in Article 113 of the subjects covered by commercial policy . . . is conceived as a non-exhaustive enumeration".[15]

The problem arises when it comes to identifying the subject matter, other than that specifically enumerated in Article 113 EEC, which falls within exclusive Community competence, in particular whether the measures adopted in respect of that subject matter extend to those not directly concerned with trade regulation but which nevertheless have an effect on trade rules, as is the case with public procurement. The necessity of determining the exact scope of Community powers is linked to the fact that where the Community has such competence, Member States no longer have the power to act.

In line with the established caselaw of the European Court of Justice, the Community's authority to enter into international commitments may arise not only from express attribution by the Treaty, as in the case of Articles 113, 114[16] and 238[17] EC, but, as stated in Case 22/70 *Commission* v *Council (ERTA)* "may equally flow from other provisions of the Treaty and from measures adopted, within the framework of those provisions by the Community".[18] The Court in Joined Cases 3, 4 and 6/76 *Kramer et al* stressed that such authority can flow by implication from other measures adopted by Community institutions within the framework of the Treaty provisions.[19]

Then in its Opinion 1/76 the Court concluded that the Community's authority to conclude international agreements could be deduced not only from the provisions of the Treaty, in conjunction with secondary legislation, or the situation where it has adopted rules within the framework of a common policy, but may extend to all areas corresponding to the objectives of the Treaty.[20] This caselaw on implied powers, often referred to as the doctrine of parallelism of internal and external competences (*in foro interno, in foro externo*), is not without further refinement.

It has been demonstrated elsewhere[21] that while the Community has the power to enter into international agreements, even in the absence of

---

[14] Opinion 1/78 of 4 October 1979 given pursuant to Article 228:1 EEC (*International Rubber Agreement*) [1979] ECR p 2871.

[15] *Ibid*, para 45; see also Case 165/87 *Commission* v *Council* of 27 September 1988 [1988] ECR 5545, para 15.

[16] Article 114 EC has since been repealed under the Treaty on European Union.

[17] Article 238 EC authorises the Community to conclude association agreements with third countries.

[18] [1971] 263 at p 274.

[19] [1976] ECR 1279 at p 1308 (paras 19–20).

[20] Opinion 1/76 of 26 April 1977 given pursuant to Article 228:1 EC (*Draft Agreement Establishing a European Laying-up Fund for Inland Waterway Vessels*) [1977] ECR 741, at p 755, para 3; reconfirmed in Opinion 2/91 of 14 March 1993 (*Convention No. 170 of the International Labour Organisation on the safety of chemicals at work*), [1993] 3 CMLR, 800, at p 816, para 10.

[21] Eeckhout, *The European Internal Market and International Trade: A Legal Analysis* (Clarendon Press, 1994), pp 38–41.

express provisions, it still leaves unanswered questions pertaining to the exact scope of Community competence in the field of external relations. Where the Community has already adopted internal common rules it has exclusive competence to negotiate and conclude international agreements. Subject matter which "affects" or "alters" the scope of these rules cannot be concluded by the Member States as demonstrated in both the *ERTA* and *Kramer* judgments.

On the other hand, Opinion 1/76 marks a departure because it is the "necessity" of concluding an international agreement with a view to achieving a "specific objective" of the Community which gives rise to exclusive Community competence. This competence must in each case be found and applied (until such time the competence remains "potential" rather than "actual"); once exercised the implied external power gives rise to external exclusivity.[22] On the basis of Opinion 1/76 there would appear to be an argument for extending the implied powers doctrine beyond the scope of the CCP contained in Article 113 EC to embrace the externalisation of public procurement policies, but the extent to which this can be done with respect to the procurement of services, or supply of services, is questionable, especially after the Court's recent Opinion 1/94[23] and in view of the fact that services are taken up in the new GPA for the first time.

The Court was called upon to examine the division of competences between the Community and the Member States in concluding the WTO Agreement, in particular with respect to new areas of trade regulation: services under the General Agreement on Trade in Services (GATS)[24] and trade-related aspects of intellectual property rights (TRIPs).[25] Although it confirmed its earlier statement in Opinion 1/78, that the enumeration of subject matter covered by the CCP under Article 113 EC, was not an exhaustive one[26], it chose to examine the matter by reference to the four modes of supply in Article 1 GATS.[27]

The cross-border supply of services is thereby considered analogous to the simple supply of goods and thus falls under the CCP and within exclusive Community competence. However, where one of the other three modes of supply exists involving (i) the movement of the service consumer towards the service supplier, or (ii) the provision of an establishment-based service, or (iii) the physical movement of persons across the border, conform with the distinction made in the Treaty between CCP at Article 3(b) and measures concerning the entry and movement of persons in

---

[22] Völker, *Barriers to External and Internal Community Trade* (Kluwer, 1993), pp 199–200.

[23] Opinion 1/94 of 15 November 1994 given pursuant to Article 228:6 EC (*Competence of the Community to conclude international agreements concerning services and the protection of intellectual property*) [1995] ECR-I 5267.

[24] Annex 1B to the WTO Agreement, *Results of the Uruguay Round*, pp 325 *et seq.*

[25] Annex 1C to the WTO Agreement, *ibid*, pp 365 *et seq.*

[26] Opinion 1/94, *supra* n 23, para 39.

[27] *Ibid*, para 43.

3(d), then competence rests with the Member States and the Community jointly.[28]

The Court then examined the proposition that if the Community's competence to conclude the GATS was not based upon Article 113 EC then it might be based upon its implied powers. In accordance with the criteria set out in Opinion 1/76, since the Community has extensive powers to regulate services in the internal market (including services, or their supply, in relation to public procurement), on the basis of Articles 57:2, 66 and 100a EC, it could be argued that the exercise of such competence on the external plane is necessary to achieve the "objective" of the internal market. However, the Court distinguished the draft GATS from the draft Agreement establishing a Laying-up Fund in its earlier Opinion 1/76. Whereas the latter dealt with the realisation of a specific economic objective (a laying-up fund for inland waterway vessels), requiring the exercise of competence to bind the Community on the external plane in the absence of a prior internal legislative act, in the case of the GATS the realisation of the objectives of freedom of establishment or freedom of movement were non-specific and were not linked to the fate of granting access to either third country nationals in the Community or to Member States' nationals in third countries.[29] This is significant because it adds a "rider" to the Court's earlier pronouncement in Opinion 1/76, by seeking to further define what it means by "specific objective".

The Court also examined two further Treaty bases from which the Community might "derive" competence to act: Articles 100a or 235 EC. In respect of Article 100a EC, it concluded that only where the competence to harmonise has been exercised by the Community on the internal plane can those harmonising measures limit the freedom of the Member States to negotiate with third countries on the external plane. Even then the internal exercise of competence must be in a specific area in order to create exclusive external competence.[30]

In the case of Article 235 EC and the realisation of a Community objective, apart from the case where competence could be exercised both internally and externally at the same time, an internal competence can only give rise to an exclusive external competence if it has already been exercised.[31] However, where Community legislation contains special rules in its legislation for dealing with third countries, or where it has expressly conferred on one of its institutions the competence to negotiate with third countries, then the Community has acquired exclusive competence for the measure so covered.[32] In all other service transactions, the Member States and the Community remain competent to act externally with respect to services' transactions.

---

[28] *Ibid*, paras 45–47.
[29] *Ibid*, para 85.
[30] *Ibid*, para 88.
[31] *Ibid*, para 89.
[32] *Ibid*, para 95.

The Court's position is not without criticism, since until such time as the Community adopts internal rules, the Member States retain the right to act individually, or collectively, in undertaking obligations with third countries.[33] Additionally, the Court's reliance on the "specificity" of the measure on the internal plane as the distinguishing feature in determining exclusive or mixed competence on the matter only serves to reinforce the notion that, even where internal measures have been adopted, each time the Community proposes action there will be a need to review the division of competences based on the specificity of the measure. This holds true in particular for public procurement.

The Court was not insensitive to the deflections in trade and the potential distortion in the functioning of the internal market to which this could lead[34] but chose to deal with the matter in summary fashion. It was of the view that nothing in the Treaty prevented Community institutions from acting in a co-ordinated manner in their relations with third countries nor from laying down policy guidelines for Member States to follow in their external policies.

It will also be recalled that there is a procedural relevance in applying Articles 57:2, 66 EC and indeed 100a EC, alongside Article 113 EC. Normally, CCP measures taken under Article 113 EC are adopted, on a proposal from the Commission, by a qualified majority decision of the Council and do not require the co-operation of the Parliament, or the involvement of the Economic and Social Committee.[35] The use of Articles 57:2, 66 and 100a EC dictates that the Council on a proposal from the Commission and in co-operation with the Parliament (thereby involving the latter in the co-decision process) acts unanimously.[36]

Autonomous Community measures in the field of public procurement

While the Community, acting under Article 113 EC, has a duty to develop a CCP and has adopted a number of measures in the conventional sphere, as discussed in the next section, a CCP in the public procurement sector in relation to third countries with which no special agreements have been reached, is lacking. Despite the Community's programme for completion of the internal market which resulted in major revisions of the Public Works and Public Supplies Directives, as well as the award of public works contracts[37], there is no elaboration of a comprehensive external policy in

---

[33] *Ibid*, paras 77.
[34] Arrowsmith, *supra*, n 13, p 5; Eeckhout, *supra*, n 21, p 41.
[35] Case C-62/88 *Greece* v *Council* [1990] ECR-I, p 1527 at p 1648 (para 11).
[36] Völker, *supra*, n 22, p 182; Eeckhout, *supra*, n 21, p 42.
[37] *Supra*, n 5.

the field of public procurement.[38] Where such measures have been taken they are usually of the trade-restricting type.

Nevertheless, a Council Resolution on third country access to Community public supply contracts was adopted during the previous GATT Tokyo Round[39] and revised in the closing stages of that Round[40], which made it clear that the Public Supplies Directive did not apply to third country imports. At the same time the Commission statement indicated that until an external policy in public procurement had been attained Member States were largely free to take such measures in the field of public supply contracts, in respect of third country products, as they saw fit and that such measures were not subject to review at Community level.[41] The Resolutions were in effect an explicit recognition of the fact that no CCP existed in the field and called upon the Commission to put forward proposals to that end while at the same time authorising Member States to continue to apply existing measures relating to third country products in supply contracts.

A further autonomous measure exists in the utilities sector with the procurement of goods and services, previously excluded from the scope of the Public Works and Public Supplies Directives.[42] The Utilities Directive opens up an external dimension, the key provision being Article 29:2 (now Article 36:2 under the consolidated Directive)[43] which operates an exclusion and preference rule with respect to third country suppliers in the excluded sectors, allowing government entities to reject a tender whenever the "third country" element exceeds 50% of the total value of the products constituting the tender.

The two key points from a commercial policy perspective are first, that it applies only to tenders from all firms which are Community-based, including subsidiaries of foreign firms in the Community, and, second, where agreements with third countries have been sought, access to Community procurement in the excluded sectors is conditional upon "comparable and effective access" for Community tenderers in third country markets. This latter aspect reinforces the notion that third country access to the Community's market in public procurement should be on the basis of "reciprocity" and highlights the fact that the provision, when adopted as Article 29 in the original Utilities Directive of 1990[44] was intended to be a market-opening device in the negotiations for a new GPA during the

---

[38] Eeckhout, *supra*, n 21, p 305.

[39] Council Resolution of 21 December 1976 concerning access to Community supply contracts for products originating in non-member countries, OJ 1977 C11/1 and Commission Statement of 21 December 1976, OJ 1977 L13/1.

[40] Council Resolution of 22 July 1980 concerning access to Community public supply contracts for products originating in third countries OJ (1980) C211/2.

[41] Eeckhout, *supra*, n 21, pp 300–301.

[42] Initially only applicable to works' contracts, services have only recently been fully taken up in Directive 93/38/EEC, *supra*, n 5.

[43] It should be noted that this Directive entered into force for all of the Members States on 1 January 1993 with the exception of Spain (1 January 1996) and Portugal (1 January 1998).

[44] *Supra*, n 5.

latter part of the Uruguay Round. The operation of the preference aspect of Article 36 requires utilities to reject a third country tender in favour of a Community tender, where there is an equivalence between the "Community" tender and the "non-Community" tender.[45]

It is possible for Member States to make an exception to the operation of the preference and exclusion rule with respect to third countries that have concluded an agreement which provides for comparable and effective market access.[46] This ensures that the criteria for determining the proportion of non-Community products, is weighted in favour of such third countries since products originating in those countries will not be taken into account in assessing the total value of products in the tender. Such an agreement, in the form of a Memorandum of Understanding was concluded by the EC with the United States on 10 May 1993 which disapplies Article 36 for tenders comprising products of US origin.[47]

The exclusion and preference rule of Article 36 has given rise to considerable controversy among some of the Community's trading partners, not least the United States with which it entered into a long and bitter dispute over the protectionist reach of the Community public procurement policies in the utilities sector, especially on telecommunications, before reaching the aforementioned agreement. The Community has refused to repeal or otherwise restrict the application of Article 36 and in the Uruguay Round trade negotiations it proved a useful bargaining chip instrument for the Community to deploy when seeking guarantees of market access for Community undertakings.[48]

However, its continued existence is not without criticism on other grounds. If the exclusion and preference rule applies equally to products imported from third countries as well as those which are in free circulation within the Community, and it appears that it does, then it is doubtful whether this approach is compatible with the principle of free movement of goods. This is reinforced by the fact that Member States can decide the fate of non-Community tenders and thus are able to interpret and apply the exclusion rules, leading to potential distortions in Member States' trade. The Article 30 EC prohibition on quantitative restrictions on imports of goods and all measures having equivalent effect[49] has received wide interpretation by the Court and has been extended into the field of public procurement.[50] It is also one of the stated objectives of the Community, as set out in the preamble to the Utilities Directive. The only permitted exception is Article 115 EC which has been retained under the Treaty on European Union and is of a transitional character because it is

---

[45] Article 36:3.
[46] Article 36:1 and 36:5.
[47] Council Decision 93/323/EEC, OJ L125/1 and Council Decision 93/324/EEC of the same date which implements the agreement, OJ L125/54.
[48] Brown, "The Extension of the Community Public Procurement Rules to Utilities" (1993) 30:4 CMLRev 721 at p 740.
[49] Also its counterpart, Article 59 EC in the field of services.
[50] For example, Case 45/87 *Commission* v *Ireland* [1988] ECR 4929.

intended to deal with situations where national measures have not yet been replaced by Community ones. The inference to be drawn from this is that Member States, on the basis of the exclusion and preference rules of Article 36 Utilities Directive, may effectively exclude tenders consisting of products in free circulation, thereby creating an obstacle to intra-Community trade. The implementation of internal protection in this way undermines the free movement of goods.

Finally, there is a further autonomous measure which warrants examination and that is a CCP measure, implementing sanctions against US contractors[51] in response to similar sanctions imposed on the Community by the US Government under Title VII of the 1988 US Omnibus Trade and Competitiveness Act.[52] The US sanctions were aimed at excluding Community firms from bidding for US Federal Procurement contracts outside their scope, or below-threshold value under the current GPA. The Community response, contained in Regulation 1461/93, is not dissimilar and applies to public supplies, public services and public works contracts awarded by central government authorities, although it only applies to supplies contracts below current GPA thresholds, whilst applying to services and works contracts below the thresholds of current EC Directives. The punitive reach of the measures extends to all firms established in and operating from the United States. It is now effectively a dead-letter since a further agreement was reached in April 1994 between the Community and the United States in order to resolve their differences, besides which the text of a new GPA has been signed. Nevertheless, it serves to demonstrate the bounds of the Community's CCP with third countries in the field of public procurement.

Conventional Community measures in the field of public procurement

We turn now to examine the extent of the Community's CCP in a series of specific agreements with designated third countries. By and large they are trade liberalising measures designed to open up access to the Community's public procurement market to third countries and equally to ensure access for Community firms to third country markets. The underlying feature of many of these agreements is an endeavour on the part of the Community to achieve a reciprocal balance with its trading partners.

However, some of these agreements are not without criticism, in particular, those which reveal a recurrence of Treaty obligation which may be divergent in principle and practice.

---

[51] Council Regulation 1461/93/EEC of 8 June 1993 concerning access to public contracts for tenderers from the United States of America, OJ 1993 L146/1.

[52] Pub. L. No. 100–418, 102 Stat. 1107 (enacted 23 August 1988); Title VII is in fact the "Buy America" legislation under the Buy America Act of 1988, *ibid.*

The new Government Procurement Agreement

The most important access agreement in the field of public procurement is undoubtedly the GPA which was originally concluded as one of the Tokyo Round Codes in 1979, with a later amendment of 2 February 1987 and which entered into force on 14 February 1988 (the "1988 GPA").[53] It is expected that the new GPA, signed at Marrakesh on 15 April 1994, finalised in parallel with the Uruguay Round, although not officially part of it[54], will bring about substantial changes in global procurement.[55] The new GPA is taken up in Annex 4 to the WTO Agreement, containing the Plurilateral Agreements[56], and is only binding on those states parties to it, of which there are currently 10.[57]

The new Agreement provides a substantially improved framework agreement which is more expansive in scope and coverage than the present 1988 GPA. Whereas the 1988 GPA is restricted in scope to supplies contracts and central/federal government entities, the new GPA has been extended to works and services as well as supplies, including certain activities in the utilities sector and embraces sub-federal and local entities, as well as certain public undertakings for the first time. Additionally, and not unimportantly it introduces improved legal remedies which extend to bid challenge procedures in WTO Members' domestic fora.[58]

The Agreement sets out a number of general principles to be applied by all the parties, including the application of the principle of non-discrimination and national treatment.[59] There are also detailed award procedures, with four basic methods of tendering (open, selective, limited and through competitive negotiations)[60] along the lines of the current GPA. Some of the other key provisions include enhanced transparency requirements governing the opening of procedures, with detailed rules on qualification of suppliers and service providers, publication of procurement notices, treatment of information prior to notice and more stringent time-limits, delivery times and so on.[61]

In accordance with Article I, the actual scope of the GPA is set out in Appendix I to the Agreement which comprises five separate Annexes, in accordance with a "positive list" approach (*i.e.* applies only to entities and procurement activities listed in the Annexes). The first three Annexes are

---

[53] GATT, *BISD* 33S/190 (1987).

[54] *Supra*, n 2.

[55] See GATT Secretariat Press Release of 22 April 1994 on *The New Agreement on Government Procurement in the GATT*.

[56] The other agreements in this Annex are the Agreement in Trade in Civil Aircraft, International Dairy Agreement and the International Bovine Meat.

[57] *Supra*, n 2.

[58] Footer, "Remedies Under the New GATT Agreement on Government Procurement" (1995) 4 *PPLR* 80–93.

[59] *Supra*, n 2, Article III GPA.

[60] Articles VII and XIV GPA.

[61] Article IX GPA.

so-called "entity Annexes": Annex 1 lists covered central government entities; for the European Union there are two institutions named – the Council of the European Union and the European Commission, besides central government purchasing entities in all the Member States. The threshold value for contracts under this Annex remains the same as under the present GPA at SDR[62] 130,000 for central government purchasing supplies and services but is set at a much higher level of over SDR 5m for construction services. New to the GPA is Annex 2 which adds sub-central government entities, *e.g.* provincial, municipal entities, or those of a prefecture. The threshold for the value of contracts which applies to this Annex is set at SDR 200,000 while for construction services the contractual threshold remains the same as under Annex 1, at SDR 5 m.

There is, however, a notable departure in Annex 3 where the scope of procurement in the utilities sector only applies to entities which carry out one or more listed "utility" activities where such entities are either "public authorities" or "public undertakings" in the sense of the Utilities Directive. In fact there was no consensus over what constitutes a "public undertaking"; indeed in the utilities sector many of the entities listed may be partially privatised. Actual coverage of individual utility sectors is not as broad as under existing Community legislation with notable exceptions in the new GPA for the distribution of gas or heat, fuel extraction and procurement of telecommunications equipment. The latter in particular because the United States remained unwilling to remove sufficient "Buy America" clauses from federally funded programmes.[63]

The threshold for the value of contracts under this third Annex is set at SDR 400,000 for the purchase of supplies and services – a higher threshold than for entities under the first two Annexes. The contractual value for purchasers of construction services again under the third Annex remains at SDR 5 m. The scope of the new GPA will extend to services and the supply of services, in Annex 4, an area previously not covered in the GPA which excluded service contracts *per se*.[64] Annex 5 covers construction service contracts which the listed entities in the first three Annexes may enter into.

However, it should be noted that the overall scope of the new GPA is limited by a number of derogations to commitments which arose because of continued disagreement between certain countries during negotiations on extension of the regulatory framework beyond central government level. The derogations are of two main types. First, there are derogations,

---

[62] Special Drawing Rights: the International Monetary Fund's international reserve unit of account.

[63] European Commission Press Release, *supra*, n 1, p7.

[64] A GATT Panel in a 1992 decision construed this wording to include services where they are "incidental to the supply of products" although necessarily still excluding service contracts *Sonar Mapping Decision (European Community v United States)*, GATT Doc. GPR.DS1 of 23 April 1992 (unadopted); for details see Footer, "GATT: Developments in Public Procurement Procedures and Practices" (1994) 3 PPLR, CS193 at 195–199.

in the form of exceptions, from the application of national treatment in Article III GPA, and the majority of signatories have contributed to the list. They reflect a desire on the part of several countries to seek absolute reciprocity on either a product, service or entity basis. Second, there are derogations in respect of services and construction services in Annexes 4 and 5. Again the listed derogations apply only to the extent that other parties to the new GPA have not provided reciprocal access for a service or construction service under the aforementioned Annexes.

In the procedural sphere, the Community has filed a further derogation with respect to United States, Japanese and Korean suppliers and service providers seeking to challenge another party under the new bid challenge procedures where the other party is classified as a small or medium sized enterprise (SMEs). This is in direct response to a similar US derogation which disapplies the procedural rules to SMEs until such time as the Community accepts that these countries no longer discriminate in favour of certain domestic small and minority businesses. The resultant picture is that the new GPA, although a multilateral framework agreement, through the inclusion of derogable provisions has achieved more the character of a set of bilateral access agreements.

Finally, there are significant additional provisions in the new GPA on remedies.[65] General consultation and dispute settlement provisions are contained in Article XXII of the new GPA, which specifically subjects disputes under the Agreement to the new integrated dispute settlement system under the WTO, the so-called "Understanding on Rules and Procedures Governing the Settlement of Disputes" (DSU) contained in Annex 2 to the WTO Agreement.[66] This is a compulsory and binding system of dispute settlement, within stringent time-limits and, contrary to its GATT predecessor, provides for appeal from panel decisions and for clear rules governing the implementation of panel rulings and decisions of the new appellate body.

The applicability of the DSU to GPA matters is subject to any special or additional rules or procedures in the Agreement which the Committee on Government Procurement may notify to the Dispute Settlement Body (DSB). The DSB is responsible for overseeing and implementing the DSU, including the establishment of panels, the adoption of panel and Appellate Body reports, the surveillance of implementation of panel rulings and recommendations and the authorisation of suspension of concessions and other obligations under the covered agreements, in this case the GPA.[67]

The new GPA also introduces challenge procedures at Article XX to allow private bidders the opportunity to complain directly against a procuring entity which has allegedly breached the rules of the Agreement and to seek redress for the infringement of rights under the GPA. This brings about two obligations for contracting parties. First, in such instances they

---

[65] See Footer, *supra*, n 58.
[66] *Results of the Uruguay Round, supra*, n 2, pp 404 *et seq.*
[67] DSU, Article 2.

are to encourage the supplier or service provider to try to resolve the complaint with the procuring entity by means of consultation but without prejudice to the instigation by the aggrieved supplier or service provider of an actual challenge procedure.[68]

Second, parties to the new GPA are under an obligation to provide in their domestic legislation for procedures before national courts or administrative bodies (in this instance including Community institutions) to allow the injured party to challenge the tender procedure or its award. The new challenge procedures are largely modelled on the Community legislation in the field of public procurement, notably the Remedies Directive and the Utilities Remedies Directive[69], and were included partly in response to experience with the inadequacies of the current 1988 GPA where there is no available remedy for situations involving a lost "opportunity to bid" rather than simply a claim against the distortion of a trade flow or the infringement of a right.[70]

Other reciprocal access agreements

EU–United States agreements

The most significant set of agreements in the bilateral sphere are the two agreements concluded between the EU and the United States, both during the Uruguay Round and after its conclusion in April 1994. The two Council decisions of 1993 which were noted earlier[71] both form part of the agreement, drawn up as a Memorandum of Understanding (MoU), which was reached between the United States and the EC in 1993, after months of disagreement over Article 29 of the newly implemented Utilities Directive (Article 36 under the consolidated version).

Under the MoU, the Community agreed to disapply the exclusion and preference rules of Article 36 with respect to tenders comprising products of US origin in the Community's electrical equipment markets (although not telecommunications equipment on which parties failed to reach agreement) in return for access by Community tenderers to five of the publicly owned federal utilities and the Tennessee Valley Authority in the United States. Additionally, the United States agreed to seek gradually to eliminate "Buy America" provisions on sub-federal funding authorities.

The MoU in fact provided the impetus for renewed negotiations on a new GPA during the Uruguay Round, after virtual deadlock between the two key negotiating partners.[72] It was followed up by a second agreement,

---

[68] GPA, Article XX, (i), section 1.

[69] *Supra*, n 5; see further Footer, *supra* n 58, pp 88–92.

[70] *Trondheim Toll Collection (United States v Norway)* of 28 April 1992, GATT doc. GPR.DS2/R (adopted); see Footer, *supra*, n 64, CS200–203.

[71] *Supra*, n 47.

[72] European Commission Press Release, *supra*, n 1, p 1.

in the form of an exchange of letters, between the EU and the United States of 13 April 1994 upon the occasion of signature of the new GPA at Marrakesh.[73] The United States improved its offer at sub-central government level for Community suppliers of goods, services and construction from 24 to 37 states, including five key states of California, New York, Illinois, Texas and Florida. This includes the grant of national treatment to such suppliers and service providers, similar to out-of-town bidders, in seven of the biggest US cities – Boston, Chicago, Dallas, Detroit, Indianapolis, Nashville and San Antonio, as well as various utilities controlled by them, such as Chicago O'Hare International Airport. Community firms will henceforth have access to US ports, in particular the Port Authorities of New York, New Jersey and Baltimore, in return for which the Community has agreed to continue to waive Article 36 of the Utilities Directive on procurement of supplies of US origin by Community ports. Finally, in the electrical sector the US has amended GPA coverage to include service contacts and has extended electrical utilities to include the New York Power Authority.[74]

Europe agreements

Of growing importance are the assocation agreements concluded by the EC and the Member States under Articles 228 EC and 238 EC (so-called ''Europe Agreements'') which extend market access in public procurement to a number of central and eastern European countries. The first two such Europe Agreements to provide access to Community markets in public procurement went into force with Hungary and Poland on 1 February 1994.[75] Since then, a further four Europe Agreements, substantially similar in scope and content to the original two with Hungary and Poland, have come into effect with the former socialist states of Romania, the Republic of Bulgaria and each of the Slovak and Czech Republics.[76]

---

[73] Commission of the European Communities *Proposal for a Council Decision Concerning the Conclusion of an Agreement in the Form of an Exchange of Letters between the European Community and the United States Government on Government Procurement*, COM (94) 251 Final/2 of 7.7.94, OJ (1994) C 291/4; approved by Council Decision 95/215/EC of 29 May 1995, OJ (1995) L 134/25, taking account of Austria, Finland and Sweden's accession to the European Union.

[74] For a detailed discussion of EU/United States relations in public procurement see Halford, ''An Overview of E.C.–United States Trade Relations in the Area of Public Procurement'' (1995) 4 PPLR 35–56 and also de Graaf and King, ''Towards a More Global Procurement Market: The Expansion of the GATT Government Procurement Agreement in the Context of the Uruguay Round'' (1995) 29:2 *The International Lawyer* 448–451.

[75] Council and Commission Decision 93/742/Euratom, ECSC, EC and Council and Commission Decision 93/743/Euratom. ECSC, EC, both dated 13 December 1993, at OJ 1993 L347/1 (approving the Europe Agreement with Hungary) and OJ 1993 L348/1 (approving the Europe Agreement with Poland); see Arrowsmith, *supra*, 13, pp 30–32.

[76] See the series of Council and Commission Decisions 94/907/ECSC, EC, Euratom, 94/908/ ECSC, EC Euratom, 94/909/ECSC/EC/Euratom and 94/910/ECSC, EC, Euratom all dated 19 December 1994, at OJ 1994 L357/1 (approving the Europe Agreement with Romania), OJ 1994 L358/1 (approving the Europe Agreement with the Republic of Bulgaria), OJ 1994 L359/1 (approving the Europe Agreement with the Slovak Republic) and OJ 1994 L360/1 (approving the Europe Agreement with the Czech Republic).

Each of the Europe Agreements contains a specific article[77] which calls for Hungarian, Polish, Romanian, Bulgarian, Slovak and Czech undertakings (including in the case of Romania and Bulgaria joint venture companies) to be granted equal access alongside Community companies on a non-discriminatory and reciprocal basis. At the same time, such market access is subject to the rules contained in the Community's directives on public procurement (including those on remedies).[78] In return Community companies have access to Hungarian, Polish, Romanian, Bulgarian, Slovak and Czech contract award procedures within a period of 10 years, or sooner, contingent upon periodic examination by the Association Councils set up under the individual agreements.

None of the Europe Agreements is specific about the procurement of services, or their supply, but instead link the matter to the general provisions regarding establishment and operations, as well as employment and movement of labour, which are tied in with the procurement and fulfilment of public works contracts.[79] However, all six Agreements make provision for the Association Councils established under the Agreements to take measures to progressively implement the liberalisation of service trade between the Community and each of Hungary, Poland, Romania, Bulgaria, the Slovak and Czech Republics and to make necessary adjustments in line with commitments taken under the new General Agreement on Trade in Services (GATS) reached during the GATT Uruguay Round.[80]

It would therefore seem likely that where the procurement of services is concerned, provided that they are linked with procurement of products which provide market access under contract award procedures, Hungarian, Polish, Romanian, Bulgarian, Slovak and Czech firms stand to benefit from Community rules on provision of works and other services, in addition to supplies. However, the extent to which any Hungarian, Polish, Romanian, Bulgarian, Slovak or Czech company may be included in the procurement of services proper, whether of a simple cross-border type, or involving more complex rights of establishment, will depend upon the degree to which any of the aforementioned countries have adopted measures to liberalise their service trade with the European Communities and taking account of specific commitments under the GATS as well as Article II GATS (most favoured nation exemptions) in certain service sectors. Similarly, the degree of enforceability of Community procurement rules by Hungarian, Polish, Romanian, Bulgarian, Slovak or Czech companies in Community courts may differ based on the foregoing factors.

---

[77] Article 66 of the Agreement with Hungary, Article 67 of the Agreement with Poland and Article 68 of the remaining Agreements with Romania, Bulgaria, the Slovak and Czech Republics.

[78] *Supra*, n 5.

[79] Article 66(3) of the Hungarian Agreement, Article 67(3) of the Polish Agreement and Article 68(3) in each of the Agreements with Romania, Bulgaria, the Slovak and Czech Republics.

[80] It should, however, be noted that Bulgaria's schedules of concessions on goods and commitments on services are still in the process of verification and approval prior to her intended accession to the WTO Agreement and this is reflected in the language of Article 59(2) of the Europe Agreement with the Republic of Bulgaria.

Conclusion

There have been significant achievements for the Community as a result of the conclusion of the Uruguay Round. The external dimensions of the Community's procurement activity will be strongly influenced by the new GPA once it comes into force on 1 January 1996 as it is by far the most liberalising trade instrument yet in the field of public procurement, although as already noted access remains largely dominated by a "reciprocal" approach.

Moreover, the new GPA has been conceived in parallel with a new international organisation on world trade (the WTO) which is intended not only to provide a proper organisational and institutional framework for world trade but also a code of conduct. Added to this, is the new improved and strengthened integrated dispute settlement mechanism. Henceforth, a more systematic treatment of public procurement at the international level can be expected due to the increase in scope and coverage of the new GPA and the available remedies thereunder. The fact that the new GPA explicitly subjects general dispute settlement, aside from the bid challenge procedures under Article XX, to the rigours of the DSU, means that the disciplines of the new WTO will have a wider reaching effect on public procurement irrespective of the fact that the GPA is a Plurilateral Agreement under Annex 4.

As for the Community's CCP in public procurement, based upon Article 113 EC, the exact scope and content of this policy remains uncertain as does its future. In the absence of a comprehensive common commercial policy in public procurement, which reflects developments in the internal market, the Community is left with a number of limited measures in place which deal with particular third countries or specific areas of procurement, as for example with the exclusion and preference rules of Article 36 of the Utilities Directive. There is uncertainty too over the extent of existing authorisations, such as the earlier Council Resolution of 1980, and potential discrepancies with internal policies in procurement, which involve the principle of non-discrimination as set out in Articles 30 and 59 EC.

MARY E FOOTER

Part 5

The EU's External Trade Policy Before the Court of Justice

Chapter 18

Individuals and the GATT: Direct Effect and Indirect Effects of the General Agreement of Tariffs and Trade in Community Law

Introduction

One of the problems which can arise in the context of the external trade relations of the European Community is the question whether, as a matter of Community law, natural or legal persons can rely before a court on a provision of an international agreement binding on the Community. In the past, individuals seeking to rely on the direct effect of GATT[1] provisions against Community and Member State measures not agreeable to them have had little success. As a rule, GATT provisions were not considered "capable of creating rights of which interested parties may avail themselves".[2] In more recent times, however, the European Court of Justice seems to be more willing to consider the possibility that GATT provisions can be invoked before a Community court. It would seem that the time has come to try and assess some of the caselaw of the Court of Justice.

This article attempts to put the question of the direct effect of GATT rules in a broader conceptual framework. Part two deals with the significance of direct effect of autonomous Community law. Against this background it will be investigated in part three whether the direct effect of international agreements concluded by the Community is determined by similar considerations, and what are the conditions under which it can be accorded. Part four examines what other, "indirect" effects Community law can have for individuals and how this can be relevant for international treaties to which the Community is a party. This also provides valuable insights into the rationale of the caselaw of the European Court of Justice on the direct effect of international agreements. In part five, the situation

---

[1] General Agreement on Tariffs and Trade. The text currently in force is in Vol. IV *BISD*, 1969.

[2] Case 9/73, *Schlüter* v *Hauptzollamt Lörrach* [1973] ECR 1135. Similarly, Cases 21–24/72, *International Fruit Company* v *Produktschap voor Groenten en Fruit* [1972] ECR 1219; Case 266/81, *Società Italiana per l'Oleodotto Transalpino (SIOT)* v *Ministero delle Finanze* [1983] ECR 731; Cases 267–269/81, *Amministrazione dello Stato* v *Società Petrolifera Italiana (SPI)* [1983] ECR 801; Cases 290–291/81, *Compagnia Singer* v *Amministrazione delle Finanze dello Stato* [1983] ECR 847.

of treaties to which only the Member States are parties is considered. Finally, in part six it is explained why it is so difficult to accord effect for individuals to GATT provisions, and what hopes there are for the future.

The significance of direct effect in the Community legal order

Direct effect is the characteristic of Community law provisions which allows them to be relied upon by individuals before their national courts. This is important to natural or legal persons, who, without it, would not be able to invoke directly before national courts any rights under Community law. Apart from this, the capacity of Community legal norms to have direct effect is also beneficial to the Community as such.

First of all, it brings Europe closer to the citizen. Europe is no longer just another bureaucracy at the other side of the border. As Europe gives the citizen rights, for instance free movement, or free trade, the idea of European integration becomes meaningful to "the people", and this in turn will increase popular interest in the objectives, aims and policies of the European institutions. Furthermore, direct effect is important for the Community as a whole because it enhances the effectiveness of Community law.

Ordinary international agreements are not always very effective. Normally, if a state does not apply a treaty, the only course of action open to its contracting partners is also to stop applying it. They could perhaps go to a competent international tribunal for a declaration that the other state is in breach of its obligations, but that is not always very diplomatic as it may adversely affect their bilateral relations. Thus, if a state breaches an international treaty the other states would very often do nothing about it.

In the EC there are basically two procedures for treaty violation. A Member State can challenge another Member State before the European Court of Justice under Article 170. That is hardly ever done, for the reasons just explained. Alternatively, the Commission can challenge a Member State before the European Court of Justice under Article 169. The Commission, which represents the Community interest, is the watchdog of the Community Treaties; but it will concentrate only on those cases which it considers most important. Apart from the fact that it has other things to do as well, this is because the outcome of the procedure under Article 169 is essentially declaratory, and the more use is made of such declarations, the less effective they become.[3]

---

[3] It is now possible for the Court of Justice to impose fines on a Member State which fails to comply with a judgment rendered under Articles 169 and 170. Although this is an improvement, it does not solve everything: apart from the fact that a Member State may be prepared to pay for a breach, it still depends on an initiative of the Commission (Art 171).

By virtue of direct effect, individuals can invoke Community law before national courts to secure observance of the rights and duties conferred or imposed by it. Direct effect (alone or in combination with supremacy or the principle that Community law overrides national law) is a much better guarantee that Community law is observed. This is so because individuals may invoke Community law even in situations the Commission and the Member States themselves would not pay attention to. Second, individuals, relying on direct effect and the supremacy of Community law, may simply decide not to obey national authorities.

Let us assume, for example, that there is a temporary shortage of wheat in the Community. A Member State that fears a steep rise in prices of wheat at home may consider prohibiting all exports. The responsible Minister knows that Article 34 forbids quantitative restrictions on exports, but, in trying to find a solution, he calculates the chances of getting away with a temporary export ban: it would take so long for the procedures under Article 169 or 170 to come into operation, that the new harvest would be in and the ban could be lifted long before that time. In the meantime the government would have achieved its aim. Yet the strongest reason why a government may not commit such violations is that it knows that exporters could simply ignore the export prohibition and, if taken before a court, could successfully invoke the EC Treaty. Individuals would simply continue exporting. In the event that they are fined by a national authority for infringement of the export ban, they could go to court to obtain a refund of the fine, and if they were prevented from exporting, they would be able to claim damages. The result is, that the export ban will not be imposed in the first place, because it is unlikely to be effective.

Direct effect is therefore very important. But how can it be that Community law has direct effect? The Treaties establishing the Communities nowhere explicitly mention that Community law can have direct effect, and many obligations are not even formulated in such a way as to explicitly confer rights on individuals. As is well known, it is the European Court of Justice that has established the principle of direct effect as a general principle underlying the Community Treaties. It did so in the celebrated *Van Gend en Loos* case[4] in 1963. A transport company had imported chemicals from Germany into the Netherlands. It had been charged a customs duty. This violated the principle of free movement of goods between Member States, specifically, Article 12 according to which Member States were to refrain from introducing new customs duties on imports or exports or charges having equivalent effect or increasing those in existence. Van Gend en Loos obviously had to pay the duty, but it claimed reimbursement of the sum before a Dutch court. In the context of these proceedings the question arose, whether the transport company could invoke Article 12 to support its claim. Article 12 is clearly addressed to Member States.

---

[4] Case 26/62, *Van Gend en Loos* v *Nederlandse Administratie der Belastingen* [1963] ECR 1.

The national court referred the question to the Court of Justice for a preliminary ruling under Article 177, and the Court held that Article 12 had direct effect. As a result, the Dutch court considered the customs duty illegal and ordered it to be reimbursed.

Van Gend en Loos was the first case in which the Court of Justice established that a Community norm had direct effect, so that the Court had to explain why this would be so. The justification given by the Court was threefold:

(i)   The Treaty establishing the European Community was not an ordinary treaty, but one which had created a new legal order. It was more than an agreement which merely created mutual obligations between the contracting parties. Its preamble referred not only to governments but to peoples. Institutions had been established with sovereign powers affecting both the Member States and their citizens.

(ii)   Although the Treaty did not provide explicitly for direct effect, it provided for a co-operation procedure between itself and national courts under Article 177. The objective of that Article was to arrive at a uniform interpretation and application of Community law. Article 177 entitled or in some cases imposed the obligation on national courts to refer questions of Community law to the Court of Justice for a preliminary ruling. In the opinion of the Court, this procedure would virtually make no sense if Community law could not be invoked before national courts.

(iii) The vigilance of individuals protecting their rights amounted to an effective supervision in addition to the one entrusted by Articles 169 and 170 to the Commission and the Member States. This argument is based on a policy consideration of the type one can find more often with the Court.

Van Gend en Loos was a revolutionary decision, since it introduced new perspectives for Community law as a whole. The enforcement of Community law would be better guaranteed, and individuals for their part found a totally new source of rights, independent of national implementation. As a consequence, provisions of the Treaty can have direct effect for individuals even if they do not explicitly provide that individuals can rely on them.

So now we know a bit more about direct effect, its importance, and its rationale. The next issue that arises is, how to determine whether a specific rule of Community law has direct effect. The Court has established in *Van Gend en Loos*, and in a long line of caselaw, that for a Community provision to have direct effect, it must fulfil several conditions:

(i)   it must be clear and unambiguous (*i.e.*, in the eyes of the courts);
(ii)   it must be unconditional (*e.g.*, no time limit or reservation);
(iii) it must not depend for its operation on further action taken by the Community or national authorities.

It is generally accepted that it is the Court of Justice that establishes whether or not a provision of Community law is directly effective. It is not at the discretion of national courts. If this was not the case, provisions of Community law would have different effects in the different Member States and the uniformity of Community law would have been compromised. A national court can resolve this question by referring a question to the European Court of Justice under Article 177.

Direct effect of international agreements concluded by the Community

The Court of Justice, when establishing the principle of direct effect, had very much in mind the effectiveness and uniform application of Community law. The same considerations have driven the Court of Justice to establish the direct effect of international agreements to which the Community is a party. The leading case is *Kupferberg*,[5] where it was argued that a German tax on wine could not be applied to imports from Portugal. Portugal had not yet entered the EC at that time, but was associated with the Community by a free trade agreement. That agreement prohibited the imposition of import duties on wine. Since the German law clearly infringed the agreement, Kupferberg sought to rely on the agreement between the Community and Portugal.

This raised the delicate question whether the provisions concerned were directly effective; the answer to this was far from obvious, since there are differences between "ordinary" international treaties and Community law. The direct effect of (autonomous) Community law is an essential characteristic of the Community legal order which the Member States have come to accept as such. However, many states would not accept the same principle for "ordinary international law", in particular intergovernmental treaties.

If we simplify reality a bit by allowing ourselves a generalisation, it is possible to distinguish two main categories of states in this respect. At the one extreme there would be the states that have accepted the so-called "monist" theory on the relationship between international law and national law. This means that all international law would, if appropriate, be applicable in the national courts. The Dutch Constitution, for example, provides for the possibility to invoke international treaties before national courts.

At the other extreme there would be the states that have a "dualist" conception of the relationship between international law and national law. In these states, international law and national law are seen as two

---

[5] Case 104/81, *Hauptzollamt Mainz* v *Kupferberg* [1982] ECR 3641.

completely different systems of law. National courts would apply only national law. Breaches of international treaties are not for national courts to solve; they are a matter of politics and diplomacy. An example of a dualist state is the United Kingdom, but many more states take the same attitude. For the United Kingdom, the direct effect of the Community Treaties and other Community law is the exception, gratefully accepted of course, because it makes Community law more effective: the British can rest assured that Community law is effectively applied not only in the United Kingdom, but also in the other Member States, where it has to have the same status and effect.

Now, if the Community concludes an international agreement with a non-member state, say for example the United States, that is a different matter. That country is a dualist state. It does not allow individuals to invoke provisions of treaties in its courts. If all the Community countries would apply the agreement in law, but the Community's contracting partners could not be forced by individuals to apply the agreement, there is a risk that the agreement will be properly applied only in the Community. That would put the Community as well as individuals in a disadvantageous position.

If countries with a dualist system occasionally accept enforceability by individuals, for instance where this is stipulated in the agreement entered into, or because a "door" is left open in their constitution – in which case the description of the system as dualist becomes debatable – they would do so only on the basis of reciprocity.

One would expect that Member States adopting the dualist approach would object to international agreements entered into by the Community being capable of having direct effect. In practice, however, matters may not be that simple, as even in monist Member States the fact an agreement may under certain circumstances be applicable within the Community legal order may have an impact on the effects of that agreement in its national courts. In fact, its effect is no longer determined by national law, but by Community law.

Yet, in spite of these possible objections, the Court established in *Kupferberg* that international agreements entered into by the Community can have direct effect, and that henceforth, if the question was not settled in the agreement itself[6] the Court would decide on a case-by-case basis whether an individual could rely on the agreement. There may be two reasons why the Court did this: first, it is a clear signal to the Community's international partners, encouraging them to negotiate international treaties with it: "conclude a treaty with us and you can rest assured it will be given full effect." Secondly, the Court considers these agreements, in the first place, to be acts of the Community institutions rather than mere international understandings, and it does not want to create a situation where such acts can be applied differently in the various Member States.

---

[6] Case 104/81, *supra*, n 5, para 17.

The principle of uniform application of Community law, in other words, is an important consideration for according direct effect to international treaties. In the light of both these arguments, the caselaw recognising the principle of direct effect of agreements concluded by the Community can be seen as an application of the doctrine of *effet utile* or the useful effect of Community law itself.

Nevertheless, the strategy of the Court is not unqualified: first, the Court left open the possibility that it would deny direct effect to an international agreement if the other party to the agreement would not reciprocate. Secondly, the judgment left the Community institutions with a pre-emptive possibility of "opting out" of direct effect. Finally, the Court did not establish a predetermined set of criteria determining the conditions in which it would grant direct effect: although these are likely to focus on the standard test of being unequivocal, unconditional and not dependent on further action, it is not clear whether these criteria are sufficient in the case of an international agreement.

Kupferberg seems to imply that, where the absence of substantive re-ciprocity (in the sense of non-performance of the agreement by the other contracting party) can be established, the Court would take this into ac-count in deciding whether an individual should be able to enforce the agreement in question,[7] in much the same way as the non-performance by one contracting party may entitle the other party under international law to suspend the execution of its obligations.[8] This solution seems to be an equitable compromise which, together with the possibility of the legislator "opting out" of direct effect by taking the necessary precautionary mea-sures, makes the principle of direct effect acceptable. One may wish to object that it is not up to the Court to decide whether the execution (or enforcement) of an agreement is suspended, but rather to the Com-munity legislator. Would not the Court be dragged into questions of an essentially political nature if it did? Yet once the principle of direct effect is accepted, there is considerable merit in Bourgeois' view that it is not out of order for a judiciary called upon to enforce an agreement to take into account manifest and substantial non-performance by the other party if that would completely upset the balance of an agreement.[9]

In *Kupferberg*, the Court also declared that it will only decide on the effects of an international agreement if the contracting parties did not settle that question in the agreement themselves.[10] It is not immediately clear exactly which aspects of an international agreement can be taken as an indication that the legislator intended to rule out direct effect. One is unlikely to find any instances where judicial review in the light of (certain parts of) an agreement is ruled out by an explicit clause in the agreement.

---

[7] Case 104/81, *supra*, n 5, para 18.

[8] Bourgeois, "Effects of International Agreements in European Community Law: Are the Dice Cast?", (1984) *Michigan Law Review* 1250–1273 at 1265–1266.

[9] *Ibid*, at 1266.

[10] Case 104/81, *supra*, n 5, para 17.

In general this is to be avoided because it is not conducive to raising confidence in the Community's negotiating partners. A more subtle way to exclude judicial scrutiny is by the introduction of vagueness, conditionality or a requirement of further implementation into the provisions of the agreement so as to prevent the provisions concerned from being justiciable. The inclusion of safeguard clauses, a framework for international consultation or dispute settlement mechanisms may not normally be a reason to deny direct effect, as they need not be used. At any rate, the Court of Justice has declined to take these aspects into account in considering the direct effect of (specific provisions of) bilateral treaties.[11] On the other hand the "structure" of an agreement can provide indications to the Court that direct effect was to be excluded. One may observe that the structural weaknesses of the GATT were among the reasons which led the Court to exclude possible direct effect of that agreement.[12] In *SPI*,[13] the Court reaffirmed that it had reached this conclusion:

"on the basis of considerations concerning the general scheme of GATT, namely that it was based on the principle of negotiations undertaken on a reciprocal and mutually advantageous basis and was characterized by the great flexibility of its provisions, in particular those concerning the possibilities of derogation, the measures which might be taken in cases of exceptional difficulty and the settlement of differences between the contracting parties."

This attention for the general scheme of the GATT[14] may have to do with the fact that GATT creates multilateral obligations. One may ask how the principle implicit in the Court's caselaw, that direct effect may be denied in case the Community's contracting partner does not perform, can be applied in the case of a multilateral treaty? In the case of a multilateral treaty, a substantive non-performance by a contracting party may not always permit the suspension of (the internal enforcement of) the Community's obligations, and there may be no international authority capable of guaranteeing the enforcement of the agreement over the contracting parties. Thus, the Court may prove much more reticent on the issue of accepting that multilateral treaties may have direct effect.

Other possible effects on individuals of treaties to which the Community is a party

The question of direct effect has to be seen in the light of other "effects" which treaties can have on individuals, in accordance with Article 164

---

[11] *Ibid*, para 21.

[12] Bourgeois, *supra*, n 8 at 1267.

[13] Cases 267–269/81, *supra*, n 2, para 23.

[14] The same considerations would seem to apply in case a Member State invokes GATT. See Case C-280/93, *Germany* v *Council* [1994] ECR I-4973.

which provides that the European Court of Justice is to ensure that in the application of the EC Treaty the law is observed.

It should be noted that this provision does not determine either the direct effect or the rank of the Community's treaties within the Community legal order. The Court of Justice, however, has indicated its willingness to test EC legislation against international treaties to which the Community is a party.[15] This is in conformity with the Court's attitude on direct effect and is based on the same considerations. On the other hand, we have seen that supremacy and direct effect need not go together; while the supremacy of treaties to which the Community is a party over Community legislation seems to be a requirement of Community law, direct effect of such a treaty provision is not a necessary corollary. Any other conclusion would defeat the possibility of direct effect being made subject to reciprocity of performance. It becomes necessary, therefore, to enquire what other effects international treaties may have.

In *Marleasing*,[16] the Court introduced the so-called "indirect effect" of Community law, more particularly of Directives. Although care must be taken, not automatically to transpose legal concepts applying within the Community to the sphere of its external relations, the concept of "indirect effect" can be of interest, as similar effects of international agreements can be derived from Article 5 EC.

The facts of the case giving rise to what scholars call "indirect effect" were as follows: Marleasing SA was seeking a declaration that the contract setting up another company, La Comercial, was void under Spanish law for "lack of cause". There was, however, a Community Directive which intended to protect companies and third parties from the adverse consequences of the doctrine of nullity of companies' statutes. The Directive listed all grounds on which such contracts could be declared void, and "lack of cause", which appeared to be an admissible ground for nullity under Spanish law, was not among them. La Comercial sought, therefore, to rely on the Directive in order to establish that "lack of cause" was not a permissible ground for nullity under Community law.

The Court held that the Directive in question had no direct effect between private parties. National courts, however, had to interpret national law, as far as possible, in the light of the wording and purpose of the Directive in order to achieve its objectives. In the words of the Court:

"the national court asked to interpret national law is bound to do so in every way possible in the light of the wording and the purpose of the directive in order to achieve the results envisaged by the directive. . . ."

Marleasing may be taken to indicate that in certain circumstances the results of direct effect and indirect effect may very well be similar. As the Spanish court had to interpret the Spanish Civil Code in the light of the

---

[15] Cases 21–24/72, *supra*, n 2.
[16] Case C-106/89, *Marleasing SA* v *La Comercial Internacional de Alimentacion* [1990] ECR I-4135.

Directive, in the end La Comercial was successful. Yet it would appear that differences do exist and these have practical implications for the use of the two principles.

What is indirect effect precisely? Narrowly conceived, indirect effect would be taken to mean that national courts are required to achieve the objectives of a non-(horizontally) directly effective Directive. The ensuing "obligations" of individuals have to be founded on national law, although they find their origin in the duty of national courts under Article 5 EC to interpret that law as far as possible in such a way that it conforms with Community law. Conse-quently, the impact of indirect effect finds its limits in the measure of flexibility of national law to adapt to the requirements of the Directive. First, if the national law leaves no room for interpretation, then the Directive will not be taken into account. Arguably, indirect effect applies only to the extent that national law can reasonably be construed, because general principles of law such as legal certainty would oppose the imposition on individuals of an interpretation of national law in a sense opposite to what it actually says. Secondly, if no national legislation exists at all on a given subject, there is no chance for Community law to have indirect effect.

The most notable distinction between direct effect and indirect effect is therefore that the latter depends on the existence and nature of national law. It follows from the limitations of indirect effect outlined above that supremacy – in the sense of the capacity of Community law to override national law which conflicts with it – applies only in the context of direct effect, not in the context of indirect effect. On the other hand, since indirect effect is achieved through construction rather than supremacy – through interpretation rather than application – the requirements for it rightly seem to be more flexible than in the case of direct effect. It must be noted that the conditions under which indirect effect applies have not been spelled out by the Court in the same way as in the case of direct effect. Notably, the Court does not require that the Community provision concerned must be clear and unambiguous to courts – although some element of it will probably have to satisfy this criterion – and it is not necessary that the provision concerned is unconditional or independent of further action taken by the Community or national authorities.

As *Marleasing* concerns exclusively the relations between individuals un-der a Directive, the question arises to what extent duties of interpretation exist also in other situations, notably, "vertical" relations under interna-tional treaties. It will hardly be contested nowadays that a general duty to interpret national law in conformity with Community law flows from Arti-cle 5 EC, and that the Community institutions are obliged to interpret Community law in conformity with "the law", as the Court of Justice has confirmed that that article is the basis of a duty of mutual solidarity.[17] That

---

[17] Cases 6, 11/69, *Commission* v *France* [1969] ECR 523; Case 230/81, *Commission* v *United Kingdom* [1979] ECR 1447. *Cf.* also Temple Lang, "Community Constitutional Law: Article 5 EEC Treaty", (1990) 27 CMLRev 645–681.

this can be of interest to individuals flows from Article 164 EC which provides that the Court shall ensure that in the application of the Treaty "the law" is observed. On account of these factors it shall be clear that international treaties to which the Community is a party can be of relevance for individuals even when they have no direct effect; individuals may, therefore, benefit indirectly from the applicability of international treaties as against the Community institutions and/or national authorities.

At this stage one might ask whether the duties incumbent on national and Community authorities under Article 5, which seem to apply in addition to direct effect, could in fact have provided an alternative for the Court, as the underlying motives are comparable to those of direct effect, in particular, the effectiveness and uniform interpretation of Community law. Indeed, Article 5 guarantees the uniform interpretation of international agreements in much the same way as in the case of direct effect, because litigation can take place at the initiative of the individual and the preliminary reference procedure can play its full role.

However, it would appear that from the viewpoint of the Community, a principle of interpreting Community law to conform to international law is not sufficient. Duties concerning the interpretation of the law are not nearly as effective as the principle of direct effect in creating confidence on the part of the Community's treaty partners, as the limits of the duties of interpretation are to be found in the flexibility of national law or Community legislation. In the absence of direct effect, international treaties cannot override contrary provisions of autonomous Community or national law.

Agreements to which only the Member States are parties

Before coming to the question of the effect of GATT in Community law, it is useful to compare the situation as summarised above to that of agreements concluded by the Member States to which the Community is not a party. This is of relevance to GATT as it was negotiated outside the Community framework, and the Community is not formally a contracting party.

Treaties to which the Member States but not the Community are parties are not part of Community law. It is important to note first of all, that because these agreements are not part of Community law, they do not have direct effect and cannot override Community legislation. This is also true for agreements concluded before the entry into force of the EEC Treaty, even in spite of Article 234.[18]

---

[18] *cf.* Case 812/79, *Attorney General* v *Burgoa*, [1980] ECR 2787, para 17, where the Court held that Art 234 did not mean that the Community was in any way bound by previous commitments of its Member States.

Would the Community authorities and courts be under an obligation to interpret Community law "in so far as possible" in conformity with treaties entered into by the Member States? An argument in favour of such an obligation would seem to be that Article 164 requires the Court of Justice to ensure that "the law" is to be observed in the application of the Treaty. The expression "the law" need not be confined to general principles of law or rules relating to the application of the Treaty. Indeed, there seems to have been developing, within the caselaw of the Court, a principle of "legislation-conform" interpretation of the Treaty,[19] which conforms both with the evolutionary character of the Community legal order and with the idea that such a principle of interpretation is a necessary ingredient of a system which is in the process of constitutionalisation. Thus, all Community acts, including international agreements to which the Community is a party can be relevant in determining the law, provided they are not in conflict with the Treaty itself.

However, with regard to the position of treaties concluded by the Member States, Article 164 provides a relatively weak argument, as a mere linguistic possibility does not *per se* give rise to a legal obligation. The arguments against it would appear to be much stronger: Community law entrusts the institutions with certain tasks for the attainment of the objectives specified therein. Admitting effects, in the Community legal order, of legal instruments which have not been adopted according to the procedures provided therein would frustrate this principle. This is even harder to accept if one takes the view that any interpretation of Community law in the light of such "alien" rules is liable to entail, directly or indirectly, obligations for individuals. The *Marleasing* case discussed above shows that even through a process of construction obligations can be imposed on individuals. In the circumstances of the case, this might be acceptable since, without interfering with the basic principle of legal certainty as regards the meaning of national legal norms, the principle of interpretation guarantees the effectiveness of Community law as such. To suppose that indirect effects can flow from agreements concluded by the Member States outside the Community framework definitely goes a step further than that. This does not seem to be justified, either in the light of requirements of Community law, or in the light of possible burdens imposed on individuals. On these grounds it would appear that agreements concluded by Member States are not only devoid of direct effect; they are also devoid of any "indirect effect". The only exception to this is where provisions of Community law explicitly refer to such agreements. In that case the need to interpret Community law in the light of such agreements will prevail. Article 234 EC may be relevant here, as the purpose of its first paragraph is:

---

[19] Case 13/61, *De Geus* v *Bosch* [1962] ECR 45; Case 48/75, *Royer* [1976] ECR 497; Case 36/74, *Walrave and Koch* v *UCI* [1974] ECR 1405; Case 13/78, *Eggers* v *Freie Hansestadt Bremen* [1978] ECR 1935; Case 15/78, *Société générale alsacienne de Banque SA* v *Koestler*, [1978] ECR 1971.

"to make it clear, in accordance with the principles of international law, that application of the Treaty does not affect the duty of the Member States concerned to observe the rights of non-member countries under a prior treaty and to fulfil its corresponding obligations".[20]

Possible effects of GATT on individuals

The Court has never given direct effect to provisions of the GATT, nor of a panel report adopted by the High Contracting Parties. There are several factors which may have rendered it difficult to give direct effect to provisions of the General Agreement as a matter of Community law.

One factor which is frequently being neglected is the fact that formally, the Community is not a contracting party to GATT; it has merely substituted the Member States by virtue of what is called, in terms of international law, a unilateral declaration combined with acceptance by the other contracting parties. Although this type of "treaty-making" is not explicitly provided for by primary Community law, it is clear that the Community would not be able to function without the acceptance of such "acts". The view taken by the Court[21] that the situation was capable of creating binding, justiciable obligations is therefore both understandable and justified. However, it is difficult on this account to establish a principle of enforcement on the initiative of individuals, because of the uncertainty as to how far the commitment and the acceptance by third states would extend and how long it lasts.[22] Thus, in spite of the fact that the Community substituted the Member States in their international obligations, it is difficult for the Court to accept the direct effect of GATT as a matter of principle.

It should be noted that the problem of according direct effect may be remedied if the Community would become a full contracting party to the GATT. As the Court is at present examining the extent and nature of the competence of the Community for the conclusion of the new agreements,[23] this matter may again become topical. It would seem that, in case the Community and its Member States jointly undertake all obligations, the effect of the provisions concerned will have to be determined according to Community law rather than according to national law.

A factor which will remain the same, however, is that GATT is a multilateral agreement. It has been suggested above that it may be more difficult for the Court to give direct effect to multilateral agreements than to

---

[20] Case 812/79, *supra*, n 18 at para 17. See also Case C-158/91, *Ministère public et Direction du travail et de l'emploi* v *J.C. Levy*, [1993] ECR I-4287, concerning ILO Convention No 89 (1948). For a dynamic interpretation of Art 234, see, *e.g.*, Micklitz and Reich, *Legal Aspects of European Space Activities, EEC Internal Market and Common Commercial Policy* (1989).

[21] Cases 21–24/72, *supra*, n 2.

[22] Under international law, unilateral declarations are valid as long as they are not withdrawn, while they may involve the responsibility of a state that does so towards states that have relied on the unilateral declaration.

[23] The Court has given its opinion on 15 November 1994; see Opinion 1/94.

bilateral agreements, and that the structure of the agreement may be taken into account in order to detect the intention of the legislator to exclude direct effect. The structure of the GATT will, of course, be reinforced by the establishment of the World Trade Organization, but whether this suffices for the purpose of conferring direct effect in the Community of the multilateral trade obligations remains to be seen.[24]

This brings us back to the question of what other effects GATT provisions can have in the Community legal order, a matter which was at issue in 1989 in *Fediol III*.[25] In this case the EEC Seed Crushers' and Oil Processors' Federation (Fediol) brought an action for the annulment of a Commission decision rejecting its complaint regarding allegedly illicit commercial practices in Argentina. On the basis of Regulation 2641/84 on the strengthening of the common commercial policy[26] the Commission can, at the request of affected individuals, take measures against practices of third states which infringe, *e.g.*, the GATT. Fediol had complained to the Commission alleging that the practice of the Argentinean authorities, impeding exports of soya beans by imposing higher duties and quantitative restrictions on exports of this product, infringed the General Agreement. The Commission disagreed and rejected Fediol's complaint. When its decision was challenged under Article 173, the Commission raised an objection of inadmissibility on the grounds that, according to the Court's own caselaw, GATT rules did not have direct effect. However, the Court held:

". . . [S]ince Regulation No 2641/84 entitles the economic agents concerned to rely on the GATT provisions in the complaint which they lodge with the Commission in order to establish the illicit nature of the commercial practices which they consider to have harmed them, those same economic agents are entitled to request the Court to exercise its powers of review over the legality of the Commission's decision applying those provisions."[27]

The Court went on to consider whether Articles III, XI, XXII(i) and XXIII GATT were applicable *in casu*.

Although it may seem at first sight as if the Court gave direct effect to the GATT provisions involved, it did not in fact change its earlier caselaw regarding the lack of direct effect of GATT. Rather, this seems to be a case of GATT-conform interpretation of Community measures required by Regulation 2641/84.

Nevertheless, *Fediol* may not adequately reflect the possibilities of individuals relying on GATT provisions. On the basis of the above it can be argued that a more general duty of GATT-conform interpretation exists. This is important as, in matters of guarantees of freedom, non-

---

[24] On the GATT-WTO dispute settlement system, see Petersmann, "The GATT dispute settlement system as an instrument of the foreign trade policy of the EC" in this volume at pp 253–277.

[25] Case 70/87, *Fediol v Commission*, [1989] ECR 1781.

[26] OJ 1984 L252/1.

[27] Case 70/87, *supra*, n 25 at para 22.

discrimination, transparent policy-making and the use of proportionate policy instruments, the GATT obligations provide norms which are much more precise than the corresponding EC provisions. Although the scope of the substitution of the Community for the Member States and the extent of the duties of interpretation resulting therefrom are uncertain, in areas where the succession by the Community is in doubt, Article 234 would still apply. The fact that the Court did not adopt this approach and confined itself to referring to the Regulation can be explained by the fact that accepting a more general duty of interpretation was not necessary in the circumstances of the case. A similar attitude of procedural economy was displayed by the Court in *Nakajima*,[28] where it merely verified the compatibility of a Council regulation with Article 2(4) and (6) of the Anti-Dumping Code – a (multilateral) treaty to which the Community is a party[29] – although the Regulation stated in its preamble that the Council had acted in order to fulfil its obligations as they resulted in particular from Article VI GATT. The judgment in this case – an indirect challenge of the Community measure through Article 184 – can be taken as an implicit denial of the justiciability of the provisions of the General Agreement in cases of possible conflict with Community measures. It does not exclude the indirect effect of GATT.

Moreover, the angle of "effects of international treaties" is arguably only one side of the coin. As may be illustrated by the caselaw of the Court concerning the European Convention on Human Rights it is important to distinguish whether a particular norm binds the Member States merely as a treaty obligation or as a general principle of law, because general principles of law can be used to override Community legislation and national measures even in the absence of direct effect. This can be relevant also in the area of external trade law. The Court has held (in connection with trading activities within the Community), for example, that:

"the principle of free movement of goods and freedom of competition, together with freedom of trade as a fundamental right, are general principles of law of which the Court ensures observance."[30]

Freedom of trade as a human right may reduce the sphere in which the Community may restrict the activity of commercial actors. According to Petersmann[31] the individual freedom of internal and external trade may therefore be restricted only if (i) Community law provides a legal basis for this; (ii) the Community powers are exercised by means of transparent,

---

[28] Case C-69/89, *Nakajima All Precisions Co Ltd* v *Council*, [1991] ECR I-2069.
[29] Agreement on the Implementation of Article VI of the General Agreement on Tariffs and Trade, OJ 1980 L71/72.
[30] Case 240/83, *ADBHU*, [1985] ECR 531 at 548.
[31] Petersmann, "Constitutional Principles Governing the EEC's Commercial Policy", in: Maresceau (ed), *The European Community's Commercial Policy After 1992: The Legal Dimension* (1993), pp 21–61 at p 37.

327

non-discriminatory and proportionate policy instruments subject to specified exceptions; and (iii) the measures are designed to protect the public interest.

The question, to what extent GATT norms apply as general principles of law is a relatively new area of research. Arguably, there are two different types of general principles in Community law: (i) any principles of law common to the legal systems of the Member States, which can be used as a means to fill gaps in the Community legal order in order to prevent a denial of justice; and (ii) those principles the observance of which is specifically required by or inherent in the Treaty, which can be used to override Community legislation. Consequently, if a GATT rule reflects a principle common to the legal orders of the Member States it can, first of all, be used as an aid in the interpretation of (non-conflicting) Community law. The possibility of invoking GATT norms as general principles of law is, however, beset with similar problems as that of direct effect. When there is no direct effect and to the extent that the effects of GATT have to be determined exclusively through Community law, no general principle of law can be taken from the legal systems of the Member States with which to fill gaps in Community law. General principles inherent in the Treaty and principles without which the Community could not function can be used to override Community law. Whether this includes the freedom of external trade is as yet uncertain. If so, one may ask what golden opportunities have already been missed for the development of the (proper) caselaw!

Conclusion

In determining the ways in which individuals can benefit from the provisions of the GATT as a matter from Community law, one ought to distinguish between various different categories of legal effects. Which of the avenues described above, direct effect, indirect effect, or perhaps general principles of law, would be the most promising way forward in a given case would appear to be an issue of particular importance.

NANETTE A E M NEUWAHL[32]

[32] The author is grateful for the encouragement given by Hans Micklitz (Fachhochschule für Wirtschaft, Berlin) and John Woodliffe (University of Leicester). Any shortcomings of this paper are, of course, solely the responsibility of the author.

Chapter 19

Judicial Review of Commercial Policy Measures after the Uruguay Round

This paper[1] looks at the approach of the Court hitherto to the task of judicial review of commercial policy measures, and raises the question what changes might be expected as a result of the Uruguay round and the entry in force of the new WTO Agreement.

The completion of the Uruguay round has already prompted, even before the entry into force of the new Agreement, a package of Community measures, affecting in particular its import regime: a series of regulations adopted on 7 March 1994 laying down common rules for imports, including new provisions for safeguard measures; common rules for imports from certain third countries (formerly referred to as State-trading countries); and common rules for imports of textile products from certain third world countries, again including new safeguard measures.[2] Of particular interest for the present topic is a regulation on the streamlining of decision-making procedures for certain Community instruments of commercial defence and amending the basic Community anti-dumping legislation.

Moreover, as part of the same package the Council finally agreed to transfer jurisdiction in anti-dumping and anti-subsidy cases from the Court of Justice to the Court of First Instance.[3]

How then is judicial review likely to be affected?

Review of anti-dumping measures

I will start with review of anti-dumping measures, where the caselaw of the Court to date is most extensive. It should be noted, however, that some of the points to be discussed on anti-dumping can be transposed to other commercial policy measures – certainly to anti-subsidy measures and, to some extent, to safeguard measures under the new import regime.

---

[1] This paper is based, with updating to October 1994, on my paper "Review by the Court of Justice of Commercial Policy Measures: Recent Trends and Future Prospects", published in Maresceau (ed), *The European Community's Commercial Policy after 1992: The Legal Dimension* (1993), pp 63–77.

[2] Council Regulation 520/94, OJ 1994 L66/1; Council Regulation 521/94, OJ 1994 L66/7; Council Regulation 522/94, OJ 1994 L66/10.

[3] Council Decision 93/350, OJ 1994 L66/29.

Dumping takes place where an exporter in a third country sells goods for export at a lower price than he charges on his home market – or, as it is put, less than "normal value". Although the issue of dumping is highly controversial, and many doubt the very justification of anti-dumping measures, the fact remains that the principal trading countries have enacted anti-dumping legislation designed to protect domestic industry against what is alleged to be a form of unfair competition, and the Council has since 1968 enacted such legislation under Article 113 which enables duties to be imposed on dumped imports so as to counter the effects of dumping. After an investigation conducted by the Commission, a provisional duty may be imposed by regulation of the Commission and a definitive duty by regulation of the Council.

Special difficulties have arisen over standing, for the purposes of judicial review: these difficulties result in part from the language of Article 173, in part from the character of anti-dumping measures. Under Article 173(4), undertakings can challenge only measures which are either decisions addressed to them or decisions which, although in the form of regulation (or a decision addressed to another person), are of direct and individual concern to them. Anti-dumping measures, although taking the form of regulations, do have elements of a decision, since the Commission will investigate individual exporters and importers and will base its findings of dumping on those investigations. But the regulations imposing the duty will necessarily be general in nature, will often extend to all imports of products from the third country in question (even if they sometimes set duties at different levels for different exporters), and will affect importers generally, all of whom are liable to pay the duty. Such regulations, although they directly concern those who are required to pay the duty, and possibly also exporters whose business suffers as a result of the duty, do not normally concern them individually: on the contrary the measures are normally, as I have said, general in their application.

The Court's approach to standing shows a significant evolution. In the very first anti-dumping cases decided by the Court, the first Japanese ball-bearings cases in 1979,[4] the Court accepted that the Japanese exporters could challenge the Council regulation in issue there. That however was a somewhat unusual regulation which named the exporters concerned, who could therefore clearly be held to be individually concerned. In *Allied Corporation* in 1984,[5] the Court went further and accepted that exporters could challenge the regulations regardless of whether they were named provided that they were "concerned by the preliminary investigations", *i.e.* took part in the Commission investigation. A similar approach was

---

[4] Case 113/77, *NTN Toyo* v *Council* [1979] ECR 1185; Case 118/77, *ISO* v *Council* [1979] ECR 1277; Case 119/77, *Nippon Seiko* v *Council and Commission* [1979] ECR 1303; Case 120/77, *Koyo Seiko* v *Council and Commission* [1979] ECR 1337; Case 121/77, *Nachi Fujikoshi* v *Council*, [1979] ECR 1363.

[5] Cases 239 and 275/82, [1984] ECR 1005.

applied to complainants, that is the Community industry seeking protection against dumping, which will usually have taken part in the proceedings before the Commission, since such proceedings are normally only started on the basis of a complaint. The Court has accepted a challenge by a party which had by a complaint instigated anti-dumping proceedings resulting in a regulation which that party considered inadequate[6] and, in the closely related field of anti-subsidy proceedings, the Court has accepted as admissible a challenge by the complainant to a refusal by the Commission to initiate proceedings.[7]

The test for the standing of importers has been more restricted: until recently the Court took the view that, if they were independent of the exporter and were members of an open class, they could not challenge a regulation directly at the Court under Article 173: their only remedy would be to wait until the national authorities adopted a decision charging the duty and to challenge that decision in the national court, with the possibility of a reference under Article 177 on the validity of the regulation.[8] It seemed that only an importer who was commercially related to an exporter, and whose retail price was used as a basis for determining the export price, could bring proceedings under Article 173.[9] However the Court accepted in the *Extramet* case[10] that in certain circumstances even an independent importer should have the right to challenge a regulation under Article 173, notwithstanding the Court's earlier caselaw on the subject.[11]

While the Court has proved relatively liberal in respect of standing, there have been until recently few cases in which challenges to anti-dumping regulations have succeeded on the substance and anti-dumping regulations have been annulled. In the first Japanese ball-bearings cases,[12] the regulations were annulled; and mention should also be made of the Opinion of Advocate General Warner in that case, whose criticisms of the procedures followed by the Commission led the Community legislature at once to amend the basic legislation to improve the procedural safeguards. Subsequently, an anti-dumping measure was annulled at the suit of the complainant on the ground that the regulation did not provide sufficient protection to the Community industry.[13] But a number of subsequent cases, including many challenges to the Commission's methodology, allegedly weighted systematically against the exporter, failed.

---

[6] Case 264/82, *Timex* v *Council and Commission* [1985] ECR 849.

[7] Case 191/82, *Fediol* v *Commission* [1983] ECR 2913.

[8] See Cases 239 and 275/82, *supra*, n 5.

[9] See for example the orders in Case 279/86, *Sermes* v *Commission* [1987] ECR 3109; and Case 301/86, *Firmodt Petersen* v *Commission* [1987] ECR 3123.

[10] Case C-358/89, *Extramet Industrie* v *Council* [1991] ECR I-2501, paras 71 to 74 per A-G Jacobs.

[11] See Arnull, "Challenging EC Anti-Dumping Regulations: the Problem of Admissibility", (1992) *European Competition Law Review* 73; Castillo de la Torre, "Anti-Dumping Policy and Private Interests" (1992) 17 ELRev 348.

[12] *Supra*, n 4.

[13] Case 264/82, *supra*, n 6.

Examples are: (i) a second series of Japanese ball-bearings cases, the "Mini ball-bearings cases", which came to judgment in 1987;[14] (ii) the Japanese Electronic typewriter cases in 1988;[15] and (iii) the Japanese Photocopier cases[16] in 1990. In those cases the Court rejected a wide variety of arguments, including arguments based on treating symmetrically the export price and the notion of normal value. The Court underlined the discretion of the Community institutions in fixing the level of the duty and in assessing the interests of the Community.

Lest it be thought that all such cases concern Japanese products, I should add that the Court also rejected a series of claims against anti-dumping duties in 1990 concerning imports of electric motors from Bulgaria, Czechoslovakia, the German Democratic Republic, Hungary, Poland, and the Soviet Union.[17] Since the goods in question were manufactured in countries with non-market economies, the issues were somewhat different from those in the series of Japanese cases, but here also the Court upheld the methods applied by the Community institutions and underlined their margin of discretion.

Recently, the Court has seemed more willing to entertain challenges to anti-dumping measures both on procedural grounds and on the substance. I will mention five examples. (1) In *Al-Jubail Fertilizer Company* v *Council* in 1991,[18] the Court annulled provisions imposing anti-dumping duties on the grounds of procedural defects. It is interesting that, in this connection, the Court relied on the principle of the right to a fair hearing in anti-dumping proceedings. That right had previously been recognised in the context of competition proceedings which could result in the imposition of fines, but the right was here recognised by the Court in the context of a dumping investigation prior to the adoption of anti-dumping measures which according to the Court might directly and individually affect the undertakings concerned and entail adverse consequences for them. The Court added

". . . with regard to the right to a fair hearing, any action taken by the Community institutions must be all the more scrupulous in view of the fact that, as they stand

---

[14] Case 240/84, *Toyo* v *Council* [1987] ECR 1809; Case 255/84, *Nachi Fujikoshi* v *Council* [1987] ECR 1861; Case 256/84, *Koyo Seiko* v *Council* [1987] ECR 1899; Case 258/84, *Nippon Seiko* v *Council* [1987] ECR 1923; and Case 260/84, *Minebea* v *Council*, [1987] ECR 1975.

[15] Case 56/85, *Brother* v *Commission* [1988] ECR 5655; Case 250/85, *Brother* v *Council* [1988] ECR 5683; Cases 277 and 300/85, *Canon* v *Council* [1988] ECR 5731; Case 301/85, *Sharp* v *Council* [1988] ECR 5813; Cases 260/85 and 106/86, *TEC* v *Council* [1988] ECR 5855; Cases 273/85 and 107/86, *Silver Seiko* v *Council* [1988] ECR 5927.

[16] Joined Cases 133 and 150/87, *Nashua* v *Commission and Council* [1990] ECR I-719; Case 156/87, *Gestetner Holdings* v *Council and Commission* [1990] ECR I-781.

[17] Cases 304/86 and 185/87, *Enital* v *Commission and Council* [1990] ECR I-2939; Cases 305/86 and 160/87, *Neotype Techmashexport* v *Commission and Council* [1990] ECR I-2945; Cases 320/86 and 188/87, *Stanko France* v *Commission and Council* [1990] ECR I-3013; Case 157/87, *Electroimpex* v *Council* [1990] ECR I-3021; and Case 323/88, *Sermes* v *Directeur des services des douanes de Strasbourg* [1990] ECR I-3027.

[18] Case C-49/88, [1991] ECR I-3187.

at present, the rules in question do not provide all the procedural guarantees for the protection of the individual which may exist in certain national legal systems."

(2) In another recent case,[19] a challenge to an anti-dumping measure succeeded, even within the limited confines of a reference for a preliminary ruling under Article 177. Here the regulation, imposing an anti-dumping duty on brushes imported from China, was ruled to be invalid on the ground that the Community authorities had not sufficiently justified their choice of Sri Lanka rather than Taiwan, as the reference country.

It seems that this was the first successful challenge to an anti-dumping regulation via the Article 177 route.[20]

(3) A challenge to anti-dumping measures which ultimately failed but marked a turning-point in the caselaw concerned a regulation imposing duties on matrix printers from Japan:[21] the judgment seems to represent a new departure in the caselaw by reviewing the compatibility of anti-dumping measures with the GATT Anti-dumping Code. At the relevant time, the basic regulation at issue in earlier cases such as Electronic typewriters and Photocopiers (Regulation No 2176/84) had been replaced by a new basic regulation, Council Regulation 2423/88,[22] which changed some of the rules for conducting an anti-dumping proceeding. However, as compared with the earlier cases, the applicant's challenge had shifted to contesting not only the compatibility of the particular proceeding with the basic regulation but also the compatibility of the basic regulation itself with the GATT rules to which it purported to give effect. This led the Court to rule that it was competent to review the compatibility of the basic regulation with the GATT rules, confirming a decision to similar effect given in relation to proceedings under the "New Commercial Policy Instrument"[23] in the *Fediol III* case.[24] In *Nakajima*, moreover, the Court accepted that the legality of the Community measures could be reviewed not only in relation to the articles of the GATT itself but also in relation to the provisions of the GATT Anti-dumping Code. In the instant case the Court held that the provisions of the new basic regulation concerning the construction of normal value were consistent with the GATT Anti-dumping Code.

(4) *Extramet* raised for the first time the interaction of anti-dumping policy with competition policy. Extramet was the main importer and the end-user of the product subject to the anti-dumping duty (calcium metal from China and the Soviet Union). Its business depended very largely on the imports caught by the duty; and it had difficulty in obtaining alterna-

---

[19] Case C-16/90, *Nölle* v *Hauptzollamt Bremen-Freihafen* [1991] ECR I-5163.

[20] *cf.*, for example, Case 246/87, *Continentale Produkten-Gesellschaft* v *Hauptzollamt München-West* [1989] ECR 1151, a preliminary ruling upholding the validity of an anti-dumping duty on imports of cotton yarn from Turkey and Case 323/88, *supra*, n 17.

[21] Case C-69/89, *Nakajima All Precision* v *Council* [1991] ECR I-2069.

[22] OJ 1988 L209/1.

[23] Council Regulation 2641/84 "on the strengthening of the Common Commercial Policy with regard in particular to protection against illicit commercial practices", OJ 1984 L252/1.

[24] Case 70/87, *Fediol* v *Commission* [1989] ECR 1781.

tive supplies from the only Community producer of the product (Péchiney), which was at the same time its main competitor for the end product, as well as being the complainant in the anti-dumping proceeding which led to the duty. It is obvious that the imposition of a heavy anti-dumping duty in such circumstances may have the effect of putting the Community producer in a dominant position going as far as a complete monopoly over the Community market which would allow it to dictate its terms or put competitors out of business. Inadequate consideration by Commission and Council of the competition issues led to the annulment of the regulation.[25]

(5) Finally, in *Rima*[26] the applicant sought annulment of a measure imposing definitive anti-dumping duties in connection with a review of anti-dumping measures concerning imports of ferro-silicone originating in Brazil. The Commission had opened a review of anti-dumping measures previously adopted; but the review was not limited to those exporters who had requested it but was extended to cover all Brazilian exporters, including Rima. Rima contended that, since the initial investigation had resulted in a finding that it had not been involved in dumping, a new investigation was unlawful, and would have been lawful only if there had been evidence of dumping on its part. The Court held that, on a proper interpretation of the basic regulation, confirmed by the provisions of the GATT Anti-dumping Code, the existence of evidence of dumping and of injury resulting therefrom was always required for the opening of an investigation, whether at the initiation of an anti-dumping proceeding, or in the course of a review of anti-dumping measures. The Court found that, in the absence of any evidence of dumping, the Community institutions had not complied with the conditions laid down by the basic regulation and annulled the measure imposing the duties.

From this brief survey of recent cases, one can see that the Court now takes an active, and perhaps it might be said a more balanced role in reviewing anti-dumping measures. The caselaw suggests that the Court will exercise control in relation to the following issues: (i) whether the procedural rules have been correctly observed, including procedural requirements which may go beyond those set out in the legislation; (ii) whether the facts have been accurately stated; (iii) whether there has been a manifest error of appraisal or misuse of powers; (iv) whether the reasoning of the regulation was adequate; and (v) whether there was a violation of any provisions of the Treaty, of the enabling legislation or of fundamental principles of Community law or indeed now, of the GATT Anti-dumping Code.

On the other hand, as already mentioned, challenges to the Commission's methodology have generally not succeeded; nor have challenges based on such matters as comparisons with sales on the domestic market, attribution of costs to domestic sales and exports, etc. It seems questionable, from such comparative surveys as have been undertaken, whether

---

[25] The Commission has opened a new proceeding and imposed a provisional duty: see OJ 23 April 1994.

[26] Case 216/91, [1993] ECR I-6303.

the courts of other jurisdictions carry out more extensive review of anti-dumping measures.[27]

What changes are likely to result from transfer of anti-dumping cases to the Court of First Instance? I will mention three points. First, while the Court of First Instance will be bound by the caselaw of the Court of Justice, both on standing and on substance, it may be expected to continue progressively to expand the test of standing, as the Court of Justice has done – and I will come back to some possible further developments on this important aspect of judicial protection. There is scope, certainly, for the caselaw on standing to become more flexible, and perhaps more coherent.[28]

Secondly, the Court of First Instance may be expected, since this is part of its *raison d'être*, to scrutinise closely the decisions of the Council and Commission.[29] This closer scrutiny has been shown, I think, to be effective in competition cases.

Thirdly whereas in the field of competition decisions of the Commission can normally be contested under Article 173 and challenge via the national courts with a reference under Article 177 is not normally an alternative route, the position is different in anti-dumping cases, because anti-dumping measures are regulations implemented by the national authorities in the Member States. Here therefore an alternative route to direct challenge under Article 173 has hitherto been available. Challenges can be made to the implementation of anti-dumping measures by the national authorities by proceedings in the national courts, combined with a reference to the Court of Justice on the validity of the Community regulations. An example has been seen in *Nölle*.[30] However a recent case in the field of state aid or subsidies under the competition rules of the Treaty raises an interesting question in that respect: this is the *TWD* case.[31] There the Commission had taken a decision finding that an aid granted by Germany was unlawful, and requiring Germany to recover the aid from TWD. TWD did not challenge the decision under Article 173 as it was entitled to do, but when recovery proceedings were taken by the German Government in the German court, TWD argued in those proceedings that the Commission decision was unlawful, and the German court referred the question of the validity of the decision to the Court of Justice under Article 177. The Court held however that the validity of the decision could no longer be challenged at that stage by an undertaking which could have challenged it under Article 173 but had failed to do so. There may therefore be a question whether similar principles apply in anti-dumping, and

---

[27] See Jackson and Vermulst (ed), *Anti-dumping Law and Practice: A Comparative Study* (1990).

[28] See Nihoul, "La recevabilité des recours en annulation introduits par un particulier à l'encontre d'un acte communautaire de portée générale", (1994) *Revue Trimestrielle de Droit Européen*, 171.

[29] See the preamble to the Council decision establishing the Court of First Instance, which recites that "in respect of actions requiring close examination of complex facts, the establishment of a second court will improve the judicial protection of individual interests."

[30] *Supra*, n 19.

[31] Case C-188/92, [1994] ECR I-833.

whether therefore an undertaking which could have challenged a regulation directly in the Court of First Instance under Article 173 but has failed to do so can do so instead in the national courts and obtain a reference to the Court of Justice under Article 177. It might be argued that such a course is not open to it, since it circumvents the more appropriate procedure of a direct action and also, since the transfer of anti-dumping cases to the Court of First Instance, avoids the appropriate forum. Caution should however be exercised before extending the *TWD* caselaw to dumping. A recipient of aid undoubtedly has standing to challenge directly a Commission decision declaring the aid unlawful. The standing of undertakings affected by anti-dumping regulations is often less certain. It would be unfortunate if an undertaking were to be denied a remedy in the national courts on the ground that it should have gone directly to the Court of Justice, unless its standing to do so were beyond doubt.

What changes may follow from the new WTO Agreement? The background is well known: the Member States were parties to the original GATT before the Community acquired its competence in the field of commercial policy but the Court has held that the Community is bound by the GATT under a doctrine of succession, having succeeded to the Member States' commercial policy powers and responsibilities.[32]

The Community is therefore bound by the GATT although not, or not yet, a party. But the Court has not been willing to give direct effect to the provisions of GATT – in contrast to certain other treaties concluded by the Community with third countries – because of the flexibility of those provisions, especially in relation to the possibilities of derogation and the arrangements for the settlement of disputes. The Court has, however, in *Fediol III* and in *Nakajima*, as we have seen, been willing to review the compatibility of the anti-subsidy and anti-dumping procedures with the GATT rules. Recently this caselaw has been confirmed in the "Bananas" case mentioned below.

One question which seems likely to be raised is whether the new WTO Agreement, by establishing a full-scale World Trade Organization, by providing for more limited possibilities of derogation and by laying down more binding dispute settlement procedures, may lead to a reconsideration of the possible direct effect of some of its provisions.

Then there is the new GATT Agreement which replaces the former Anti-dumping Code: the "Agreement on implementation of Article VI of GATT 1994", which contains far more detailed specifications of the determination of dumping, the determination of injury, the procedures to be followed, etc. The Community legislation will no doubt need to be further amended, and will no doubt frequently be tested against the GATT Agreement. And there are the revisions already made in the March 1994 package to the Community legislation on anti-dumping, and other commercial policy measures, with perhaps ominous reference to streamlining the decision-making procedures. Here, in the event, the Council did not

---

[32] Cases 21–24/72, *International Fruit Company* [1972] ECR 1219.

accept the Commission's proposal that the Commission, as well as its responsibility for provisional anti-dumping duty, should also take over from the Council the power to impose definitive duty.[33] But the Council did decide, reportedly against the wishes of certain governments, to amend the basic regulations so that definitive duty could be imposed by simple rather than qualified majority. Will this lead to a readier use of anti-dumping measures – and perhaps to more challenges? Other changes may also have an impact on judicial review. Time limits are imposed on the various stages in anti-dumping proceedings – subject to more staff being made available to the Commission. As well as exporters, importers and complainants, the new regulation recognises – some would say belatedly – the interests of users and of consumer organisations. In 1991 the Court declined to entertain a complaint made on behalf of a European consumers' organisation, when the Commission refused it access to the non-confidential file in anti-dumping proceedings.[34] Another question then is whether the current concern for transparency, under which all Community documents are said in principle to be accessible to everyone, with of course appropriate reservations for commercially confidential information and the like, will change the Commission's practice in this respect; whether the right to information for importers, exporters and complainants upheld in *Al-Jubail* will extend more widely; and whether the recognition in the new legislation of the interests of users and of consumer organisations will lead to recognition in some circumstances of their standing before the Court.

It is clear therefore that the review of anti-dumping and related measures will raise many new questions in the future; and the transfer of anti-dumping and anti-subsidy cases to the Court of First Instance may mark a new stage in the development of judicial review.

Other commercial policy measures

Let me turn now to recent cases concerning certain other measures in the field of trade with non-member countries. Here, I will not attempt to focus specifically on the implications of the Uruguay Round, but I will examine judicial review of protective measures, especially but not exclusively in the agricultural sector. A case of some interest here is a case concerning import of apples from Chile, in which the Court held that the Commission had not justified its action in suspending imports already in transit, annulled the Commission regulations to that extent, and ordered the Community to pay damages to the applicant in respect of its losses.[35] That case

---

[33] This proposal was somewhat implausibly presented as a *quid pro quo* in return for transferring jurisdiction to the Court of First Instance.

[34] Case C-170/89, *BEUC* v *Commission*, [1991] ECR I-5709.

[35] Case C-152/88, *Sofrimport* v *Commission* [1990] ECR I-2477.

stands out as one of the few in which the applicant managed to clear all the hurdles set by the Court's caselaw for the establishment of liability on the part of the Community and in addition cleared those standing in the way of admissibility of an annulment action by an undertaking. In order to obviate a threat of serious disturbances to the Community market in apples, the Commission had suspended import licences for dessert apples originating *inter alia* in Chile, by three regulations adopted under the basic legislation in the field, in particular Council Regulation No 2707/72 laying down the conditions for applying protective measures for fruit and vegetables.[36] Article 3(3) of that Regulation provides that such measures "shall take account of the special position of products in transit to the Community". The applicant, Sofrimport, was a French company which had shipped a consignment of dessert apples from Chile just before the suspension took effect, and when a few days later it applied for import licences it found that it could not obtain them owing to the adoption of the Commission regulations in question. The Court held that Sofrimport had standing to challenge the validity of those measures, notwithstanding that they were regulations, because they were of direct and individual concern to it within the meaning of the second paragraph of Article 173 of the EEC Treaty. The Court held that the legislation concerned Sofrimport directly inasmuch as it required national authorities to reject pending applications for import licences, leaving them no discretion; and it concerned Sofrimport individually inasmuch as the persons concerned constituted a restricted group which was sufficiently well defined in relation to any other importer of the same product and could not be extended after the suspensory measures took effect, and inasmuch as Sofrimport derived specific protection from Article 3(3) of Regulation No 2707/72 which it had to be able to enforce in legal proceedings.

On the substance, the Court held that Article 3(3) of Regulation No 2707/72 had the effect of enabling an importer whose goods were in transit to rely on a legitimate expectation that in the absence of an overriding public interest no suspensory measures would be applied against him; and accordingly it annulled the three Commission regulations in question in so far as they had failed to make provision for goods in transit.

The Court went on to find that the imposition of protective measures on goods in transit in the circumstances of the case was sufficient to give rise to liability on the part of the Community for the harm thus caused to Sofrimport. It held that the adoption by the Commission, without invoking any overriding public interest, of protective measures in the fruit and vegetable sector concerning imports from non-member countries without taking any account whatsoever of the position of traders whose goods are in transit to the Community, thus disregarding the legitimate expectation created by Article 3(3) of Regulation 2707/72, constituted a sufficiently serious breach of a superior rule of law giving rise to non-contractual

---

[36] OJ (Special ed) (28–30 December) 1972 p 3.

liability on the part of the Community. It further held that any damage resulting from the adoption of such measures in those circumstances went beyond the limits of the economic risks inherent in the business in issue inasmuch as the purpose of Article 3(3) was precisely to limit those risks with regard to goods in transit. Thus the criteria of a sufficiently serious breach of a superior rule of law for the protection of the individual resulting in harm to the applicant, on which so many claims for damages have come to grief before the Court, were in this instance held to be fulfilled; and the Court ordered the Community to make good the damage suffered by Sofrimport. The parties were to inform the Court of any agreement on the amount of compensation, which they subsequently did. The judgment shows that it is possible for an applicant to succeed in a damages claim against Community legislation, but at the same time exemplifies the extremely narrow circumstances in which this may be the case. For present purposes it is interesting to note that the case took place in the field of common commercial policy.

In a group of three other cases also concerning protective measures on imports of agricultural products, the Court held that the levy imposed on imports of mushrooms from China infringed the principle of proportionality and was invalid.[37] In those cases, German companies had imported large quantities of mushrooms from China without, as it subsequently emerged, valid import certificates. They were accordingly charged a supplementary import levy which the Commission had introduced by way of a protective measure to preserve the Community mushroom market from the risk of serious disturbances. That measure was based on legislation comprising Council Regulation 521/77 laying down the conditions for applying protective measures for processed products derived from fruit and vegetables,[38] Article 2(2) of which provided that such protective measures could be adopted only to the extent and for the time strictly necessary and that they could be limited to certain places or countries of origin, certain destinations, qualities or packages. That wording is a specific expression, as the Court held, of the general principle of proportionality.

Having regard to the purpose of the protective measures in question (*viz* to protect the Community market in mushrooms from the risk of excessive disturbances) the Court held in its judgments that the Commission had set the level of the charge too high. The charge was set at a flat rate (175 ECU *per* 100 Kg) equivalent to the full cost of production of top-quality mushrooms in France – the Community's main producer. It was not reduced to take account of lower grades of quality and was payable in addition to a customs duty of 23%. This did not equalise the prices of the imported and Community products, but made the cost of the Chinese

---

[37] See Case C-24/90, *Hauptzollamt Hamburg-Jonas* v *Faust* [1991] ECR I-4905; Case C-25/90, *Hauptzollamt Hamburg-Jonas* v *Wünsche* [1991] ECR I-4939; and Case C-26/90, *Hauptzollamt Hamburg-Jonas* v *Wünsche* [1991] ECR I-4961.

[38] OJ 1977 L73/28.

mushrooms much more than that of the French product. The Court held that the level of the charge was therefore out of proportion to the aim pursued and accordingly rendered the Commission regulations at issue invalid in so far as the amount of the charge was concerned. This was the first time that the Court had decided the central question, namely the disproportion of the charge on the imported mushrooms, even though the case had come before it on previous occasions.[39]

If those judgments indicate a deepening of the Court's review of commercial policy measures, mention might be made of a case which may point towards a possible widening of its scope. In *Richardt*,[40] the Court was led to approach the sensitive field of defence and it did not draw back from dealing with the issue to the extent that it impinges on Community law. In that case a French undertaking bought a piece of technologically advanced equipment from a United States manufacturer for onward sale to the then Soviet Union. The goods were dispatched from Paris for shipment via Luxembourg where the authorities seized them for lack of an export licence under the Grand Ducal Regulation of 17 August 1963. That Regulation was adopted to give effect to arrangements within the framework of COCOM (Co-ordinating Committee for Multilateral Export Controls) the purpose of which was to control the export to Communist countries of goods of strategic importance. The Court held that the public security exception in Article 36 extended to Member States' external, as well as internal security, and therefore authorised Member States to subject exports of strategically important material to special authorisation such as that provided for by the Grand Ducal Regulation. The Court, however, added an interesting rider concerning the sanctions which may be applied for breaches of such national provisions in order to be consistent with Community law. It held that such sanctions may be justified under Article 36 only if no other measure less restrictive of the free movement of goods would enable the same objective to be attained. In this regard, it held, seizure or confiscation of the goods might be judged disproportionate, and therefore incompatible with Article 36, in so far as returning the goods to the Member State of their departure would suffice.

A case of some political importance which should be mentioned is the *Anastasiou* case,[41] even though it does not fall squarely within the field of commercial policy. The case arose out of the division of the island of Cyprus following the Turkish invasion. On a reference from the English High Court on the interpretation of the Association Agreement with Cyprus, the Court ruled that the authorities of the Member States must

---

[39] See Case 126/81, *Wünsche* [1982] ECR 1479; Case 245/81, *Edeka* [1982] ECR 2745; Case 52/81, *Faust* [1982] ECR 3745; Case 345/82, *Wünsche* [1984] ECR 1995; and Case 69/85, *Wünsche* [1986] ECR 947.
[40] Case C-367/89, [1991] ECR I-4621.
[41] Case C-432/92, [1994] ECR I-3087.

not accept, in the context of phytosanitary controls, certificates emanating from the *de facto* administration of the northern part of Cyprus, but only those issued by the competent authorities of the Republic of Cyprus.

Another recent case of some importance concerned bananas. Both the Federal Republic of Germany and a number of importers challenged the Council regulation establishing a common organisation of the market in bananas. The actions by the importers were rejected for lack of standing under Article 173, while the action by Germany was rejected on the substance.[42] The German Government had contended, among other arguments, that the regulation infringed certain fundamental provisions of the GATT. The Court held that the GATT could not be invoked for that purpose; a Community measure could be challenged for breach of the GATT rules only where the Community had intended to implement a specific GATT obligation or where the measure referred expressly to specific provisions of the GATT, as in *Nakajima* and *Fediol III* cited above.[43] The judgment confirms on this point the limited effect of GATT in Community law, in the light of the characteristics of the GATT system. It remains to be seen, as mentioned above, whether the new WTO Agreement will affect that situation in any respect.

Finally, the Court has apparently reversed its caselaw in relation to the import of goods for purposes of scientific research. To give effect to its international commitments (*e.g.,* under the Florence Convention) the Community admits scientific instruments or apparatus (as well as educational and cultural materials) free of customs duties, provided among other things, that "instruments or apparatus of equivalent scientific value are not being manufactured in the Community".[44] A German university, the Technische Universität München, ordered a scanning electron microscope from a Japanese company and applied for its duty-free admission. The request was refused following a Commission decision to the effect that an instrument manufactured by Philips in the Netherlands was of equivalent scientific value. The university did not agree that it was of equivalent scientific value and the German Bundesfinanzhof, being inclined to the same view, referred the question to the Court of Justice. In its previous caselaw the Court had set narrow limits to its review of such matters, declining to find fault with the substance of such a decision, save in the event of manifest error of fact or law or misuse of power.[45] In this case, however, the Court held that the decision was invalid on no fewer than three grounds: first, that the procedure for examining such applications was defective; secondly, that no adequate reasons had been given for the decision; and thirdly, that the importing university had not been given

---

[42] Case C-280/93, [1994] ECR I-4973.
[43] Paragraph 111 of the judgment.
[44] See Council Regulation 1798/75, OJ 1975 L184/1, as amended.
[45] See *e.g.*, Case 303/87, *Universität Stuttgart* v *Hauptzollamt Stuttgart-Ost* [1989] ECR 705.

the opportunity to make its views heard.[46] The result of the case constitutes a turning point on the importer's right to be heard in such duty-free admission procedures. Without burdening the Court with a duty to look into highly technical questions for which it is ill-qualified, the judgment also effectively widens the scope of the Court's judicial review, extending it in particular to ensure basic requirements of due process in the working methods of the Commission's Committee on Duty-Free Arrangements.

In conclusion, it emerges from this brief survey of the recent caselaw of the Court of Justice in the field of commercial policy that, whatever may be the allegations or fears of protectionism on the part of the political institutions of the Community, it cannot be said that in its recent caselaw the Court of Justice has shown any such disposition.

Postscript: the principle of Community preference

A question of general interest was raised in a recent case: that of the scope and effect of the principle of Community preference, according to which, it has been suggested, preference must always be given to intra-Community trade as compared with trade with third countries.[47] Recently Community regulations on soya beans were challenged on the ground, among others, that they infringed the principle of Community preference.[48] Rejecting that challenge, the Court held that, while the principle could be taken into account by the Community legislature as an element in the common agricultural policy, it could not affect the legislature's decision until all the economic factors influencing world trade had been evaluated; and that Community preference was not in any event a legal requirement the violation of which would result in the invalidity of the measure in question.[49]

The approach of the Court in this case, and elsewhere in its recent caselaw, seems consistent with the liberal principles of commercial policy stated in the Treaty. Thus Article 110 recites that, by establishing a customs union between themselves, the Member States "aim to contribute, in the common interest, to the harmonious development of world trade, the progressive abolition of restrictions on international trade and the lowering of customs barriers." These aims will no doubt acquire even greater importance after the entry into force of the new regime for world trade resulting from the Uruguay Round.

FRANCIS G JACOBS

---

[46] See Case 269/90, *Technische Universität München-Mitte* [1991] ECR I-5469.
[47] See Toth, *The Oxford Encyclopaedia of European Community Law* (1990), vol. I, p 102.
[48] Case C-353/92, *Greece* v *Council* [1994] ECR I-3411.
[49] Paragraph 50 of the judgment.

Chapter 20
The Scope of the Common Commercial Policy: A Coda on Opinion 1/94

Introduction

The successful conclusion of the Uruguay Round of Multilateral Trade Negotiations in December 1993 brought to a head a long-running dispute over the scope of the European Community's common commercial policy. According to Article 3(b) EC, that policy constitutes one of the "activities" of the Community and it is the subject of Title VII, Part Three, of the Treaty, which consists of Articles 110–116. None of those provisions contains what might be called a definition of the common commercial policy. The closest approximation is Article 113(1), according to which:

"The common commercial policy shall be based on uniform principles, particularly in regard to changes in tariff rates, the conclusion of tariff and trade agreements, the achievement of uniformity in measures of liberalisation, export policy and measures to protect trade such as those to be taken in the event of dumping or subsidies."

That provision does little to answer a question raised in stark form by the Final Act embodying the results of the Uruguay Round, namely whether the common commercial policy is confined to trade in goods or whether it extends to associated areas such as trade in services and trade-related aspects of intellectual property. The importance of the answer to that question lies in the exclusive competence which Article 113 confers on the Community for negotiating and concluding agreements which fall within the scope of the common commercial policy.[1]

Proponents of treating trade in services as part of the common commercial policy do not deny that there are important differences between goods and services.[2] International trade in services will often entail the movement of individuals across national borders. Some types of service transaction may require the supplier to establish a commercial presence in the country of the consumer. These matters have implications for immigration control. By contrast, trade in goods does not necessarily imply the

---

[1] See *e.g.* Opinion 2/91, [1993] 3 CMLR 800 (ILO Convention No 170 concerning safety in the use of chemicals at work), para 8.

[2] See further Eeckhout, *The European Internal Market and International Trade: A Legal Analysis* (1994) ch. 1.

343

movement of people across national frontiers. Moreover, unlike goods, services cannot generally be stored, with the result that "production and consumption coincide".[3]

Notwithstanding the undeniable differences between goods and services, the two are closely related. The products of manufacturing industry may contain not only raw materials but also services provided by independent contractors in the course of the manufacturing process. Sale of the products may involve transport, marketing, insurance and other services. The writing of computer software, for example, may be preserved on disk and sold with a computer along with technical support. The link between goods and services is reflected in the caselaw of the Court of Justice, where a remarkable parallelism has developed between Article 30 EC and Article 59 EC.[4] Moreover, the service sector is now of considerable economic importance, particularly in the developed world. As a result, the argument runs, it would be unrealistic to attempt to construct a trade policy with non-member countries which did not deal with trade in services.

There is also a close link between intellectual property protection and trade in goods. Intellectual property rights have traditionally been regarded as barriers to trade because of the territorial exclusivity they grant to the holder. However, the absence of protection for such rights in a particular national market can be as effective as tariffs or quotas in excluding imports, since producers of goods which incorporate a high degree of intellectual creativity will be reluctant to place them on markets where they cannot be protected against counterfeiting. Under pressure from the developed world, deficiencies in intellectual property protection have therefore assumed a central place in the international trade debate.[5]

Support for the view that matters such as these fall within the scope of the common commercial policy seemed to be provided by Opinion 1/78,[6] which concerned a draft International Agreement on Natural Rubber. There the Court stated that Article 113 could not be interpreted so as "to restrict the common commercial policy to the use of instruments intended to have an effect only on the traditional aspects of external trade to the exclusion of more highly developed mechanisms such as appear in the agreement envisaged. A 'commercial policy' understood in that sense would be destined to become nugatory in the course of time." The Court added that "A restrictive interpretation of the concept of common commercial policy would risk causing disturbances in intra-Community trade

---

[3] *Ibid*, p 11.

[4] Compare Case 120/78, *Rewe* v *Bundesmonopolverwaltung für Branntwein* ("Cassis de Dijon") [1979] ECR 649, with Case C-288/89, *Collectieve Antennevoorziening Gouda* [1991] ECR I-4007, and Case C-353/89, *Commission* v *The Netherlands* [1991] ECR I-4069. For a recent decision concerning the borderline between Articles 30 and 59 EC, see Case C-275/92, *Schindler* [1994] ECR I-1039.

[5] See Govaere, "Intellectual Property Protection and Commercial Policy" in Maresceau (ed), *The European Community's Commercial Policy After 1992: The Legal Dimension* (1993), 197–222 at 199.

[6] [1979] ECR 2871, at 2913, paras 44 and 45.

by reason of the disparities which would then exist in certain sectors of economic relations with non-member countries.''

The Final Act embodying the results of the Uruguay Round

Evidence of the economic link between goods, services and intellectual property is to be found in the Uruguay Round Final Act signed in Marrakesh on 15 April 1994. Annexed to that Act is, *inter alia*,[7] the Agreement Establishing the World Trade Organization (WTO), which is to "provide the common institutional framework for the conduct of trade relations among its Members in matters related to the agreements and associated legal instruments included in the Annexes to this Agreement."[8] There are four such annexes. The first is divided into three parts: Annex 1A is entitled "Multilateral Agreements on Trade in Goods" and includes the GATT 1994, an adapted and consolidated version of the 1947 version of the GATT; Annex 1B contains the new General Agreement on Trade in Services (GATS); Annex 1C contains the new Agreement on Trade-Related Aspects of Intellectual Property Rights (TRIPs). Annex 2 contains an Understanding on Rules and Procedures Governing the Settlement of Disputes and Annex 3 contains a Trade Policy Review Mechanism. These three annexes, referred to as "Multilateral Trade Agreements", constitute integral parts of the WTO Agreement and are binding on all Members.[9] Annex 4 contains a series of so-called Plurilateral Trade Agreements. Their status differs from that of the Multilateral Trade Agreements in that, by virtue of Article II(3) of the WTO Agreement, they do not create obligations or rights for Members that have not accepted them.

According to the Ministerial Declaration of 20 September 1986 which formally launched the Uruguay Round, the negotiations were to be treated as "a single undertaking". The interdependence of each element of the package eventually signed at Marrakesh is strikingly illustrated by the creation of a single institutional structure to administer the Multilateral Trade Agreements and by the Understanding on the settlement of disputes. That Understanding covers[10] both the WTO Agreement and the Multilateral Trade Agreements,[11] as well as the Plurilateral Trade Agreements (subject to the terms of a decision by the parties to each such

---

[7] Also annexed to the Final Act are a number of Ministerial Decisions and Declarations and an Understanding on Commitments in Financial Services.

[8] Art II(1) of the WTO Agreement.

[9] Art II(2) of the WTO Agreement.

[10] See Art 1(1) and Appendix 1.

[11] With the exception of Annex 3, which is not intended to serve as a basis for the enforcement of specific obligations or to impose new policy commitments on Members: point A.(i).

agreement). The Understanding envisages that a complaining party may request authorisation to retaliate against a Member which has been found to be in breach of its obligations. Such retaliation need not be confined to the agreement which has been infringed or to the sector in which the infringement took place.[12] This possibility of so-called "cross-retaliation" significantly strengthens the provisions on the settlement of disputes.

It was not until the conclusion of the Uruguay Round that the institutions and the Member States confronted the question whether the package of agreements it produced fell within the scope of the common commercial policy. That question had arisen in the context of the Tokyo Round of Multilateral Trade Negotiations which came to an end in 1979, but it had not been definitively resolved: a compromise led to all the agreements agreed in that Round being concluded by the Community, two of them also being concluded by the Member States.[13]

The issue spilled over into the new Round of trade negotiations which began at Punta del Este in 1986. From the outset, these took place on the basis that the question of the competence of the Community and the Member States on particular issues should not be prejudged. Thus, the Ministerial Declaration which formally launched the new Round was approved by both the Council, acting on the basis of a Commission recommendation, and by the Governments of the Member States. However, the negotiations themselves were conducted by the Commission alone on behalf of the Community and the Member States.

The Final Act embodying the results of the Uruguay Round and the WTO Agreement were finally signed in Marrakesh on behalf of the Community by the President of the Council and the Commissioner for External Economic Relations. However, the Member States took the view that the Act and the WTO Agreement covered areas that also fell within national competence. They therefore proceeded to sign them in Marrakesh alongside the Community.

The reference to the Court of Justice

Although, apparently for political reasons, the Commission had not opposed the participation of the Member States as original Members of the WTO,[14] it made it clear that, in its view, the Final Act and the WTO Agreement fell within the exclusive competence of the Community. Accordingly, on 6 April 1994 the Commission submitted a request to the

---

[12] See Art 22 of the Understanding.
[13] See further Bourgeois, "The Tokyo Round Agreements on Technical Barriers and on Government Procurement in International and EEC Perspective" (1982) 19 CMLRev 5–33 at 21.
[14] See Art XI(1) of the WTO Agreement.

Court under Article 228(6) with a view to securing a definitive ruling on the matter.[15] Article 228(6) provides as follows:

"The Council, the Commission or a Member State may obtain the opinion of the Court of Justice as to whether an agreement envisaged is compatible with the provisions of this Treaty. Where the opinion of the Court of Justice is adverse, the agreement may enter into force only in accordance with Article N of the Treaty on European Union."

Article N of the TEU sets out the procedure for amending the Treaties.

The procedure followed by the Court under Article 228(6) is the subject of Articles 107 and 108 of its Rules of Procedure.[16] Where a request is presented by the Commission, the Council and the Member States have the right to submit observations. That right was exercised by the Council and the Governments of Denmark, Germany, Greece, Spain, France, the Netherlands, Portugal and the United Kingdom. The Rules make no express provision for observations to be submitted by the European Parliament but, at the Parliament's request, the Court allowed it to do so, following the precedent set in the proceedings which led to the Court's second Opinion on the draft EEA Agreement.[17] It may be noted that the third countries or international organisations with which the Community intends to conclude the agreement concerned have no right to take part in the proceedings.

The questions referred to the Court concerned two particular issues. First, they were designed to establish whether or not the Community had exclusive competence to conclude the Multilateral Agreements on Trade in Goods, in so far as those Agreements related to products covered by the ECSC and Euratom Treaties. Secondly, and more importantly, they were concerned with the problem of whether the Community had exclusive competence to conclude GATS and TRIPs. As the Council pointed out, the WTO Agreement, which does not comprise any provisions of a substantive nature, did not give rise to any particular problems of competence: competence to participate in the institutional arrangements depended on competence to conclude the substantive provisions laid down elsewhere.

There was no dispute over the desirability of concluding the WTO Agreement and its Annexes. Moreover, it was common ground that, because the WTO Agreement established a specific institutional framework, Article 228(3) EC would require the assent of the European Parliament to be obtained. There also seemed to be agreement that the Council should act unanimously.[18]

---

[15] See Opinion 1/94 1, [1994] ECR I-5267. The following account is confined to the main issues discussed by the Court.

[16] See further Lasok, *The European Court of Justice: Practice and Procedure* (1994, 2nd ed), pp 590–592; Brown and Kennedy, *The Court of Justice of the European Communities* (1994, 4th ed), pp 240–243.

[17] Opinion 1/92, [1992] ECR I-2821.

[18] See Art 228(2).

Preliminary matters

Before addressing the main issues raised by the Commission, the Court dealt with a number of preliminary matters. It will be observed that Article 228(6) does not expressly provide for the Court's Opinion to be requested on the extent to which an agreement falls within the competence of the Community. According to Article 107(2) of the Court's Rules of Procedure, however, "The Opinion may deal not only with the question whether the envisaged agreement is compatible with the provisions of the E[E]C Treaty but also with the question whether the Community or any Community institution has the power to enter into that agreement." The Rules of Procedure evidently cannot alter the scope of the jurisdiction conferred on the Court by the Treaty, but the Court pointed out[19] that it had consistently held that the extent of the Community's power to enter into an agreement may be considered under Article 228(6). The Court did not share the doubts expressed by the Council and the Netherlands Government over whether an agreement which had already been signed constituted "an agreement envisaged" for the purposes of Article 228(6). As long as the Community's consent to be bound by the agreement in question had not been finally expressed, the Court declared that it could be asked for an Opinion in accordance with that Article.

According to Article VII of the WTO Agreement, each member is to contribute to the expenses of the WTO. Since the Member States were to be original members of the WTO, the Portuguese Government maintained that this was enough to justify the conclusion of the Agreement by the Member States. That argument allowed the Court to address an apparent conflict between two of its earlier Opinions. In Opinion 1/75, it was held that the Community had exclusive competence by virtue of Article 113 to take part in the Understanding on a Local Cost Standard drawn up under the auspices of the OECD. The Court considered it "of little importance that the obligations and financial burdens inherent in the execution of the agreement envisaged are borne directly by the Member States."[20] By contrast, in Opinion 1/78 the Court ruled that, if the financing of the draft International Agreement on Natural Rubber was to be the responsibility of the Member States, "that will imply the participation of those States in the decision-making machinery or, at least, their agreement with regard to the arrangements for financing envisaged and consequently their participation in the agreement together with the Community. The exclusive competence of the Community could not be envisaged in such a case."[21] The Commission pointed out that the WTO's budget was simply a consequence of the pursuit of the organisation's general objectives. The Court therefore concluded:

---

[19] See para 9.
[20] [1975] ECR 1355 at 1364.
[21] [1979] ECR 2871, at 2918, para 60.

"Given that the WTO is an international organisation which will have only an operating budget and not a financial policy instrument, the fact that the Member States will bear some of its expenses cannot, on any view, of itself justify participation of the Member States in the conclusion of the WTO Agreement."[22]

Article 113 and The Multilateral Agreements on Trade in Goods

The Commission and those who submitted observations were broadly in agreement that, to the extent that the Multilateral Agreements on Trade in Goods affected goods which fell within the scope of the EC Treaty, those Agreements were covered by the exclusive competence enjoyed by the Community under Article 113.[23] Even in so far as they extended to Euratom products, the exclusive competence of the Community was not contested. Since the status of such products had been raised by the Commission, however, the Court remarked:

"Article 232(2) of the EC Treaty states that the provisions of that Treaty 'shall not derogate from those of the Treaty establishing the European Atomic Energy Community.' Since the Euratom Treaty contains no provisions relating to external trade, there is nothing to prevent agreements concluded pursuant to Article 113 of the EC Treaty from extending to international trade in Euratom products."[24]

The question of products covered by the ECSC Treaty proved more controversial. The Council and most of the Member States argued that, in so far as the Agreements on Trade in Goods covered such products, those Agreements had to be concluded by the Member States in view of Article 71 ECSC. According to the first paragraph of that Article, "The powers of the Governments of Member States in matters of commercial policy shall not be affected by this Treaty, save as otherwise provided therein." By virtue of Article 232(1) of the EC Treaty, that Treaty does not affect the ECSC Treaty, in particular as regards the rights and obligations of Member States and the powers of the institutions.

The Court pointed out that Article 71 ECSC could only have been intended to apply to coal and steel since, when the ECSC Treaty was drawn up, the EEC was not yet in existence. Accordingly, that Article could only preserve the international competence of the Member States in relation to agreements which dealt specifically with those products. It was the EC which had exclusive competence under Article 113 to conclude international agreements of a general nature covering all goods, even if they extended to coal and steel.[25] Since none of the Multilateral Agreements on Trade in Goods was concerned specifically with coal or steel, it followed

---

[22] Para 21.
[23] The Council, the European Parliament and the United Kingdom Government thought that recourse to Art 43 was also necessary because agricultural products would be affected, a view rejected by the Court: see paras 28–31. Had it been accepted, the exclusive competence of the Community would not in any event have been called into question.
[24] Para 24.
[25] cf. Opinion 1/75, *supra*, n 20 at 1365.

that the Community's exclusive competence to conclude them was not affected by the fact that they covered those products.

The Court therefore concluded that the Community had exclusive competence under Article 113 to conclude the Multilateral Agreements on Trade in Goods.

Article 113 and GATS

The Commission's view that GATS fell within the exclusive competence of the Community by virtue of Article 113 was vigorously contested by the Council, by the Member States which presented observations and by the European Parliament. The Court looked first at services other than transport and then at transport services.

The Court accepted that the increasing importance of the services sector in international trade and the "open nature of the common commercial policy"[26] meant that trade in services could not be excluded as a matter of principle from the ambit of Article 113. In order to establish the precise extent to which trade in services was covered by that Article, it was necessary to consider the definition of "trade in services" given in Article I(2) of GATS. The Court explained that that definition embraced four ways in which services could be supplied:[27]

"(1) cross-frontier supplies not involving any movement of persons; (2) consumption abroad, which entails the movement of the consumer into the territory of the WTO member country in which the supplier is established; (3) commercial presence, *i.e.* the presence of a subsidiary or branch in the territory of the WTO member country in which the service is to be rendered; (4) the presence of natural persons from a WTO member country, enabling a supplier from one member country to supply services within the territory of any other member country."

The Court observed that, in the case of cross-frontier supplies, the service is provided by a supplier established in one country to a consumer resident in another. An example given by the Council was the supply of an electrical installation project by a firm of architects established in country A to a firm of engineers established in country B. In a situation such as this, the supplier does not move to the country of the consumer and the consumer does not move to that of the supplier. There was, said the Court, an analogy between that situation and trade in goods, which unquestionably fell within the scope of the common commercial policy. There was no reason why such a supply of services should not also be covered by that policy.

The position with regard to the three other modes of supply of services covered by GATS was different. Article 3 EC distinguished between the

---

[26] Para 41.
[27] Para 43.

common commercial policy, mentioned in paragraph (b), and "measures concerning the entry and movement of persons . . .", referred to in paragraph (d). This indicated that the treatment received by nationals of third countries when they crossed the external frontiers of the Member States could not be considered an aspect of the common commercial policy. In more general terms, the Court saw in the presence in the Treaty of Chapters devoted specifically to the free movement of persons confirmation that, where the supply of a service involved the movement of a natural or legal person across a national frontier, it fell outside the scope of the common commercial policy.

As far as transport was concerned, the Court observed that this was the subject of a separate Title of the EC Treaty, Title IV, which was distinct from Title VII on the common commercial policy. The Court noted that it was in the context of transport policy that it had held in the *ERTA* case[28] that the Community may derive exclusive competence in the international field not only where it is expressly conferred by the Treaty, as in the case of Articles 113 and 238 (which concerns association agreements), but also under other provisions of the Treaty and from legislation adopted by the Community institutions. As the Court pointed out, "The idea underlying that decision is that international agreements in transport matters are not covered by Article 113."[29]

The Court refused to accept that a distinction could be drawn between agreements dealing with safety rules, such as the one at issue in *ERTA*, and agreements of a commercial nature.[30] No such distinction had been drawn in the *ERTA* case. Moreover, the approach taken there had been followed in Opinion 1/76,[31] which concerned an economic agreement unconnected with the laying down of safety rules. It was irrelevant that a series of embargoes[32] involving the suspension of transport services had been adopted on the basis of Article 113. Those measures were concerned principally with the import and export of goods and would have been ineffective had they not involved the suspension of transport services, which was to be seen as "a necessary adjunct to the principal measure."[33] In any event, the practice of the institutions could not be decisive as to the choice of the correct legal basis.[34] The Court therefore concluded that international agreements in the field of transport also fell outside the scope of the common commercial policy.

---

[28] Case 22/70, *Commission* v *Council* [1971] ECR 263, at 274, paras 16–18.

[29] Para 48.

[30] A distinction of that type was advocated by Van Rijn, "Transport Policy and Commercial Policy" in Maresceau (ed), *op cit*, n 5, 249–266 at 260–262.

[31] [1977] ECR 741 (draft Agreement establishing a European laying-up fund for inland waterway vessels).

[32] Listed in para 51 of the Opinion.

[33] *Ibid.*

[34] See Case 68/86, *United Kingdom* v *Council* [1988] ECR 855, at 898, para 24.

Article 113 and TRIPs

The Commission's claim that the Community had exclusive competence to conclude TRIPs was also vigorously contested. The Court noted that Section 4 of Part III of TRIPs, which concerns the enforcement of intellectual property rights, contained special requirements relating to border measures. That Section corresponded to Council Regulation 3842/86 laying down measures to prohibit the release for free circulation of counterfeit goods.[35] That Regulation had been correctly based on Article 113: it was concerned with the measures to be taken by customs authorities at the Community's external borders. Because measures of that nature could be adopted by the Community institutions on the basis of Article 113, it was for the Community alone to enter into international agreements on such matters.

With the exception of the provisions of TRIPs concerned with prohibiting the release for free circulation of counterfeit goods, the Commission's point of view could not, according to the Court, be sustained. The Court acknowledged that there was a link between intellectual property and trade in goods. That link was not sufficient to bring intellectual property rights within the scope of Article 113, however, since such rights were not concerned specifically with international trade: they affected internal trade "just as much as, if not more than, international trade."[36] The principal objective of TRIPs was to strengthen and harmonise the protection of intellectual property rights on a global scale. As the Commission had admitted, since TRIPs laid down rules in areas which had not been harmonised at the Community level, its conclusion would facilitate such harmonisation and thereby contribute to the functioning of the common market. On the internal level, the Community had the power to harmonise national laws on intellectual property under Articles 100 and 100a EC. It could also use Article 235 to create new rights over and above those existing under national law. That Article had been used as the basis for Regulation 40/94 on the Community trade mark.[37] The use of these provisions of the Treaty was subject to voting rules and procedural requirements which differed from those laid down by Article 113. If the Court were to accept that the Community had exclusive competence to conclude agreements with third countries designed to harmonise the protection of intellectual property which resulted in such harmonisation within the Community, the Community institutions would be able to evade the procedural requirements and voting rules to which they were subject internally.

The Commission sought to rely on a number of cases[38] in which reliance had been placed on Regulation 2641/84,[39] the so-called new

---

[35] OJ 1986 L357/1.
[36] Para 57.
[37] OJ 1994 L11/1.
[38] See para 62 of the Court's Opinion.
[39] On the strengthening of the common commercial policy with regard in particular to protection against illicit commercial practices, OJ 1984 L252/1 (legal basis: Art 113). See Govaere, *supra*, n 5 at 201–202.

commercial policy instrument, in order to defend the interests of the Community in the field of intellectual property. However, the Court pointed out that the measures which could be taken under that instrument enabled the Community to react to the absence of protection in third countries for the intellectual property rights of Community undertakings and against discrimination against such undertakings in that field. Such measures fell by their very nature within the scope of the Community's commercial policy. They were not connected with the harmonisation of intellectual property protection, which was the main objective of TRIPs.

The Commission also sought to rely on measures taken by the Community to suspend generalised tariff preferences accorded to a third country which was discriminating between its trading partners in connection with the protection of intellectual property. The Court did not find that argument convincing either. Both the grant and the suspension of generalised tariff preferences constituted measures of commercial policy,[40] but that did not mean that the Community had exclusive competence under Article 113 to conclude with third countries agreements designed to harmonise intellectual property protection on a global scale.

The Court therefore concluded that, apart from the provisions concerning the prohibition on the release for free circulation of counterfeit goods, TRIPs fell outside the scope of the common commercial policy.

Implied powers

The Commission argued that, even if the Community did not enjoy exclusive competence by virtue of Article 113, such a competence derived from either (a) the provisions of the Treaty giving the Community internal competence, or (b) the existence of legislation adopted by the institutions intended to implement those provisions, or (c) the need to conclude international agreements in order to achieve an objective for which the Community was responsible internally. The Commission also maintained that, if adequate powers could not be derived from specific provisions of the Treaty or from acts of the institutions, exclusive competence flowed from Articles 100a and 235 EC. While accepting that the Community had certain powers, the Council and the Member States which presented observations denied that they were exclusive in nature.

GATS

The Commission maintained that the Community had powers to take internal measures in all the areas covered by GATS. Those powers were to be found in the Chapters on the right of establishment and the freedom to

---

[40] See Case 45/86, *Commission* v *Council* [1987] ECR 1493, at 1522, para 21; Govaere, *supra*, n 5 at 203.

provide services and in the Title on transport. The Community's internal powers implied the existence of exclusive external competence.

The Court did not agree. As far as transport was concerned, it had been accepted in *ERTA*[41] that, because Article 75(1)(a) covered international transport to or from non-member States, the Community's competence extended to the conclusion of international agreements. However, the Court had made it clear that the Member States only lost their power to enter into agreements with third countries to the extent that common rules had been established within the Community which might be affected by such agreements. Only where common rules had been laid down internally did the Community's competence become exclusive. Not all transport matters had yet been made the subject of common rules. It was no answer to say that, if the Member States remained free to enter into bilateral agreements with third countries, the result would be to distort the flow of services and undermine the internal market. The Court pointed out that there was nothing in the Treaty to prevent the institutions from establishing, within the framework of common rules, a concerted approach to third countries or from laying down the approach to be taken by Member States to the outside world.

Unlike the Title on transport,[42] the Chapters on establishment and services contained no provision expressly giving the Community competence to conclude international agreements. The sole objective of those Chapters was to confer on the nationals of the Member States the right of establishment and the freedom to provide services. They contained no provisions dealing with the right of nationals of third countries to establish themselves for the first time in the territory of a Member State or with their right to provide services. It could not therefore be said that those Chapters conferred on the Community exclusive competence to conclude with third States an agreement designed to liberalise the right of first establishment and access to the market for services other than those which could be provided on a cross-border basis, which had already been held to fall within the scope of Article 113.

The Commission pointed out that, according to the Court's subsequent caselaw, the principles laid down in *ERTA* were not confined to situations where the Community had laid down rules within the framework of a common policy. According to Opinion 1/76,[43] where Community law conferred on the institutions internal powers to achieve a particular objective, the Community had implied power to act at the international level. It was enough if the participation of the Community in an international agreement was necessary to achieve one of the objectives of the Community. According to the Commission, the proper functioning of the

---

[41] [1971] ECR 263, at 275, para 27.

[42] *Sic* see para 81 of the Opinion. In fact, the Court held in *ERTA* that the Treaty did not expressly confer on the Community authority to enter into international agreements in the sphere of transport policy, but that such authority flowed from the general system of the Treaty.

[43] *Supra*, n 31 at 755, paras 3 and 4.

internal market would be prejudiced if the Community did not have exclusive competence to conclude GATS and TRIPs.

The Court was unconvinced. The circumstances which had given rise to Opinion 1/76 were different: there the involvement of third countries was indispensable if the agreement envisaged was to achieve its objective. It was for that reason that the Court had held that the Community had external competence even in the absence of internal legislation and that that competence became exclusive once it was exercised. In the case of GATS, however, there was not necessarily any link between (a) the right of establishment and the right to provide services of nationals of the Member States within the Community, and (b) the rights of nationals of third countries in the Community and of nationals of the Member States in third countries.

The Court then turned to Article 100a. When the Community's power to harmonise national laws had been exercised, the Court acknowledged that measures taken under that Article could have the effect of limiting the freedom of the Member States to negotiate with third countries or even of removing that freedom completely. However, there could be no question of the Community's power to harmonise internally creating an exclusive external competence in areas where that power had not been exercised. As for Article 235, that provision could not in itself confer on the Community exclusive competence to conclude international agreements. With the exception of cases where internal competence could only be usefully exercised at the same time as external competence, such as the circumstances which gave rise to Opinion 1/76, an internal competence could only give rise to external competence once it had been exercised. That principle applied equally to Article 235.

Although the sole objective expressly mentioned in the Chapters on the right of establishment and the freedom to provide services was the achievement of those rights for nationals of the Member States, it did not follow that the Community institutions had no right to use their powers under those Chapters to regulate the treatment of nationals of non-member States. Indeed, a number of measures adopted by the Council[44] under Articles 54 and 57(2) contained provisions on that subject or conferred on the Community institutions power to negotiate with third countries. Whenever that was the case, the Court concluded that the Community acquired exclusive external competence in the field covered by the legislation concerned. Even in the absence of provisions expressly conferring on its institutions power to negotiate with third countries, the Community enjoyed such competence where it had achieved complete harmonisation of the rules governing access to a given self-employed activity, because the common rules thereby laid down might be affected within the meaning of the *ERTA* case if the Member States remained free

---

[44] For examples, see paras 92–94 of the Opinion. The Court appeared to reproach the Council for not having mentioned the measures in question: see para 90.

to negotiate with third countries. However, as the Commission had acknowledged, the Community had not adopted legislation of that nature for all service sectors. The Court therefore concluded that competence to conclude GATS was shared between the Community and the Member States.

TRIPs

Here again the Commission sought to rely on the *ERTA* case, on Opinion 1/76 and on Articles 100a and 235. The Court did not consider Opinion 1/76 helpful: the unification or harmonisation of intellectual property rights within the Community did not have to be accompanied by agreements with third countries in order to be effective. As for Articles 100a and 235, the Court reiterated that these were not enough in themselves to confer exclusive competence on the Community.

Was there Community legislation which was liable to be affected within the meaning of the *ERTA* case if TRIPs was concluded by the Member States? The Court observed that, in some fields covered by TRIPs, the harmonisation which had been achieved within the Community was only partial and that, in others, no harmonisation was envisaged. For example, Directive 89/104 on the harmonisation of the laws of the Member States relating to trade marks[45] was confined, according to its preamble, to national laws "which most directly affect the functioning of the internal market." In other areas covered by TRIPs, no harmonising legislation had been adopted by the Community. Examples were the protection of undisclosed information, industrial designs, for which proposals had merely been presented,[46] and patents. In relation to patents, the Commission had only referred to intergovernmental conventions rather than Community acts: the Convention on the Grant of European Patents and the Agreement relating to Community Patents.[47] The latter was in any event not yet in force.

Some of the Member States argued that the provisions of TRIPs on the enforcement of intellectual property rights,[48] in particular those relating to the guarantee of fair and equitable procedures, evidence, the opportunity to be heard, the reasoning of decisions, the right of appeal, injunctions and damages, fell within national competence. The Court remarked that, if that argument was to be understood as meaning that those matters fell within "some sort of domain reserved to the Member States",[49] it could not be accepted. There was no doubt that the Community was competent to harmonise national laws on those matters where, in the

---

[45] OJ 1989 L40/1.
[46] See OJ 1993 C345/14; OJ 1994 C29/20.
[47] OJ 1989 L401/1.
[48] See Part III of TRIPs.
[49] Para 104.

words of Article 100 EC, they "directly affect the establishment or functioning of the common market." None the less, the Community institutions had not yet exercised their powers in the field of the enforcement of intellectual property rights, except in the case of Regulation 3842/86 on counterfeit goods.

The Court therefore concluded that competence to conclude TRIPs was also shared between the Community and the Member States.

The duty of co-operation

The Court concluded its Opinion with some remarks on the duty of the Member States and the Commuity institutions to co-operate with each other in the framework of the Uruguay Round Agreements. The Commission had emphasised the practical difficulties which would inevitably arise in the implementation of those Agreements if the Court found that competence to conclude them was shared. The Court acknowledged that that concern was a legitimate one, but refused to accept that difficulties of that nature could have the effect of altering the answer to be given on the question of competence, "that being a prior issue."[50]

The Court recognised that it was important to ensure that there was close co-operation between the institutions of the Community and the Member States in giving effect to international agreements for which competence was shared. The duty to co-operate was "all the more imperative"[51] in the present case in view of the inextricable link between the Agreements annexed to the WTO Agreement and of the system of cross-retaliation for which provision was made in the Understanding on the settlement of disputes. In the absence of such co-operation, the Community and the Member States might not be able to take advantage of that system: if the Community obtained the right to retaliate in the goods sector but was unable to exercise it, it would not have the power to retaliate in the fields covered by GATS or TRIPs, since those fell within the competence of the Member States. Conversely, if a Member State, having been authorised to retaliate in the fields covered by GATS or TRIPs, wished to do so in the field of trade in goods, it might be unable to do so since the latter fell within the exclusive competence of the Community. The Court did not, however, offer any practical suggestions as to how the necessary co-operation might be ensured,[52] presumably taking the view that that issue fell within the competence of the political institutions and the Member States.

---

[50] Para 107.
[51] Para 109.
[52] Although this was the subject of one of a series of questions put by the Court to those who took part in the proceedings.

Comment

Because the Community's external competence mirrors its internal competence, the significance of the procedure laid down in Article 228(6) is not confined to the sphere of external relations. That procedure has become one of the principal mechanisms for identifying the fields where the Community shares competence internally with the Member States and where, in accordance with the second paragraph of Article 3b of the Treaty, the principle of subsidiarity is applicable. That issue provides fertile ground for conflict between the Commission and the Member States.

Notwithstanding the welcome it received from Sir Leon Brittan, the Commissioner responsible for external trade,[53] Opinion 1/94 joins a growing catalogue of spectacular errors of judgment by the Commission. In Opinion 1/91,[54] the Court found that the system of judicial supervision contained in the draft EEA Agreement, which had been painstakingly negotiated by the Commission with the countries of the European Free Trade Association and with Liechtenstein, was incompatible with the EEC Treaty. In Opinion 2/91,[55] the Court rejected the Commission's contention that the Community had exclusive competence to conclude ILO Convention 170 concerning safety in the use of chemicals at work. In the notorious *BASF* case, a series of procedural errors led the Court of First Instance to find a Commission decision on the application of Article 85 EC non-existent.[56] An appeal by the Commission to the Court of Justice was only partly successful, the Court declaring the contested measure void.[57] Although the outcome protected the Commission from a potentially unlimited number of claims submitted outside the time limit laid down in Article 173, a prospect opened up by the judgment of the Court of First Instance, the Court did not endorse the Commission's apparently cavalier attitude to its own Rules of Procedure.

It is a matter for considerable disquiet that, in the approach to 1996, the Commission should appear to be so out of touch with the mood of the other institutions and of the Member States. The Court's conclusion in Opinion 1/94 that an extended definition of the common commercial policy was incompatible with the Community's exclusive jurisdiction under Article 113 had been foreshadowed in the literature.[58] Had the Court accepted the Commission's view that Article 113 extended to any international agreement which was liable to produce a direct or indirect effect on

---

[53] See *Europe* and the *Financial Times* of 16 November 1994.

[54] [1991] ECR I-6079.

[55] *Supra*, n 1.

[56] Joined Cases T-79/89 etc., *BASF and others* v *Commission* [1992] ECR II-315.

[57] Case C-137/92 P, *Commission* v *BASF and others* [1994] ECR I-2555.

[58] See Gilsdorf, "Portée et délimitation des compétences communautaire en matière de politique commerciale" (1989) RMC, 195–207 at 197–198; Van Rijn, *supra*, n 30 at 263–265. *Cf.* Eeckhout, *op cit*, n 2 at 32–34; Mengozzi, "Trade in Services and Commercial Policy" in Maresceau (ed), *op cit*, n 5, 223–247 at 234–243.

the volume or structure of commercial trade, the result would have been to transform the common commercial policy into a common policy on external economic relations. A number of those who submitted observations pointed out that a Commission proposal to amend the Treaty along those lines was rejected at the Intergovernmental Conference on Political Union.[59] Given the close connection between commercial policy and foreign policy in the general sense,[60] for the Court to have accepted the Commission's claim to exclusive competence would have been quite out of keeping with the spirit underlying Title V of the Maastricht Treaty, which is essentially intergovernmental in character.

In the absence of a proper Treaty basis, the Court has traditionally been reluctant to interfere with the right of Member States to control immigration from outside the Community.[61] That reluctance is reflected in its unwillingness to allow the movement of third country nationals across the Community's external borders to be regulated as part of the common commercial policy. Article 100c EC, introduced at Maastricht, now provides a legal basis for the Council to regulate aspects of such movement. Opinion 1/94 shows that the Court remains unwilling to bring that subject within the scope of other provisions of the Treaty which were not specifically designed to deal with it.

The Court's reliance on the discrepancy between the voting rules and procedural requirements laid down by Articles 100, 100a and 235 on the one hand, and Article 113 on the other, to justify excluding the harmonisation of intellectual property protection from the scope of the common commercial policy is not entirely convincing. That discrepancy merely reflects the lack of coherence in the voting rules and procedural requirements laid down by the various provisions of the Treaty which confer legislative powers on the institutions. That issue may be addressed in 1996 when, according to a declaration made at Maastricht, the establishment of an appropriate hierarchy between the different categories of Community act is to be considered. Should such a hierarchy be established, the procedural requirements laid down by a particular provision might give some indication of the substantive scope it is intended to have. In the meantime, the Court's Opinion seems to imply that disputes over the legal basis of a proposed act should be determined, not by the substantive scope of the competing bases, but by the procedural requirements they lay down. That approach is difficult to reconcile with the *Titanium Dioxide* judgment,

---

[59] See Maresceau, "The Concept 'Common Commercial Policy' and the Difficult Road to Maastricht" in Maresceau (ed), *op cit*, n 5, 3–19.

[60] See Gilsdorf, *supra*, n 58 at 196. Arts C and J.1(4) TEU, which concern the external activites of the Union, were cited by the Council in connection with the practical difficulties which, according to the Commission, joint competence would entail.

[61] See *e.g.* Joined Cases 35 and 36/82, *Morson and Jhanjan* v *State of the Netherlands* [1982] ECR 3723; Joined Cases 281, 283 to 285 and 287/85, *Germany, France, Netherlands, Denmark and United Kingdom* v *Commission* [1987] ECR 3203. For a useful short discussion, see Weatherill and Beaumont, *EC Law* (1993) 503–506.

where the Court said that the choice of legal basis had to be based on objective factors such as the aim and the content of the measure in question.[62]

The rejection by the Court of the argument of some Member States that the provisions of TRIPs on the enforcement of intellectual property rights fell within national competence might be taken as an encouragement to the Commission to bring forward legislation under Article 100 EC harmonising the conditions in which claims against Member States under the *Francovich*[63] ruling may be brought. Discrepancies between the laws of the Member States on matters such as evidence, injunctions, damages and other remedies, all covered by Part III of TRIPs, directly affect the functioning of the common market. The Court's Opinion confirms that the necessary legislation can be adopted under Article 100 of the Treaty and that no specific legal basis is required.

Reference has already been made to the procedure followed by the Court under Article 228(6).[64] One of the most striking features of that procedure is that no formal Advocate General's Opinion is delivered. By virtue of Article 108(2) of the Rules of Procedure, the Court delivers its Opinion "after hearing the Advocates General", but their views are not made public. In practice, however, the advice of the Advocates General is normally embodied in a document of some kind. There may either be separate documents submitted to the Court by each Advocate General or a single document on which they have all agreed. It is submitted that neither arrangement is as satisfactory as the normal procedure under which a single Advocate General is assigned to a case: the delivery of multiple "Opinions" dilutes their effect, especially if they take different approaches; a collective "Opinion" is liable to be the product of compromise. Be that as it may, when the views of the Advocates General are expressed in written form, they should be published.

ANTHONY ARNULL

---

[62] See Case C-300/89, *Commission v Council* [1991] ECR I-2867. *Cf.* Eeckhout, *op cit,* n 2 at 29.
[63] Joined Cases C-6/90 and C-9/90, [1991] ECR I-5357.
[64] See *supra,* n 16 and accompanying text.

Part 6

The EU and China:
A Continuing Saga

Chapter 21
Legal Aspects of Trade Between The European Union and China: Preliminary Reflections

Introduction

Trade between the European Union (EU) and the People's Republic of China (PRC, China) is set to increase dramatically during the next decade. With this prospect in mind, the European Commission recently issued a Communication to the Council proposing a new Asian strategy.[1] It concluded, among other things, that the EU should give Asia a higher priority, place greater emphasis on pro-active economic co-operation, and help countries such as China, which are moving from state controls to market-oriented economies, to integrate into the market-based world trading system.[2] Thus, the EU might benefit from the fact that, together with other Asian countries, China is expected to provide half of the growth in the global economy by the year 2000.[3]

What is the role of law in these changes? This question underlies a research project of which this paper presents some preliminary reflections. In trying to answer the question, it will doubtless be necessary to distinguish between the viewpoints of the two trading partners, the EU and China, and that of an outside observer.[4] In the light of east Asian legal history, particularly that of China since World War II,[5] the outside observer might be tempted to discount the importance of law. It has recently been asserted, however, that law has been among the most important factors in the Pacific economic boom.[6] With this in mind, one may advance the following hypothesis: law, legal processes and legal culture will

---

[1] Commission of the European Communities, "Towards a New Asian Strategy" (Communication from the Commission to the Council), COM(94)314 final, Brussels, 13 July 1994.

[2] *Ibid* at 24. A concrete illustration of the new strategy in the field of economic co-operation is the Financing Agreement signed on 31 January 1995 regarding the second phase of the EC-ASEAN COGEN Programme concerning the transfer of technology in the field of energy production. See European Commission Spokesman's Service, 31 February 1995.

[3] *Ibid* at 1; see also United Nations, *World Economic and Social Survey 1994* (1994).

[4] On Chinese academic perspectives on Europe as of 1987, see Kapur, *As China Sees the World: Perceptions of Chinese Scholars* (1987).

[5] For example, see Chen, "A Review of Third Years of Legal Studies in New China", (1988) 2 *Journal of Chinese Law* 181; Lubman, "Studying Contemporary Chinese Law: Limits, Possibilities and Strategy", (1991) 39 *American Journal of Comparative Law* 293; Zheng, "The Evolving Role of Lawyers and Legal Practice in China", (1988) 36 *American Journal of Comparative Law* 423.

[6] Yasuda, "The Evolution of the East Asian Law Region", unpublished paper (1994), at 1.

play an important, though rarely determinative, role in future relations between the EU and China.

Against this background this paper discusses some legal aspects of trade between the EU and China. It begins with a brief sketch of the historical context. Then it describes the evolution of framework trade agreements, the common rules on imports and special rules concerning textiles. A subsequent section considers some controversial current issues. The last section sets forth several general conclusions.

Historical overview

Trade relations between Europe and China have a long history.[7] For the present purposes, however, it is sufficient to begin after World War II.[8] Trade between China and Western Europe has continued, despite an embargo imposed by the United States, since the early 1950s.

A series of important changes occurred during the 1970s. They were stimulated by the accession of new Member States to the European Community (EC), the resumption by China of its seat in the UN in October 1971, and the establishment by a number of EC Member States (Italy, Belgium, Federal Republic of Germany, Luxembourg) of diplomatic relations with China. At the end of 1974 the trade agreements between the EC Member States and various so-called "state-trading countries" were due to expire. At that time, the EC and China expressed the wish for a trade agreement. In May 1975 Sir Christopher Soames, then the Vice-President of the Commission, visited Beijing. This visit established a basis for diplomatic relations between the EC and China, beginning on 16 September 1975. It also led to an expansion of trade and economic relations between the two parties. In 1983 these relations were expanded to include the ECSC and Euratom. A delegation of the EC Commission was established in China in May 1988.

Trade relations between the EC and China increased especially in 1978 and 1985–86. In 1978, the "four modernisations" programme in China focused on science and technology, industry, agriculture and defence. It led to the conclusion of the first Trade Agreement between the EEC and the People's Republic of China.[9] A special agreement on trade in textiles was signed in the same year.[10] Then, in 1985–86, Chinese imports of EC goods increased, as did EC investments in and loans to China. This led to

---

[7] See, *e.g.*, Thompson, *Silk, Carpets and the Silk Road* (1988).

[8] For a historical account of political and economic relations between the EC and China, see Kapur, *Distant Neighbours: Europe and China* (1990).

[9] Trade Agreement between the European Economic Community and the People's Republic of China, OJ 1978 L123/1. See also the EEC-China Textile Agreement, OJ 1986 L389/3.

[10] EEC-China Textile Agreement, OJ 1986 L389/3.

the conclusion in 1985 of a new Trade and Economic Co-operation Agreement.[11]

During the past decade trade relations between the EC and China have continued steadily, interrupted only (and even then not entirely) by the immediate post-Tianenmen Square period of EC trade sanctions between 4 June 1989 and 22 October 1990. As of 1992 China ranked eleventh in the world in terms of export volume. The EC was China's second largest trading partner, ranking ahead of the United States and (if Hong Kong is not counted separately) behind only Japan. It supplied 12% of Chinese imports and absorbed 9% of Chinese exports.[12] It was also the third largest investor in China, following the United States and Japan (and again not counting Hong Kong separately). It was the leading supplier of high-technology know-how and equipment to China.[13] Despite these factors, the EU has a growing trade deficit with China: by 1992 it amounted to approximately ten billion ECUs.[14]

Trade and co-operation agreements

The general legal framework of EU-China trade relations consists of EU (EC) law, the law of the EU Member States, Chinese law and the GATT.[15] The following discussion concentrates mainly on the first source, which falls within the common commercial policy.

The first Trade Agreement between the European Economic Community and the People's Republic of China (the Trade Agreement) was signed in 1978.[16] It was the first trade agreement concluded by the EC with a state-trading country. It provided a general legal framework for EC-China trade.

The cornerstone of EC-China trade, as provided in the Trade Agreement, was a most-favoured-nation (MFN) clause. The MFN clause did not apply, however, to treatment accorded to other members of customs unions or free trade areas, to neighbouring countries, or to measures taken to meet obligations under international commodity agreements. More restrictive than the MFN clause in the GATT, this clause placed

---

[11] Trade and Co-operation Agreement between the European Economic Community and the People's Republic of China, OJ 1985 L250/1.

[12] European Communities, *Eurostat* (31st edn, 1994), table 6.15, p 321.

[13] Xiao, *The EC and China* (1993), pp 3–4.

[14] The EU trade deficit with China declined to approximately nine billion ECU by 1993; see *Agence Europe*, no 6179 (n.s.), Saturday 26 February 1994, p 5.

[15] For a more detailed analysis of the period prior to 1993, see Hu, *Legal and Policy Issues of the Trade and Economic Relations between the China and the EEC: A Comparative Study* (1991) and Xiao, *The EC and China* (1993), on which this section is partly based.

[16] Trade Agreement between the European Economic Community and China, OJ 1978 L123/1. See also Council Regulation 3421/83 laying down certain detailed rules for the implementatation of the Trade Agreement between the Community and China, OJ 1983 L346/91.

China in a relatively disadvantageous position compared to most of the EU trading partners. It was accompanied, however, with a commitment by the EC to "strive" to remove quantitative restrictions on imports from China. Its most significant effect has been to remove discriminatory tariff barriers.

The Trade Agreement stated that the parties would make every effort to attain balance in their bilateral trade. It included a price clause, which specified that trade was to be effected at market-related prices; this protective measure was designed to prevent China from selling in the EC at a low price. The Agreement also provided a safeguard clause and consultation procedure. From the EU standpoint, the safeguard clause was complemented by the availability of quantitative restrictions on imports, antidumping measures and special commercial policy instruments as trade protection and management measures. The Trade Agreement also established a Joint Committee, comprising representatives of both the EC and China. Its role was to monitor the functioning of the Agreement, examine problems and make recommendations regarding EC-China trade.

In 1985 the Trade Agreement was replaced by the EEC-China Trade and Economic Co-operation Agreement (the Co-operation Agreement).[17] Its trade provisions comprised an MFN clause, a safeguard clause, a price clause and a balance of trade clause in virtually the same terms as in the Trade Agreement. The Co-operation Agreement also established a new Joint Committee concerning EC-China relations.

The Co-operative Agreement was broader in scope than the Trade Agreement. In addition to dealing with trade, it was designed to facilitate economic co-operation in numerous sectors between the EC and China at EC level. It also referred to numerous methods and forms of co-operation, such as joint ventures, the transfer of technology and the organisation of seminars and symposia. These measures were stated in general terms, however, and the elaboration of specific schemes was left to the parties. In addition, the Co-operation Agreement included an investment clause; the parties agreed to promote and encourage mutually beneficial investment and to encourage the extension of investment promotion and protection arrangements based on the principles of equity and reciprocity.

The EC Member States, as well as the EC itself, have trade relations with China. Consequently, the Co-operation Agreement provided that it, and any action taken under it, shall in no way affect the powers of any of the EC Member States to undertake bilateral activities with China in the field of economic co-operation and to conclude, where appropriate, new economic co-operation agreements with China (art 14).

---

[17] Council Regulation 2616/85 concerning the conclusion of a Trade and Co-operation Agreement between the European Economic Community and the People's Republic of China, OJ 1985 L250/1; Agreement on Trade and Economic Co-operation between the European Economic Community and the People's Republic of China, OJ 1985 L250/2.

Rules on imports into the EU from China

The framework agreements have been complemented by more specific rules on imports into the EU from China. Leaving textiles for later discussion, these rules comprised until recently two sets of regulations.

First, certain imports from China not subject to quantitative restrictions were originally covered by common EC rules on goods from state-trading countries.[18] Subsequently, however, special rules were enacted for imports from China.[19] Even after the more general rules were revised,[20] such special rules continued to apply to China.[21] Additional products were included in the common liberalisation list by means of Commission regulations.[22] Secondly, certain goods were subject to quantitative restrictions. Common rules dealing with products which were not liberalised applied to China as well as to all other non-market economy countries.[23]

Recently, however, these two sets of regulations were replaced by a single regulation.[23a] It was designed to strengthen the common commercial policy yet at the same time protect certain sensitive sectors of Community industry. Products from *inter alia* China may be imported freely and without quantitative restrictions, with the exception of (a) safeguard measures and (b) quantitative quotas on specified products. Imports of other specific products are subject to Community surveillance. Despite the MFN clause, the EC thus still imposes quantitative restrictions on certain imports from China.

A recent controversial example of such restrictions concerns toys. In March 1994 the EU adopted a new quota system, based on a system of licences issued by the Member States in line with quantitative criteria

---

[18] Règlement no 109/70 du Conseil portant établissement d'un régime commun applicable aux importations de pays à commerce d'Etat, JO 1970 L19/1.

[19] Council Regulation 2532/78 on common rules for imports from the People's Republic of China, OJ 1978 L306/1.

[20] Council Regulation 1765/82 on common rules for imports from State-trading countries, OJ 1982 L195/1.

[21] Currently Council Regulation 1766/82 on common rules for imports from the People's Republic of China, OJ 1982 L195/21; amended by Council Regulation 1243/86 amending Regulations 288/82, 1765/82 and 1766/82 on common rules for imports, OJ 1986 L113/1.

[22] See Commission Regulation 35/83 adding other products to the Annex to Council Regulation 1766/82 on common rules for imports from the People's Republic of China, OJ 1983 L5/12; Commission Regulation 101/84 adding other products to the Annex to Council Regulation 1766/82 on common rules for imports from the People's Republic of China, OJ 1984 L14/7; Commission Regulation 268/85 adding other products to the Annex to Council Regulation 1766/82 on common rules for imports from the People's Republic of China, OJ 1985 L28/39; Commission Regulation 1409/86 adding other products to the Annex to Council Regulation 1766/82 on common rules for imports from the People's Republic of China, OJ 1986 L128/25.

[23] The basic rules were established in Council Regulation 3286/80 on import arrangements in respect of State-trading countries, OJ 1980 L353/1, as amended by Commission Decision 81/248, OJ 1981 L115/1. It was replaced by Council Regulation 3420/83 on import arrangements for products originating in State-trading countries, not liberalised at Community level, OJ 1983 L346/6.

[23a] Council Regulation 519/94 on common rules for imports from certain third countries and repealing Regulations (EEC) 1765/82, 1766/82 and 3420/83, OJ 1994 L67/89.

established at Community level.[24] This reform resulted in the unilateral removal of 6,417 national quantitative restrictions, including 4,700 concerning China, and the introduction of EU quotas on seven categories of products from China, including toys.[25] Neither EU toy producers nor importers of Chinese toys, however, were satisfied.[26] The United Kingdom brought an action under Article 173 to annul the Chinese toys quota, arguing, in particular, that the EU toy industry was concentrated in only one country, namely Spain, and that it was "inappropriate" to transpose such an existing national restriction into an EC restriction.[27] An increase in the quota was proposed by the Commission.[28] The Member States disagreed.[29] On the one hand, Germany, the United Kingdom, the Netherlands and Ireland sought a global solution to the Chinese quota problem, embracing not only toys but also textiles and other products. On the other hand, France, Spain, Portugal and Greece rejected the Commission proposal, both in itself and as a dangerous precedent, claiming that it favoured traders as against manufacturers. In the event a compromise solution was adopted by the Council.[30] Subsequently, however, the European subsidiaries of an American toy manufacturer brought an action in the Court of First Instance to annul the toy quota and to obtain compensation for injury.[31]

These import rules do not apply to agricultural products, except in a complementary way and in so far as Member States are still allowed to impose quantitative restrictions. Agricultural products are governed instead by rules enacted within the framework of the EC Common Agricultural Policy, in particular concerning the common organisation of agricultural markets; processed agricultural products are governed by specific rules adopted under Article 235.

Garlic provides a recent example of the former group. Imports of garlic from China into the EU between January and November 1993 amounted to 21,951 tonnes, which represented an increase of 121% since 1992 and 254% more than the average for the same period between 1988 to 1990.[32] Following a request by France for safeguard measures under the common organisation of the market in fruit and vegetables, the EU by Commission

---

[24] Council Regulation 520/94 establishing a Community procedure for administering quantitative quotas, OJ 1994 L66/1.

[25] *Agence Europe*, no 6272 (n.s.), Wednesday 13 July 1994, p 9.

[26] It may be noted that the then European Commissioner for External Relations, Sir Leon Brittan, announced changes in EU trade policy instruments on the occasion of a speech before the annual Conference of Toy Manufacturers; see *Agence Europe*, no 6347 (n.s.), Saturday 29 October 1994, p 1.

[27] See *Agence Europe*, no 6276 (n.s.), Mon/Tues 18/19 July 1994, p 13.

[28] *Agence Europe* no 6272 (n.s.), Wednesday 13 July 1994, p 9.

[29] *Agence Europe*, no 6275 (n.s.), Saturday 16 July 1994, p 14. For the contrasting viewpoint of traders associations, see *Agence Europe*, no 6289 (n.s.), Saturday 6 August 1994, p 8.

[30] *Agence Europe*, no 6277 (n.s.), Wednesday 20 July 1994, p 13.

[31] Case T-268/94 *Tyco Toys (UK) Ltd and Others* v *Commission and Council*, OJ 1994 C254/14; see also *Agence Europe*, no 6317 (n.s.), Saturday 17 September 1994, p 13.

[32] *Agence Europe*, no 6240 (n.s.), Monday/Tuesday 30/31 May 1994, p 9.

regulation imposed a quantitative restriction amounting to 40.3% of the quantity for which import licences had been applied.[33] Imports were thus limited to 10,000 tonnes for the period from 2 June 1994 until 31 May 1995, including a maximum of 5,000 tonnes before 31 August 1994.[34] Subsequently the Commission suspended garlic imports from Burma until 31 May 1995, on the ground that such imports in fact originated in China; similar restrictions were applied to Taiwan and Vietnam.[35]

Trade in textiles

Textiles form one of the most important areas of trade between the EU and China. This trade from China to the EU is governed by a special legal framework, consisting of the 1979 Textile Agreement, a 1984 Additional Protocol and the 1988 Textile Agreement.[36] This framework was drafted in line with the Arrangement Regarding International Trade in Textiles, the so-called Multi Fibre Arrangement (MFA),[37] agreed within the framework of the GATT in 1974. In accordance with the MFA, the EC has concluded numerous bilateral arrangements on textiles with third countries, particularly developing countries; these agreements are implemented in the EC by Council regulations. The MFA has been repeatedly renewed;[38] an extension at the end of the fourth MFA was concluded in 1992.[39] China was not originally a member of the MFA and acceded to it only in January 1984.[40]

---

[33] Commission Regulation 1270/94 concerning the issue of import licences for garlic originating in China, OJ 1994 L138/32, amended by Commission Regulation 2021/94, OJ 1994 L203/11.

[34] *Agence Europe*, no 6240 (n.s.), Monday/Tuesday 30/31 May 1994, p 9.

[35] Commission Regulation 2091/94, OJ 1994 L220/8 (Taiwan and Vietnam); see also *Agence Europe*, no 6327 (n.s.), Saturday 1 October 1994, p 11.

[36] Recently, European trade unions in the textile industry have also called for codes of good conduct in agreement with third countries. Such codes would require the inclusion in all textile agreements of a clause imposing respect of ILO working norms, in particular a ban on child labour and forced labour as well as the freedom of association and negotiation. See *Agence Europe*, no 6363 (n.s.), Thursday 24 November 1994, p 14.

[37] GATT, *Basic Instruments and Selected Documents*, 21 *Supplement* (1974), at 3.

[38] The 4th MFA was agreed in 1986: see Conclusions of the Textiles Committee adopted on 31 July 1986, OJ 1986, L341/35; Protocol extending the arrangement regarding international trade in textiles, OJ 1986 L341/34; Council Decision 86/590 concerning the conclusion of the Protocol extending the Arrangement regarding international trade in textiles, OJ 1986 L341/33.

[39] Decision by the Textiles Committee to maintain in force the Arrangement regarding international trade in textiles for a period of 12 months, OJ 1993 L38/35; Protocol maintaining in force the Arrangement regarding international trade in textiles, OJ 1993 L38/34; Council Decision on the conclusion of the Protocol maintaining in force the Arrangement regarding the International trade in textiles (MFA), OJ 1993 L38/33. See also GATT, *Basic Instruments and Selected Documents*, 39 Supplement (1993), at 4.

[40] GATT, *Basic Instruments and Selected Documents, 31 Supplement* (1985), at 294–297.

The 1979 Textile Agreement was the first EEC-China textile agreement.[41] It replaced a system of import quotas decided on an annual basis. The 1979 Textile Agreement established quantitative limits on exports of different categories of textile products from China to the EC. It specified annual growth rates for imports of textile products, as well as mechanisms to provide flexibility among products within a given year and between one year and the next. It also provided that the EC could ask for consultation in order to fix a quota if exports of a product which was not subject to quantitive restrictions exceeded a certain threshold level; this so-called "basket exit" or "basket extractor" mechanism could be applied between China and a single EC region or regions, not just the EC as a whole. The Textile Agreement also included a price clause, as well as a clause (similar to an anti-surge clause, *infra*) to ensure that. Chinese exports of textile products were distributed as regularly as possible over the year. It provided for double administrative control or "double checking system", that is, exports of textiles from China were subject to an export licence issued by the Chinese authorities and to an import licence or equivalent document issued by the EC Member State of import.

The Textile Agreement also included two unusual features. First, it sought to guarantee the supply of certain raw materials to the EC by an undertaking on the part of China to supply minimum guaranteed quantities of textile raw materials to the European textile and clothing industry on conditions determined by market practice and at the normal trade price; these materials included pure silk, angora and cashmere. Secondly, in order to stimulate exports to China from the EC, the Agreement provided that, in return for increasing its quotas into the EC, China should encourage and facilitate the import into its own market of textiles originating in the EC. Finally, the Textile Agreement established a Textile Committee to oversee the operation of the Agreement.

In 1984 the EC and China reached agreement on a Supplementary Protocol to the 1979 Agreement.[42] The Supplementary Protocol incorporated various amendments so as to ensure consistency with the third MFA, then in force. It thus included an anti-surge clause, designed to prevent a sudden increase in import levels, even within the agreed total quantities. If such a sudden increase occurred, the EC could request the opening of consultations, which were to lead to the suspension of flexibility, changes in quantitative limits and corresponding compensation. The Supplementary Protocol also introduced an anti-circumvention clause. This provision was intended to prevent circumvention of the Agreement by transship-

---

[41] Council Decision 86/669 concerning the conclusion of the Agreement between the European Economic Community and the People's Republic of China on trade in textile products, the Protocol of Adaptation and the Supplementary Protocol thereto, OJ 1986, L389/1; Agreement between the European Economic Community and the People's Republic of China on trade in textile products, OJ 1986 L389/2.

[42] Council Regulation 2072/84 on common rules for imports of certain textile products originating in the People's Republic of China, OJ 1984 L198/1.

ment, re-routing or other measures. However, the price clause included in the 1979 Agreement was omitted from the 1984 Protocol.

In 1988 the 1979 Agreement was replaced by a new Textile Agreement.[43] It took account of the conclusion in 1986 of the fourth MFA. The 1988 Textile Agreement increased the quotas for certain products, while introducing new quotas for others which had not previously been subject to quantitative restrictions. It replaced the anti-surge clause, which had been severely criticised, with provision for consultation in the event of an "excessive concentration" of imports. It also abandoned the rigid formula based on values between EC exports to China and Chinese exports to the EC as a way of increasing EC exports to the Chinese market. The 1988 Textile Agreement ran until the end of 1992. It continues to be applied on a provisional basis pending the formal conclusion of a subsequent agreement.[44]

In March 1994 the Council enacted common rules for imports from certain countries, including China, of textiles not covered by bilateral agreements, protocols, other arrangements or other specific EC import rules.[45] These rules were intended to help complete the EC's common commercial policy. In addition, following the conclusion of the GATT Uruguay Round negotiations, they were designed to prepare for the integration of the textile and clothing sector into normal WTO rules and disciplines, beginning 1 January 1995 and to be completed by 2005.[46] With regard to China and so far as textiles were concerned, they put an end to the existence of two separate regulations, one for products subject to quantitative restrictions and the other for products not subject to such restrictions.[47] Textile imports from China are not included however in the liberalisation of imports.[48] Instead they are subject to annual quotas, which are either established in advance or may be fixed by the regulatory committee procedure.[49] Their entry into free circulation is subject to an

---

[43] Council Decision 88/656 concerning the provisional application of the Agreement between the European Economic Community and the People's Republic of China on trade in textile products, OJ 1988 L380/1; Agreement between the European Economic Community and the People's Republic of China on trade in textile products, OJ 1988 L380/2.

[44] See Council Decision 92/625 on the provisional application of agreements between the European Economic Community and certain third countries on international trade in textiles, OJ 1992 L410/1; Agreement in the form of an exchange of letters amending the Agreement between the European Economic Community and the People's Republic of China on trade in textile products, OJ 1992 L410/103.

[45] Council Regulation 517/94 on common rules for imports of textile products from certain third countries not covered by bilateral agreements, protocols or other arrangements, or by other specific Community import rules, OJ 1994 L67/1; see also Commission Regulation 2980/94 opening quotas for imports from China of certain categories of textile products and amending certain annexes of Council Regulation 517/94, OJ 1994 L315/2.

[46] See United Nations, *World Economic and Social Survey 1994* (1994), at 80.

[47] See recital 25, Council Regulation 517/94, OJ 1994 L67/1.

[48] Council Regulation 517/94, arts 1, 2(1), Annex II, OJ 1994 L67/1.

[49] Depending on the product concerned, either the "net"\(*filet*) or the "safety net" (*contrefilet*) procedure is used; see Council Regulation 517/94, arts 3(3), 25, Annex IV; OJ 1994 L67/1.

import authorisation.[50] With regard to the information and investigation procedure and surveillance and safeguard measures, more stringent rules apply to imports from China, and the Commission is invested with greater discretion.[51]

In January 1995 the European Commission and China completed negotiations for a new textile agreement.[52] It covers all trade in textiles between the EU and China. This trade now amounts to approximately five billion ECUs or two million US dollars per year. The agreement adapts quotas to take account of EU enlargement, settles some cases of circumvention, limits imports of certain additional categories of products and adapts certain economic provisions in the current bilateral textiles agreement in view of China's possible accession to GATT/WTO. Of particular importance, it is the first agreement on trade in silk and linen products, which previously were covered by an autonomous regime.[53] The agreement has yet to be approved by the Council.

Some current issues

A number of current issues concerning EU-China trade raise significant, indeed enduring problems of trade law and policy.[54] They can be classified into two groups. The first group refers to problematic aspects of EU law as seen from a Chinese perspective. The second group encompasses problematic aspects of Chinese law as seen from an EU perspective. Together they present contrasting views on EU-China trade relations.

Among the problematic aspects of EU law as seen from a Chinese perspective is the fact that, within the framework of EU trade relations, China is currently classified by the EU as a non-market economy country. The amended Constitution of the PRC of March 1993, however, refers not to the "centrally planned economy" but to the "socialist market economy". As a result of the recent economic reforms in China,[55] it may be suggested that the EU classification now needs to be reconsidered.

In addition, EU relations with China are expanding in scope, but with regard to some forms of co-operation the boundaries between the powers of the EC and the powers of the Member States are not entirely clear. We

---

[50] Council Regulation 517/94, art 3, OJ 1994 L67/3.

[51] See Council Regulation 517/94, arts 10(2), 11(2), 12(2), OJ 1994 L67/1.

[52] European Commission Spokesman's Service, "The EU has completed textile negotiations with China" (20 January 1995); *Agence Europe*, no 6403 (n.s.), Saturday 21 January 1995, p 7.

[53] Council Regulation 517/94, OJ 1994 L67/1.

[54] On EC trade law generally, see Hawkes and Snyder, *Customs Law and Commercial Policy in Europe* (forthcoming, 1996).

[55] See Kim, "Mainland China in a Changing Asia-Pacific Regional Order", (1994) 30 *Issues and Studies* 1; Cheng, "Mainland China's Transition from a Planned Economy to a Market Economy: New Breakthroughs and Hurdles", (1994) 30 *Issues and Studies*, 74; Perkins, Dwight, "Completing China's Move to the Market", (1994) 8 *Journal of Economic Perspectives* 23.

may consider in particular the scope of the implied powers of the EC; the question as to whether EC competence is exclusive or concurrent; and, in the case of concurrent competence, the division of responsibility between the EC and the Member States.

These issues have long been of concern to the EU's trading partners.[56] Most recently, with regard to the first two issues, it will be recalled that in Opinion 2/91 the Court of Justice took a very broad view of the EC's implied powers in the field of external relations; it also held, in effect, that the exclusive competence of the EC may extend to virtually any area of positive EC law.[57] With regard to the third issue, the Court of Justice ruled very recently that, while including some areas of exclusive EC competence, the WTO also embraces areas in which the EC and its Member States have concurrent competence, and that in these areas there is an "obligation to co-operate [that] flows from the requirement of unity in the international representation of the Community."[58] It may be suggested that, to the EU's trading partners, the boundaries of the EU's role in external relations remain far from clear.

From the same perspective, some related aspects of EU constitutional law and trade law are even less certain. First is the distinction between the acts of the Council of the European Union and the acts of the representatives of the Member States meeting in the Council.[59] A second concerns the powers of the Commission to conclude international agreements[60] and to manage and police international economic markets.[61] A third refers to the division of legal labour between the EC institutions, and in particular the fact that the EC legal systems lacks a clear distinction between legislative and administrative acts, institutions or functions.[62] From the viewpoint of an outsider, these aspects of the EU legal system need to be clarified.

A second group of issues concerns Chinese law as seen from the EU perspective. One issue, which obviously raises issues for both trading part-

---

[56] See, *e.g.*, Song, "Treaty-Making Power of the European Communities", LLM thesis, European University Institute (1994).

[57] Opinion 2/91 *Re ILO Convention 170 on Chemicals at Work* [1993] 3 CMLR 800, at 816, paras 9–11 *per curiam*.

[58] Opinion 1/94 *Agreement establishing the World Trade Organisation*, 15 November 1994, para 108 [English transcript], nyr; see also *Agence Europe*, no 6357, Wednesday 16 November 1994, p 9.

[59] See, *e.g.*, Joined Cases C-181/91 and C-248/91, *European Parliament* v *Council and Commission* [1993] ECR I-3685.

[60] See Case C-327/91, *France* v *Commission* [1994] ECR I-3641; see also *Agence Europe*, no 6291 (n.s.), Wednesday 10 August 1994, pp 1–2.

[61] For a case study, see Snyder, "European Community Law and International Economic Relations: The Saga of Thai Manioc", in R StJ Macdonald (ed), *Essays in Honour of Wang Tieya* (1993) 753–769.

[62] See, for example, Snyder, "The Taxonomy of Law in EC Agricultural Policy: A Case Study of the Dairy Sector", EUI Working Paper LAW No. 95/- (1995).

ners, refers to China's relation to the GATT/WTO.[63] In 1986 China applied formally to resume its status as a contracting party. A Working Party established in 1987 concluded that a number of areas required action before China could accede to the GATT. In particular, trade laws were not uniformly administered, many of China's trade rules were un-published internal regulations and thus lacked transparency, and dis-criminatory measures existed with regard to foreign companies and trade in services. In addition, tariffs were high, quantitative restrictions on imports and exports were widespread, both mandatory and non-mandatory standards and inspections were employed, subsidies were provided to various companies, and intellectual property rights lacked effective protection.[64]

China's request concerning the GATT was supported by the European Commission. At the same time the Commission argued in favour of transi-tional provisions, including a selective safeguard clause and transitional maintenance of some quotas for imports of Chinese products, a ceiling for Chinese customs duties, gradual liberalisation of the right to engage in foreign trade and the right to invest.[65] The negotiations for China to become a founding member of the World Trade Organization (WTO) were not successful.[66] Eventually, however, Chinese membership of the WTO is likely to lead to substantial changes in EU-China relations.

Another problematic aspect of Chinese law as seen from the EU stand-point concerns industrial counterfeiting. In July 1993 the Commission submitted a proposal for measures to prohibit the release for free circula-tion, export or transit of counterfeit and pirated goods.[67] Subsequently the European Commissioner responsible for Fiscal and Customs Policy, Mrs Scrivener, met with Chinese Deputy Minister for External Trade and Economic Co-operation, Mr Gu Yongjiang. Among the main topics for discussion was customs co-operation, in particular joint action against in-

---

[63] See McDonnell, "China's Move to Rejoin the GATT: An Epic Transition", (1987) 10 *World Economy* 331; Yu-Li, "Resumption of China's GATT Membership", (1987) 21 *Journal of World Trade* 25; Shu, "China's Membership of GATT: A Practical Proposal", (1988) 22 *Journal of World Trade* 53; McKenzie, "China's Application to the GATT: State Trading and the Problem of Market Access", (1990) 26 *Journal of World Trade* 133; Chiu, "China and GATT: Implications of International Norms for China", (1992) 26 *Journal of World Trade* 5; Cai, "China's GATT Member-ship: Selected Legal and Political Issues", (1992) 26 *Journal of World Trade* 35; Zhang, "Les aspects juridiques des relations commerciales de la Chine avec les Etats-Unis et la CEE", (1992) 4 *Revue Internationale de Droit Comparé* 957; Qin, "China and GATT: Accession instead of Redemption", (1993) 27 *Journal of World Trade* 77; Fouquoire-Brillet, "La Chine et le GATT", (1993) 49 *Défense Nationale* 143; Wang, "China's Return to GATT: Legal and Economic Implications", (1994) 28 *Journal of World Trade* 51.

[64] See Industrial Structure Council Japan, *1994 Report on Unfair Trade Policies by Major Trading Partners: Trade Policies and WTO* (1994), pp 48–53.

[65] *Agence Europe*, no 6179 (n.s.), Saturday, 26 February 1994, p 5 (Sir Leon Brittan); *Agence Europe*, no 6216 (n.s.), Friday 22 April 1994, p 6 (Mrs Scrivener).

[66] *Agence Europe*, no 6384 (n.s.), Thursday 22 December 1994, p 12.

[67] See Draft Counterfeit Goods Regulation (Proposal for a Council Regulation laying down measures to prohibit the release for free circulation, export or transit of counterfeit and pirated goods, COM(93)329 final (13 July 1993)), [1994] 1 CMLR 37.

dustrial counterfeiting.[68] The EU is especially concerned to ensure what it considers to be adequate protection of intellectual property rights.

A further issue refers to human rights. Following the United States, the EU stated, with regard to the GATT negotiations, that there was no automatic and direct link between trade and human rights.[69] However, on 9 February 1994 the European Parliament adopted a Resolution which, among other things, called for China to respect human rights and fundamental freedoms, introduce internationally respected social standards and an environmental protection policy, and establish a multiparty political system.[70] From the Chinese standpoint, these points may constitute differing degrees of interference in domestic matters, much as if the EU's trading partners showed undue concern for unemployment, income distribution or the "economic constitution" in Europe.

A final issue concerns dumping. The economic changes now underway in China are likely to lead to a growing number of anti-dumping actions in the European courts.[71] EU policy in such actions is closely linked to its view that China remains a non-market economy. A recent example is *Gao Yao*,[72] in which the Hong Kong distributor of lighters produced by a mainland Chinese manufacturer sought to challenge anti-dumping measures imposed on the latter. Advocate-General Lenz suggested that the distributor should have *locus standi*, on the ground that the the distributor and the producer constituted a single economic entity.[73] The Court of Justice, however, did not agree. It held that the distributor was an independent entity and could not challenge anti-dumping measures imposed on the mainland producer. From the Chinese perspective, the case involved legal recognition of its changing company structures, together with the opening of channels for its increasing ability to compete, not only economically but also through the European courts. From the EU standpoint, however, the case exemplified dumping by a non-market economy country with low labour costs, as well as the difficulties of analysing and evaluating legal and economic relations between companies in a very different context.

---

[68] *Agence Europe*, no 6216 (n.s.), Friday 22 April 1994, p 6.

[69] See *Agence Europe*, no 6239 (n.s.), Saturday 28 May 1994, p 12.

[70] European Parliament, Resolution on relations between the European Union and the People's Republic of China, OJ 1994, C61/71; see also (1994) 1 *Bulletin of the European Union* 82 (point 1.3.72).

[71] For a survey to 1991, see Vermulst and Graafsma, 'A Decade of European Community Anti-Dumping Law and Practice Applicable to China', (1992) 26 *Journal of World Trade* 5.

[72] Case C-75/92, *Gao Yao (Hong Kong) Hua Fa Industrial Co. Ltd* v *Council*, [1994] ECR I-3141.

[73] Case C-75/92, *ibid* at 3152–3153.

Conclusion

This brief paper presented some preliminary reflections based on a research project that is now in its initial stages. The project has three purposes. The first purpose is to monitor and analyse the development of the legal aspects of trade relations between the EU and China. The second purpose is to understand the causes and implications of these legal changes. The third purpose is to use the law as a learning device.

A basic assumption of the project is that changes in the content and the use of law affect the way each party views its partner. Conversely, the way each party views its partner may lead to changes in the content and use of law. Changes in law, legal processes and legal culture with regard to trade thus provide a mirror of – and contribute to – changing economic relations between the two trading partners.

At the same time, we can use le regard (juridique) de l'autre to learn more about our own legal system. For example, students of EU law can learn a great deal about the EU, its legal system, its constitutional development and its role in the world economy by examining more closely the ways in which these matters are perceived by the EU's trading partners. Similarly, it may be suggested that students of Chinese law have much to gain by considering the way in which this legal system is refracted and reflected in EU law. Many of these conceptions are expressed in legal principles, social practices with regard to the law, and recourse to litigation in trade-related matters, whether at national, EU or international level.

Though highly selective, this paper aimed to convey the significance and interest of a study of the legal aspects of trade between the EU and China. Even such a brief discussion provides the basis for two general conclusions.

First, trade between Europe and China is becoming increasingly "Europeanised", in the sense that the EU, as distinct from its Member States, is assuming an increasingly significant role. This process is not unique to trade.[74] It stems from two factors. On the one hand, the completion of the internal market of the EC as part of the EU has provided a major impulse. On the other hand, it has recently gained momentum as a result of the strengthening of economic organisation and legal discipline at international level, in particular by means of the WTO. This process is likely to be reinforced by China's eventual membership of the WTO.

Second, there remain a number of significant outstanding issues in trade relations between the EU and China. Some of these issues are conjunctural and only of passing importance. Others are structural and reflect more fundamental differences. Both affect trade and, reciprocally, are influenced by it. In this paper, mainly for the sake of brevity and

---

[74] See, for example, Joerges, "European Economic Law, the Nation-State and the Maastricht Treaty", in Dehousse (ed), *Europe after Maastricht: An Ever Closer Union?* (1994) pp 29–62.

convenience, these conjunctural and structural issues have usually been presented from the standpoint of one side. A more complete analysis would need to consider them from the perspectives of both trading partners. In this way we may combine these contrasting perspectives in order to understand more clearly the increasingly complex legal aspects of trade between the EU and China.

FRANCIS SNYDER[75]

---

[75] The author wishes to thank Vassil Breskovski, Jason Coppel, Emir Lawless, Angela Ward, Wolf Sauter, Anne-Lise Strahtmann and Song Ying for their contributions to this paper.

Index